WITHDRAWN

Carnegie Mellon

sixarchitects

PETER GIESEMANN
CARLOS LARA
RAUL MINONDO H.
ERNESTO PORRAS
RODOLFO SOLARES
RAFAEL TINOCO

sixarchitects

Direction and Editing
BENJAMÍN VILLEGAS

Photography
ANGE BOURDA

Design
CARMEN LUCÍA SOLARES

This book has been produced and
published in Colombia by
VILLEGAS ASOCIADOS S. A.
Avenida 82 No. 11-50, Interior 3
Bogotá, D. C., Colombia.
Telephone (57 -1) 616 1788
Fax (57 -1) 616 0020 / 616 0073
e-mail: informacion@VillegasEditores.com

© SOLARES & LARA
© MINONDO & GIESEMANN
© TINOCO & PORRAS
© VILLEGAS EDITORES, 2002

Seis Arquitectos S. A.
7 ave. 11-63 zona 9 Edificio Galerías España.
Sótano oficina C1
Guatemala, Guatemala. 01009
(502) 331-9886 , 332-2351
e-mail: info@seisarquitectos.com

Art Department
ENRIQUE CORONADO, Villegas Editores

Translation
JIMMY WEISKOPF

All rights reserved.
No part of this book may be reproduced,
stored in a retrieval system or transmitted,
in any form or by any means, electronic,
mechanical, photocopying, recording
or otherwise, without the prior
permission of Villegas Editores.

First edition
November, 2002

ISBN
958-8156-09-2

VillegasEditores.com

www.seisarquitectos.com

Front Jacket,
Atlantis building, Guatemala City.
Pages 2/3,
(from left to right). The architects
Rodolfo Solares, Raúl Minondo,
Peter Giesemann, Carlos Lara,
Ernesto Porras and Rafael Tinoco.

720.97281
S625

tableofcontents

introduction

solares&lara

minondo&giesemann

seisarquitectos

workinprogress

technicalinformation

curriculumvitae

introduction

Formed in 1997, Seis Arquitectos (Six Architects), is a group of professionals whose individual accomplishments have left a significant mark on Central American and, especially, Guatemalan architecture. Formerly working in three independent groups, the members of Seis Arquitectos saw an affinity between their respective ways of thinking and their search for an optimum response to the current problems of architecture. To begin with, the differences in their architectural languages were evident, but as soon as they joined forces a new collective architecture came into being, which responded in a novel and inventive way to the specific needs that have emerged in this new era of globalization. Today, Seis Arquitectos is a solid firm, made up of people whose positive approach to the challenges of the future and great sense of respect for the memory of the past lead them to work as a team who share the same work table, around which they analyze, discuss and propose a series of solutions that lead to a synthesis of the best ideas and strategies for the project on which they are working. In the era of globalization the role of the architect goes beyond the creativity of an individual who confronts a defined and predictable problem. Competition and the complexity of the current market, intensified by the quick and efficient spread of information, mean that architecture necessarily becomes the assembling of the work of experts in each of the specialized areas that make up this discipline. In this context, the Seis Arquitectos firm has also assumed this new role in order to find and train groups of expert professionals who intensively participate in every one of the projects that are developed in their office. This form of cooperative work, led by six renowned and highly-experienced architects, allows the firm to carry out both the functional/economic aspects of a project and the formal/cultural ones with great care and effectiveness. In a context in which it possible to take advantage of the great heritage of Mayan architecture, on the one hand, and European architecture, on the other, the architecture of Seis Arquitectos seeks to respond to specific situations within a cultural surrounding, rather than utilize a specific language. It is an architecture whose constant concern for light, spatial qualities and detail – which is evident in all of the projects presented here – reflects its suitability to a particular context, while it recognizes, at the same time, current changes and transformations in the international ambit.

solares&lara

SOLARES & LARA

The symbolic character of the Banco Internacional is expressed through four shining towers that resemble piles of diverse metallic coins and are joined to form a front that is articulated in terms of both height and depth. The use of leading-edge technology in the building is seen in the fact that it is the first project in Guatemala that uses cellular concrete and also because it has an "intelligent" system to ensure the optimum functioning of the complex. Located at a strategic point in Guatemala City, facing the "Monumento a

BANCO INTERNACIONAL

los Próceres" (which commemorates the founding fathers of the republic of Guatemala), the elegant headquarters of the Banco Internacional is subtly adapted to the plaza where the monument stands, which determines its curvilinear shape. In this way, the form of the main front of the building reflects the urban lines to which it responds, while the visual effect produced by the reflective surface echoes back and becomes an extension of the plaza, providing a visual enlargement of the vistas around it.

This gentle curved movement of the glass surfaces causes its clean volumetrics to vanish into the sky, nearly leading us to recall the poetic words of the Popul Vuh: "Perfectly they saw, perfectly they knew everything under the sky, whenever they looked. The moment they turned around and looked around in the sky, on the earth, everything was seen without obstruction." In this way, the building becomes part of the context through a pure geometrical language, expressing the spatial richness of its interior and underlining its identity as a landmark in Guatemala City.

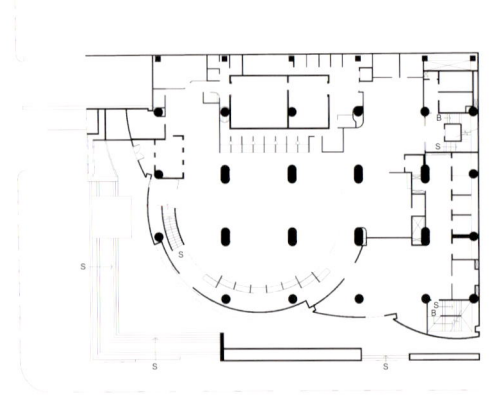
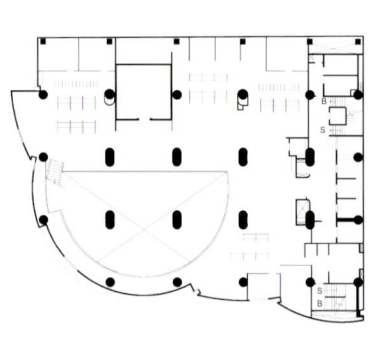
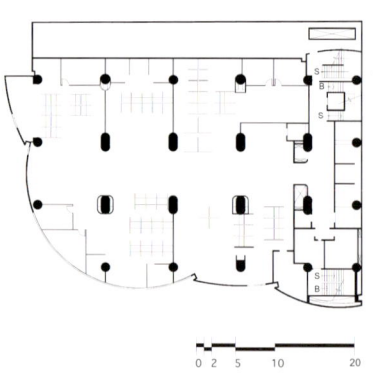

0 2 5 10 20

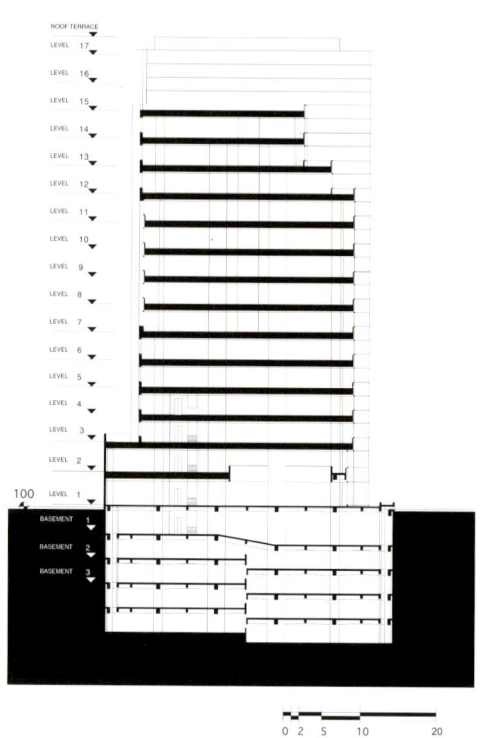

The architectural design of the Banco de Occidente began by turning the building at a 45 degree angle toward the main avenue, so that its front would be able to command a view of a plaza that would provide a large public space. Having considered different options for the materials of the exterior cladding, fired-clay brick was chosen, because it is one of the most traditional and vernacular building materials in our social environment. In this way, the walls and the weft of

BANCO DE OCCIDENTE

their texture form an excellent contrast with the blue reflecting glass that encloses the atrium and the steel framework that supports it. This dialogue between traditional and contemporary elements makes the Banco de Occidente an outstanding example of an architecture that seeks to reflect contemporary ideas while recognizing, at the same time, the esthetic value of our regional materials.

The access and exit ramps of the underground car-park were designed so that they would run parallel to the avenue and not perpendicular to it, as is usual. This innovative strategy uses the sidewalk space and the set-back line for the location of the ramps and, by relocating that space on private property, protects the pedestrian from vehicular traffic while inviting him to utilize the plaza in front of the building. What is more, the linear pattern of the texture of this plaza is introduced into the main atrium, creating a rhythmic language that eases the relationship between the interior and exterior at the main entrance. This sensation is further strengthened by the use of overhead lighting in the atrium, which captures and directs the natural light in the interior of the building to create a subtle transition towards the exterior. The visitor enters the building by means of a bridge over a pool of water beneath the projecting glass cylinder, an effect which helps to dematerialize the borders of the atrium's entrance, while the institutional solidity of the whole building becomes evident when you look at it from the outside, since the brick cube suggests the shape of two hands that seem to hold and protect the glass cylinder. These elements create an appropriate synthesis between mass and void, interior and exterior and the private and the public, emphasizing the quality of the transitional spaces and upholding the strength of the bank's image.

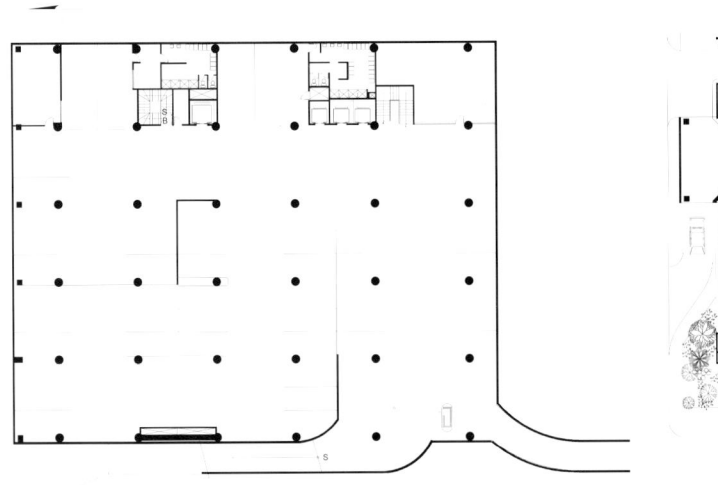
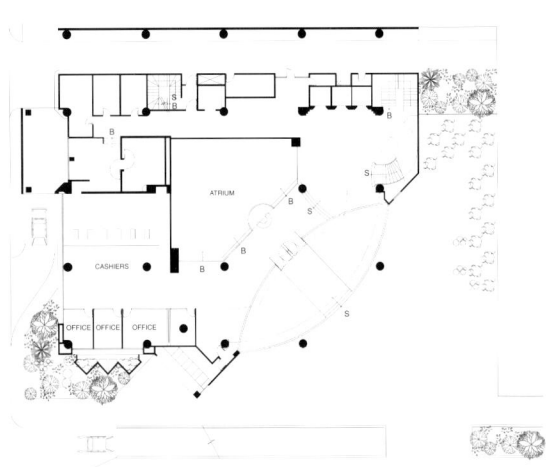
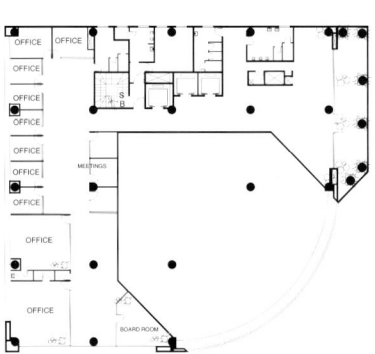

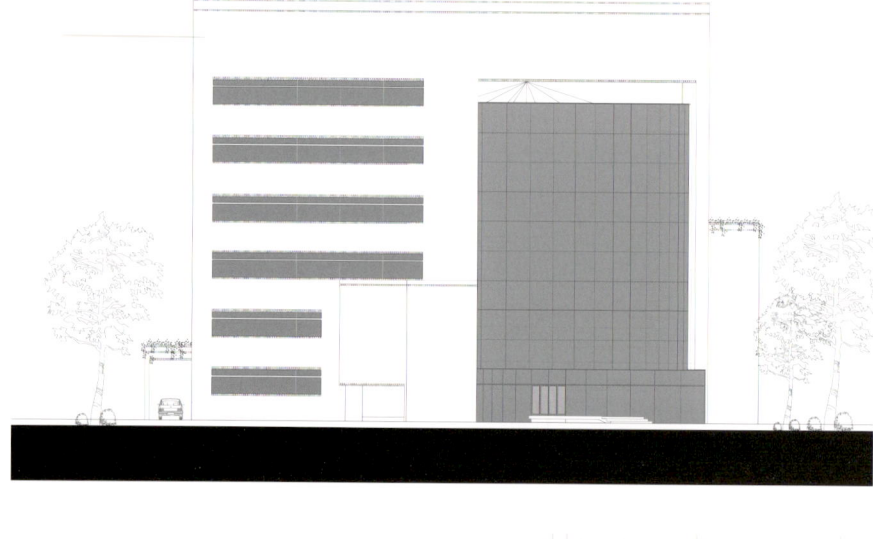

The initial design concept for the Banco SCI utilizes as a metaphor the image of a rising statistical bar graph, a symbol that reflects the continual progress and evolution of the company since its foundation. In addition to the representational character of its forms, the concept provided a variety of spatial advantages for the building. Due to restrictions imposed by the site's location within the area of approach paths for planes using the city's airport, the height of the building was limited to 12 stories, but this meant that the proportions of the volume would run the risk of taking on too massive an appearance. To avoid this result, Solares & Lara adopted a different

BANCO SCI

strategy: they took advantage of the original concept to break up the volume into five slender glass bars, slightly separated from one another, that gradually grow in height and depth, thus emphasizing the effect of their articulation. Utilizing the same pattern of gradation in the floor plan, the building gives way to a public space in the corner of the terrain, which is formed by a road intersection: from there one obtains a clearer view of the building. The opposite end of the joined bars terminates in a tower, of rustic-faced concrete block, which houses the building's service area.

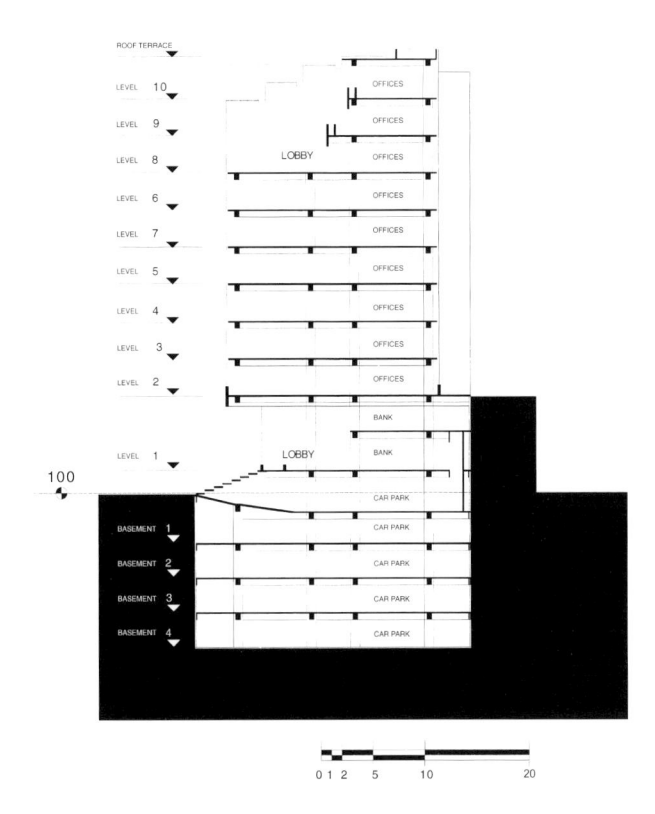

The Banco SCI is the first building in Guatemala which, for security purposes, uses two lobbies and two systems of vertical circulation. The second lobby, located on the ninth floor, serves the corporation's offices on the three upper levels and is the place at which the vertical circulation is interrupted as it passes by a control point. Using the advantage of the ninth floor, which is the highest point of the first tower, the roof of the lobby gradually rises in glass tiers which also illuminate the rest of the offices. In the main space, the different conference rooms, with glass partitions, have a panoramic view of the city and adjoin the pool of water that runs along the waiting rooms and blends into the vegetation of the indoor gardens. In addition, a curtain of water running down the exterior walls of the elevator shaft falls into the pool, creating a natural oasis nine stories above the ground. On one occasion Frank Lloyd Wright declared that "Form and function must be one, joined into a spiritual union", and the final result of the design for the Banco SCI expresses this special quality of unified architectural elements.

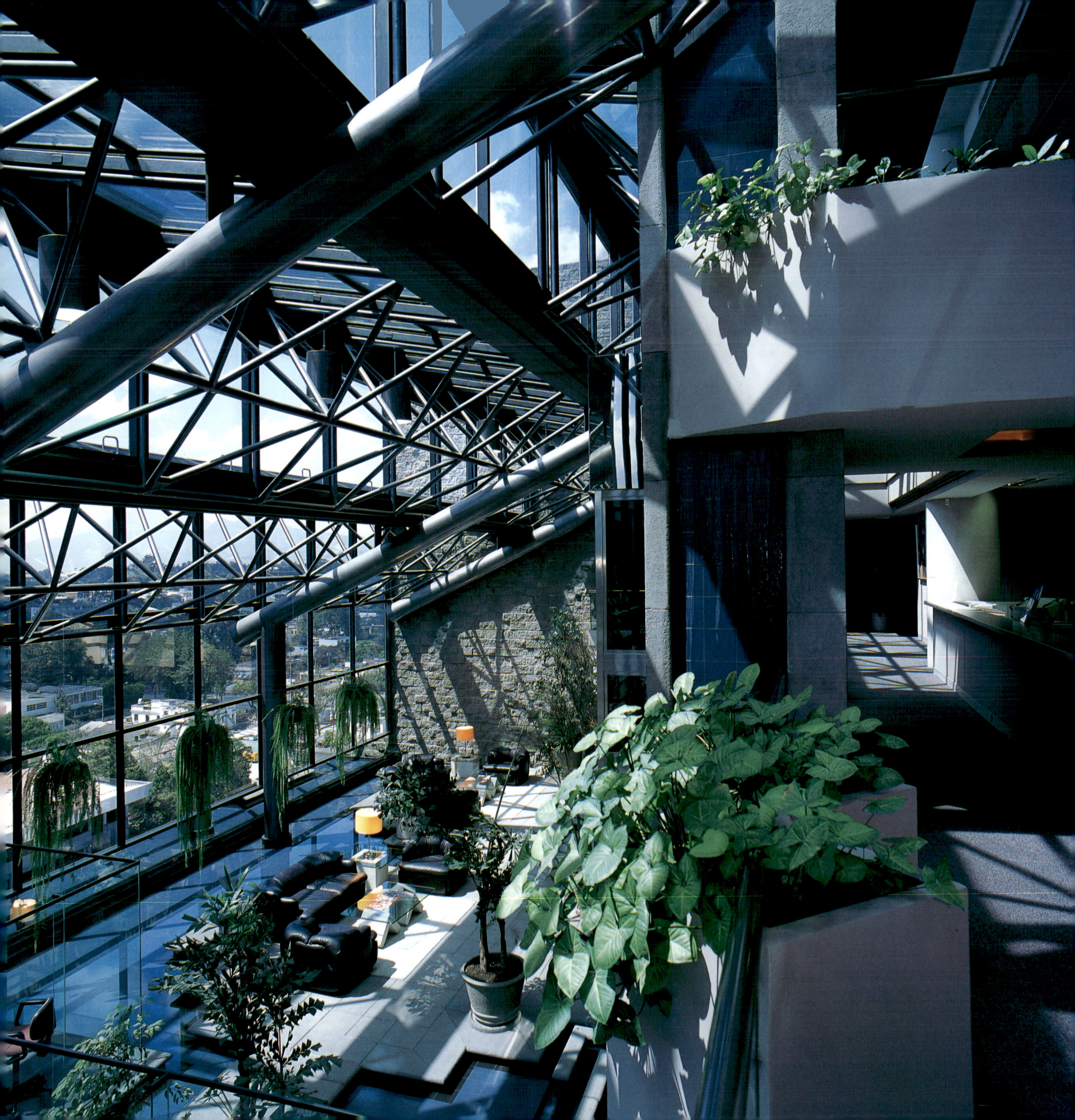

PRE-PROJECT

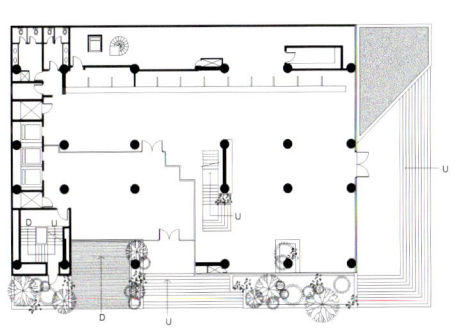

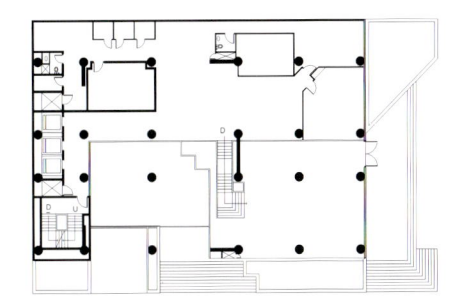

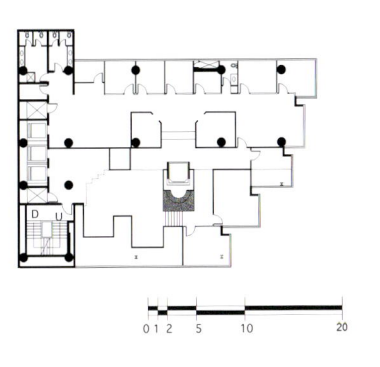

BANCO REFORMADOR

reflective glass, which seems to merge into the blue of the sky, makes all of the opaque volumes that compose the building, whether vertical or horizontal, stand out as solids that float in the air in defiance of gravity. The interior of the main atrium, which is three-stories-high, has natural illumination from the roof and bathes in light the wall that acts to close the vista from the entrance. This important interior view is adorned by indoor gardens, which provide the space with a touch of nature. The look of the cubic volume of rustic-block, together with the blue glass that reflects the garden outside, give the building an aspect of solidity which echoes the steady progress of one of the most prosperous banks in the Guatemalan financial system.

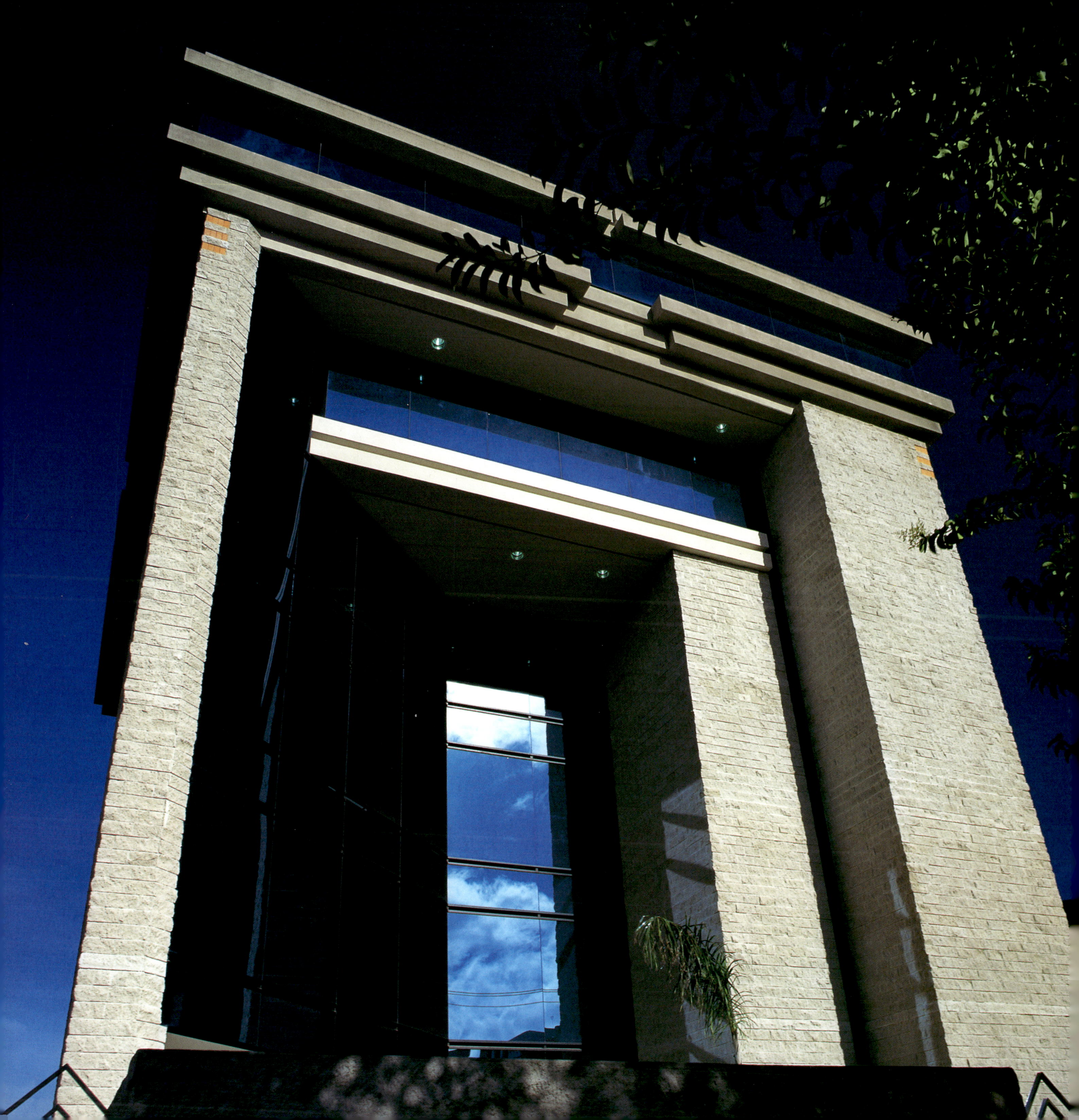

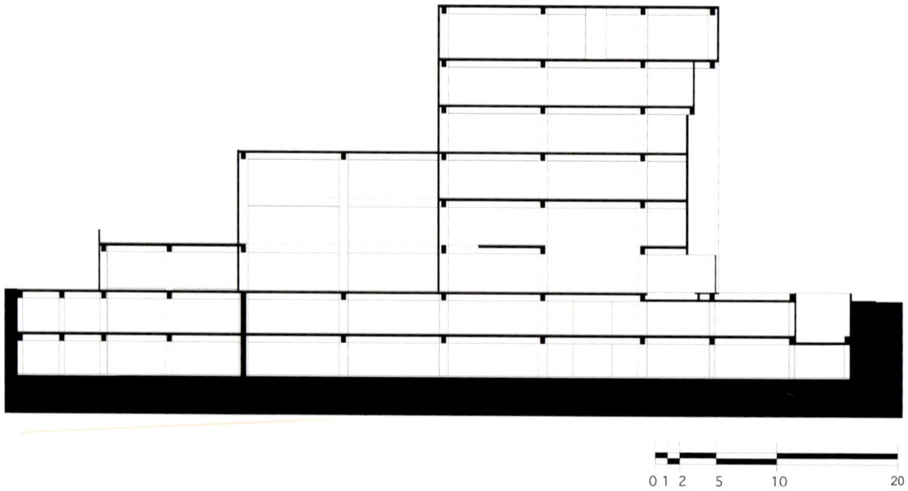
0 1 2 5 10 20

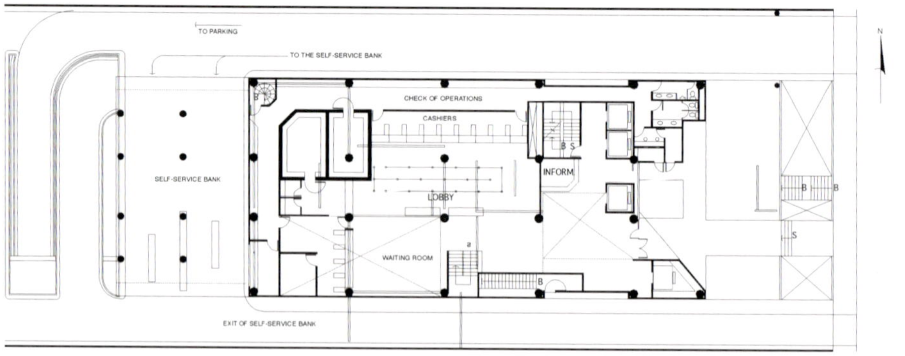
TO PARKING
TO THE SELF-SERVICE BANK
CHECK OF OPERATIONS
CASHIERS
SELF-SERVICE BANK
INFORM
LOBBY
WAITING ROOM
EXIT OF SELF-SERVICE BANK
N

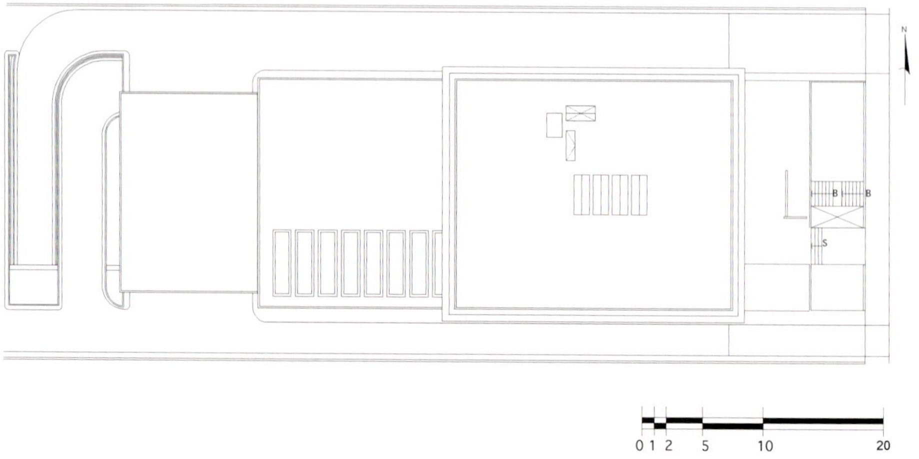
N
0 1 2 5 10 20

0 1 2 5   10   20

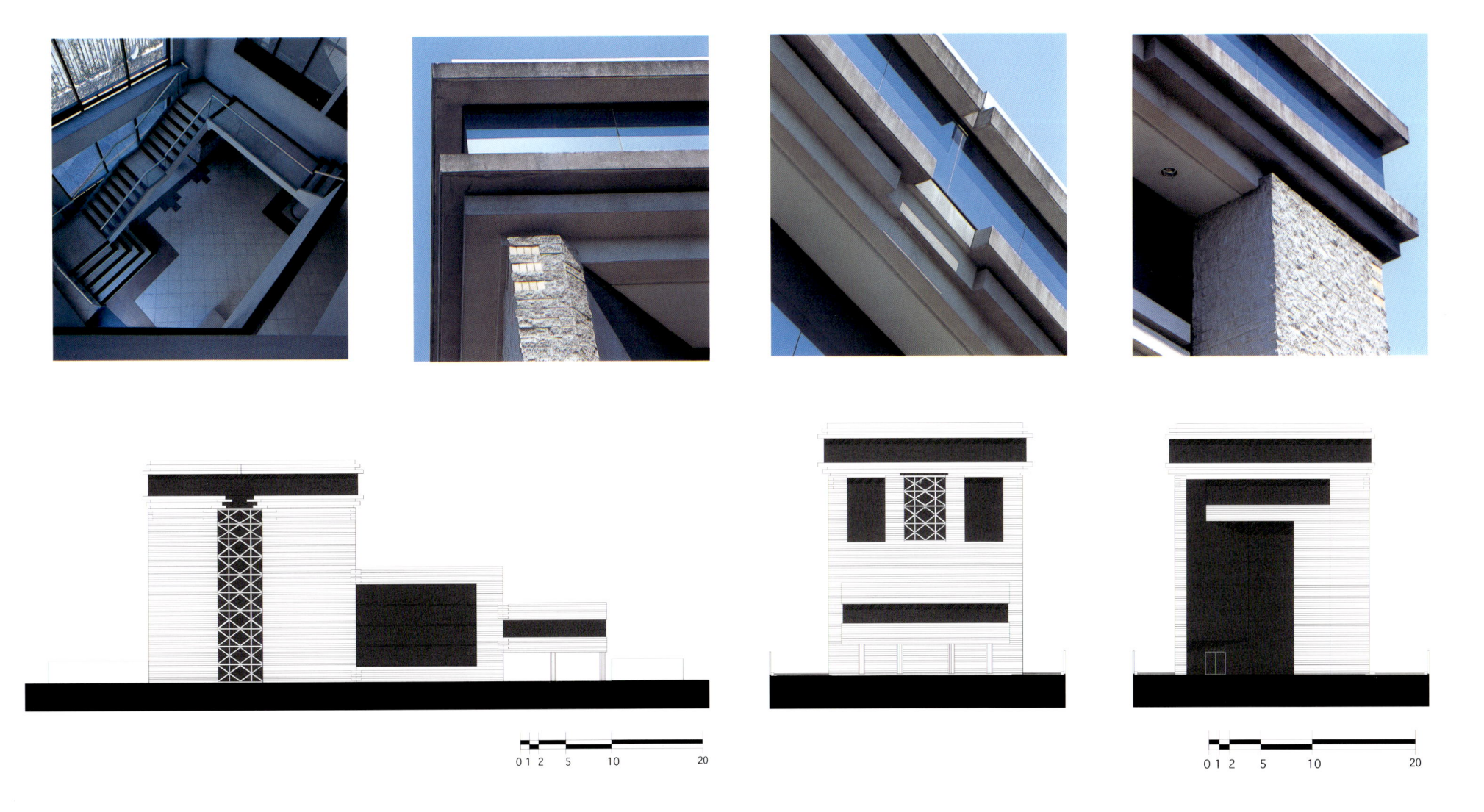

0 1 2 5   10   20

added, a steel frame construction which bears the load of an added curved roof. This roof emphasizes its rank both as the central space of the composition and the upper part of the building. This space houses a new lobby for public events. At the present time, it is used for a great variety of art exhibitions and installations of experimental art. On the outside the central axis of the main front is accentuated through the use of a blue glass that contrasts with the red utilized on either side of it, a gesture that directs one's attention towards the center of the building and highlights its symmetry.

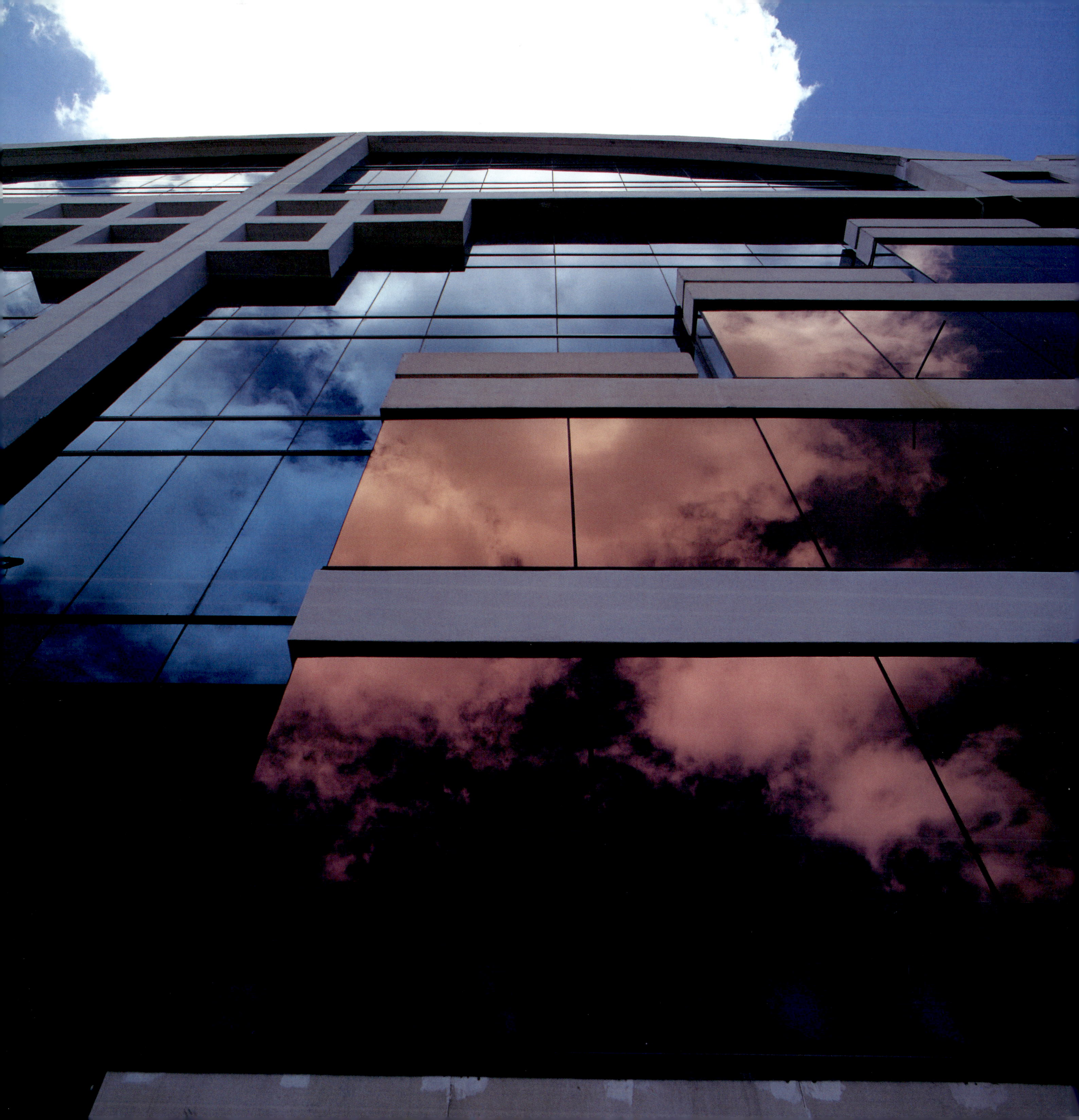

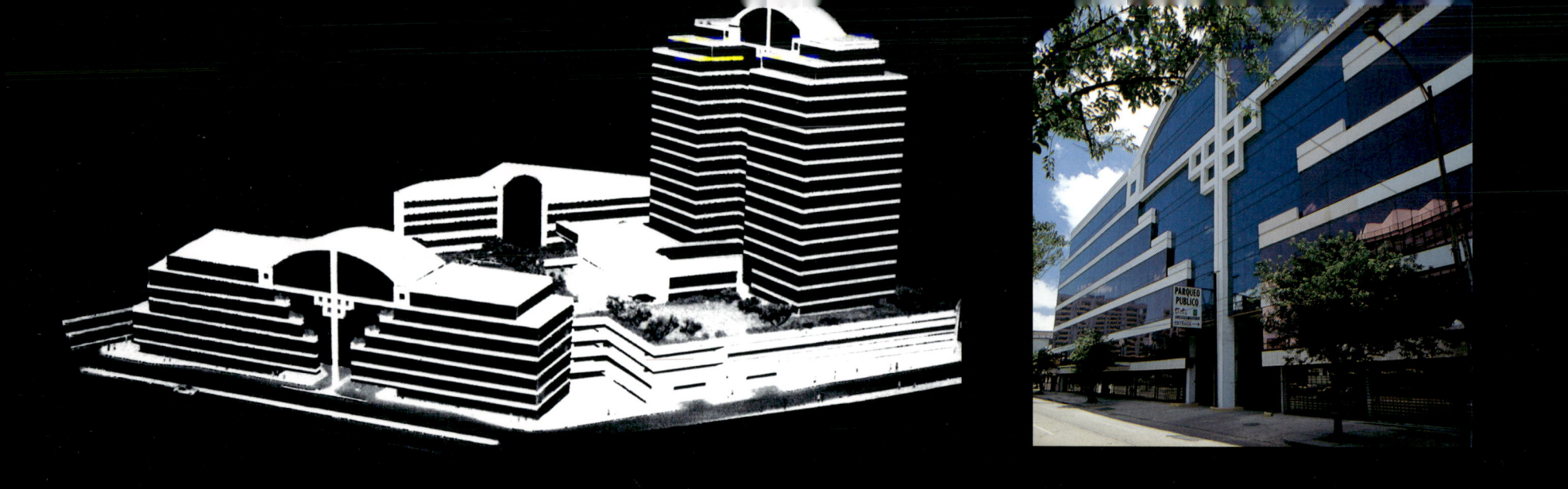

RUTA 2 ZONA 4

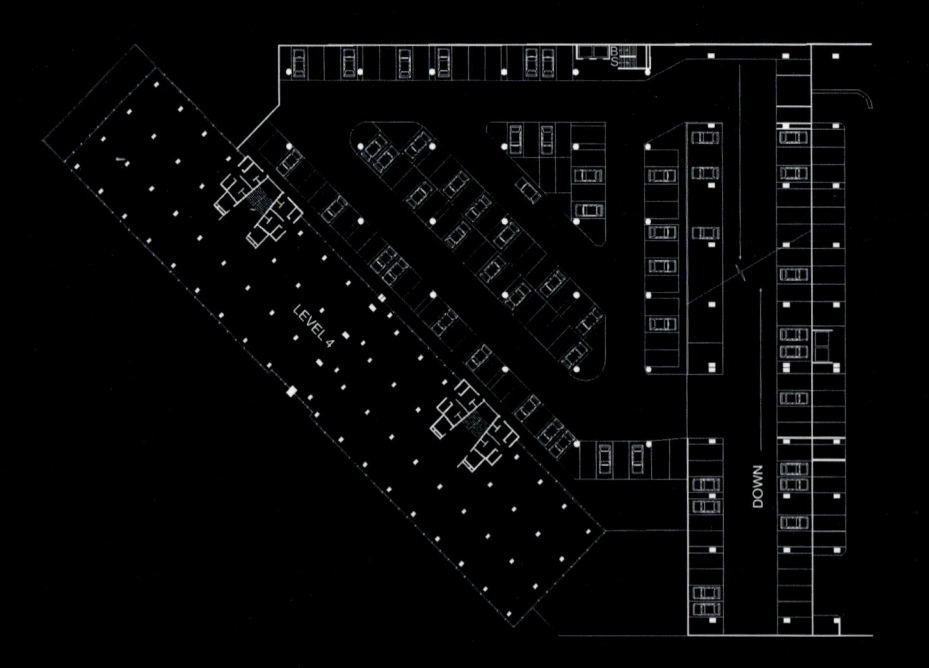

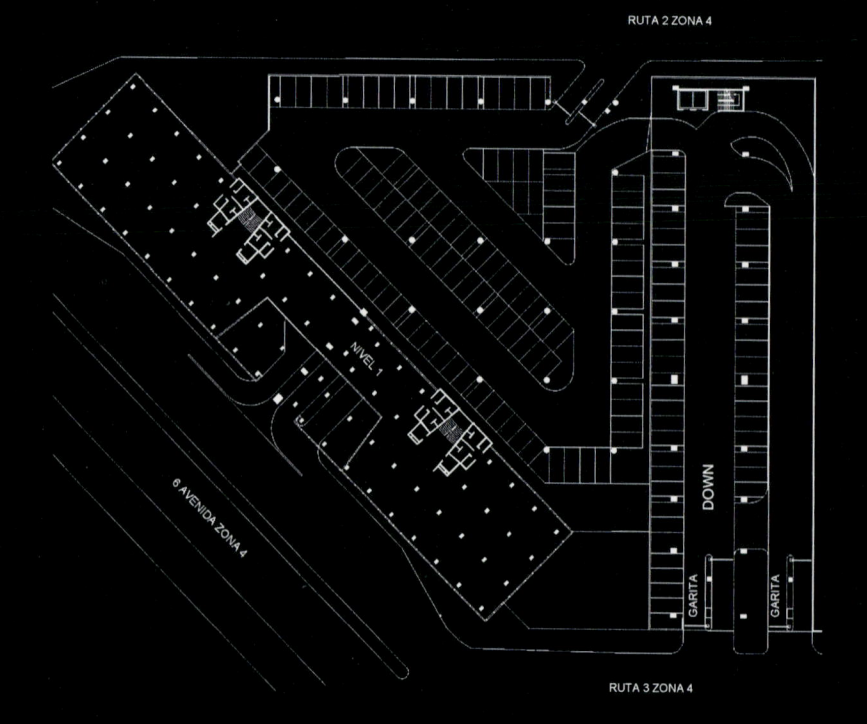

LEVEL 4

NIVEL 1

6 AVENIDA ZONA 4

DOWN

DOWN

GARITA GARITA

RUTA 3 ZONA 4

"And when they came to fruition, they came out human. They talked and they made words, they looked and listened, they walked, they worked. They were good people, handsome, with looks of the male kind. Thoughts came into existence and they gazed; their vision came all at once. Perfectly they saw, perfectly they knew everything under the sky, whenever they looked. The

effect of reflected light on its surface. The design of this building is made up of a volume of blue glass and two blocks of rustic-faced block that define the area of the stairways and elevators. Due to the visual block caused by the proximity of the existing building, the architects Solares & Lara designed one of the fronts so that the staggered

MURANO CENTRE

wall of glass would provide adequate angles of lateral view from the interior. The first two floors are devoted to shopping areas, while the third holds a multi-purpose hall which meets the needs of the different events and meetings that take place in the offices. The use of a bluish glass in the building allows the natural surroundings to be reflected on the lower part, while the upper part seems to break into fragments that vanish into the infinite, like a crystal that forms a hybrid with the blue sky.

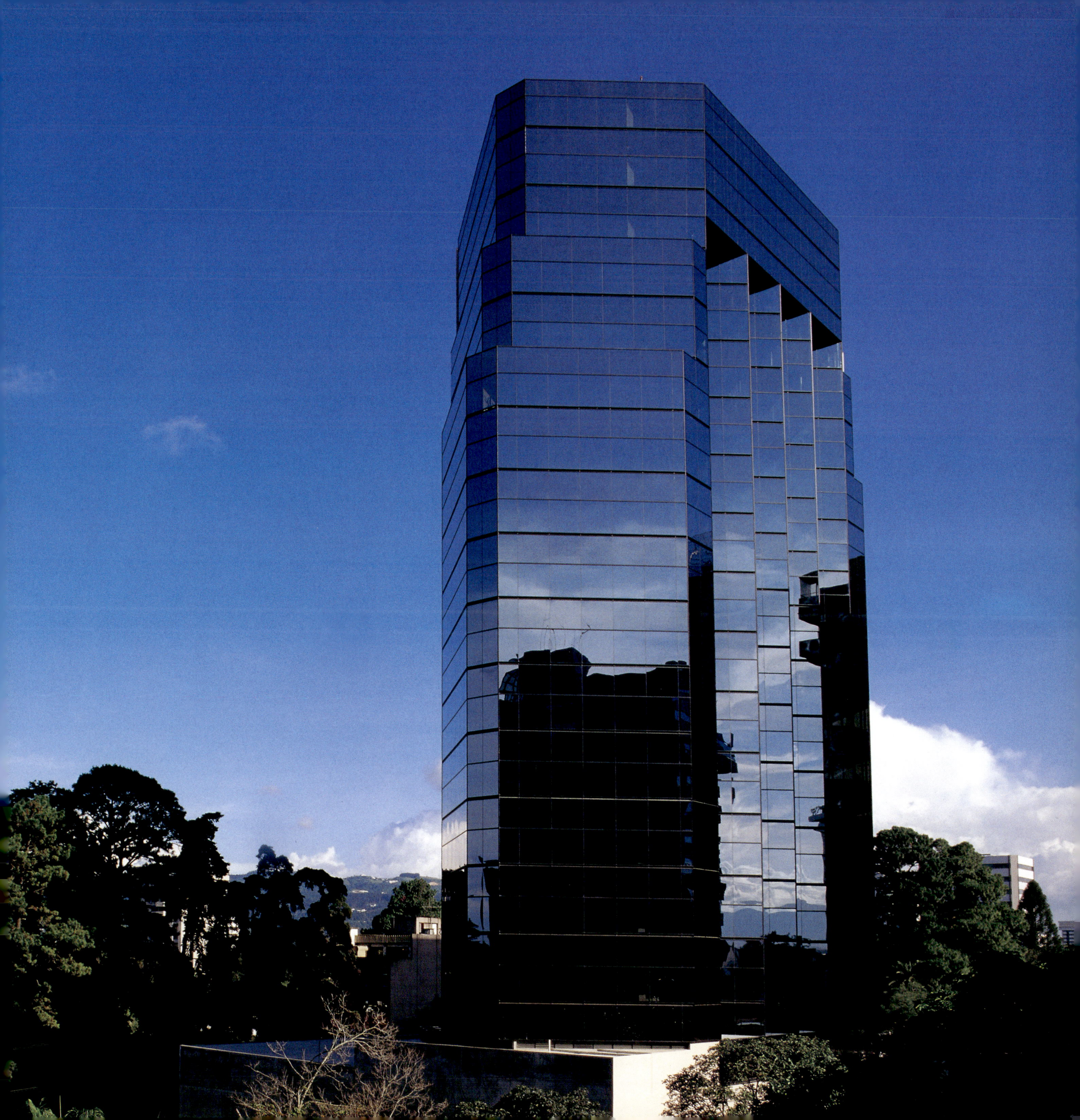

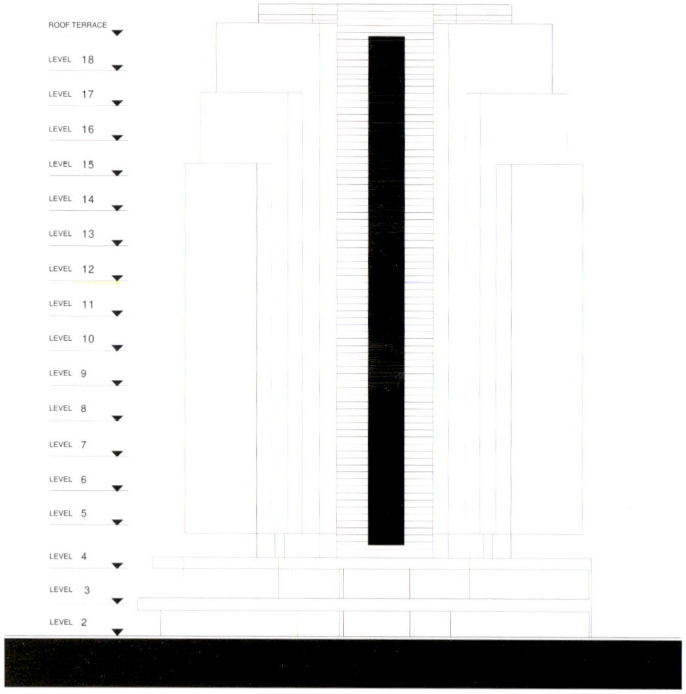
ROOF TERRACE
LEVEL 18
LEVEL 17
LEVEL 16
LEVEL 15
LEVEL 14
LEVEL 13
LEVEL 12
LEVEL 11
LEVEL 10
LEVEL 9
LEVEL 8
LEVEL 7
LEVEL 6
LEVEL 5
LEVEL 4
LEVEL 3
LEVEL 2

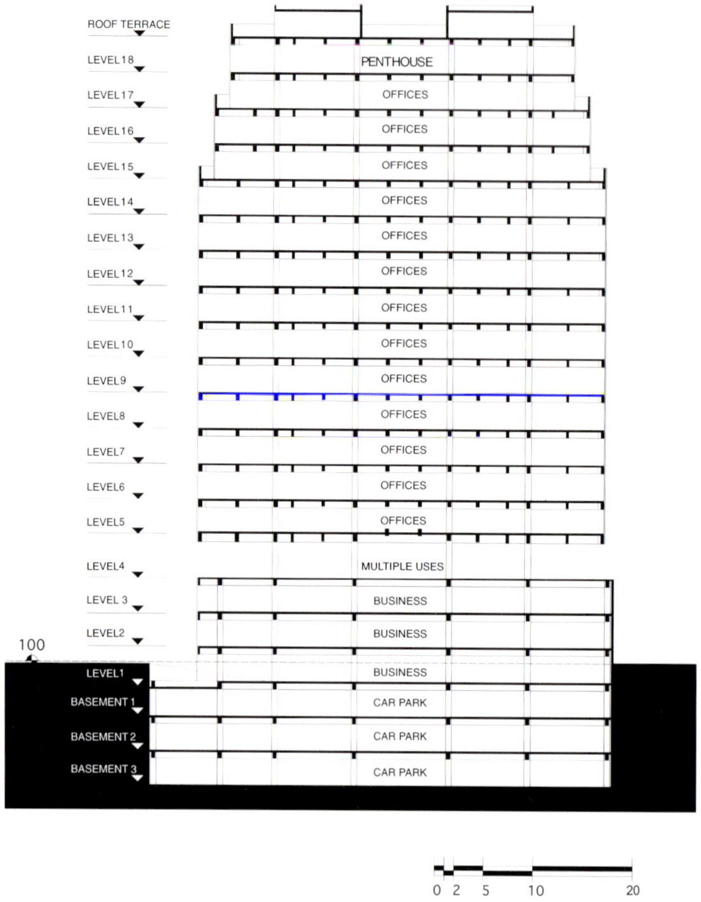
ROOF TERRACE
LEVEL18
PENTHOUSE
LEVEL17
OFFICES
LEVEL16
OFFICES
LEVEL15
OFFICES
LEVEL14
OFFICES
LEVEL13
OFFICES
LEVEL12
OFFICES
LEVEL11
OFFICES
LEVEL10
OFFICES
LEVEL9
OFFICES
LEVEL8
OFFICES
LEVEL7
OFFICES
LEVEL6
OFFICES
LEVEL5
OFFICES
LEVEL4
MULTIPLE USES
LEVEL 3
BUSINESS
LEVEL2
BUSINESS
100
LEVEL1
BUSINESS
BASEMENT 1
CAR PARK
BASEMENT 2
CAR PARK
BASEMENT 3
CAR PARK
0 2 5 10 20

N

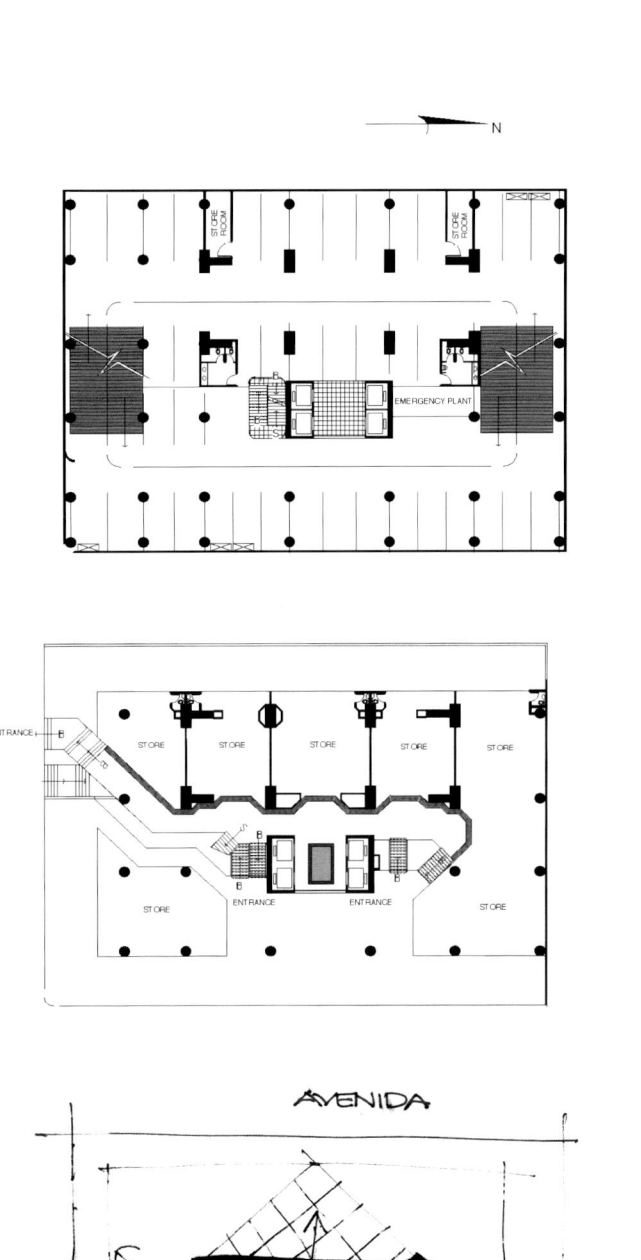

AVENIDA

VISTA

CALLE

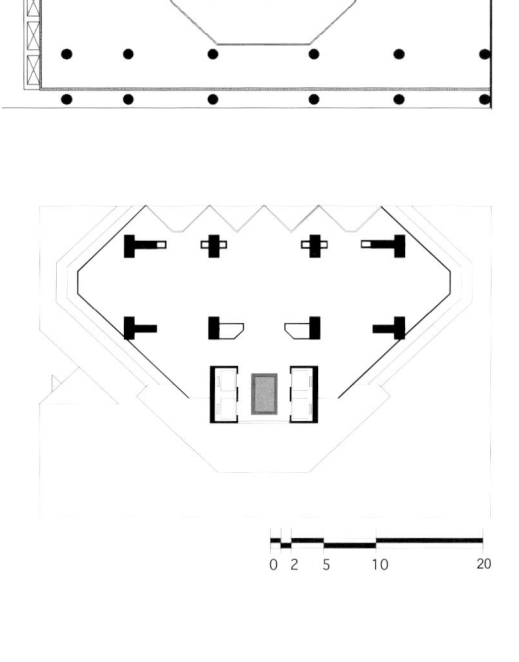

0 2 5 10 20

Located in zone 10 of Guatemala City, this 16-story building was the first in Guatemala to use a curtain wall in an apartment building. The railings of the balconies on each floor are made up of window panes topped by an aluminum handrail, a detail that prevents a blocking of the exterior view from the apartments. In addition, the continuous strip of dark glass makes the back of the balconies stand out in form and color, which gives both fronts a light touch. This contrasts, in turn, with the robust volumes of rustic-block at both ends. The play of texture and window detail that characterizes

TIFFANY BUILDING

its design stands out even more through a detail of vertical lines formed by the same material and dark glass, which create the aspect of a vertical latticework. They allow light to enter into the ambits, which do not require the use of very large windows. In addition, these lines emphasize the verticality which articulates the corners that unite the two volumes, creating a geometrical rhythm that complements the horizontality of the balconies made of glass and white slabs. The building also has a social area, a gymnasium and an underground car park with a continuous ramp.

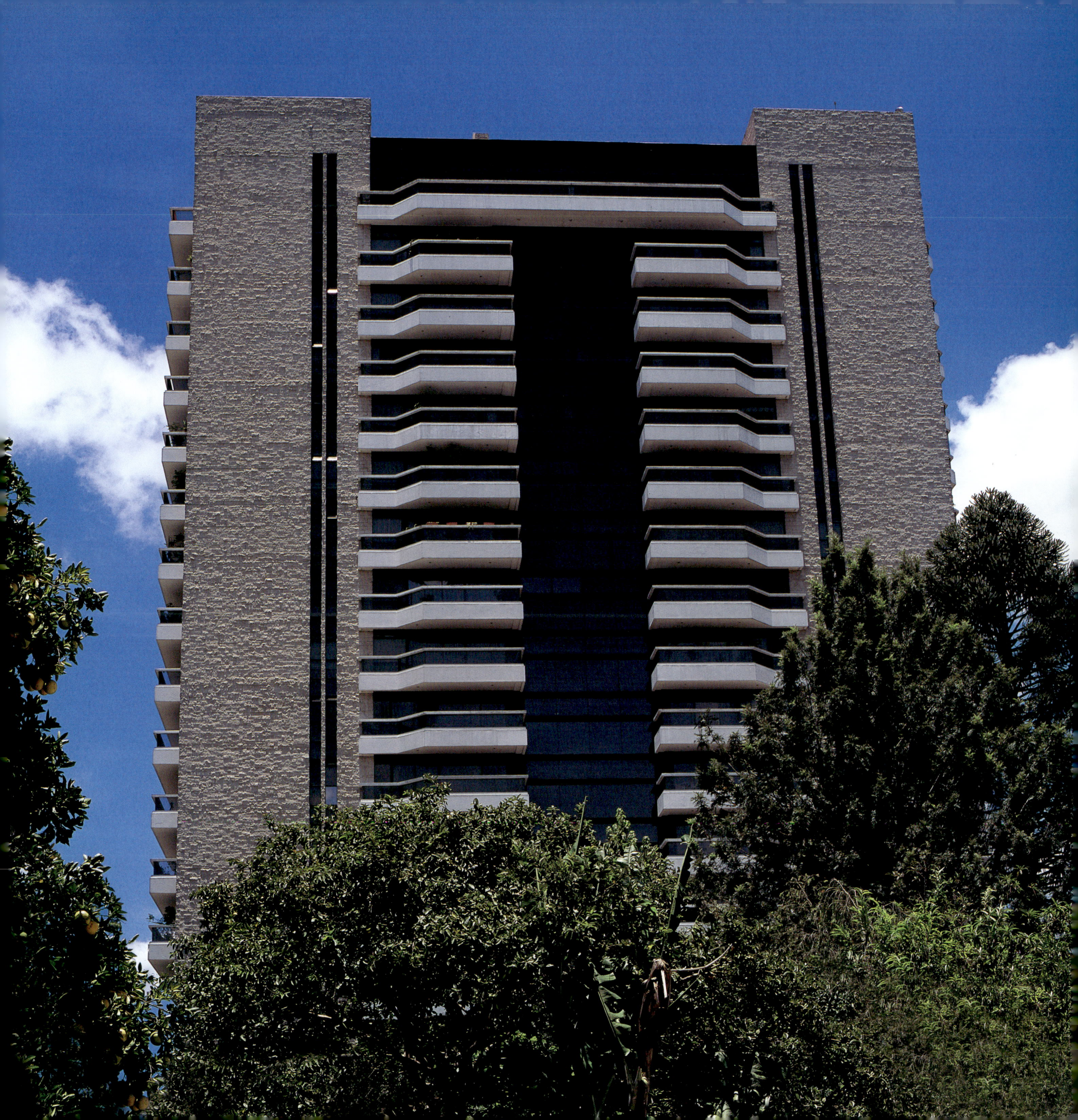

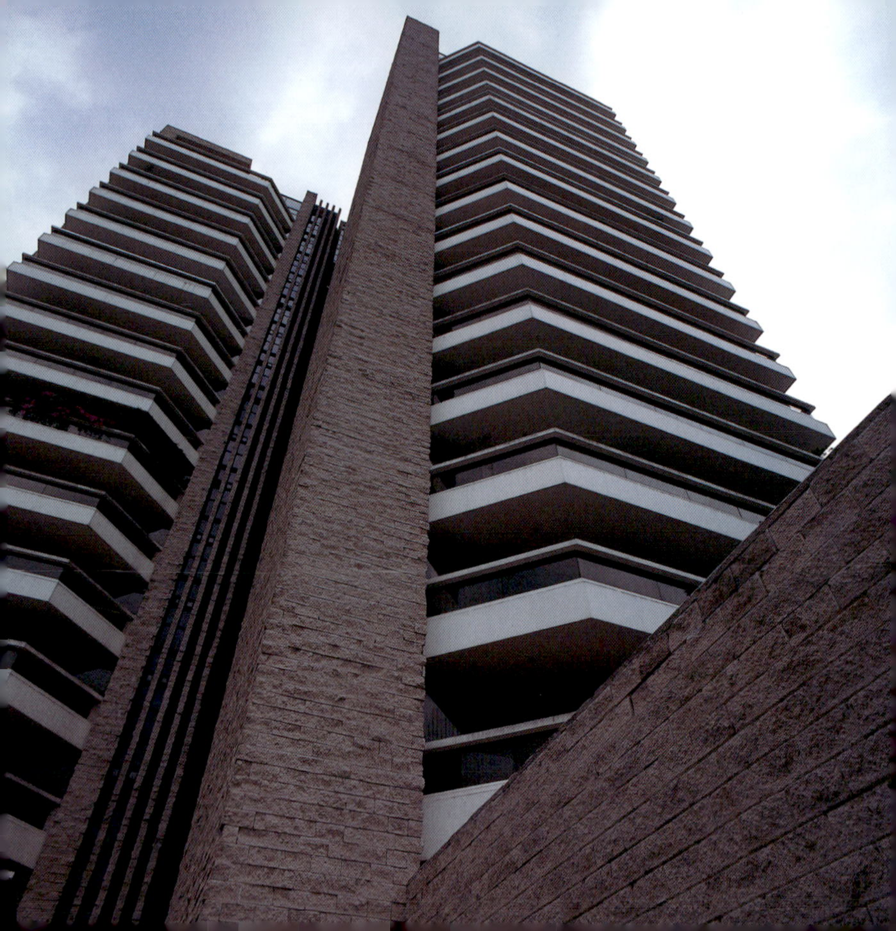

Tiffany is an example of a residential architecture that suitably responds to the urban setting in which it stands, giving a special attention, at the same time, to the architectural detail of its composition.

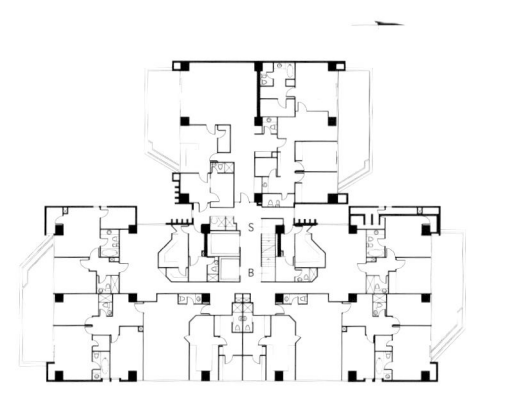

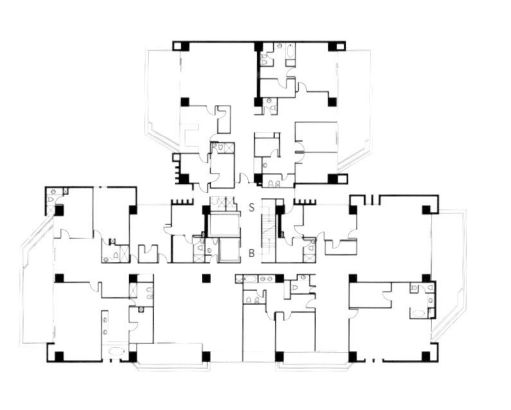

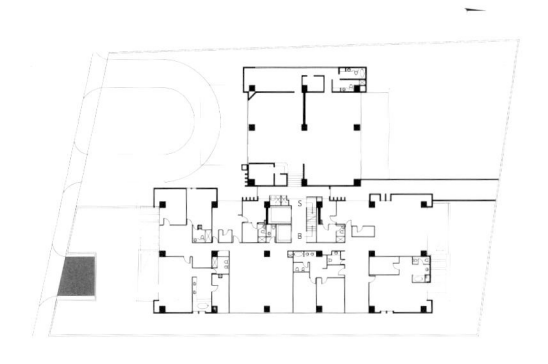

through broad open terraces adorned with plants and flowers that give a touch of nature to each apartment. In this context, the balconies of this building maintain a geometry of horizontal elements that articulate the vertical body of its volume. Oriented in a north-south direction, the building, which is structurally symmetrical, is made up of four volumes turned at a 45 degree angle at each corner, which allows the

L'EXCELLENCE BUILDING

interior spaces to give way to ample corner balconies. This structure reveals a play of columns and walls in the center of the block, which allowed for a great freedom of design and layout in each apartment. The three upper floors are differentiated by means of slanting corners that terminate, on the highest, in sloping roofs that strengthen the image of a residential building that is suitable for Guatemala City.

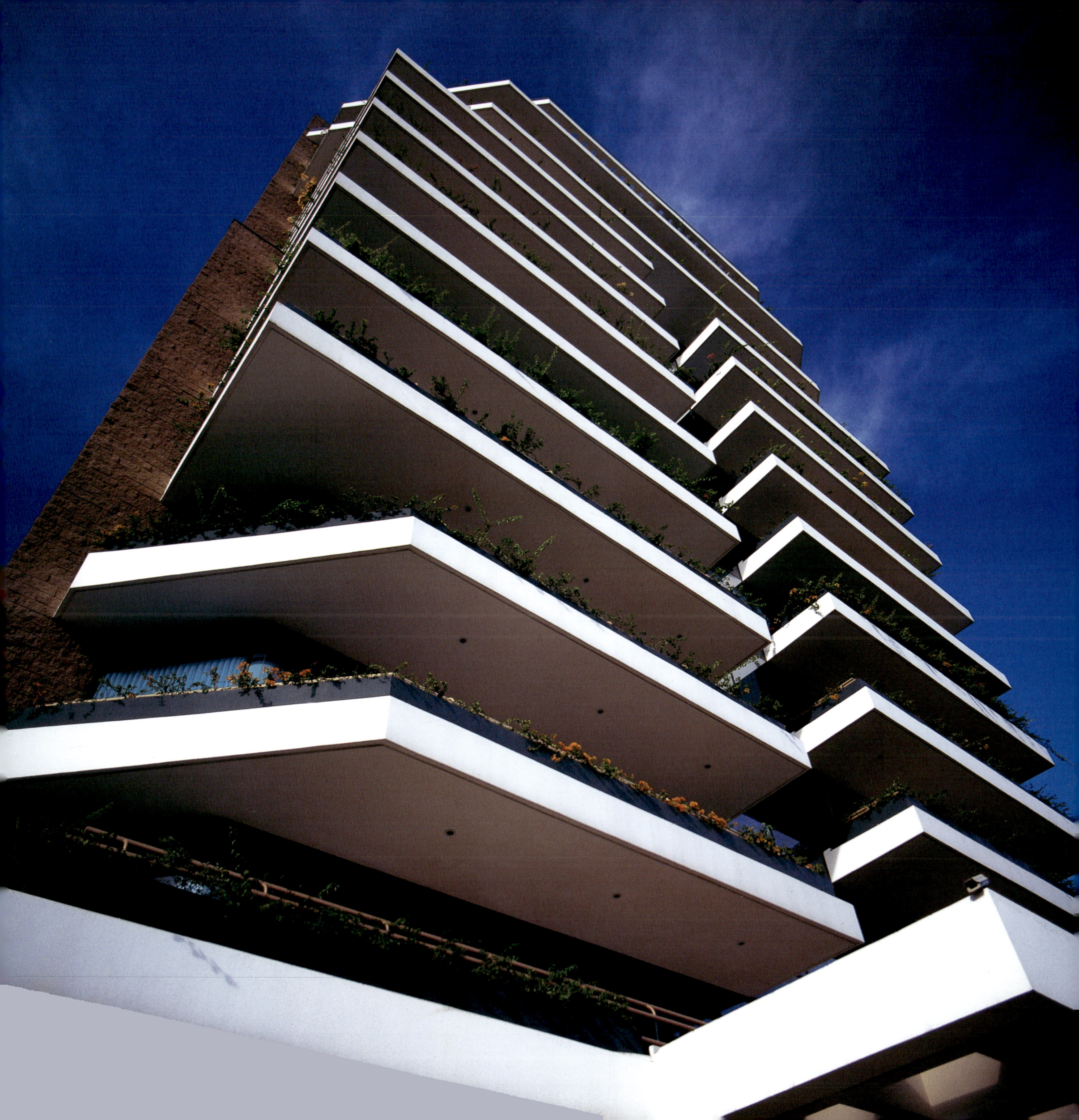

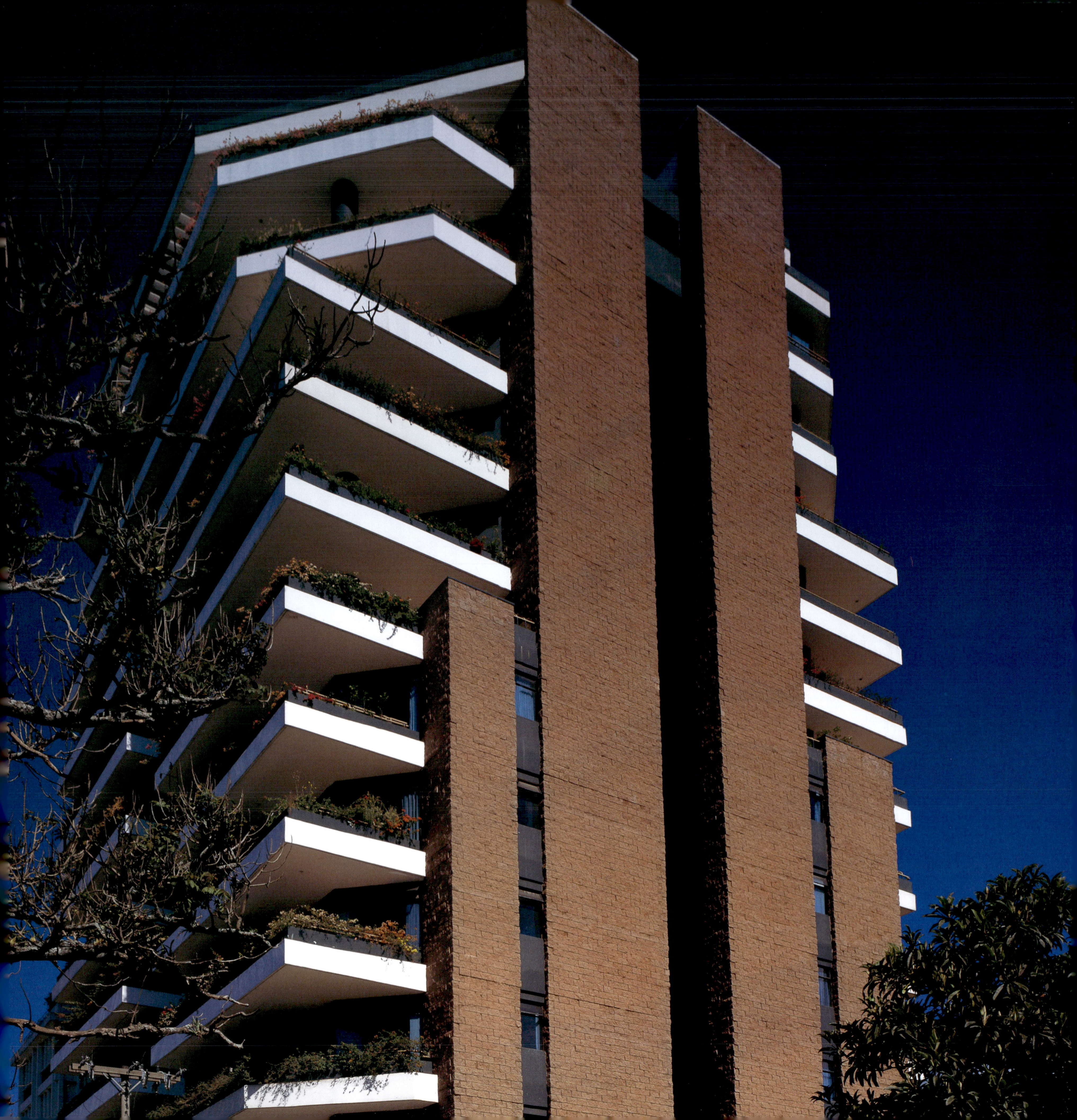

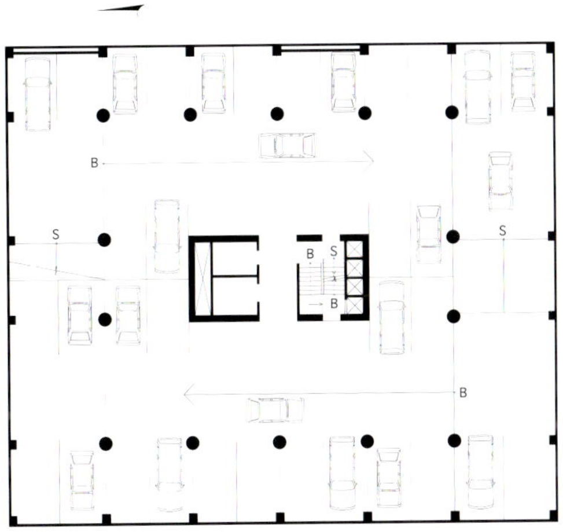

B
S
S
B
S
B
B

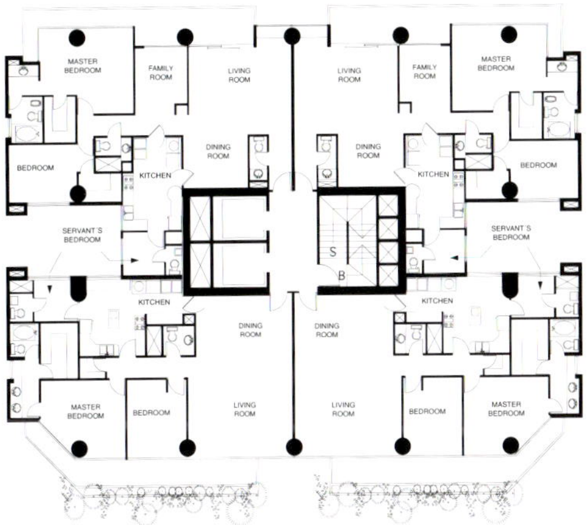

MASTER BEDROOM
FAMILY ROOM
LIVING ROOM
LIVING ROOM
FAMILY ROOM
MASTER BEDROOM
DINING ROOM
DINING ROOM
BEDROOM
KITCHEN
KITCHEN
BEDROOM
SERVANT'S BEDROOM
SERVANT'S BEDROOM
S
B
KITCHEN
KITCHEN
DINING ROOM
DINING ROOM
MASTER BEDROOM
BEDROOM
LIVING ROOM
LIVING ROOM
BEDROOM
MASTER BEDROOM

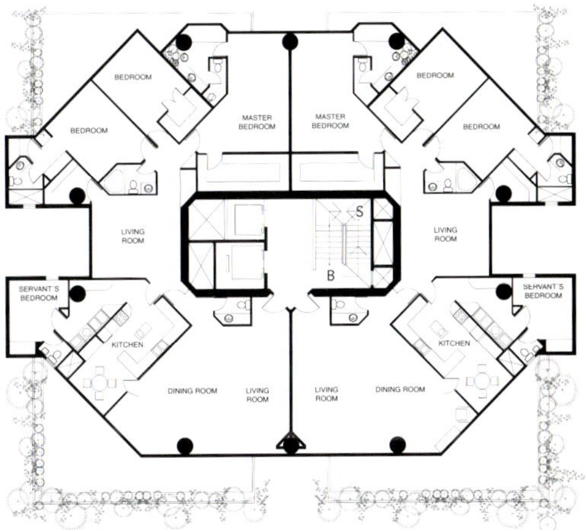

BEDROOM
BEDROOM
MASTER BEDROOM
MASTER BEDROOM
BEDROOM
BEDROOM
LIVING ROOM
S
LIVING ROOM
B
SERVANT'S BEDROOM
SERVANT'S BEDROOM
KITCHEN
KITCHEN
DINING ROOM
LIVING ROOM
LIVING ROOM
DINING ROOM

0 1 2 5 10 20

L'Excellence

Under the concept of a complex of townhouses organized around a plaza of gardens, the Cantabria Condominium expresses a European architectural style. The plaza-garden is raised half a level above the underground car park, allowing the individual units to enjoy a view over the green area. It is possible to gain access to the different two-story houses both from the plaza and the car park, which means that there is an adequate functionality both for visitors to and residents of the condominium. The stairways leading to the second-story apartments are placed within volumes that project towards the plaza, creating intermediate spaces that

CANTABRIA CONDOMINIUM

provide greater privacy for the residents. The stair landings in each of these projecting volumes extend out towards the plaza, forming a garden-like balcony with a view of nature. In the twenty-six units that make up the complex, the bedrooms of the upper area are located in an attic, a strategy which allows the houses, when seen from the garden, to maintain a horizontal proportion suitable for residential uses of this kind. The natural materials and shingle roofs of the architectural language turn the Cantabria Condominium into a European-style complex which nevertheless reflects the characteristic traits of the buildings of Solares & Lara.

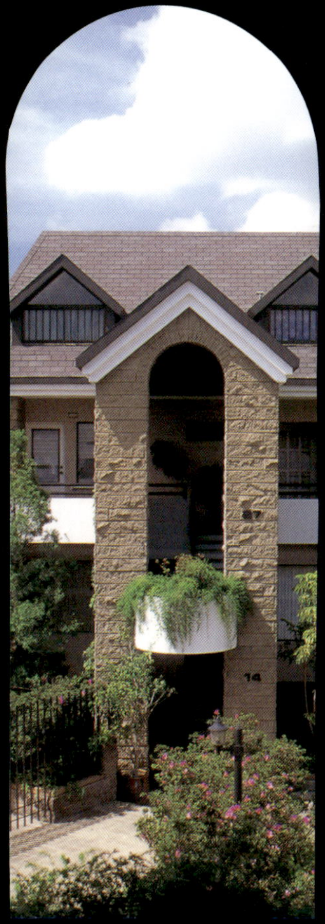

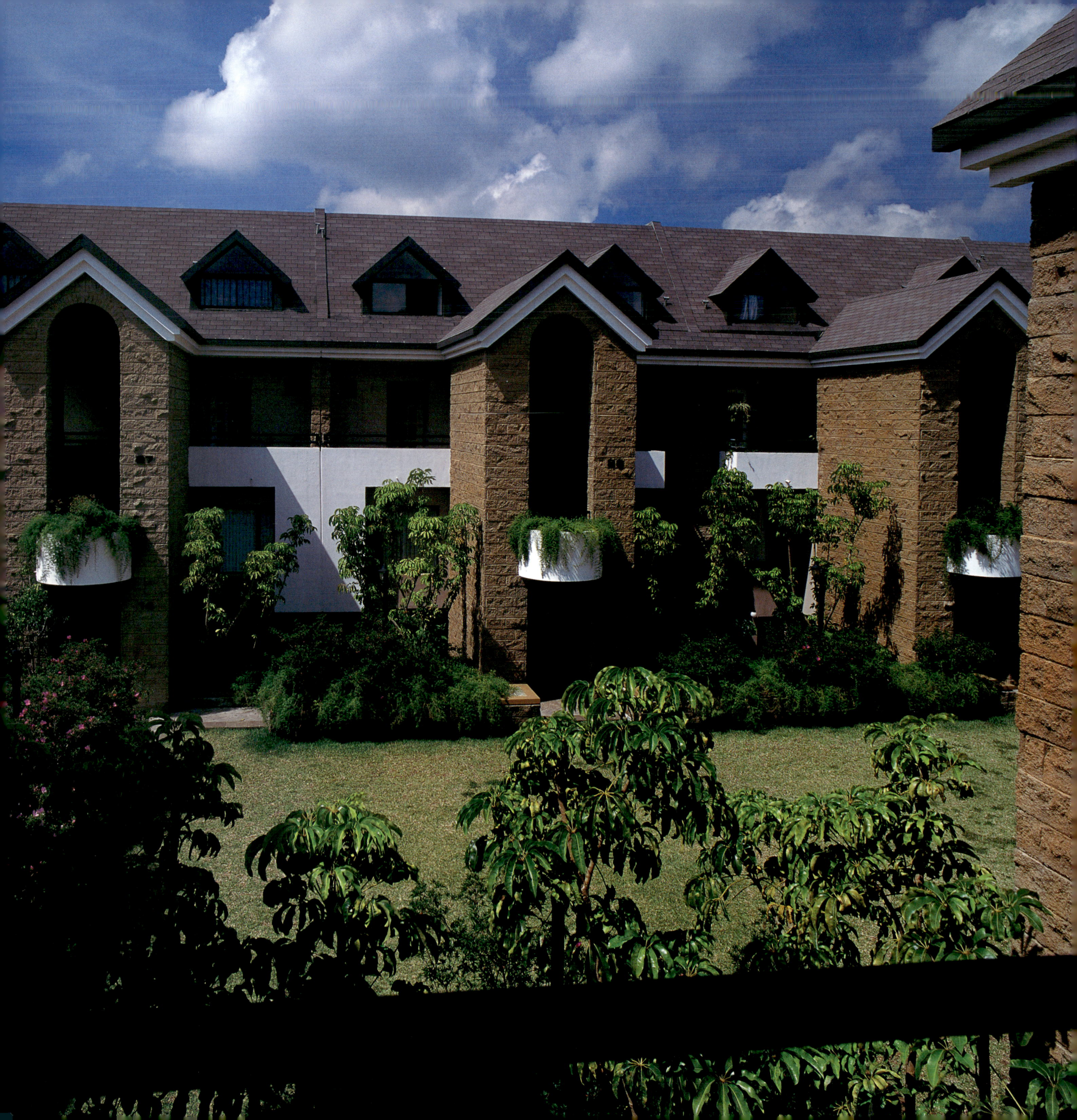

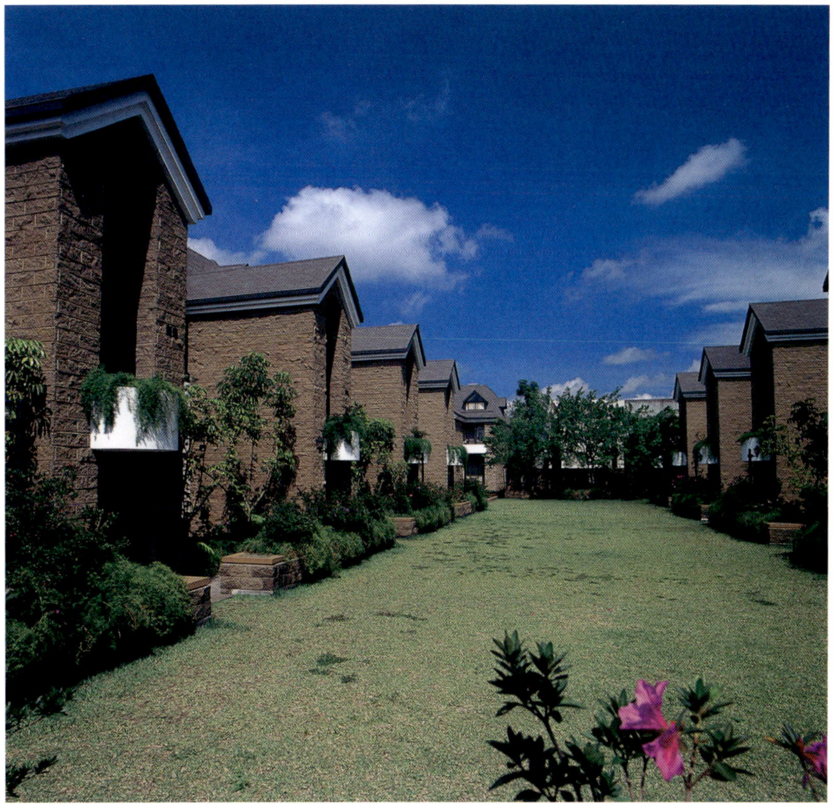

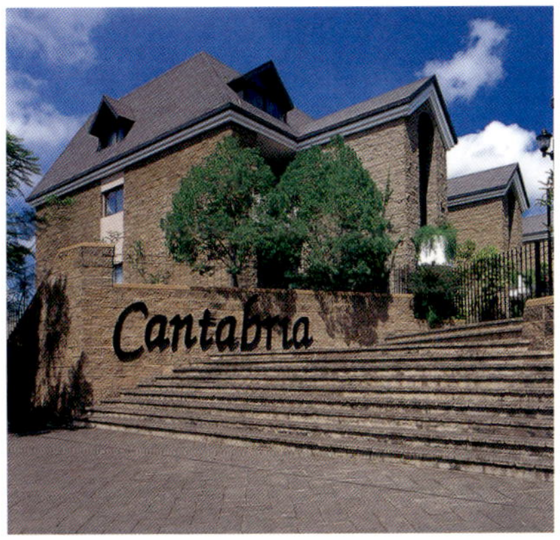
Cantabria

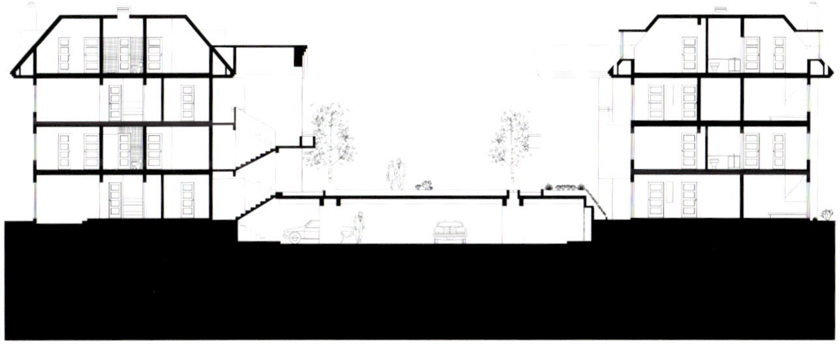

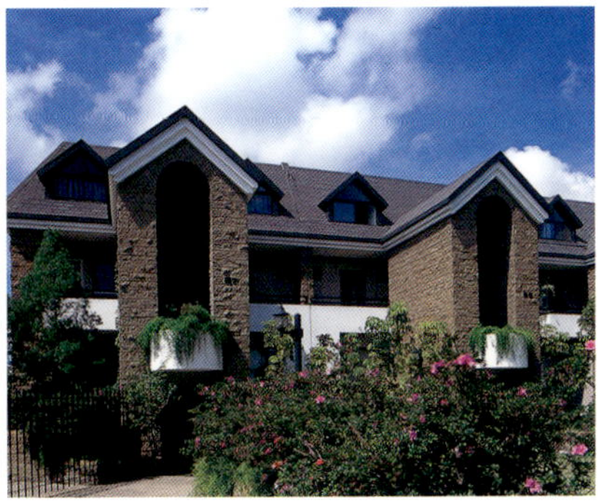

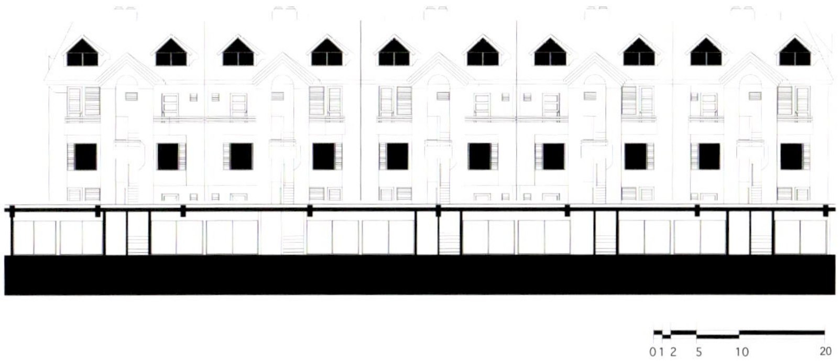
0 1 2 5 10 20

Located on the beach of Chulamar on the Pacific coast, this hotel was designed in the form of several modules, separated by ample areas of surrounding gardens. From these gardens radiate the main corridor, the entrance building and the swimming pools of the complex, as well as the wet-bar, which has a mezzanine with a panoramic view of the sea. The bedrooms are situated in the rear, in three-and four-story buildings with a four-slope roof thatched with palm, while the villas or suites are on the periphery. Some of the latter face a river that runs through the site, the María Linda, which divides the hotel into two sectors: one private, for guests and the other,

HOTEL VILLAS DEL PACÍFICO

mixed, which welcomes visitors. The design of the swimming pools has an organic shape, with the characteristic gently curving lines, giving rise to alternate spaces that divide the vegetated areas from those which are set aside for sunbathing and games. The overall architecture is made up of big, heavy walls, with very ample bays, little texture and fresh-toned colors. The structures of tied logs which support the palm-leaf roofs integrate the architectural elements into the natural setting, thus achieving a series of ample and well-ventilated interior spaces.

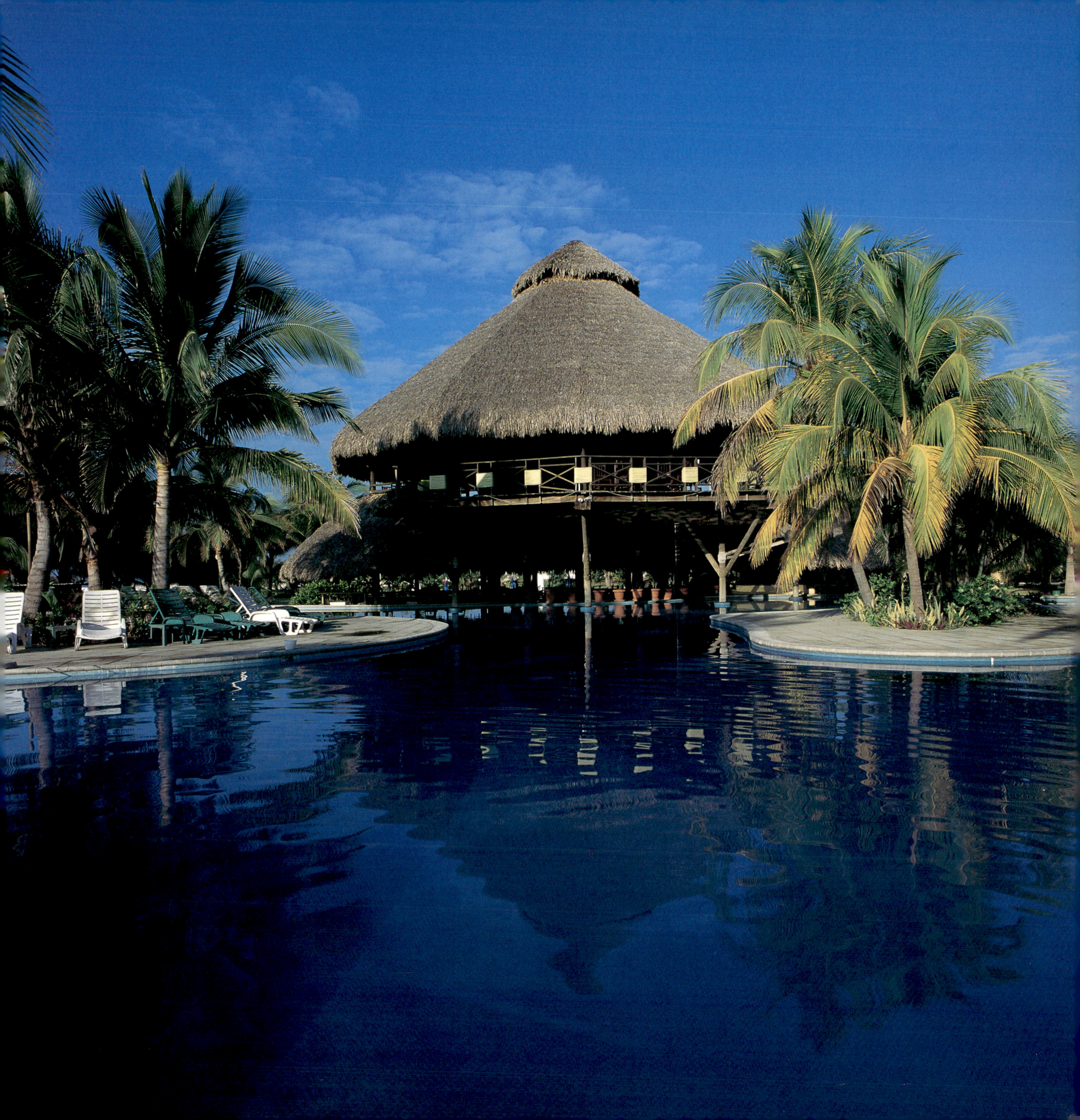

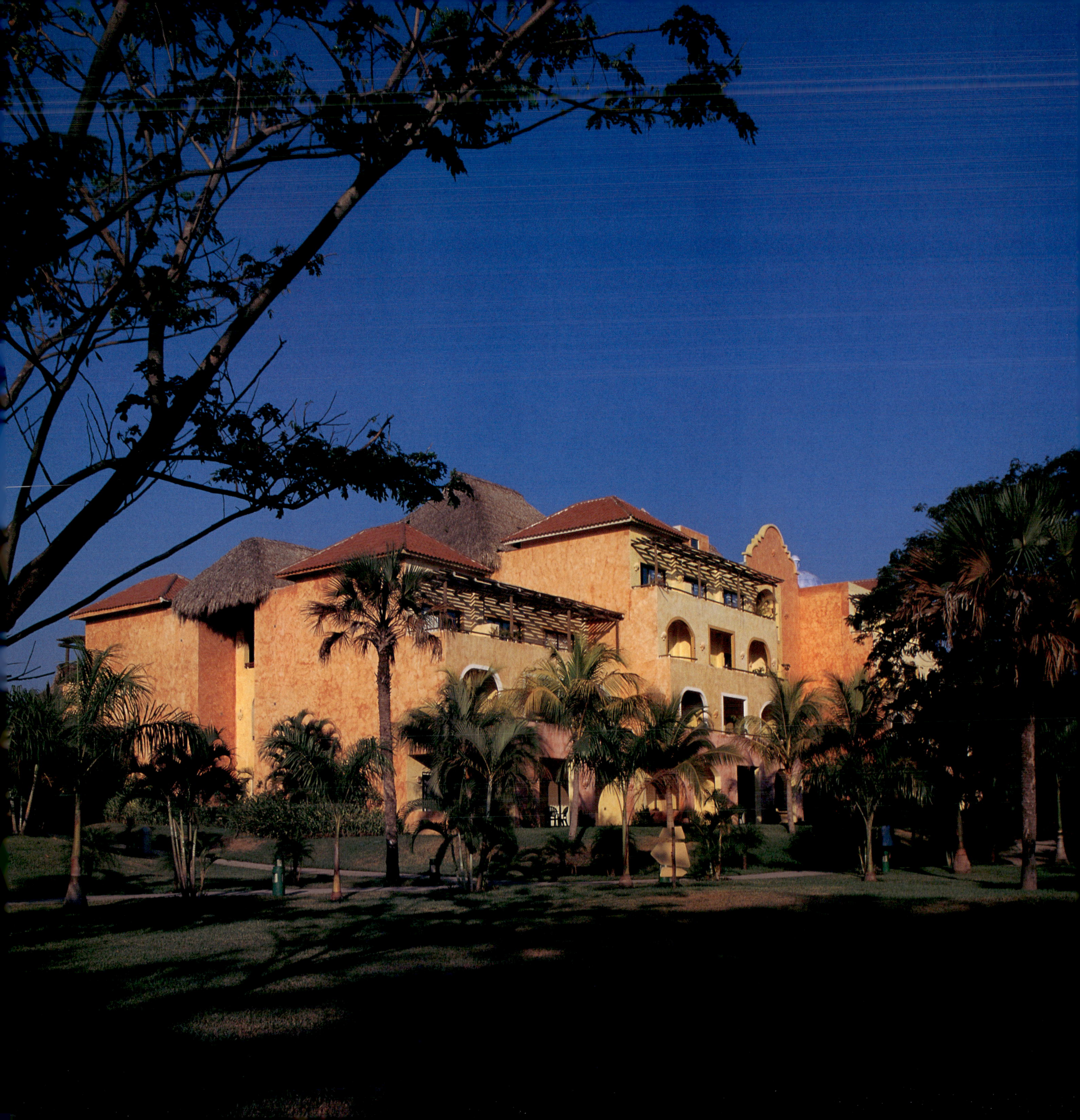

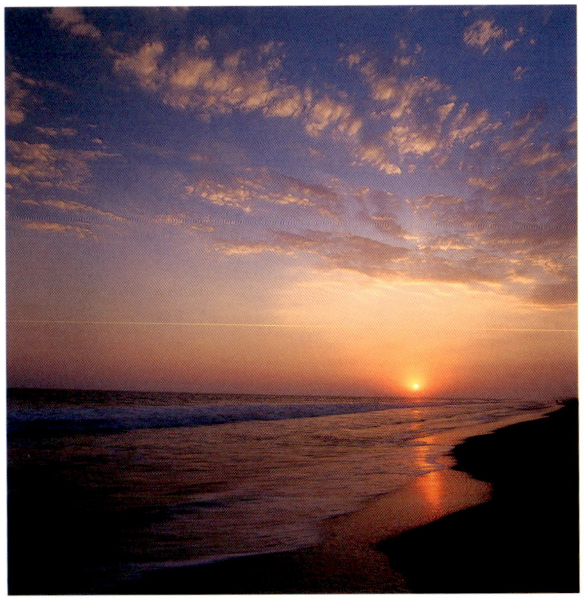

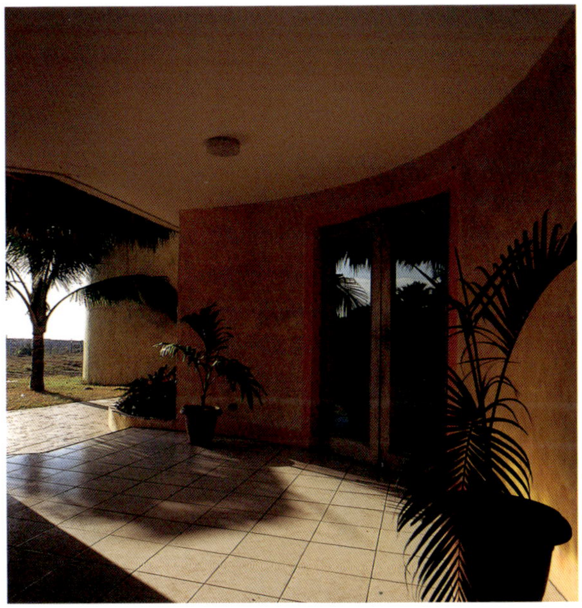

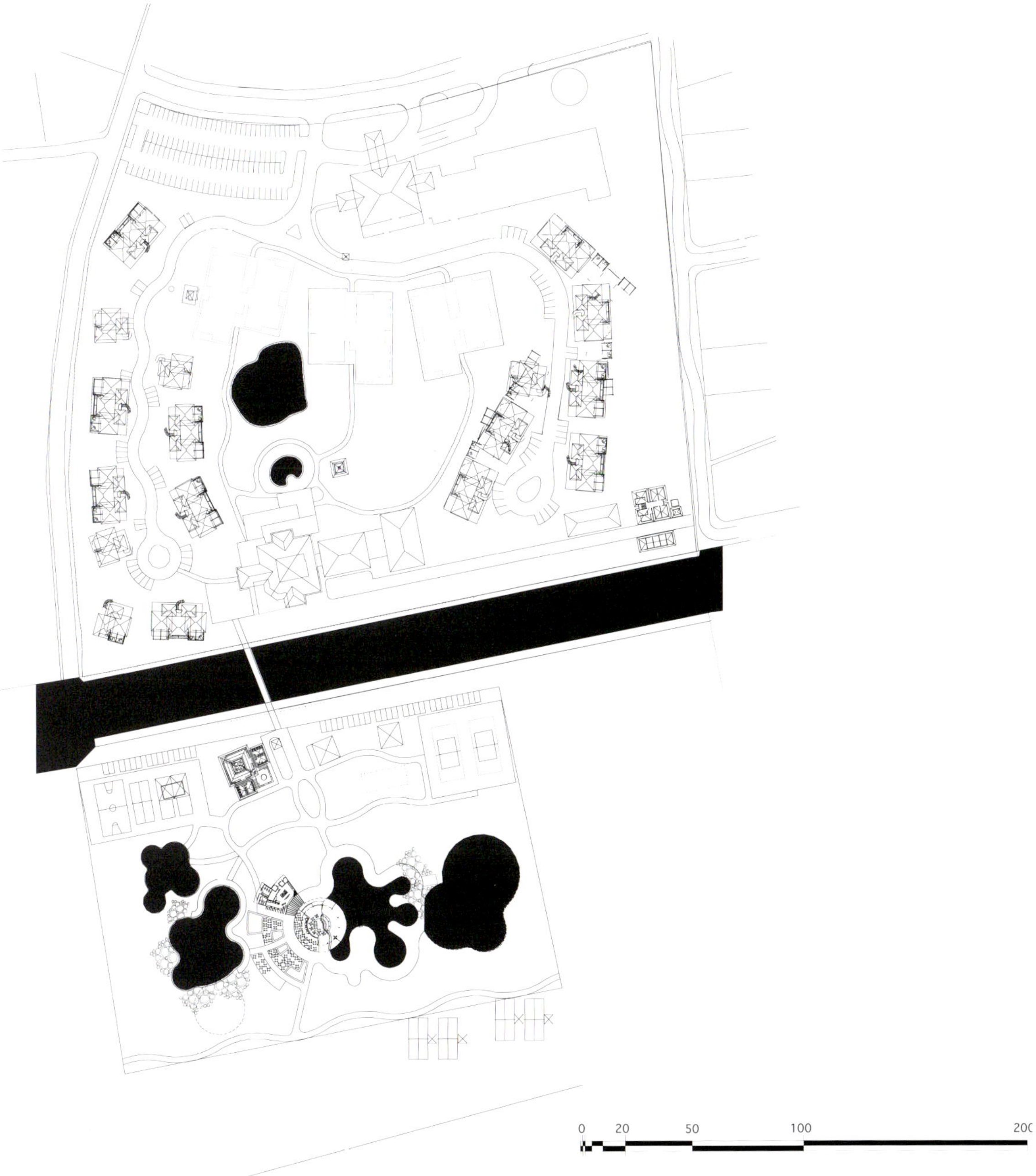
0
20
50
100
200

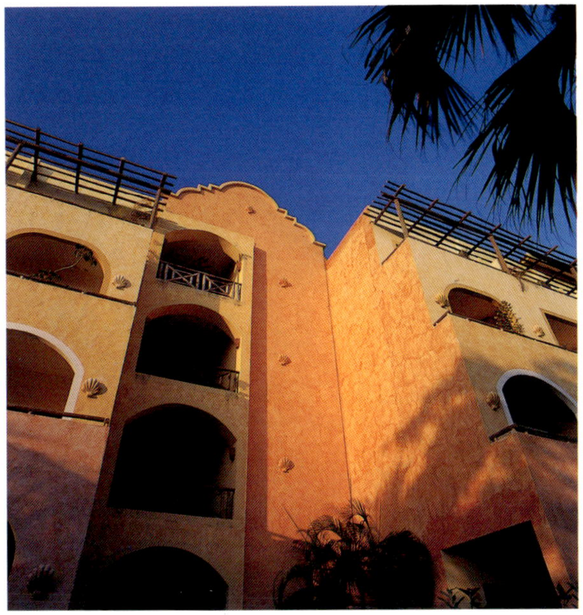

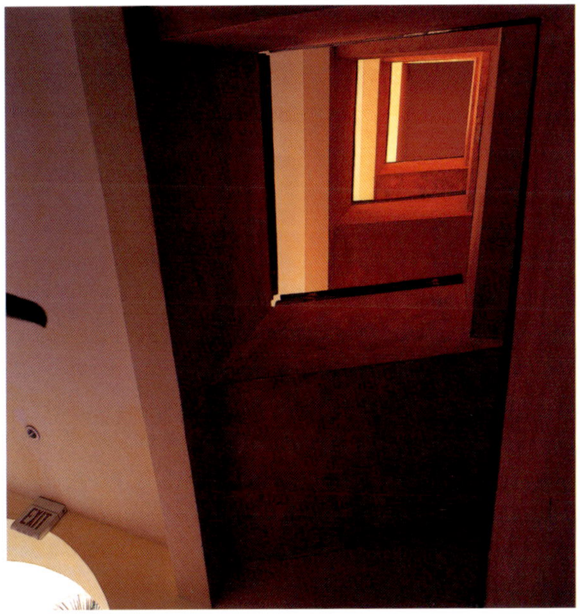

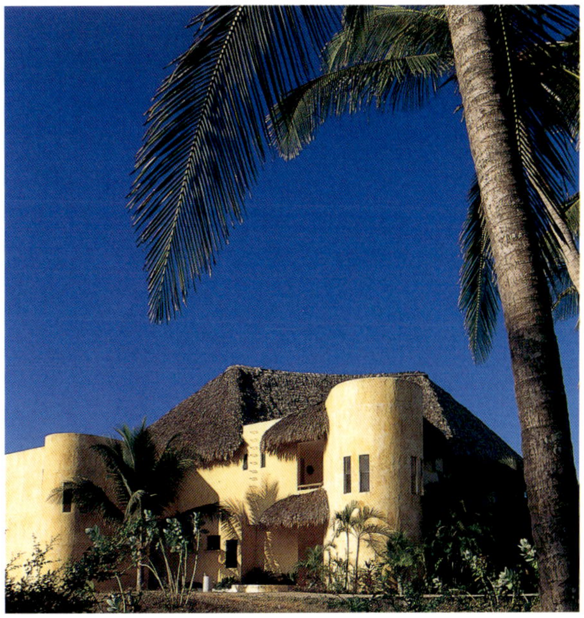

This vacation home is set in a rocky terrain of the bay of Tzanguacal, on the shores of Lake Atítlan. The main design idea arose in an intuitive way and was shown to the clients in a paper model. A white sail over blue water inspired the creation of a white concrete roof, the lower part of which rests on an inverted-scissors steel truss, lined in mahogany wood, which gives warmth to the ambits. The house was given a north-westerly orientation to protect it from the wind, which also allows for a view of the broadest part of the lake. From this point, one may enjoy a view of the sun setting over the Cerro de Oro ("Golden Mountain"), a scene of singular beauty. On entering the

HOUSE IN THE BAY OF TZANGUACAL

house, the visitor descends a number of stairs, whose placement reveals and frames the view over the lake and its surroundings through the overlaps formed by the layers of the roof. Reaching the two-story-high living room, decorated with a mural by the artist Jake Demburg, you encounter glass doors which open onto the exterior space to integrate the living room with the exterior. There, an ample projecting terrace, which rests on walls of carved local stone, terminates in a stone bench covered with blue ceramic tiles that seem to merge into the tranquil blue waters of the lake.

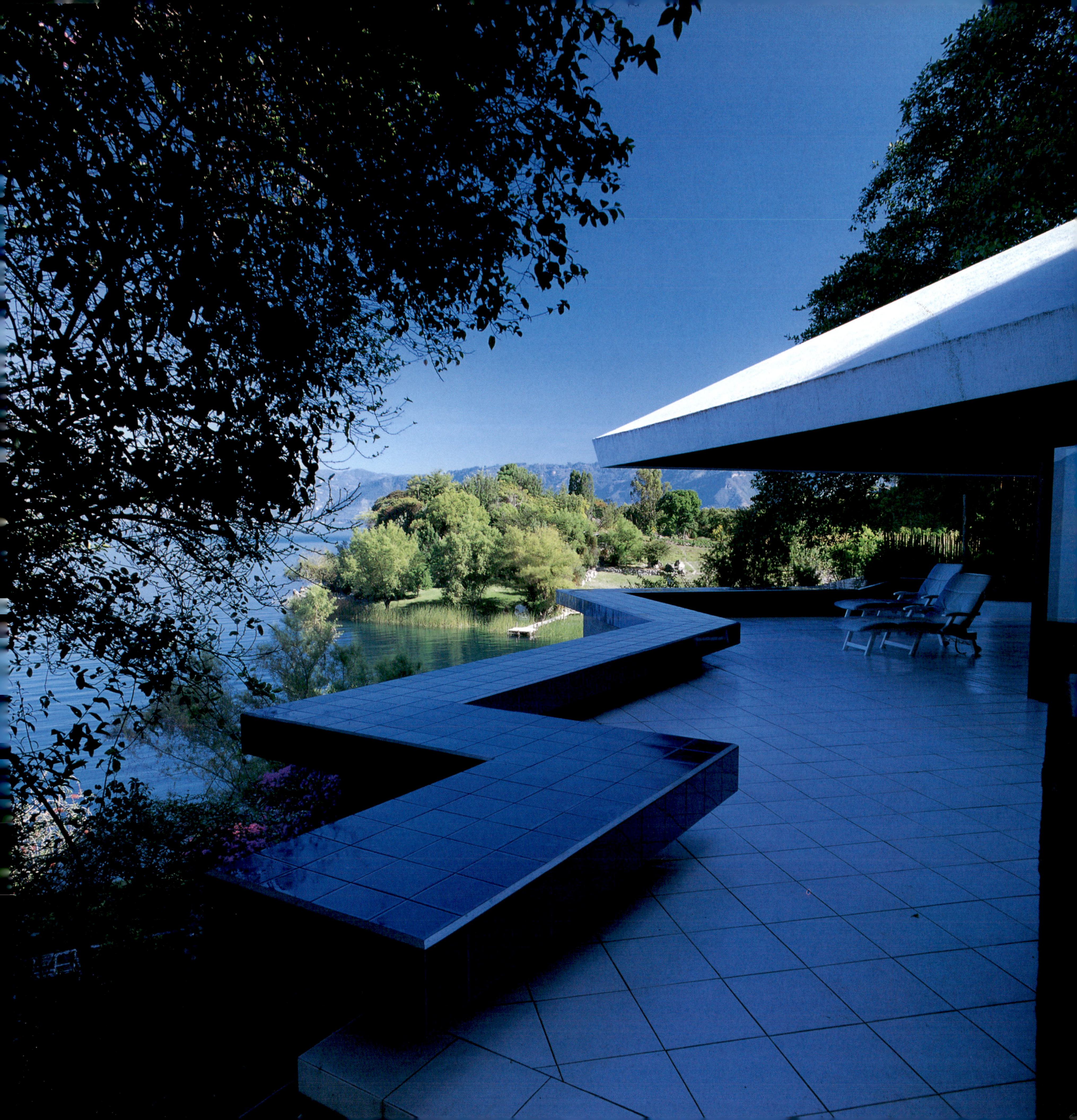

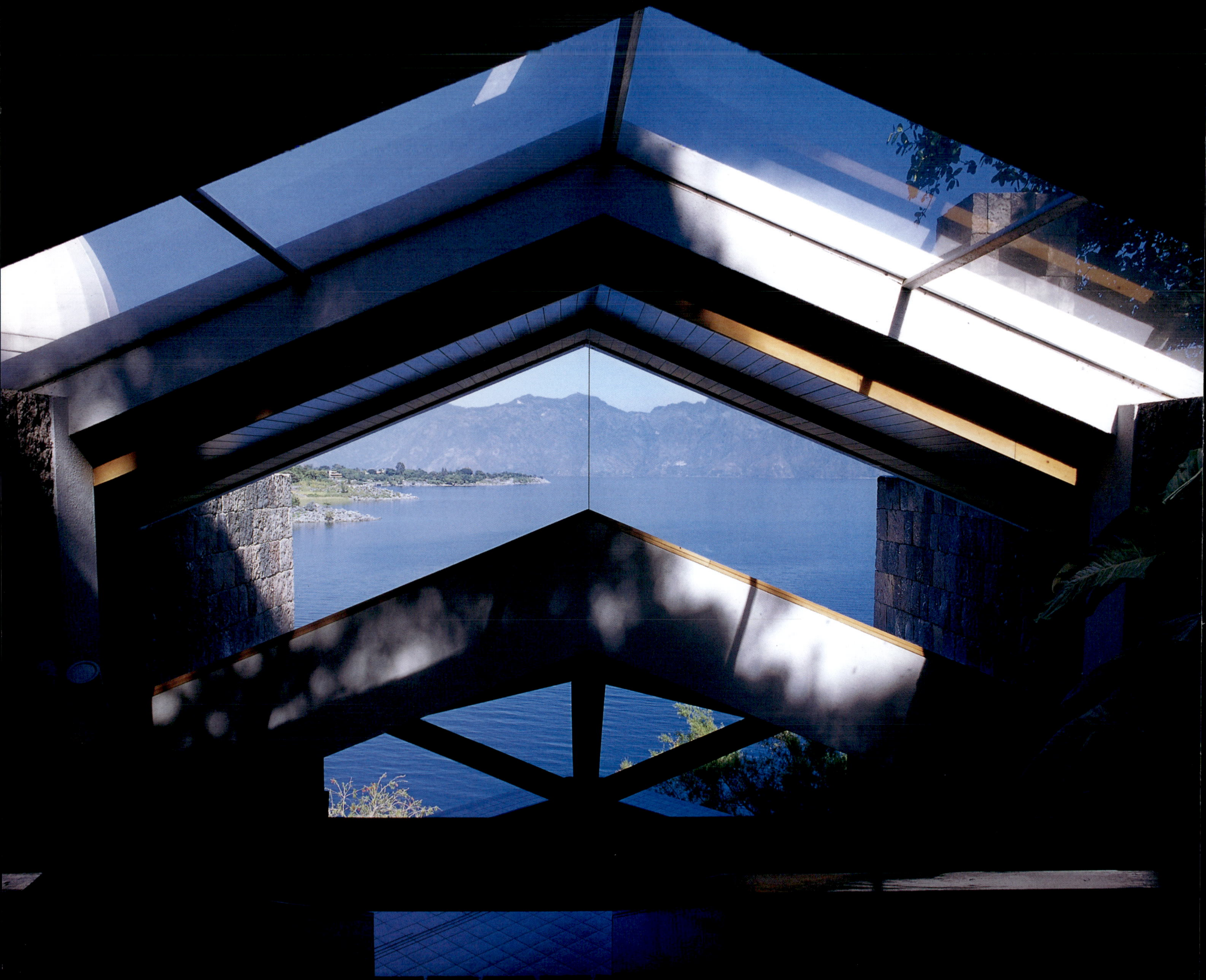

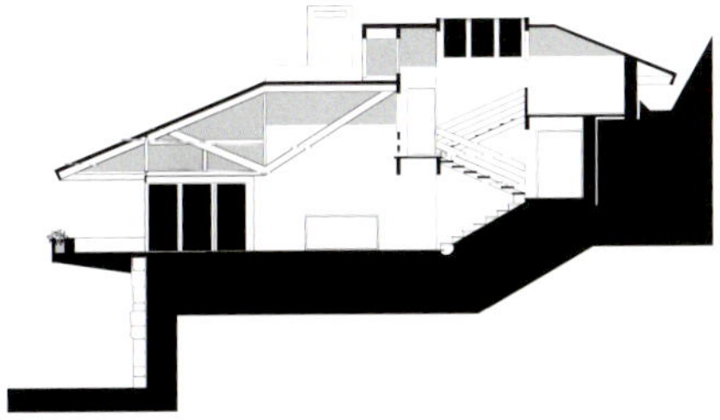

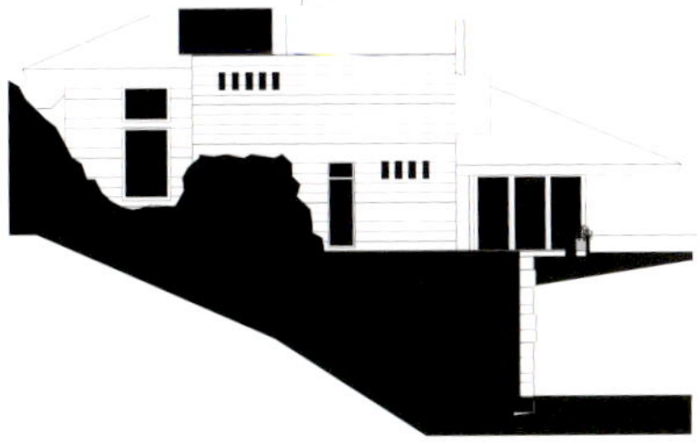

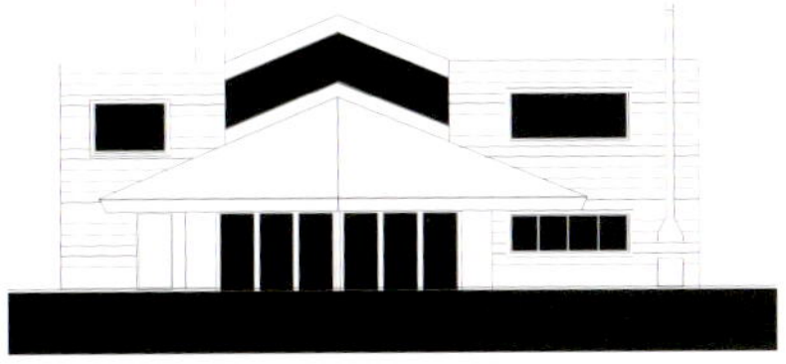

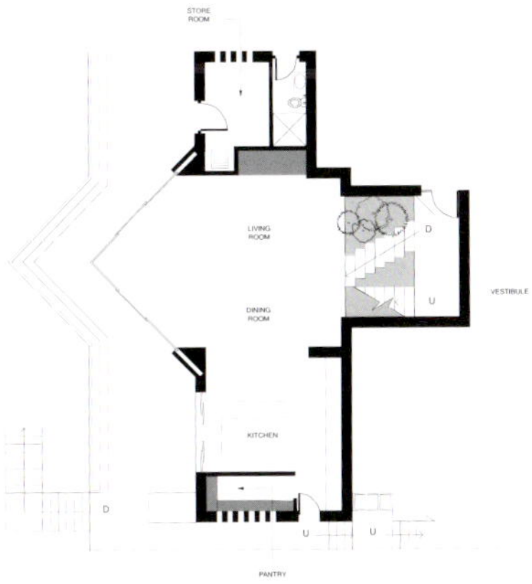

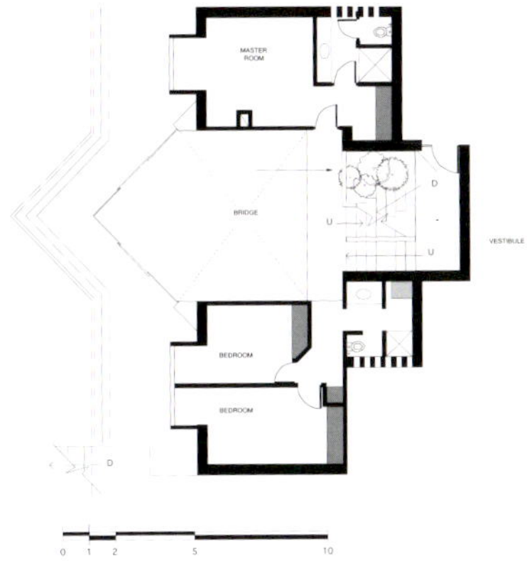

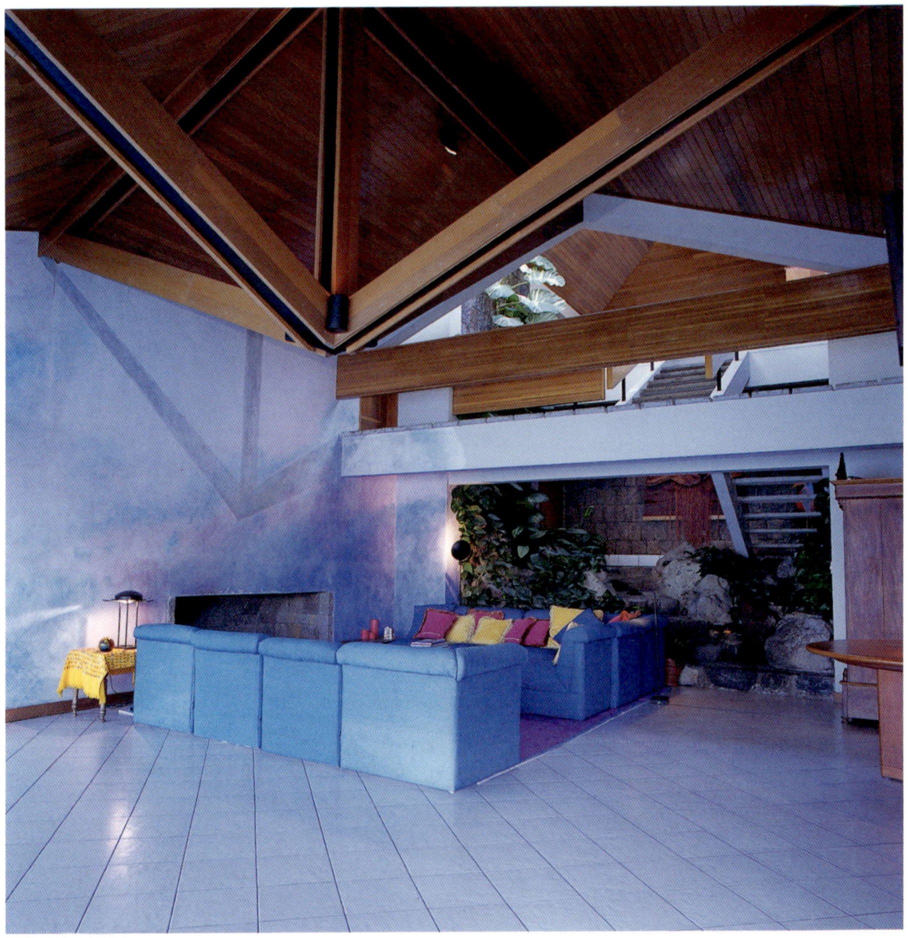

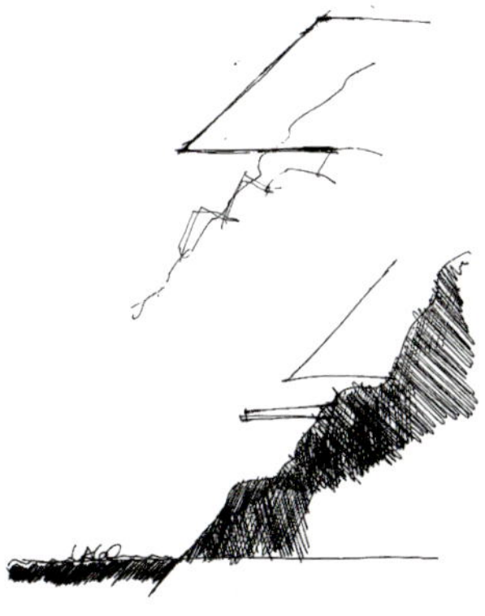

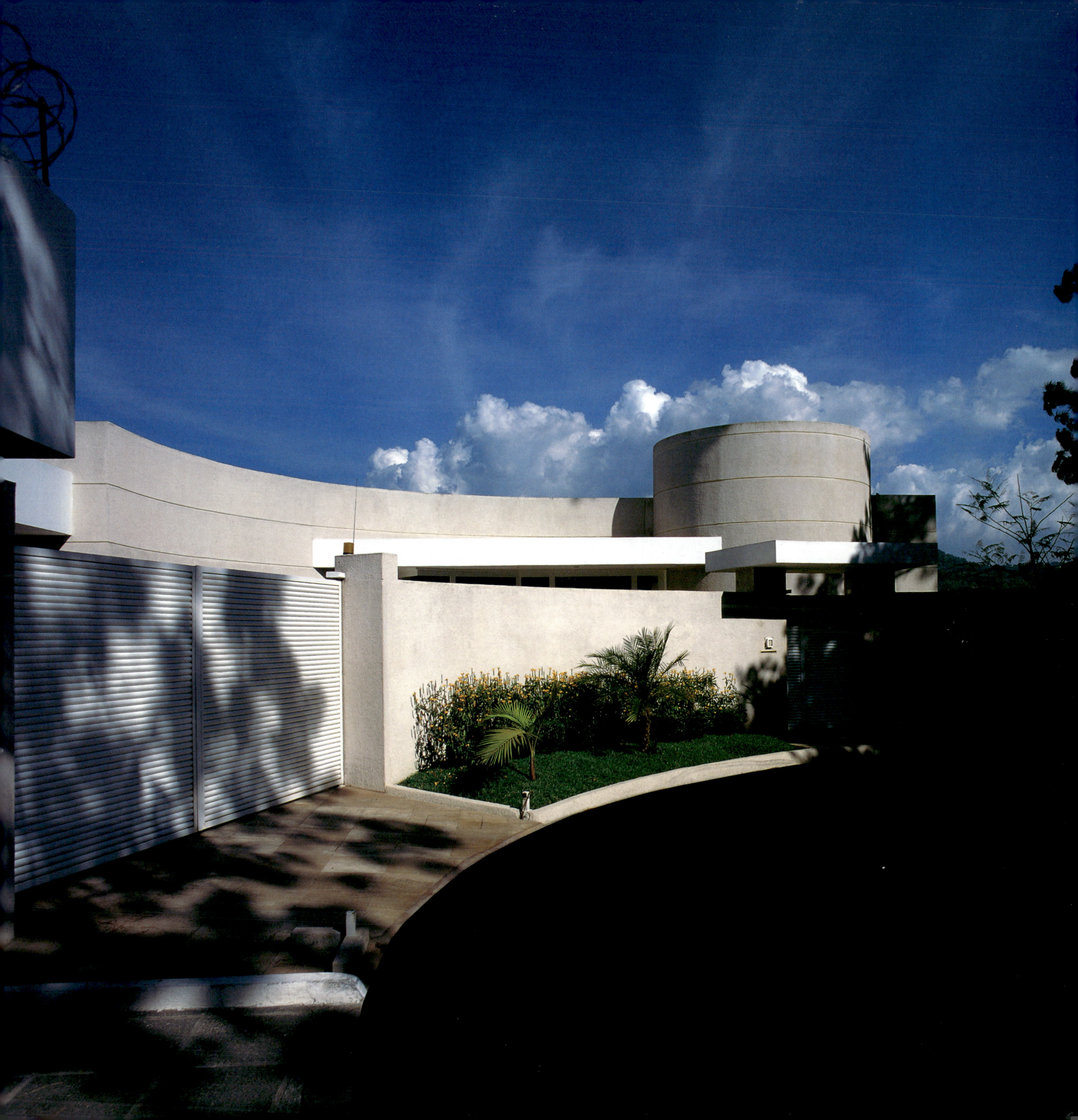

Designed by a young couple from Guatemala City, the Casa de la Rotonda (the "Rotunda House") runs lengthwise along the side of one of the ravines that are characteristic of the local topography. This orientation permits the views to be divided into panoramic vistas of nature, on one side, and vistas towards the garden, on the other. The view towards the ravine from the living room is articulated, in turn, by the rectilinear volume of the chimney, which acts to partly divide the social space from the balcony which runs along the second floor of the rear face. When the windows are opened, the living room is integrated into the exterior space of the balcony to complete the view towards the swimming pool and the garden on the lower level, while, at the same time, the balcony provides shade for the rooms on that floor.

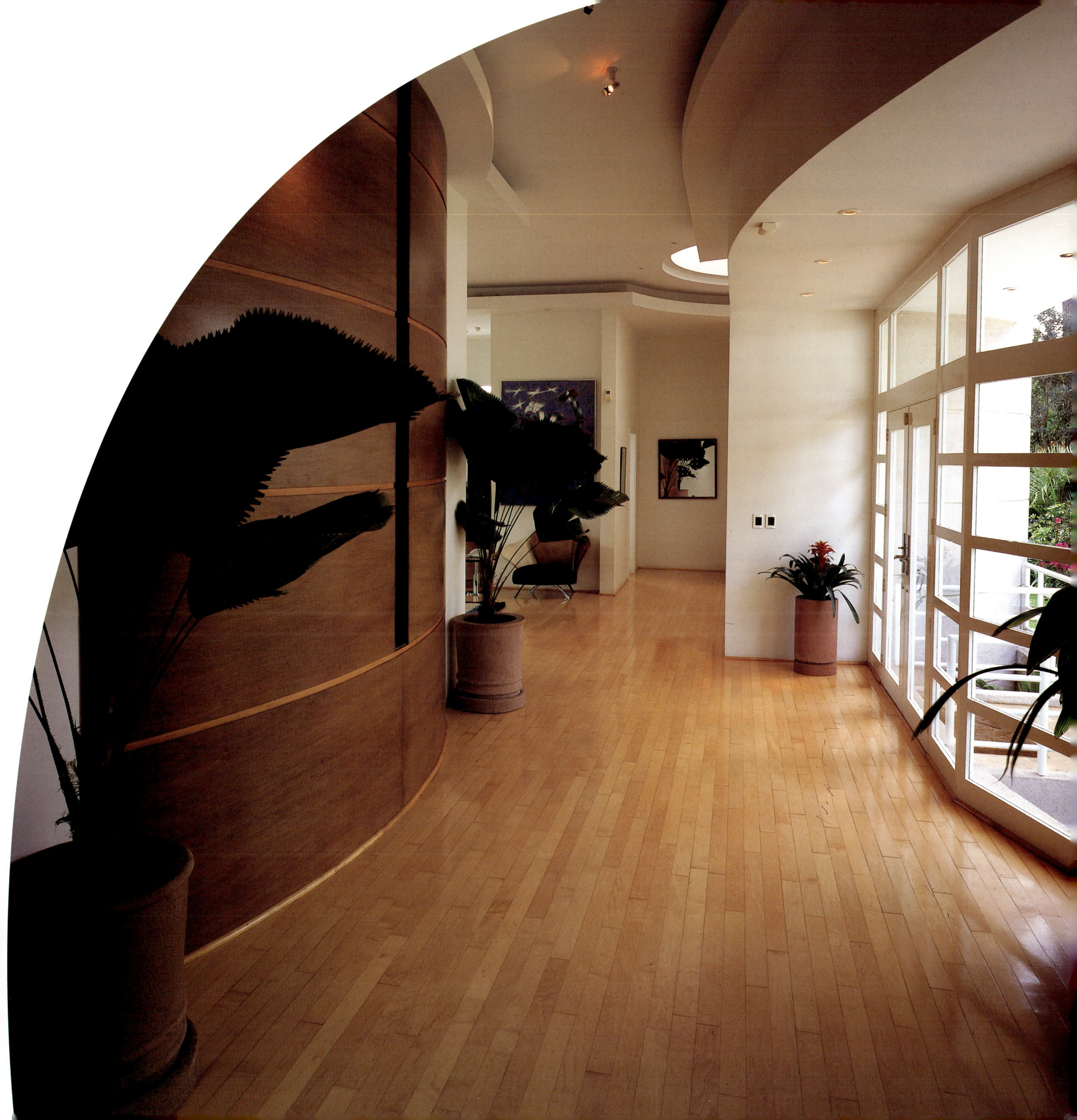

The overall geometry used in this design works with a long horizontality in the elevation, which is then broken by a vertical cylinder topped by a glass dome. By virtue of its prominence, this cylinder indicates the location of the main entrance; it also provides light for the main stairwell and the first-and second-floor vestibules. The presence of natural light in this space is further taken advantage of through the use of a semi-cylindrical-shaped vertical duct which channels the illumination towards the main walk-in closet. In addition, the uniformly hammered concrete texture of the main façade contrasts with the horizontal lines of the cylinder, which articulate their geometry so as adapt to the linear form of the elevation. The floor plan shows a broadly-curved front façade which responds to the public space of the street, on the one hand, and the curvature of the private space of the cylinder, on the other. Since the couple who designed the house love to coouk, the kitchen was designed to open onto the social spaces so that there would be a visual and physical communication between them. The architecture of the Casa de la Rotonda, with its innovative spatial arrangement and clean shapes and materials, makes us recall the words once uttered by Le Corbusier, when he was talking about modernity: "Modern life demands a new plan for the house and the city." And in the same way, Casa de la Rotunda becomes a new plan that articulates the distribution of its impeccable geometric volumes.

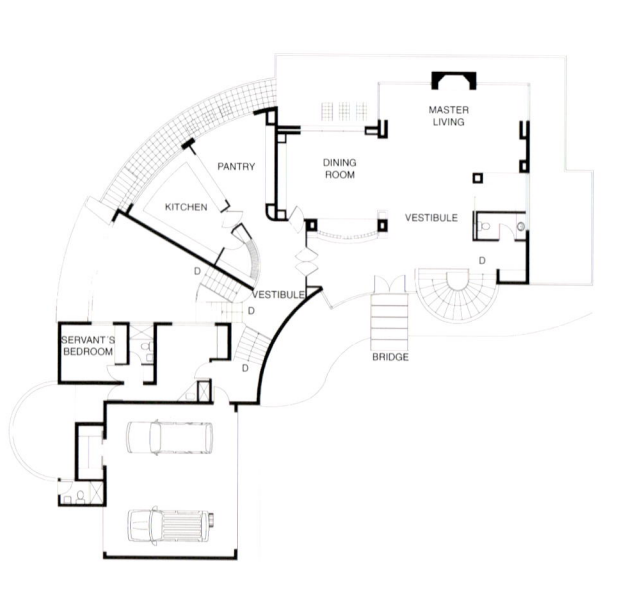

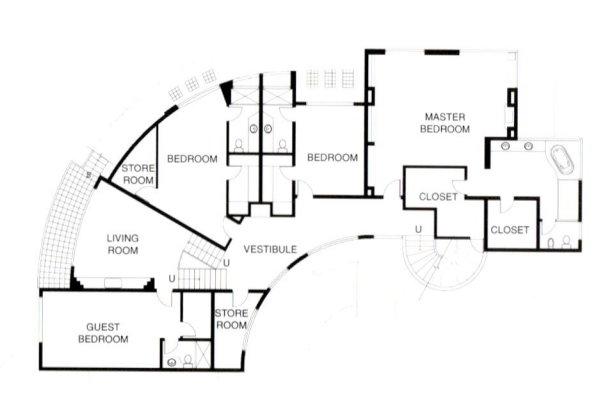

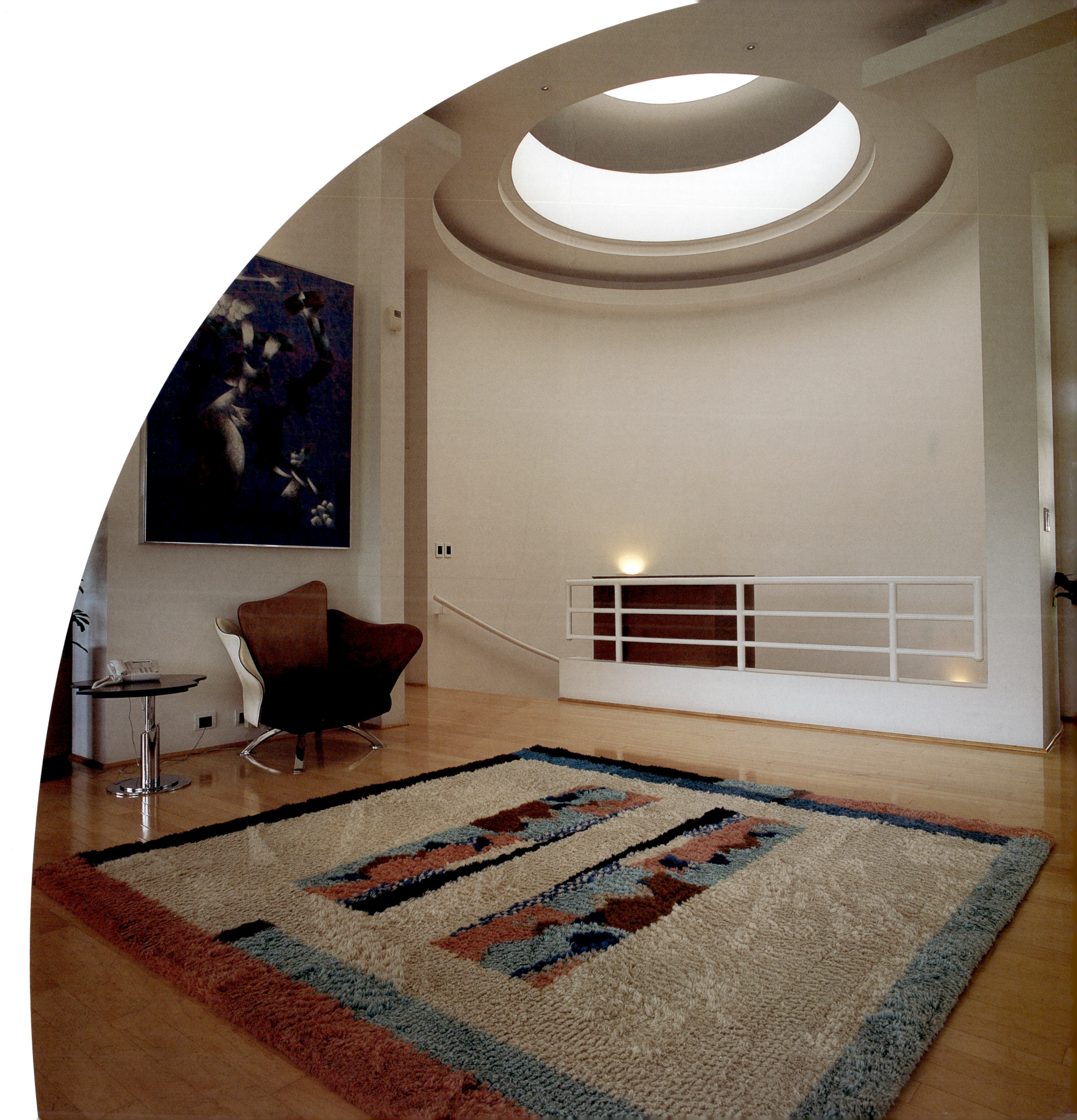

Approaching a minimalist simplicity, the Casa de los Árboles ("House of the Trees") is completely delineated by clean right-angled lines. Designed for an artist chef, it has a two-story-high kitchen and despite the fact that it is not a country house, this ample kitchen helps to create the social ambit that forms the nucleus of the spatial organization of its interiors. The windows in the social area are also high, so that one may appreciate the verticality of the tall trees that surround the house, and thus work to fit the house into its natural setting. The exterior was given a smooth rust-red plaster finish to soften the harshness of the volumes. The

CASA DE LOS ÁRBOLES

characteristic concern for detail of Solares & Lara led them to design a front door reminiscent of a monochromatic painting by Mondrian. Its rust-steel color vanishes into the rust-red of the smooth plaster of the walls, while the burnished steel on the inside of the door merges with the glass and stainless steel utilized for the details within the house. This characteristic is especially seen in the use of the glazed panels that support the handrails in the different passageways, which remove visual obstructions in those areas. To accentuate this spatial fluidity, the continuous cork floor, without seams or grid lines, gives a harmonic unity to all of the elements.

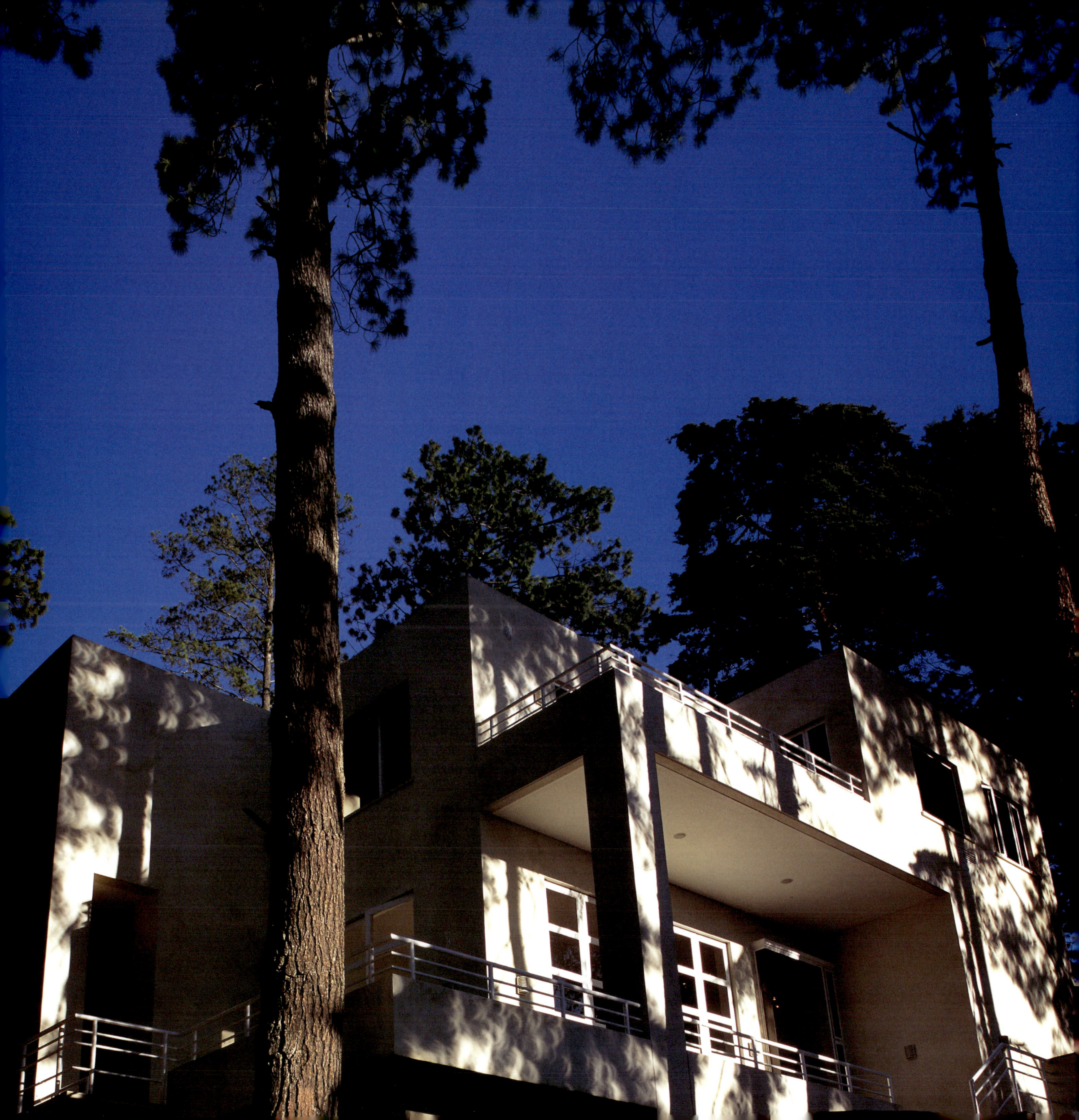

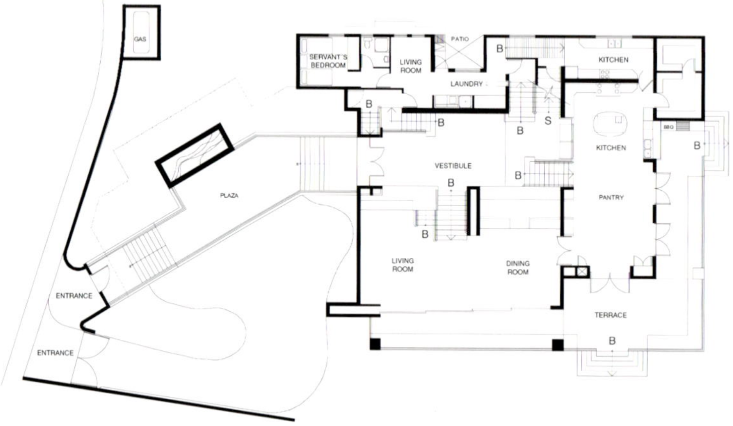
GAS
SERVANT'S BEDROOM
LIVING ROOM
PATIO
LAUNDRY
KITCHEN
PLAZA
VESTIBULE
KITCHEN
BBQ
PANTRY
LIVING ROOM
DINING ROOM
ENTRANCE
ENTRANCE
TERRACE

LIVING ROOM
VISITORS BATHROOM
W.C.
BATHROOM
MASTER BEDROOM
BEDROOM
GAMES ROOM
BEDROOM

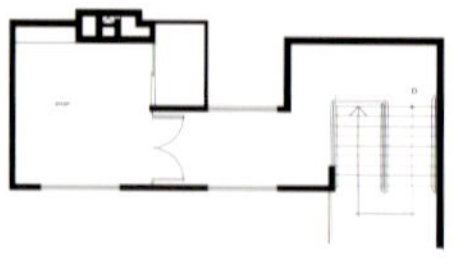

0 1 2 5 10

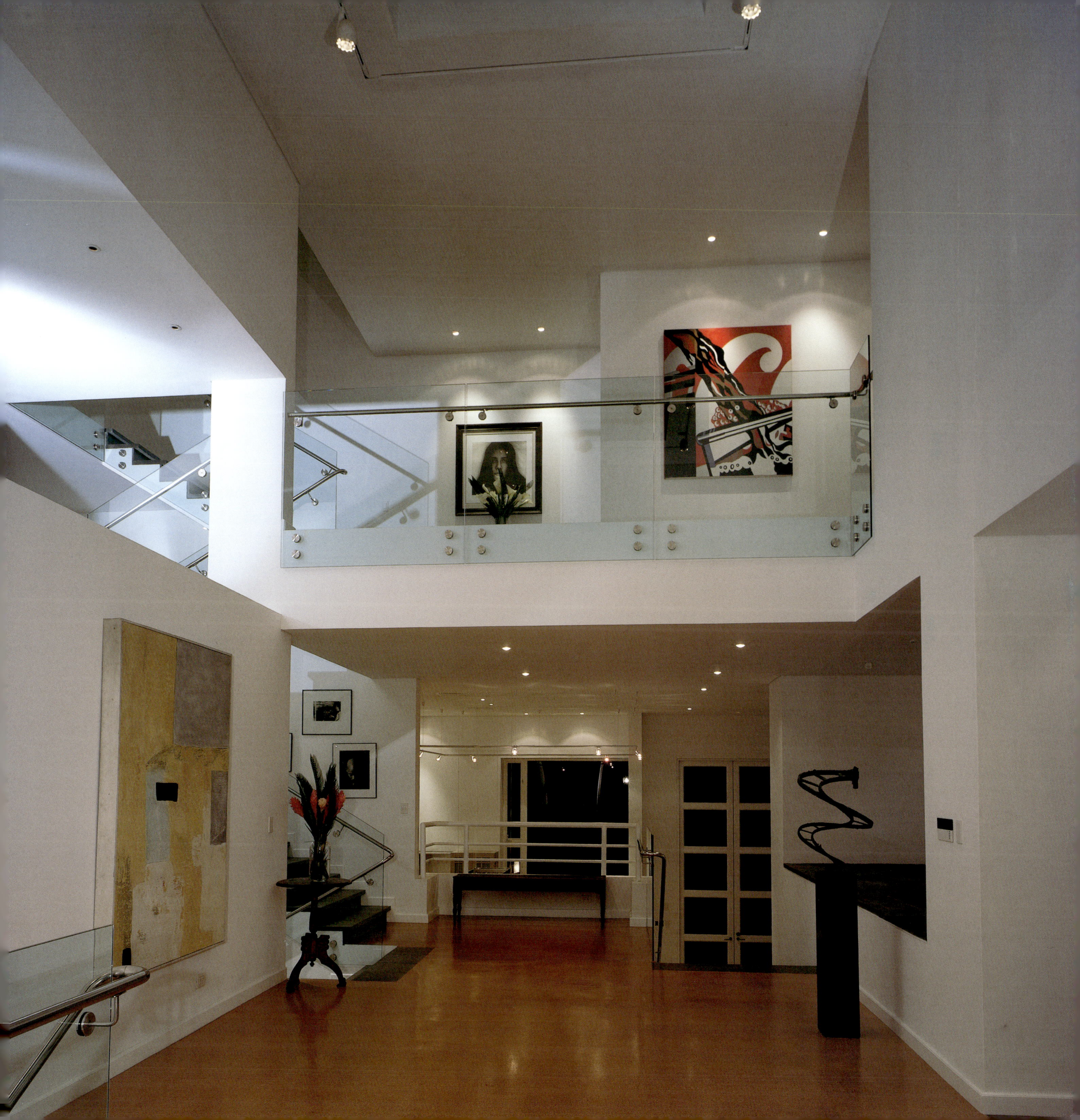

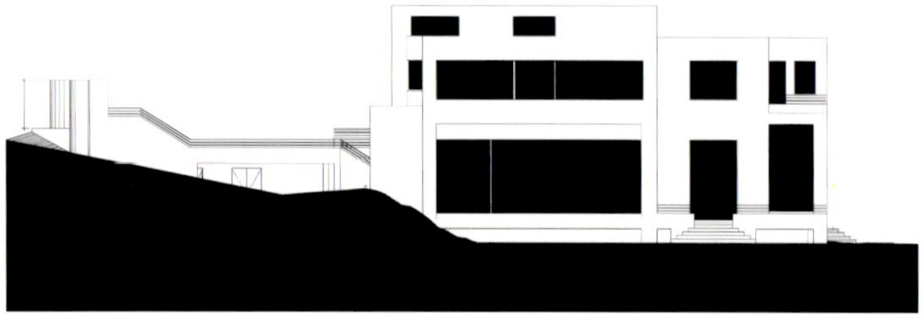

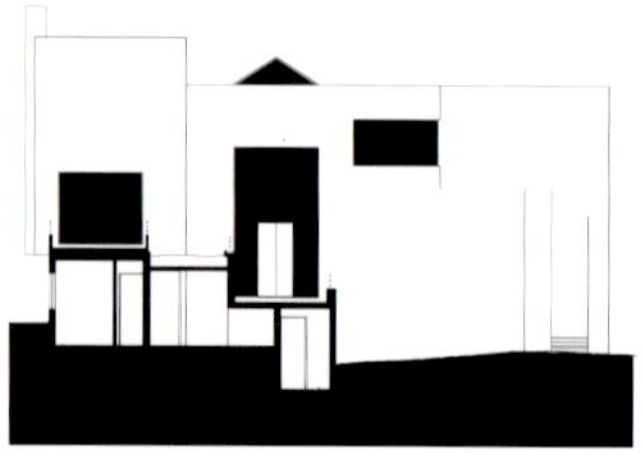

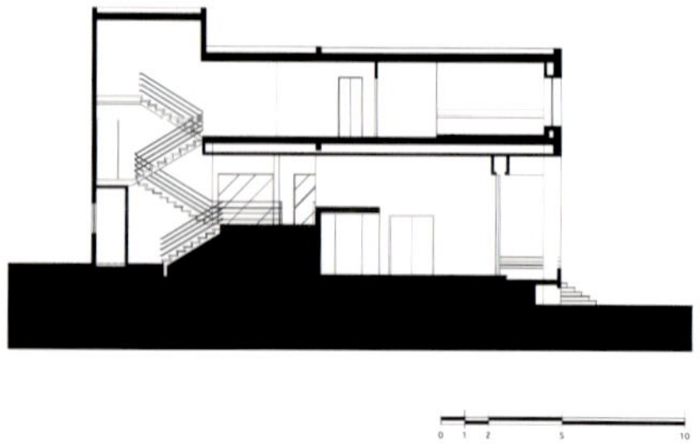

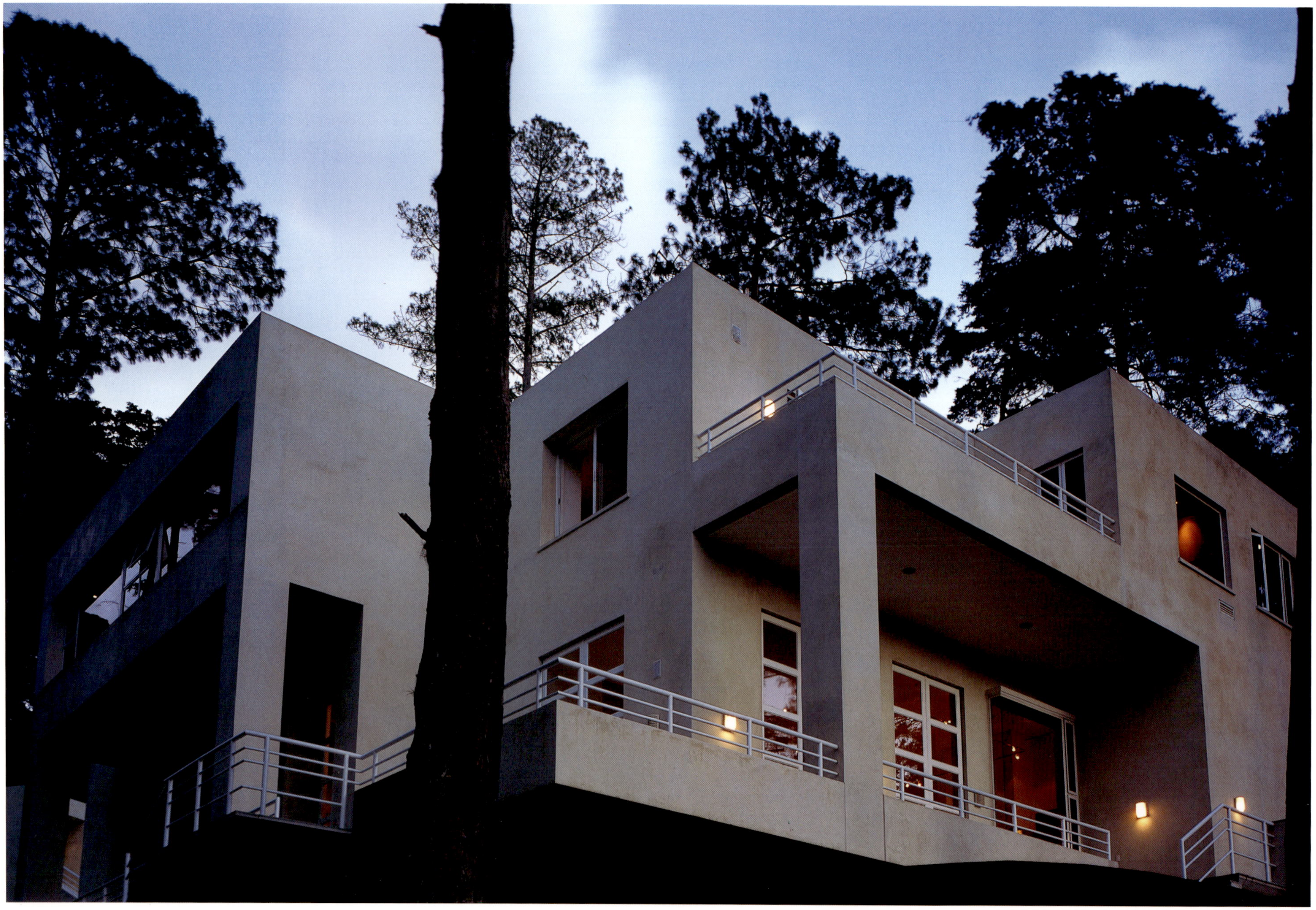

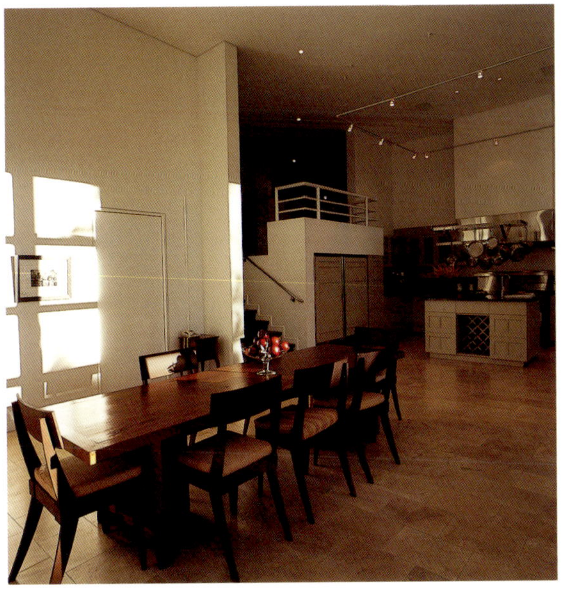

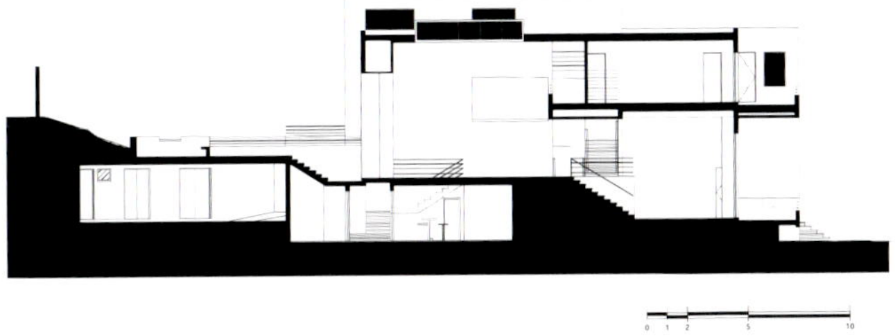

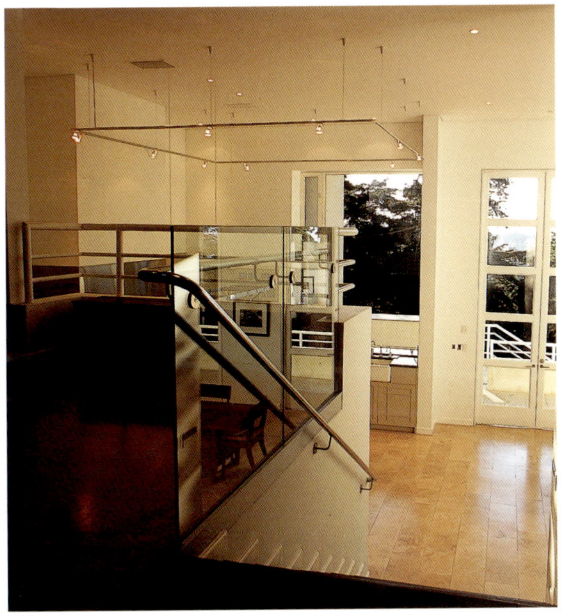

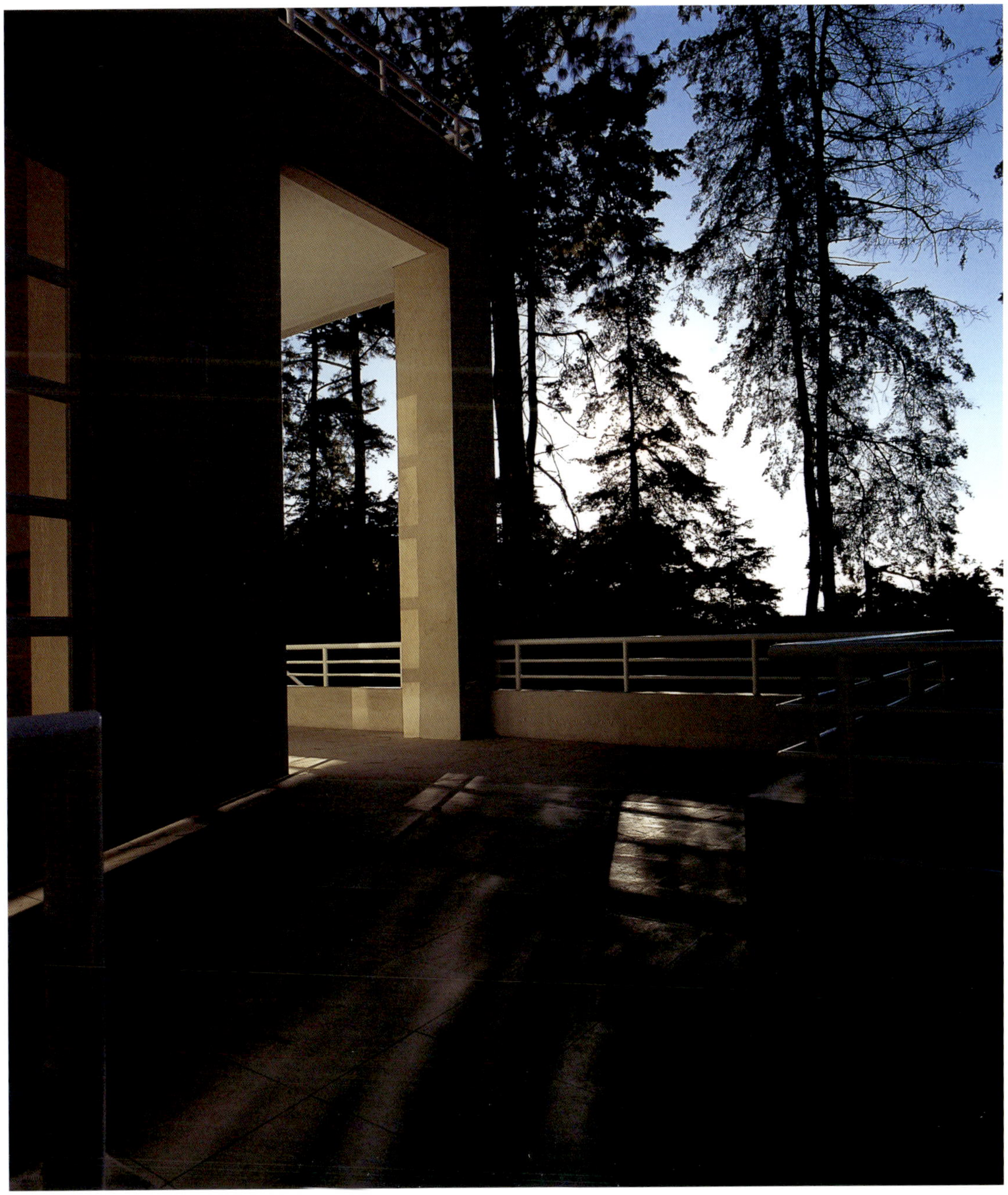

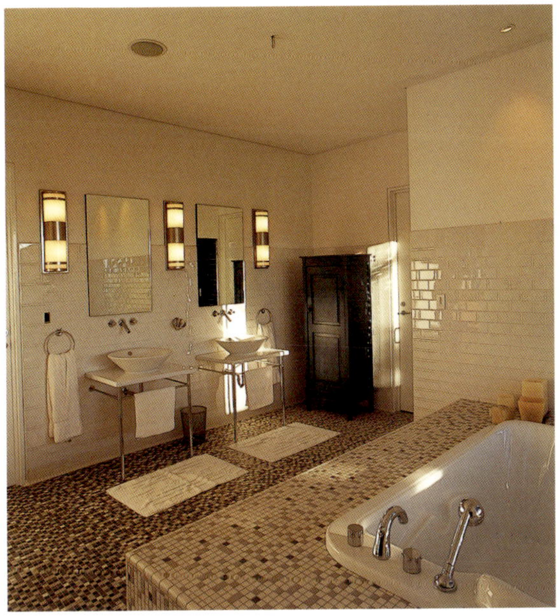

While Frank Lloyd Wright correctly said one time that "the inner space becomes the reality of the building," the Casa de Los Eucaliptos (The House of the Eucalyptuses) is an example of the sobriety of exterior architecture and the wealth of spaces within. When the house is seen from the garden entrance, the slightly inclined roofs display a character similar to the topography of the natural setting. Once inside, the space begins to open up, starting with the entrance to an atrium with natural light above, and invites one to enter a two-story-high hall, whose walls are horizontally staggered with the aim of creating a play of light and shadow that underscores the

CASA LOS EUCALIPTOS

depth of the space. At the main entrance, a vestibule frames the spiral staircase that leads to the central studio on the second floor, which is also lit by a glass skylight. This spatial arrangement winds up achieving an effect of broken light upon the main entrance, completing the circuit of interior light. As is the case with many of the buildings designed by Solares & Lara, the materials used in this house are left in a raw state so that they may "weather along with the building." As they explain, through this meticulous job of choosing the appropriate materials and their constant concern for the quality of the light, spaces and volumes of their buildings, their architecture manages "to speak for itself and be its own expression."

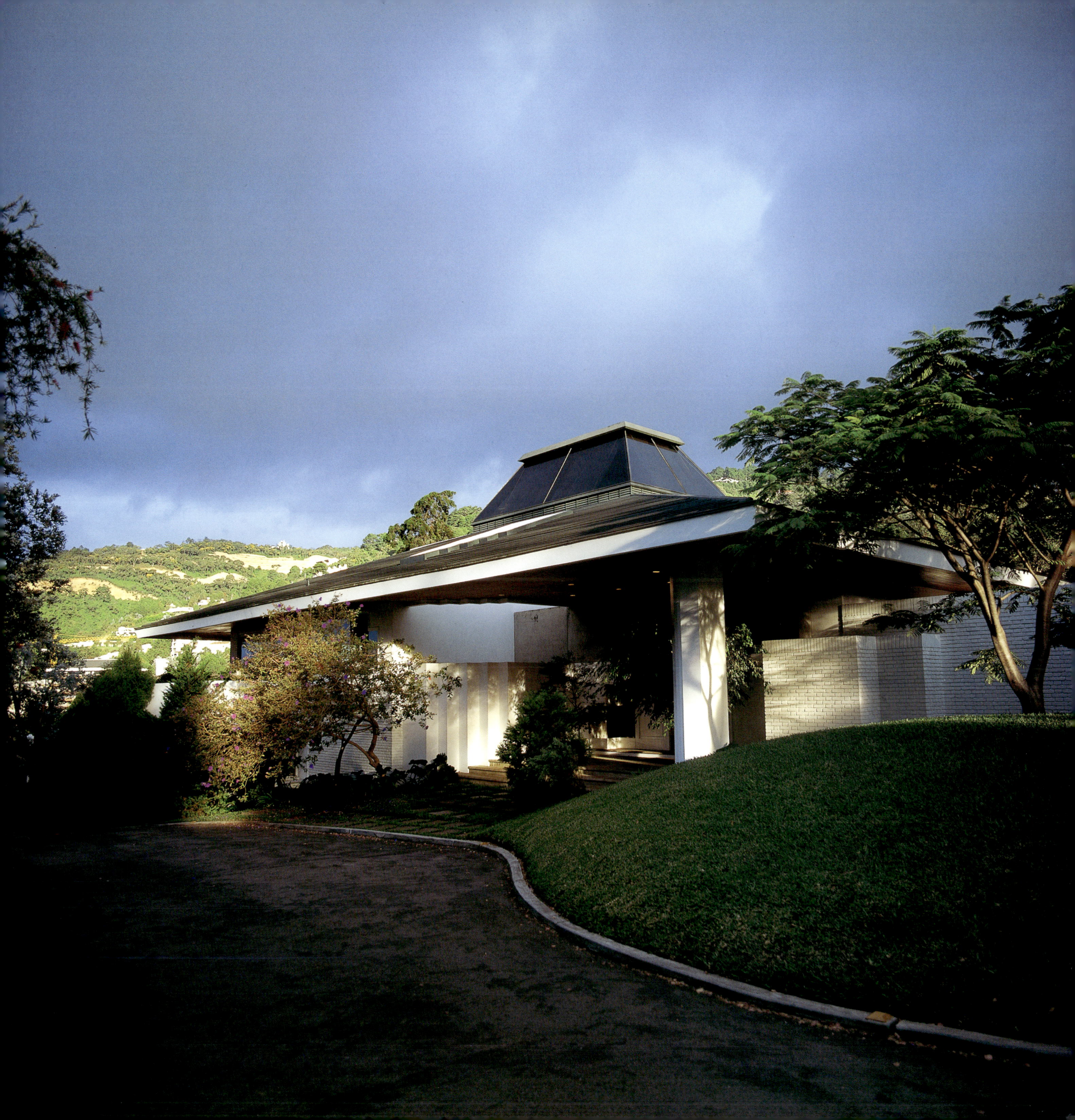

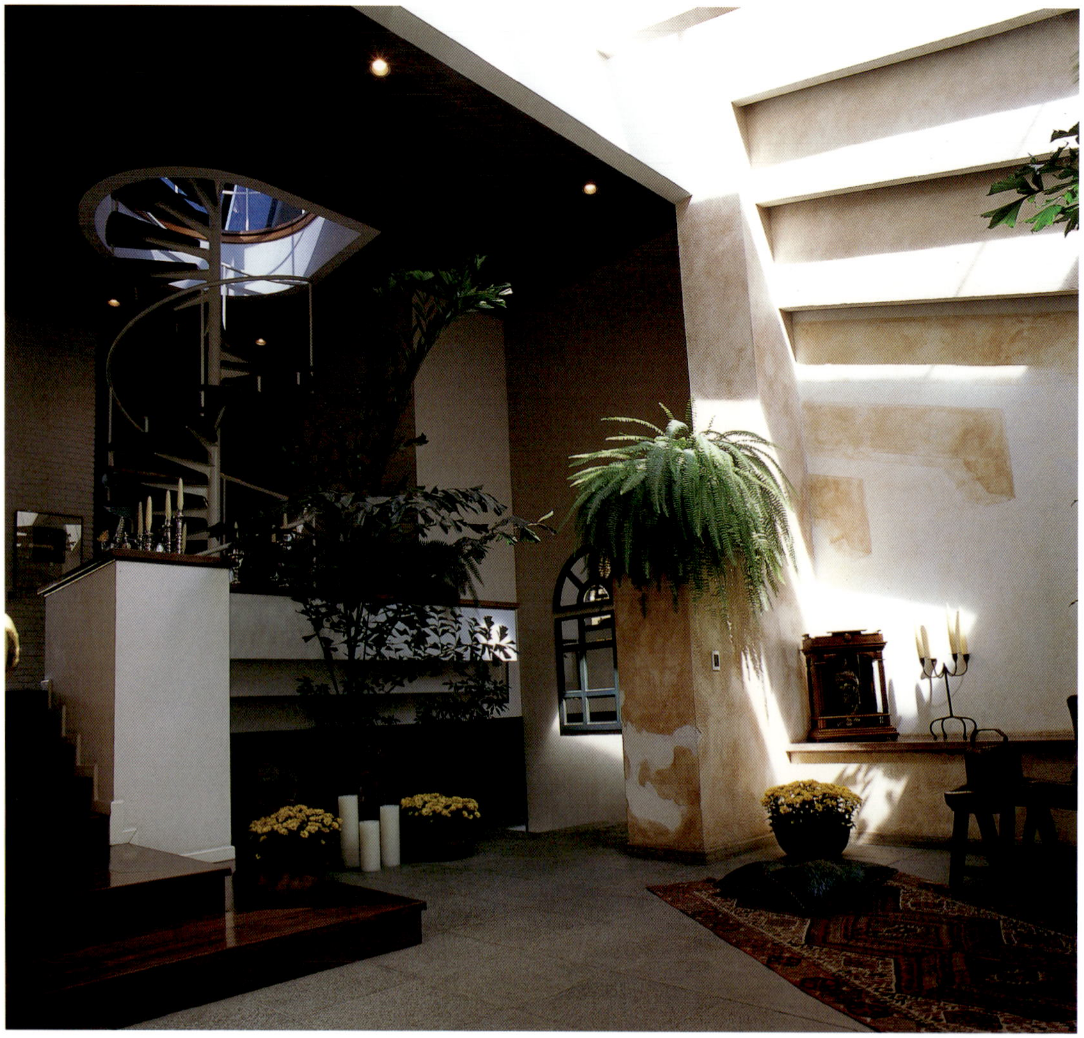

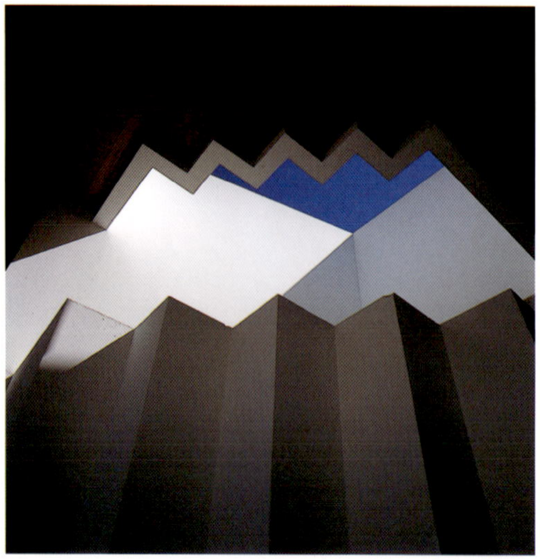

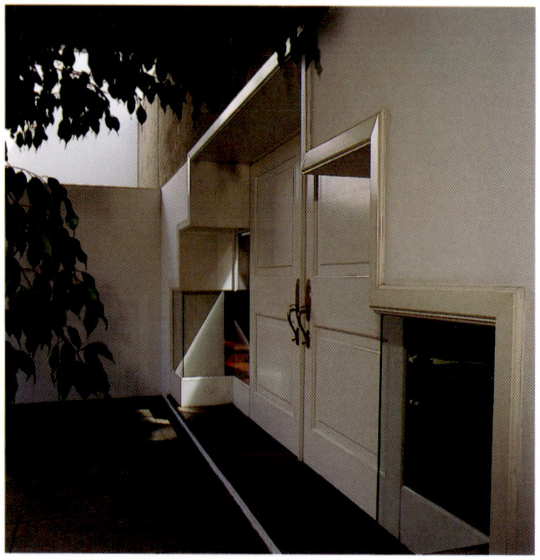

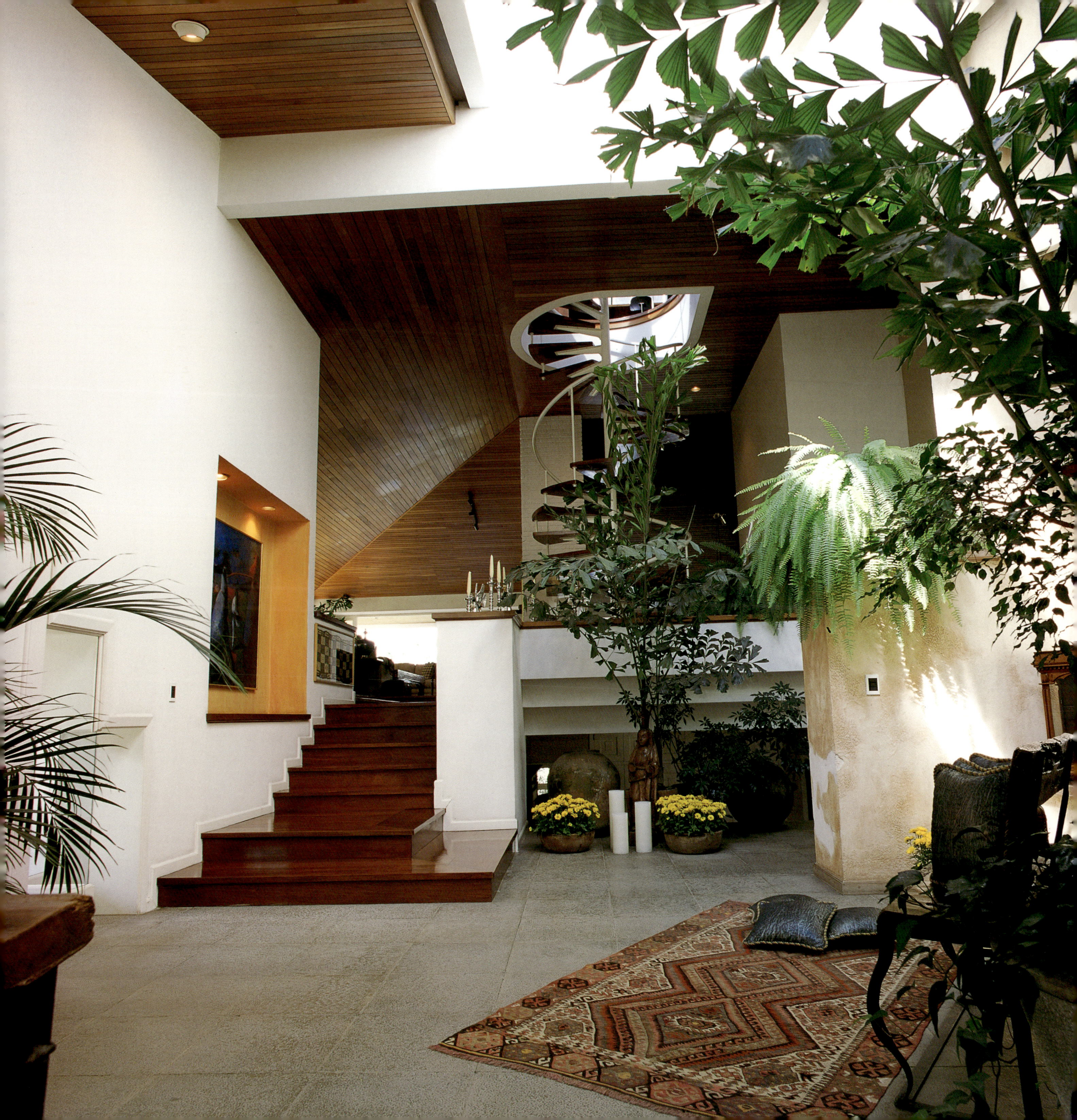

On the shores of Atitlán Lake one finds the Cerro de Oro (Golden Mountain), so-called because of its color in the season when the stalks of maize planted there are left to dry after the corn has been harvested. Built on the slopes of this famous mountain, this vacation house is situated in a rocky terrain whose stones were used as a construction material both for the façades and the floor in the exterior area. In this way, the architecture is integrated into its natural setting as a volume of geometrically-cut stone that is perforated by windows with large panes which provide views towards the lake and the villages that surround it. As a protection

CASA CERRO DE ORO ATITLÁN

against the sun, a number of concrete pergolas with big projections were employed, which provide shade both for the inner ambits and the terrace of the social area. By adapting the form of the house to the topography of the site, the design achieved an architecture whose placement respects the vegetation of the setting and also preserves the existing trees. The organic shape of the swimming pool contrasts with the right-angled elements of the house and creates a ribbon of water which looks out towards the lake, creating a sensation of infinite blues and greens.

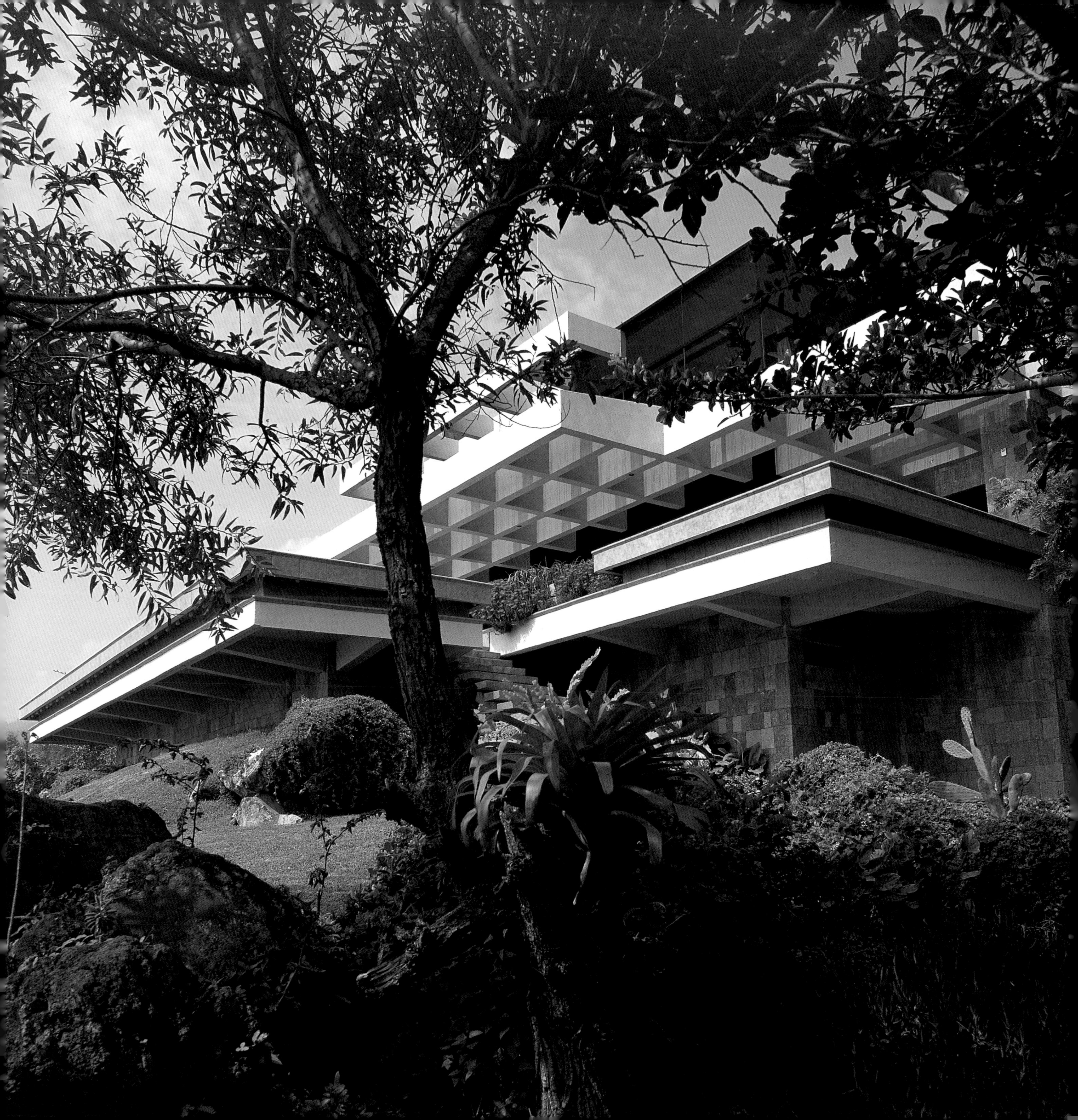

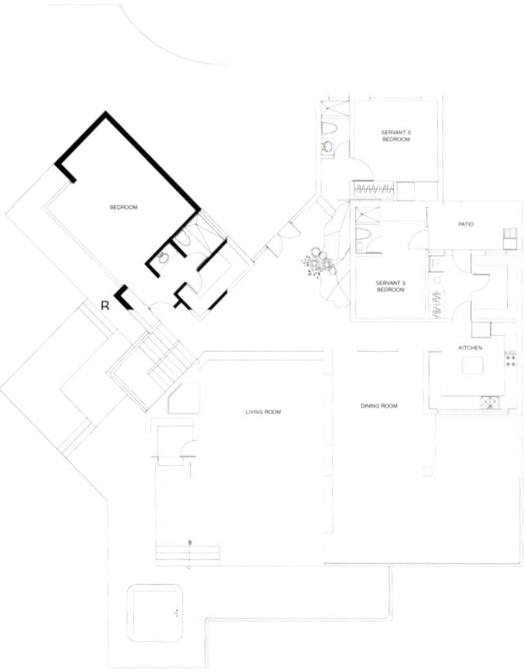

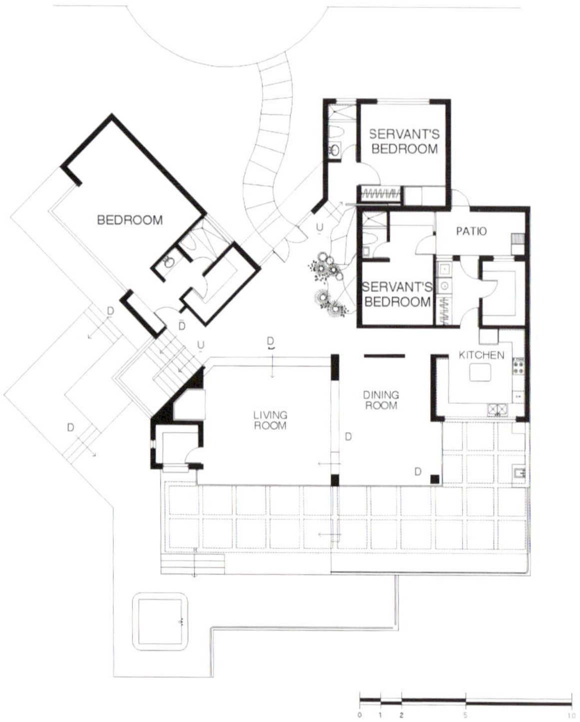
SERVANT'S BEDROOM
BEDROOM
PATIO
SERVANT'S BEDROOM
KITCHEN
LIVING ROOM
DINING ROOM

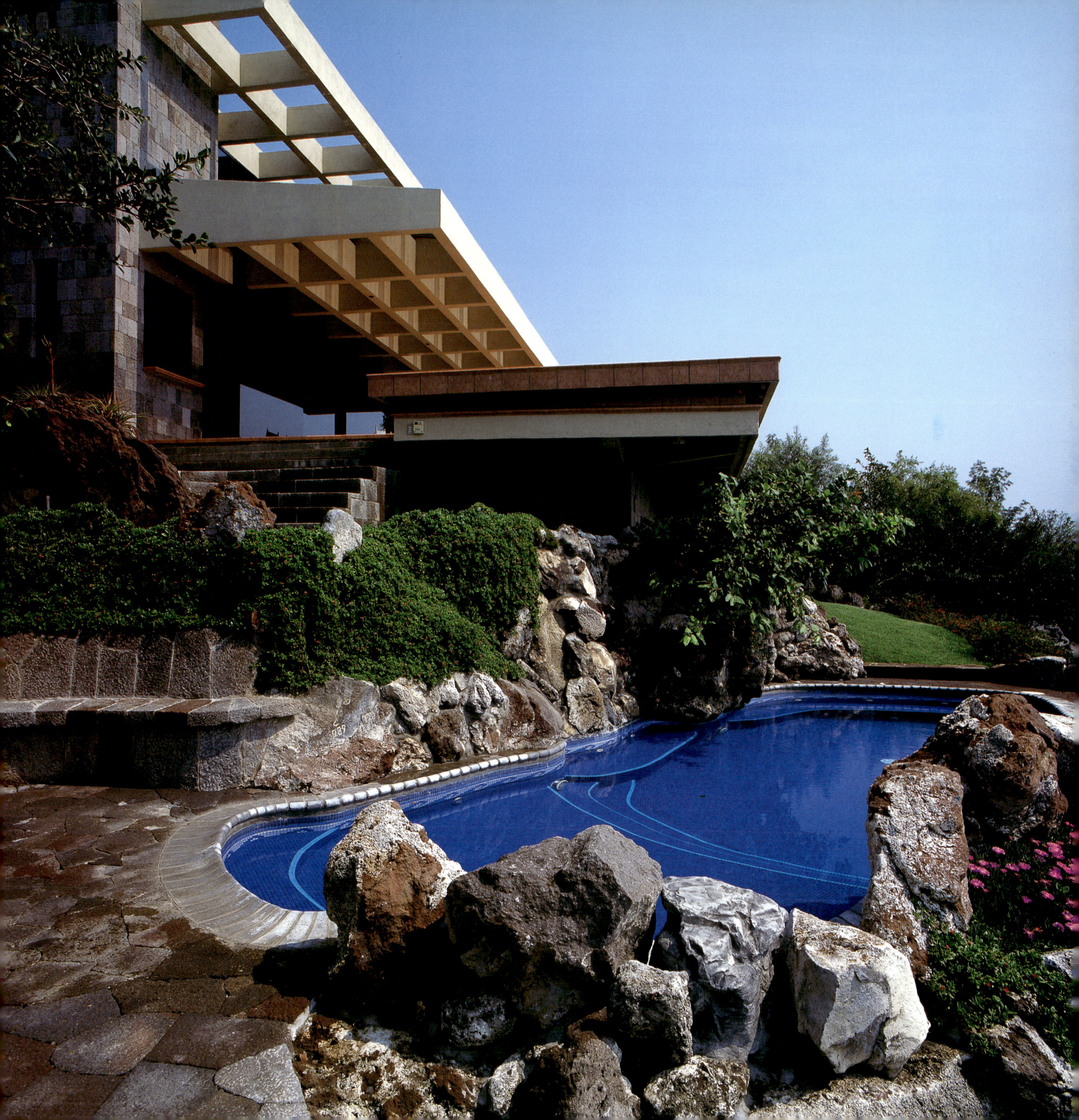

The architecture of this house reflects a traditional European style which has been adapted to Guatemala City. The two-story-high vestibule is illuminated by a number of windows that are placed so that the light reflects on the surface of the walls, creating a play of lights and shadows that highlight the characteristics of the materials used in the interior. When you enter the house from the stone-paved

CASA LA CAÑADA

patio, the view is directed through the vestibule towards a garden in the rear part of the house, creating a feeling of spatial amplitude. The façade of rustic, hand-made bricks contrasts with the clean, simple lines of the interior spaces, whose smooth white walls, marble floors and wooden ceilings create an elegant space that displays the spatial characteristics of the architecture of Solares & Lara.

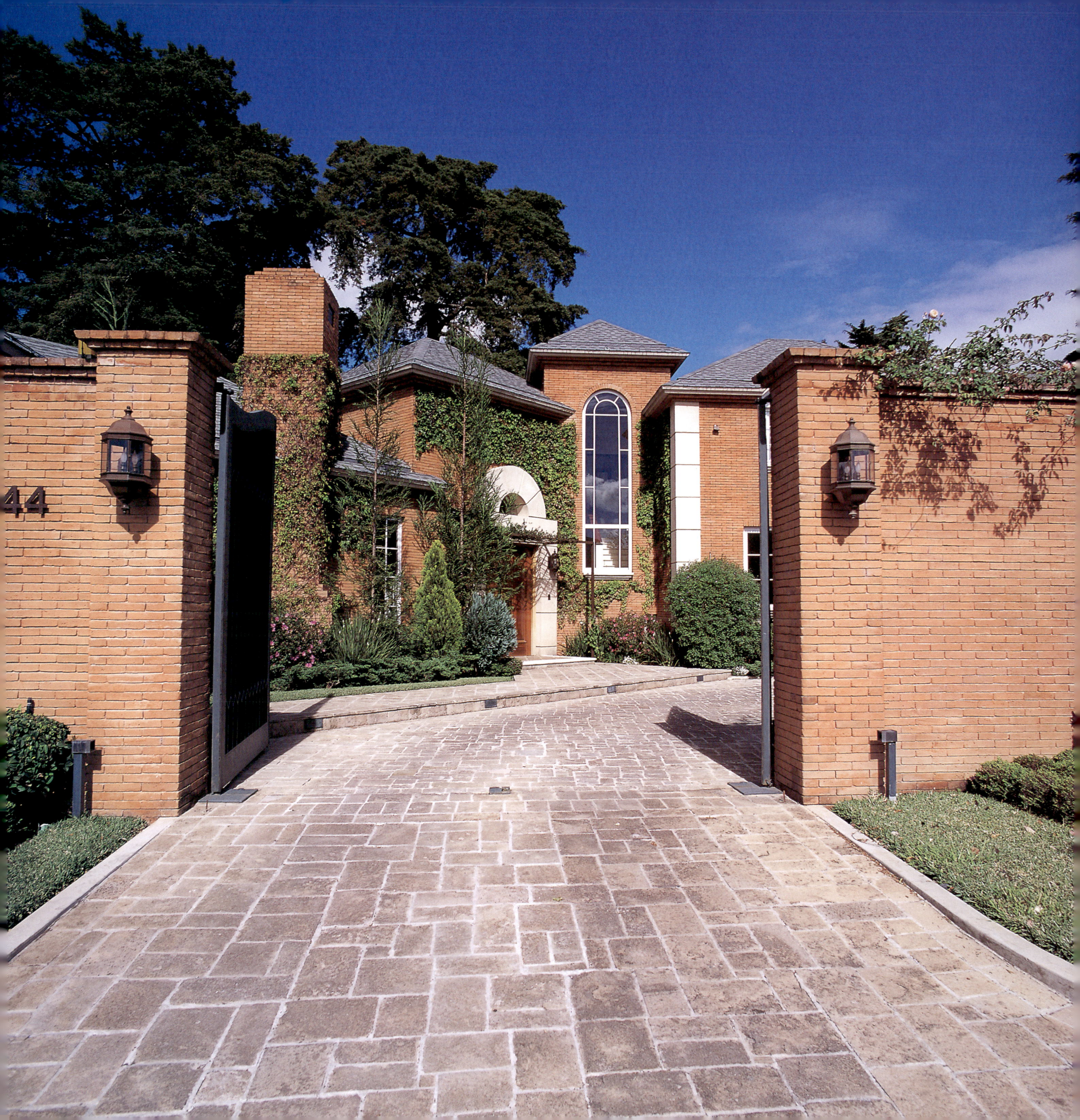
44

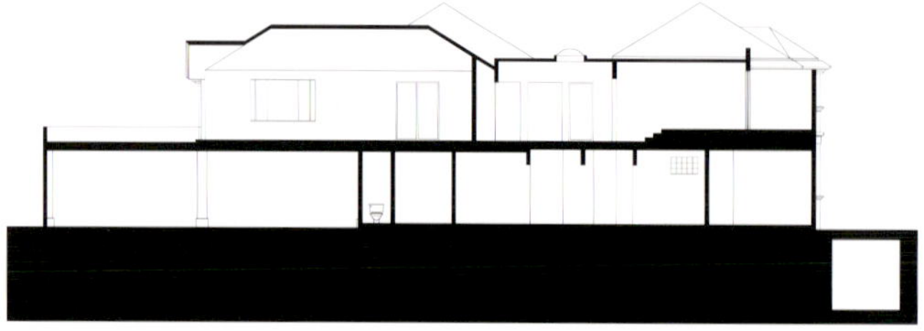

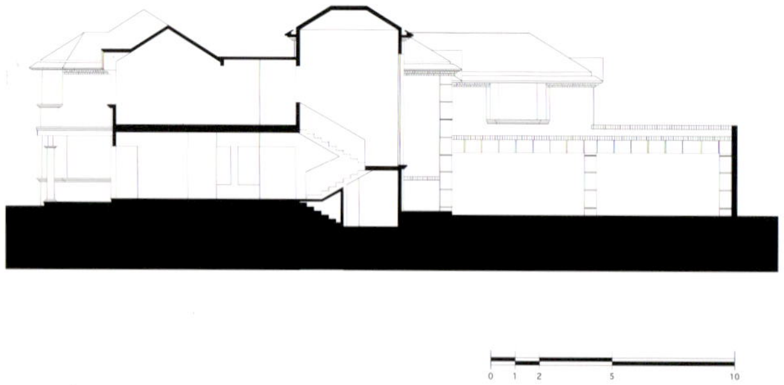

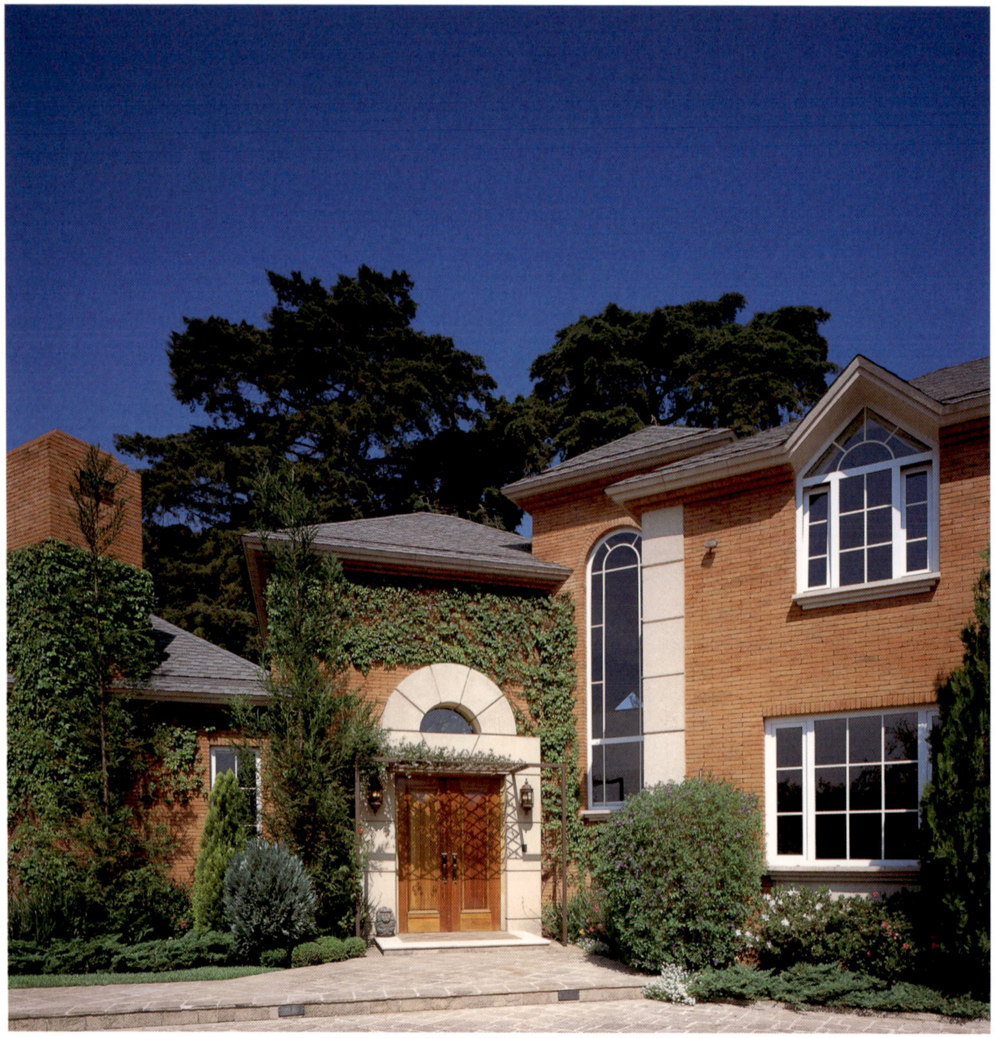

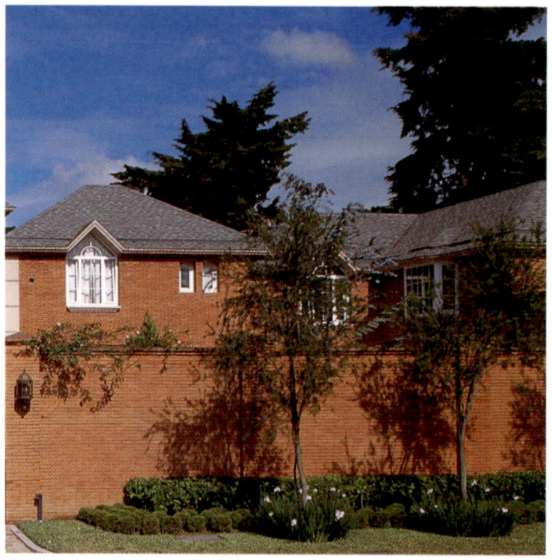

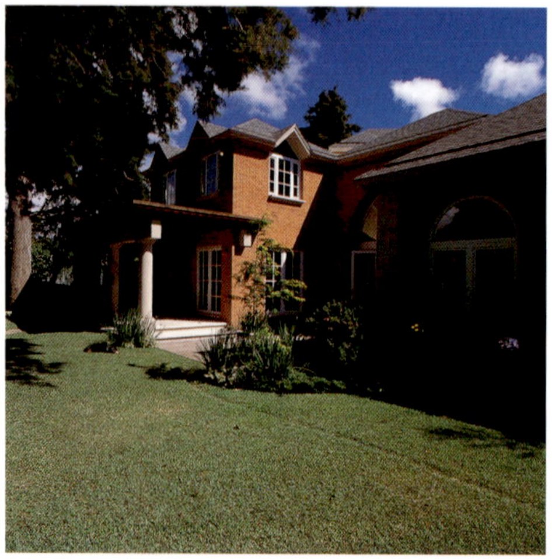

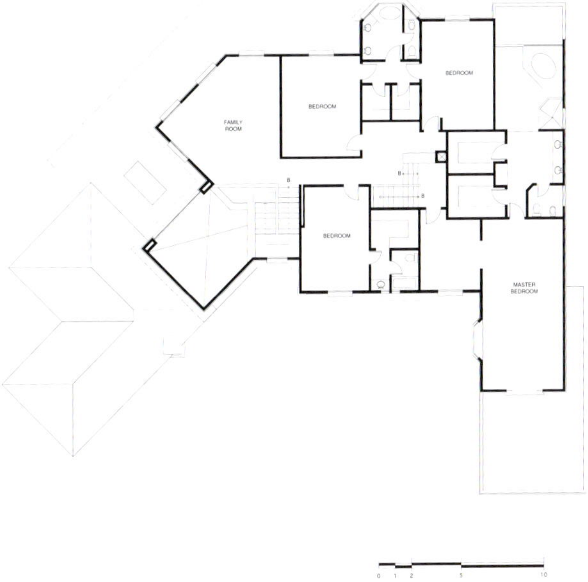

FAMILY ROOM
BEDROOM
BEDROOM
BEDROOM
MASTER BEDROOM
0 1 2 5 10

PANTRY
LAUNDRY
DINING ROOM
KITCHEN
SERVANT'S
SERVANT'S
SERVANT'S
VESTIBULE
STUDY
GARAGE
LIVING ROOM
GARAGE
0 1 2 5 10

The Casa de Grillos was built on the land of a coffee plantation in the Calvario district, which lies outside the historic center of Antigua Guatemala. It was designed with the idea of being a studio-apartment, which is why the kitchen-bar, dining room, living room and work area are joined into a single ambit. Managing to maintain a minimalist character, the Casa de Grillos was constructed with materials that

CASA DE GRILLOS, ANTIGUA GUATEMALA

exemplify the colonial architecture of Guatemala and are characterized by their soft colors. The sanded clay floor tiles recall the traditional floors of the Capuchin Convent of the same city, while the rustically-finished walls suitably combine with the wooden beams that support the tile roof to give the building an original colonial-style touch.

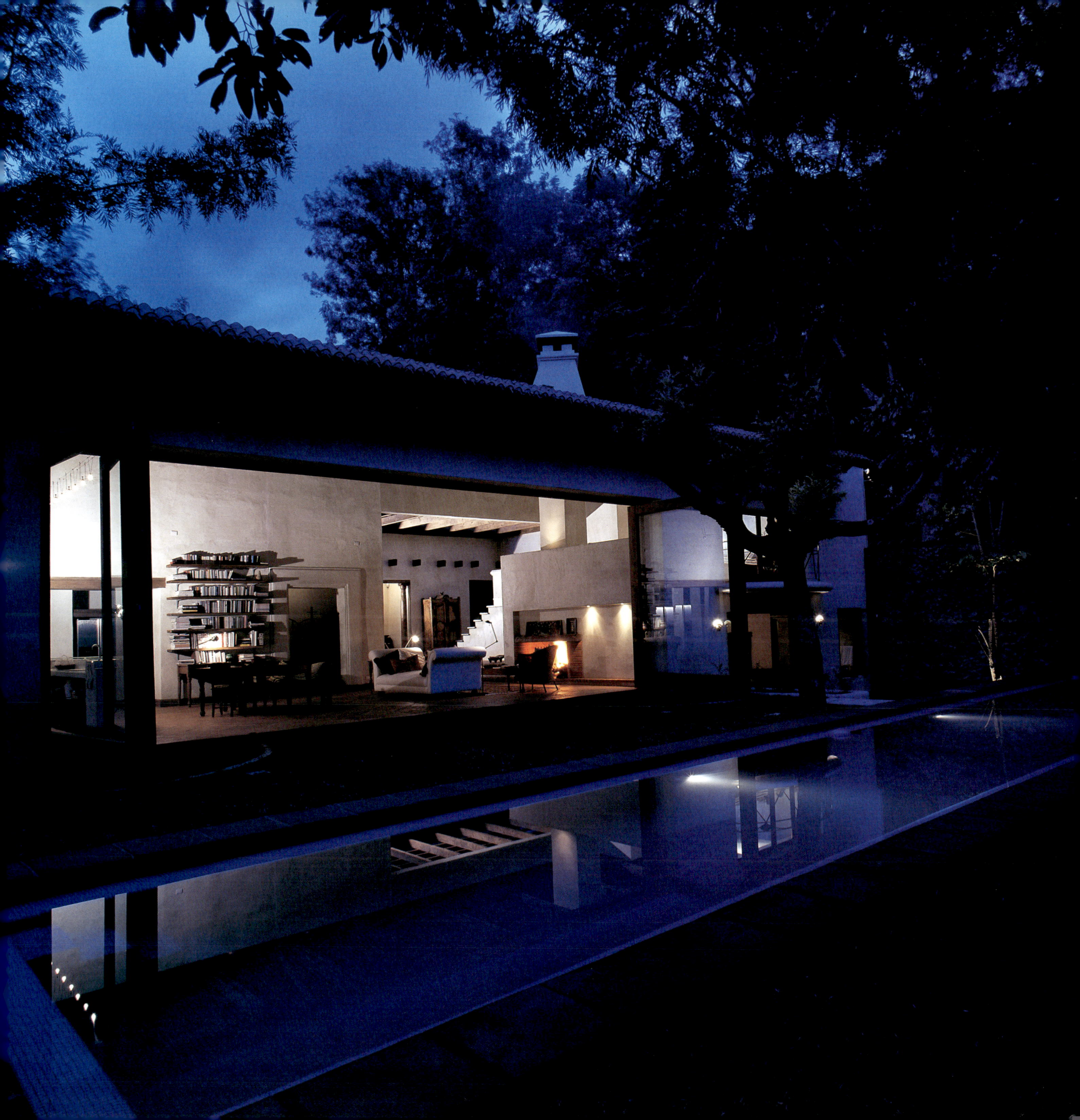

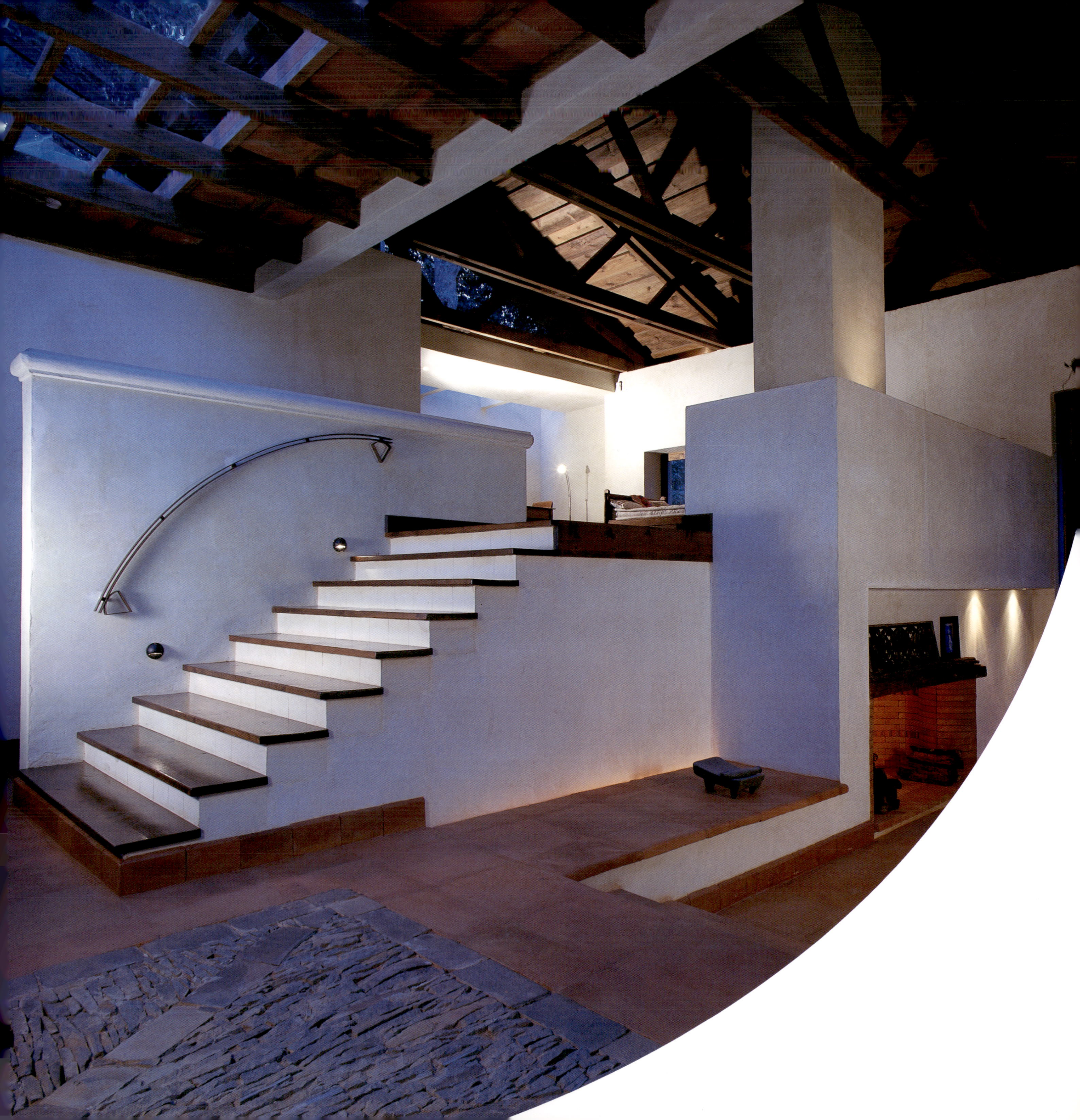

The vestibule, illuminated by a skylight, has a cobblestone floor that is reminiscent of those used in the entrance halls of traditional, colonial-style buildings. The studio located in the mezzanine is separated from the social areas by a chimney with a simple and austere geometry that strengthens the minimalist character of the composition. From the social area, four large sliding doors open with a mechanism of rails and rollers, creating a bay with a twelve meter span that joins the interior and exterior into a single ambit. Outside, the placement of the lap-pool enables it to reflect the same breach in the front, creating a subtly modern aspect. Casa de Grillos achieves a synthesis between formal contemporary elements and the colonial atmosphere that characterizes the historic city of Antigua Guatemala.

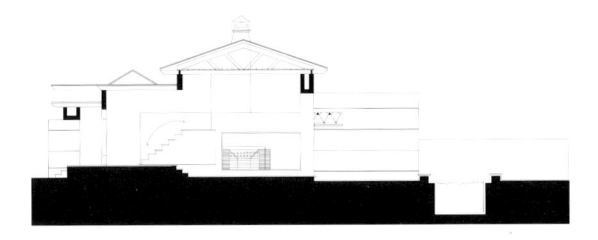

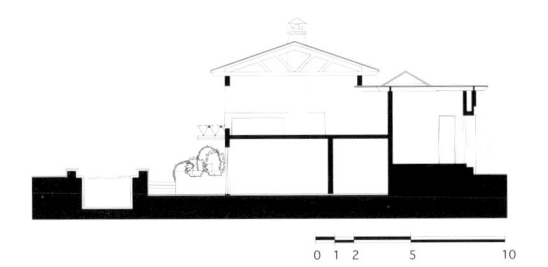

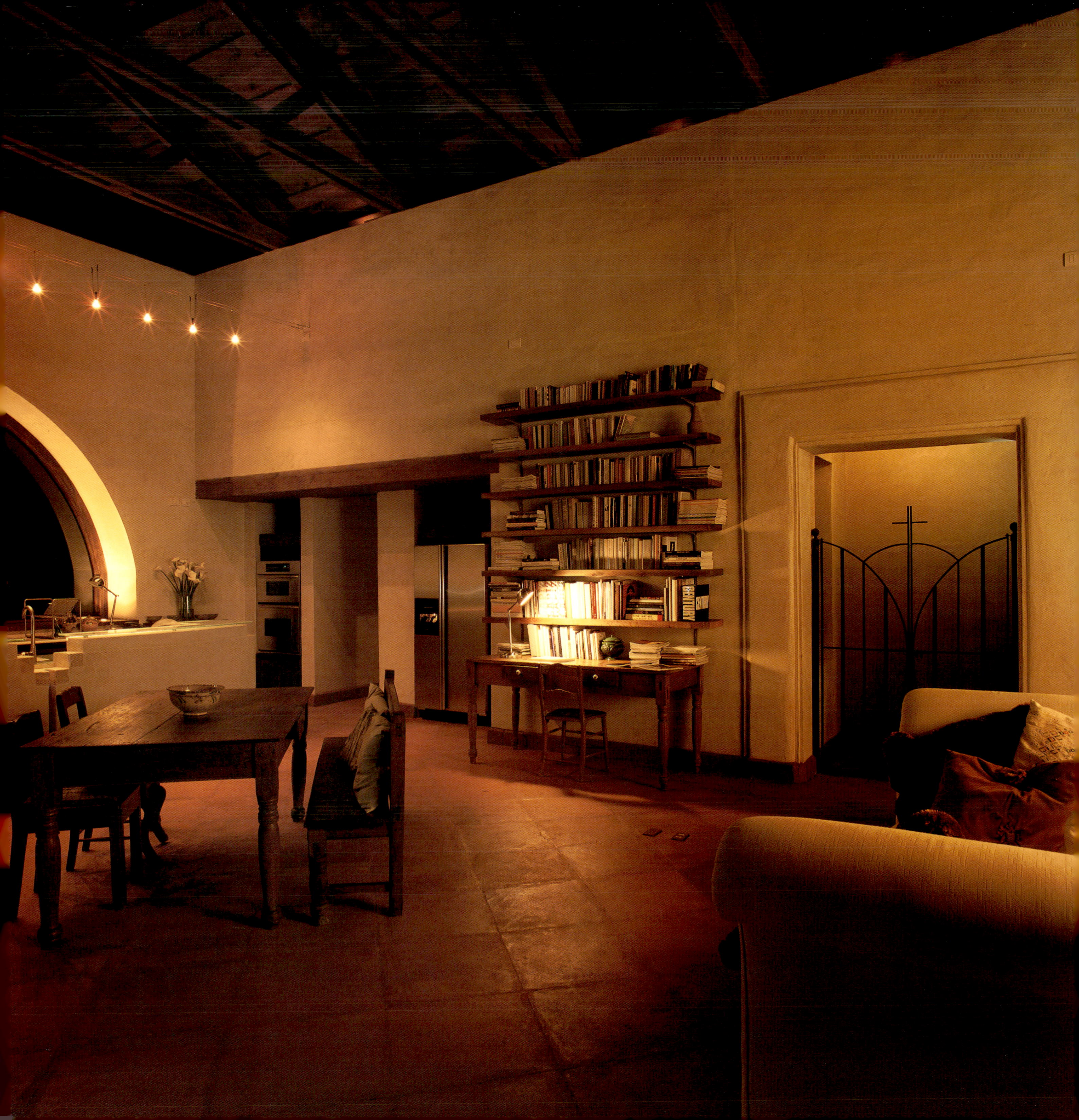

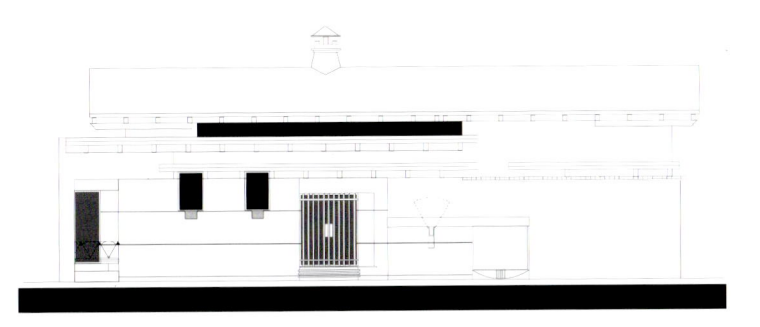

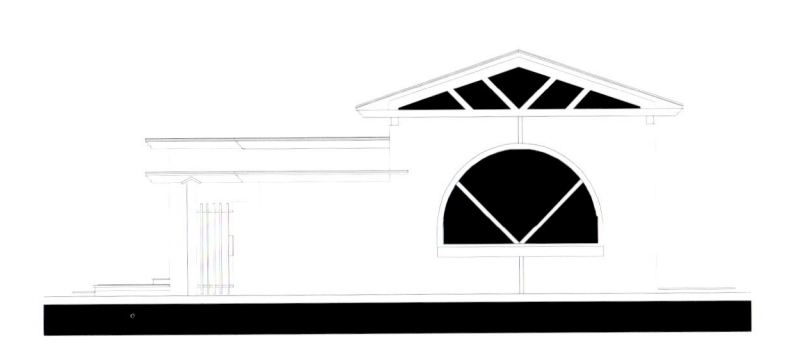

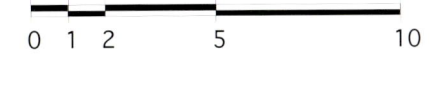

0 1 2 5 10

Although its clean surfaces reflect modern characteristics, the Casa de la Poza Azul ("House of the Blue Pool") has a strong affinity with the architecture of the old house that was incorporated into it and, especially, with the existing colonial ruin. After carrying out the necessary excavations, it was discovered that the ruin was of a kiln for ceramics and it was decided to make it one of the most important elements of the new house, integrating it into the whole by means of a glass roof that rests on a

CASA DE LA POZA AZUL

wooden framework. The kiln begins to demarcate the end of an axis where there is a great stone arch that serves as a transition between the existing house – which would contain the bedrooms, the kitchen and the dining room – and the new house that would contain the social areas. Maintaining the proportions and the thickness of the walls of the new addition, the architects have created a coherent and creative composition that nevertheless preserves the past and respects the distance of time.

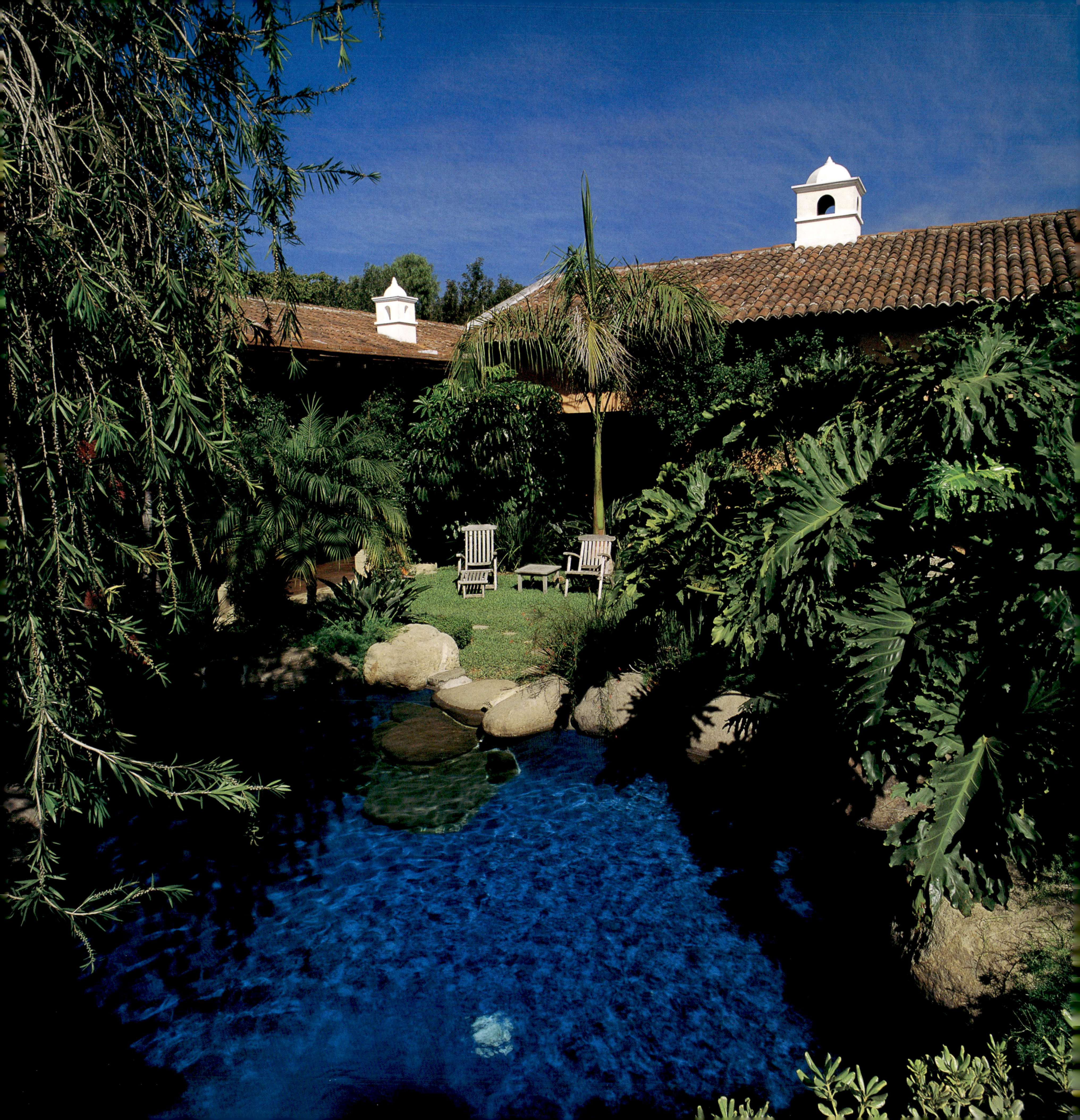

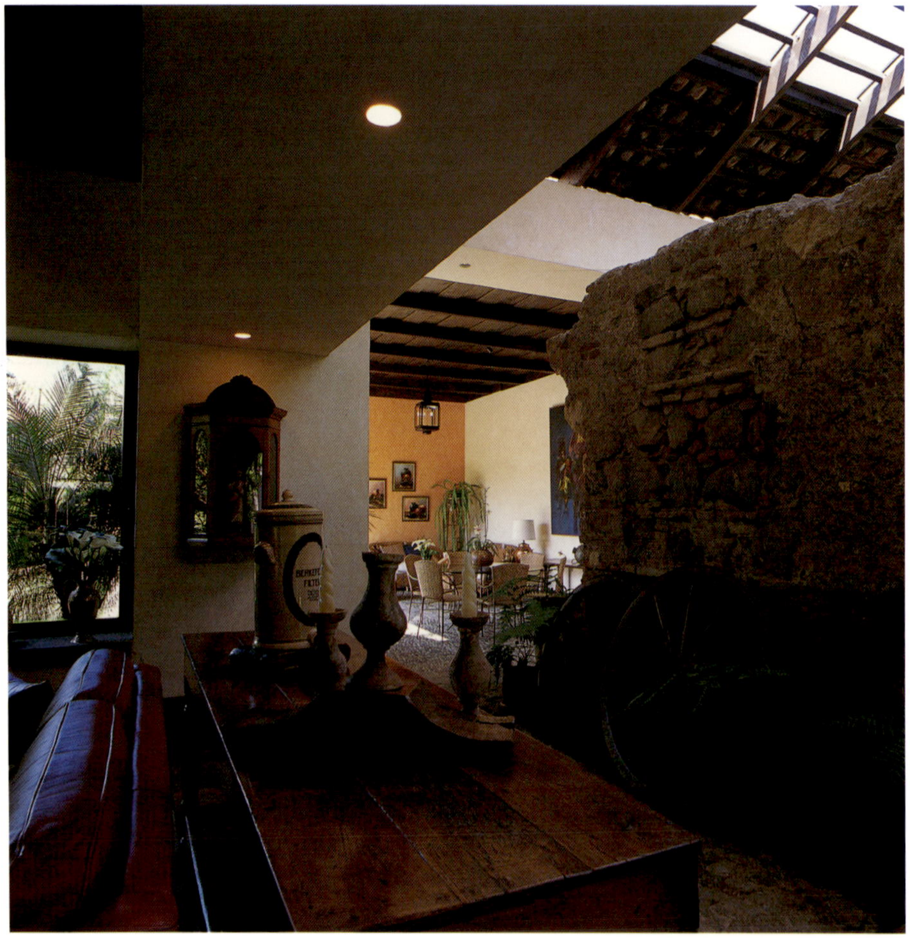

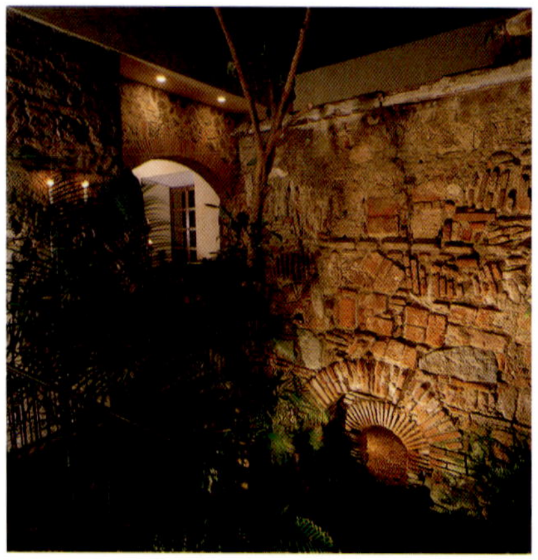

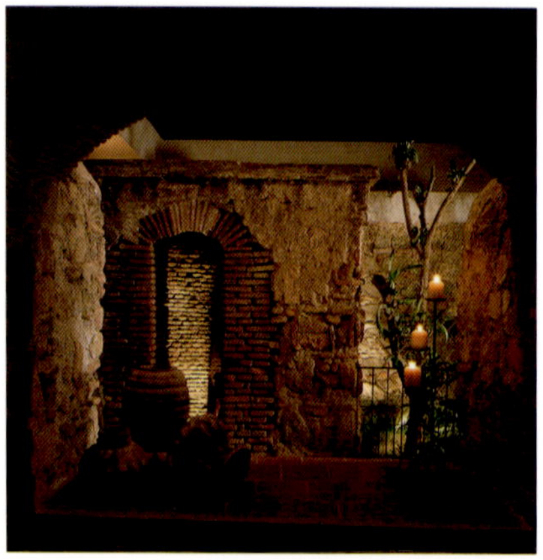

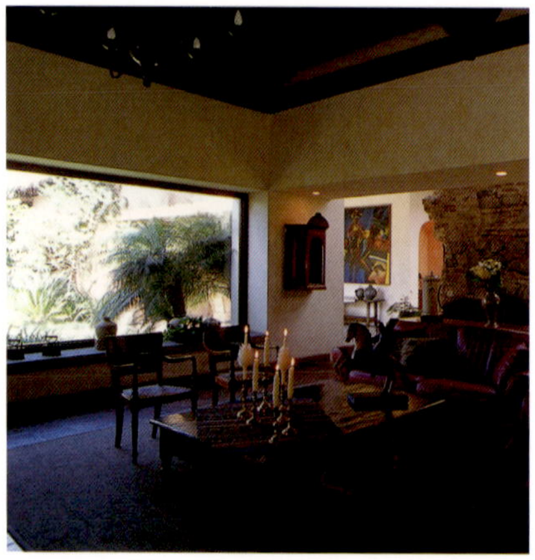

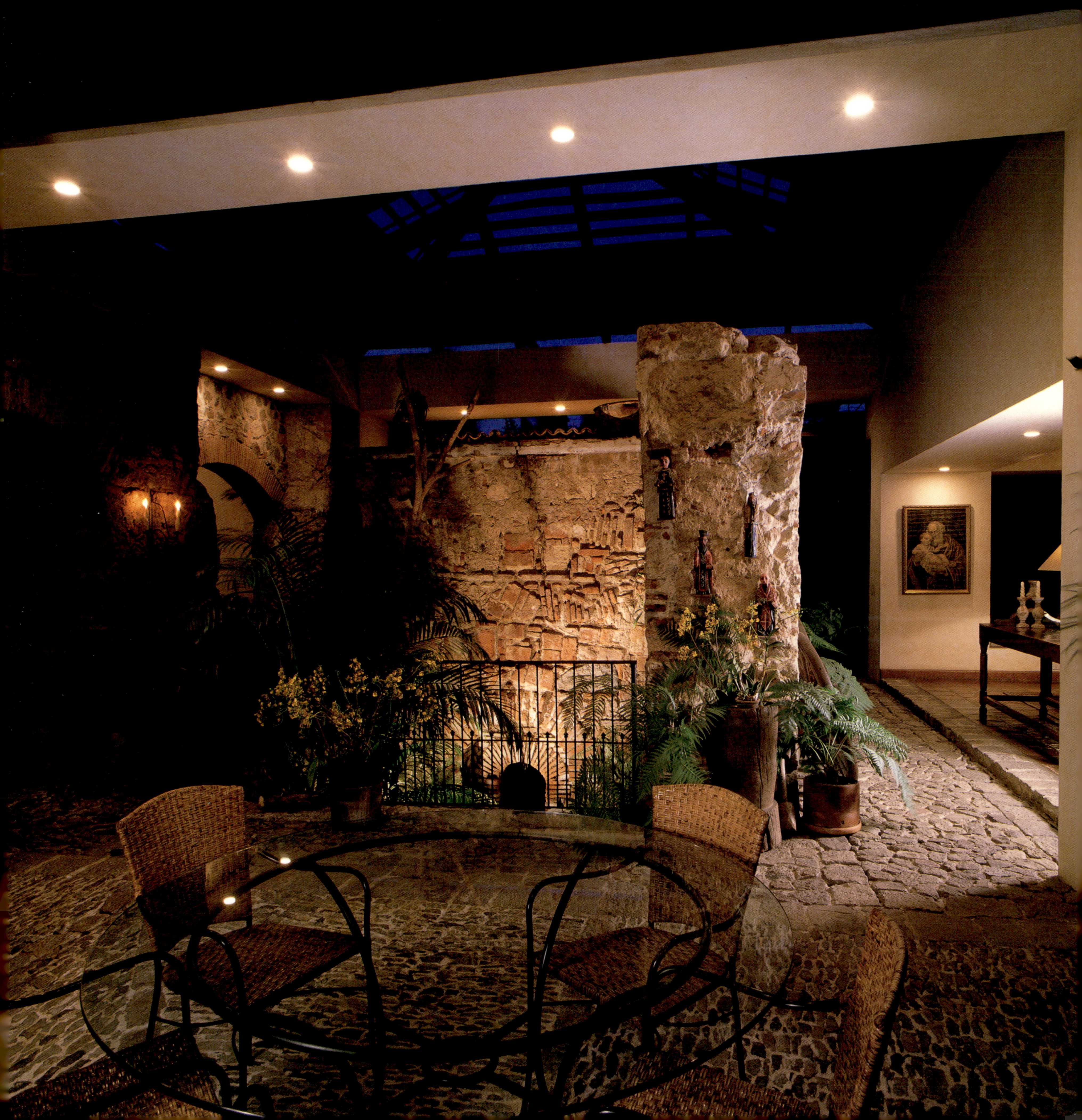

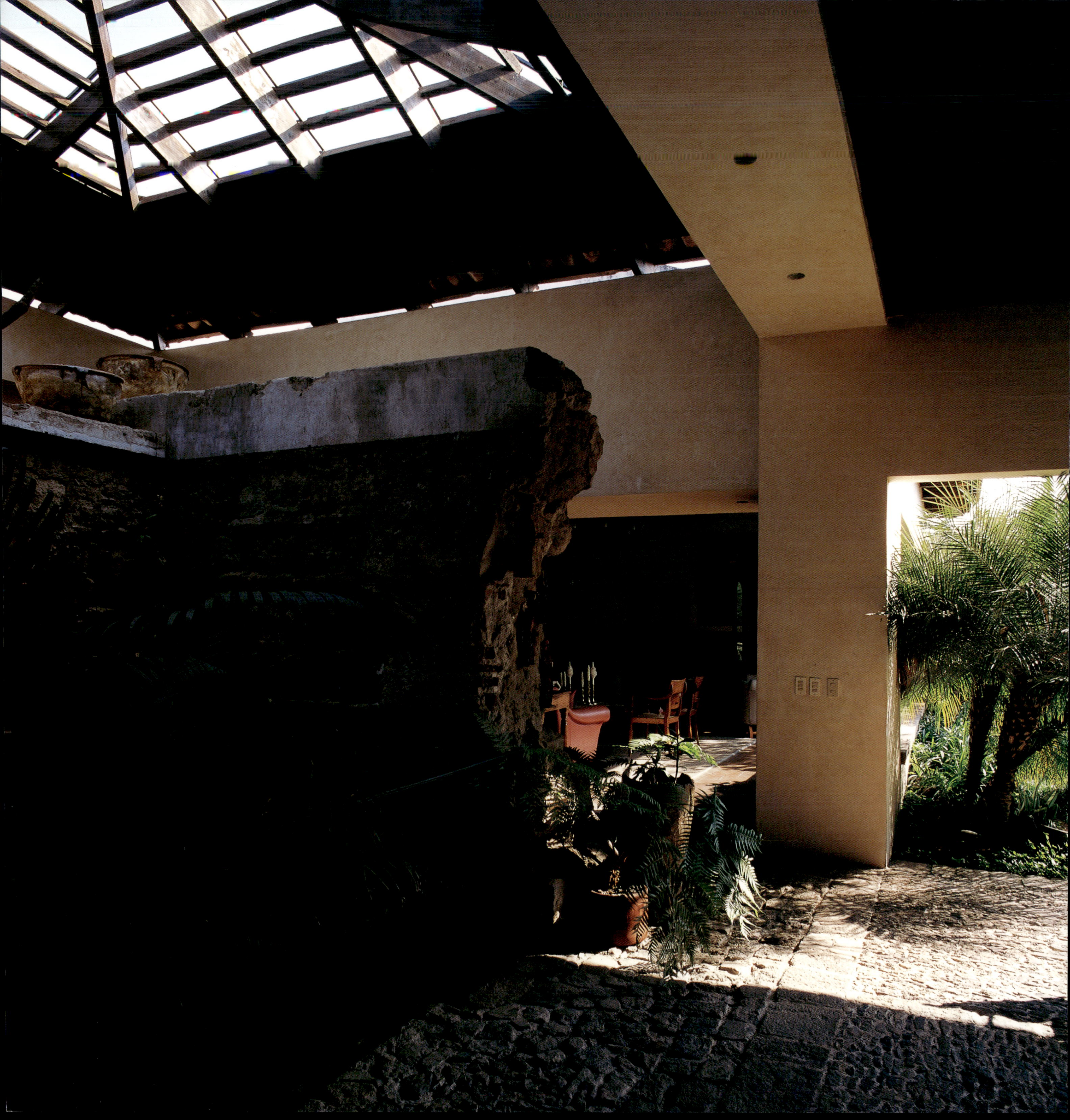

painted many centuries ago. Its meaning is hidden from the person who reads and ponders it. The book explained how the whole of the heaven and the earth was finally formed. Its essence was quartered into equinoxes and solstices, its essence was divided into four parts: white, yellow, red and north, that is, north, south, east and west; its essence was marked by placing each star and planet in its place, establishing their orbits... and how the Creator with his thought and with the force of his Word alone engendered and maintains all of the beauty that there is in the heavens, the earth, the lakes and seas." (Excerpt from the POPOL VUH, introduction).

This unusual work is built on the beaches of Punta de Palma, in Amatique Bay and surrounded by a rich and dense tropical jungle. Showing a great respect for the natural setting, the house in Punta de Palma makes a formal integration between a contemporary orthogonal architecture and the vernacular architecture of the region in which it is found. Making use of cross-shaped roofs thatched with *manaco*-palm leaf, constructed by local inhabitants, and white walls that form the different spaces of the house, the design seeks to achieve a synthesis of both of the above languages. In addition, the use of *manaco*-thatch creates an unusual spaciousness, because

CASA, PUNTA DE PALMA

there is no need to employ steel in the roof structure, which exclusively relies instead on the light but strong mangrove-pole framework. Acting as a chimney, its height allows it to expel hot air and it thus provides natural ventilation for the social areas. On entering, the interior opens into a space of great height made up of the areas of the living room, dining room and a guest bedroom. A double set of stairs leads from the vestibule to a leisure room on the mezzanine and from there you reach the other bedrooms, where triangular openings in the roof provide vistas of the surroundings.

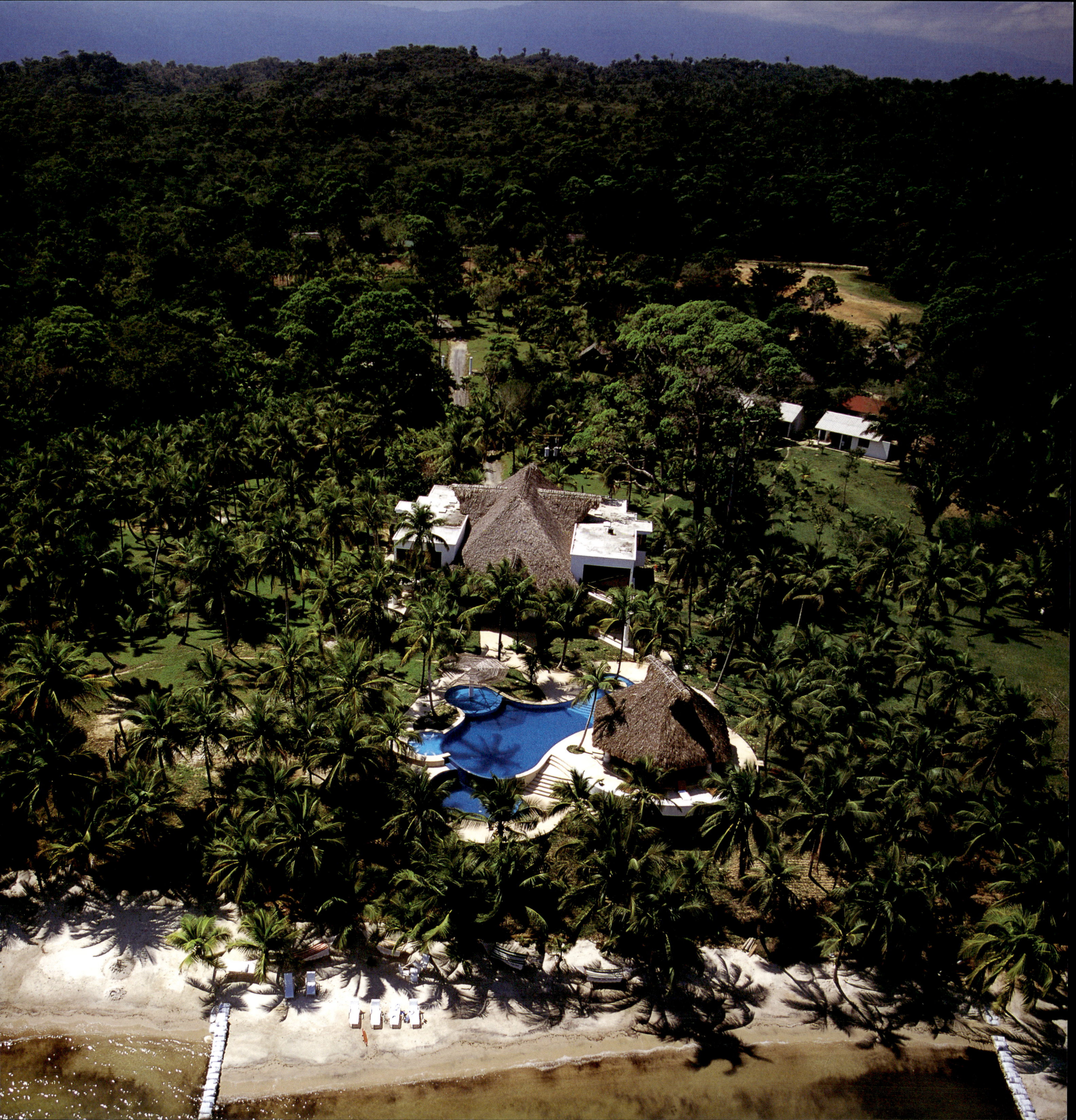

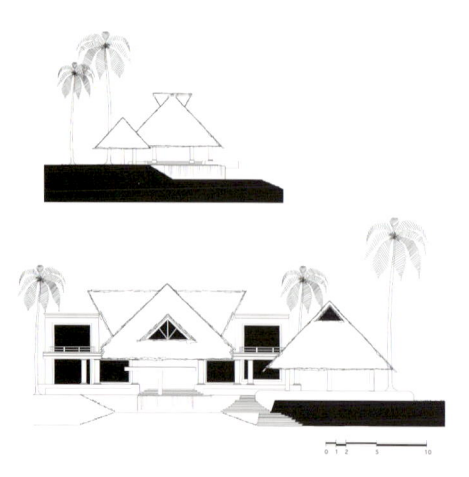

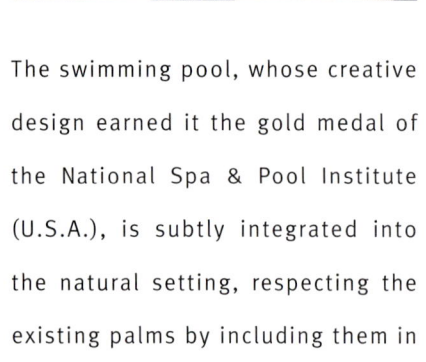

The swimming pool, whose creative design earned it the gold medal of the National Spa & Pool Institute (U.S.A.), is subtly integrated into the natural setting, respecting the existing palms by including them in islets arranged in an organic form.

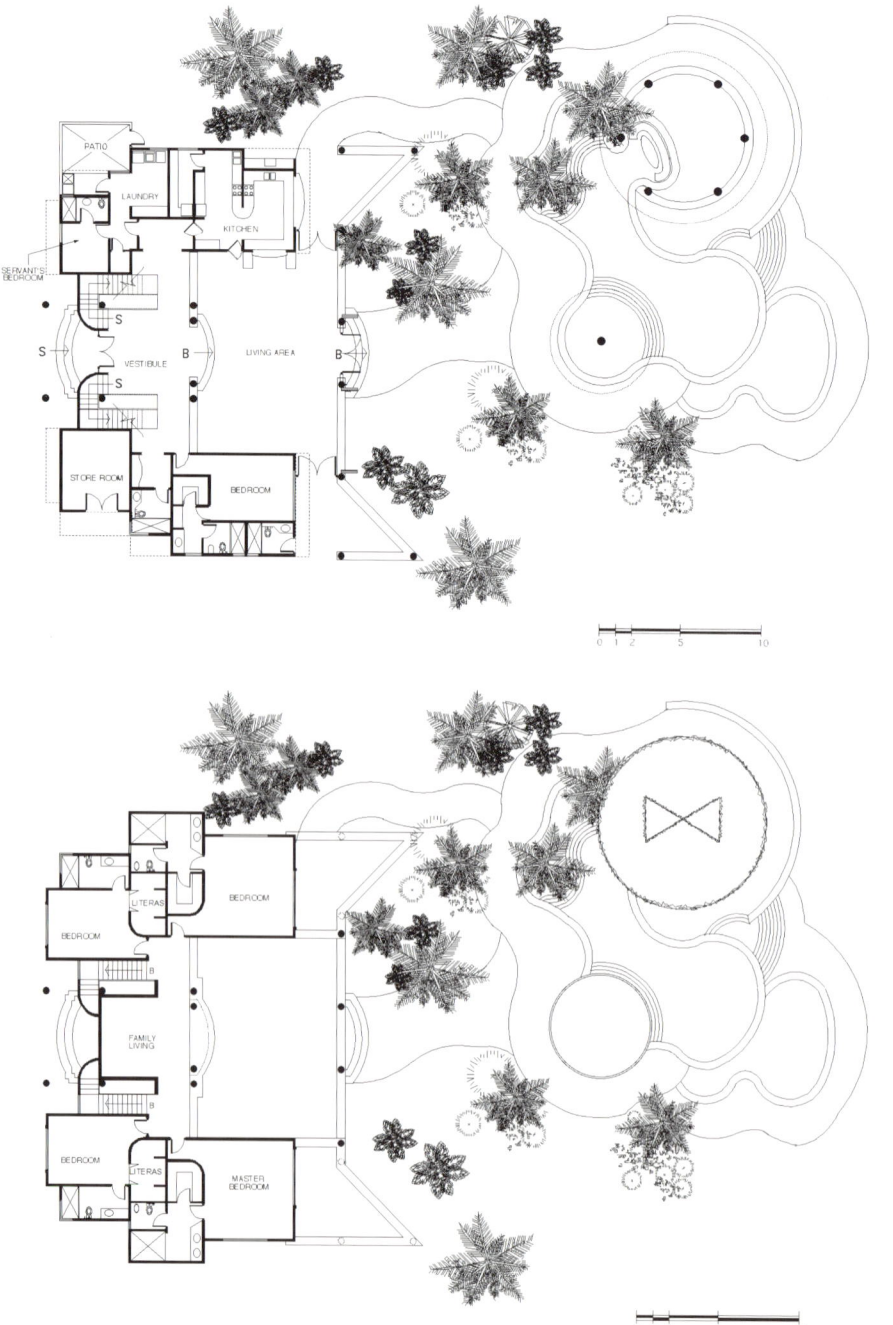

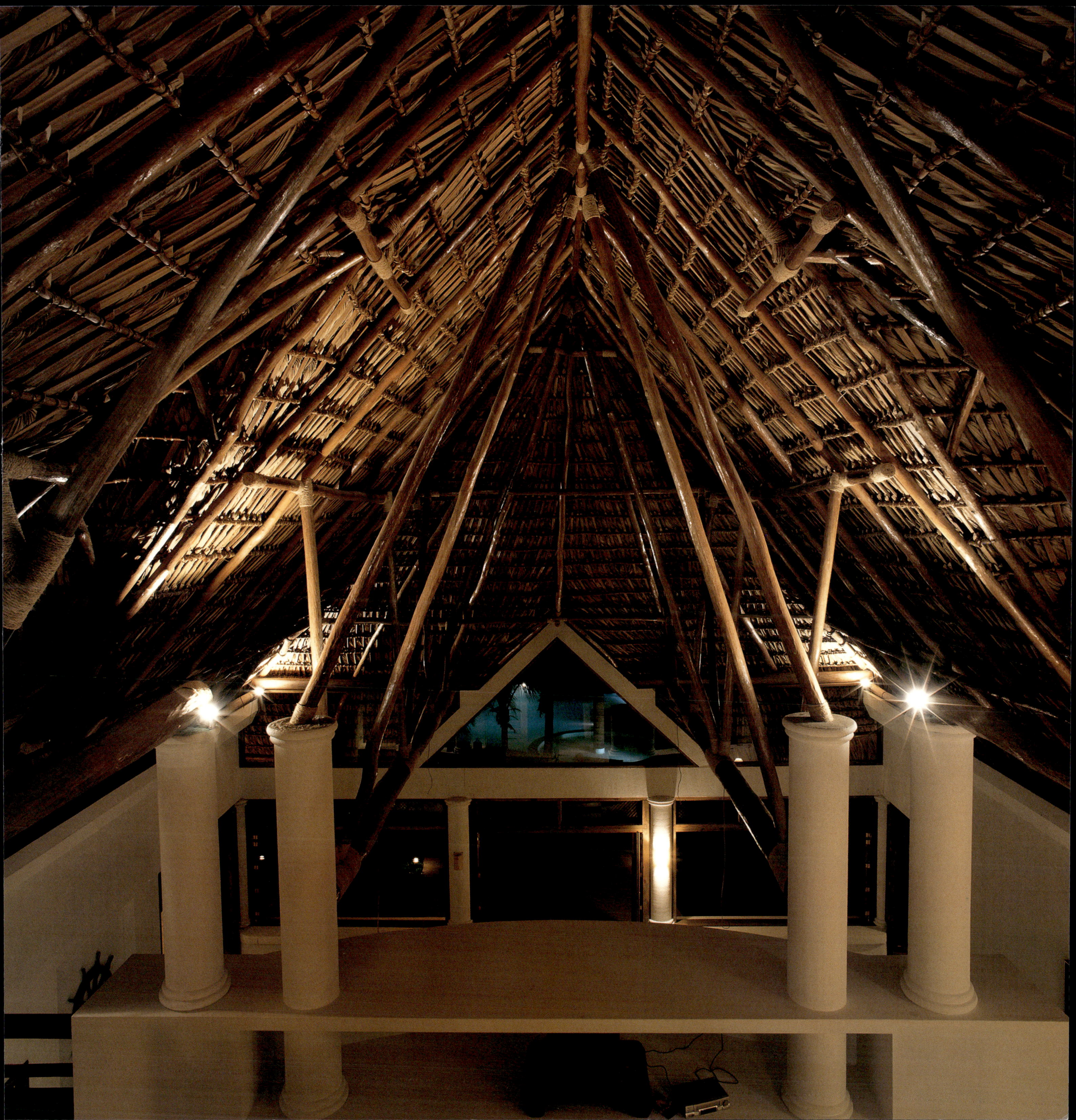

Because the house is situated on the beautiful beaches of the Pacific Ocean, one of the architectural priorities in the composition of the Casa Las Olas ("Waves House") was to provide the best possible views of the landscape. Due to the extreme flatness of the terrain, the architects Solares & Lara adopted the strategy of creating a four meters-high landfill on the building site. This allowed the six bungalows that house the bedrooms and the main social areas to enjoy a panoramic view of the beach and the tropical surroundings. Going through the entrance of the house, on the second floor, the visitor passes between the two main thatched huts, where his gaze is drawn

CASA LAS OLAS

towards a vestibule that enjoys a view of both the swimming pool on the lower level and the landscape that serves as a backdrop to the visual composition. The bungalows, each with its own terrace, are linked by wooden bridges that pass over the thick vegetation and thus provide a natural ambit in the areas of circulation. The swimming pool, with cascades that flow down the different levels, surrounds the perimeter of the social areas, like the games room and the aqua-bar on the lower level, and the master bedroom, whose terrace overlooks the bays that make up the swimming pool.

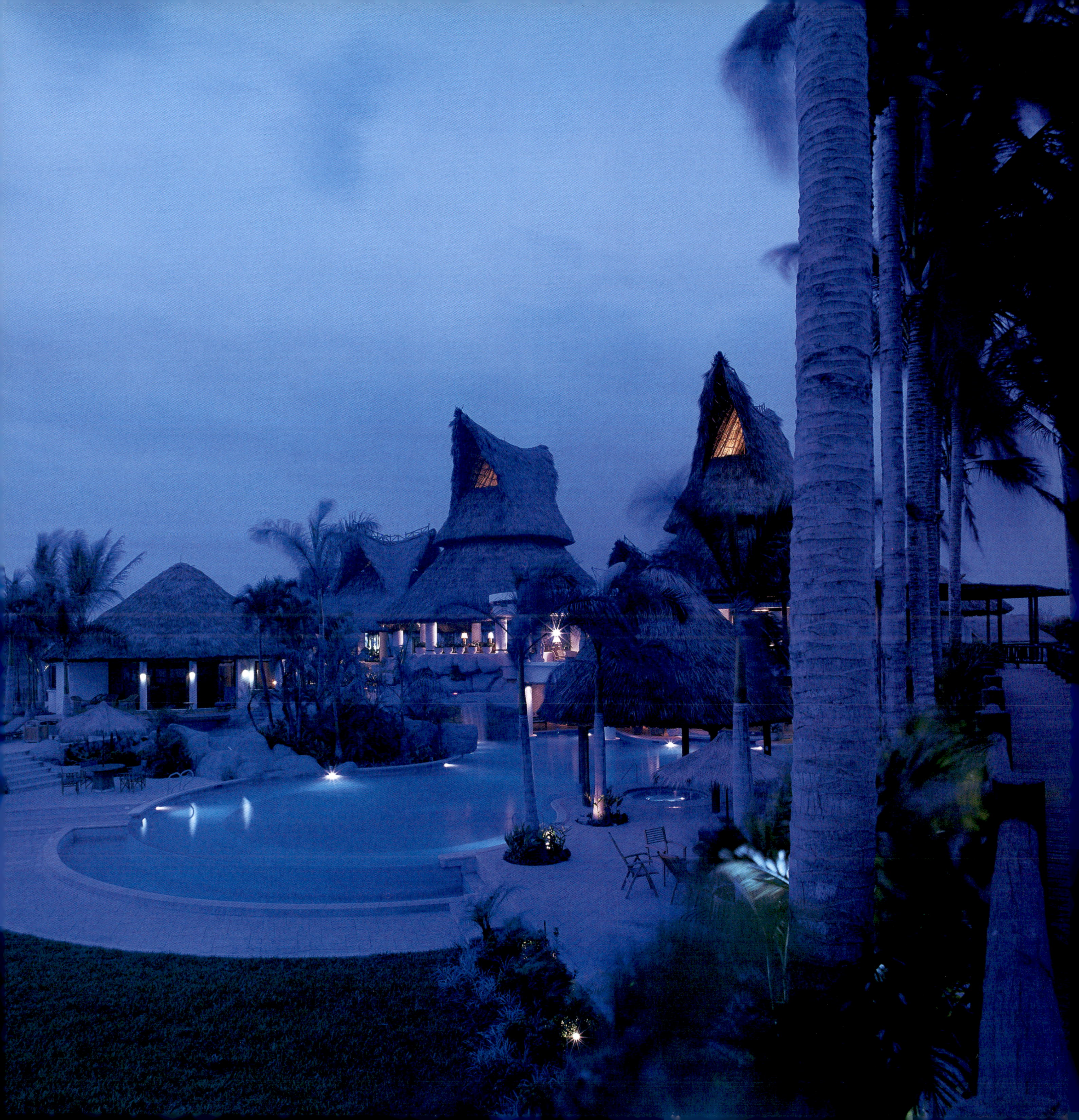

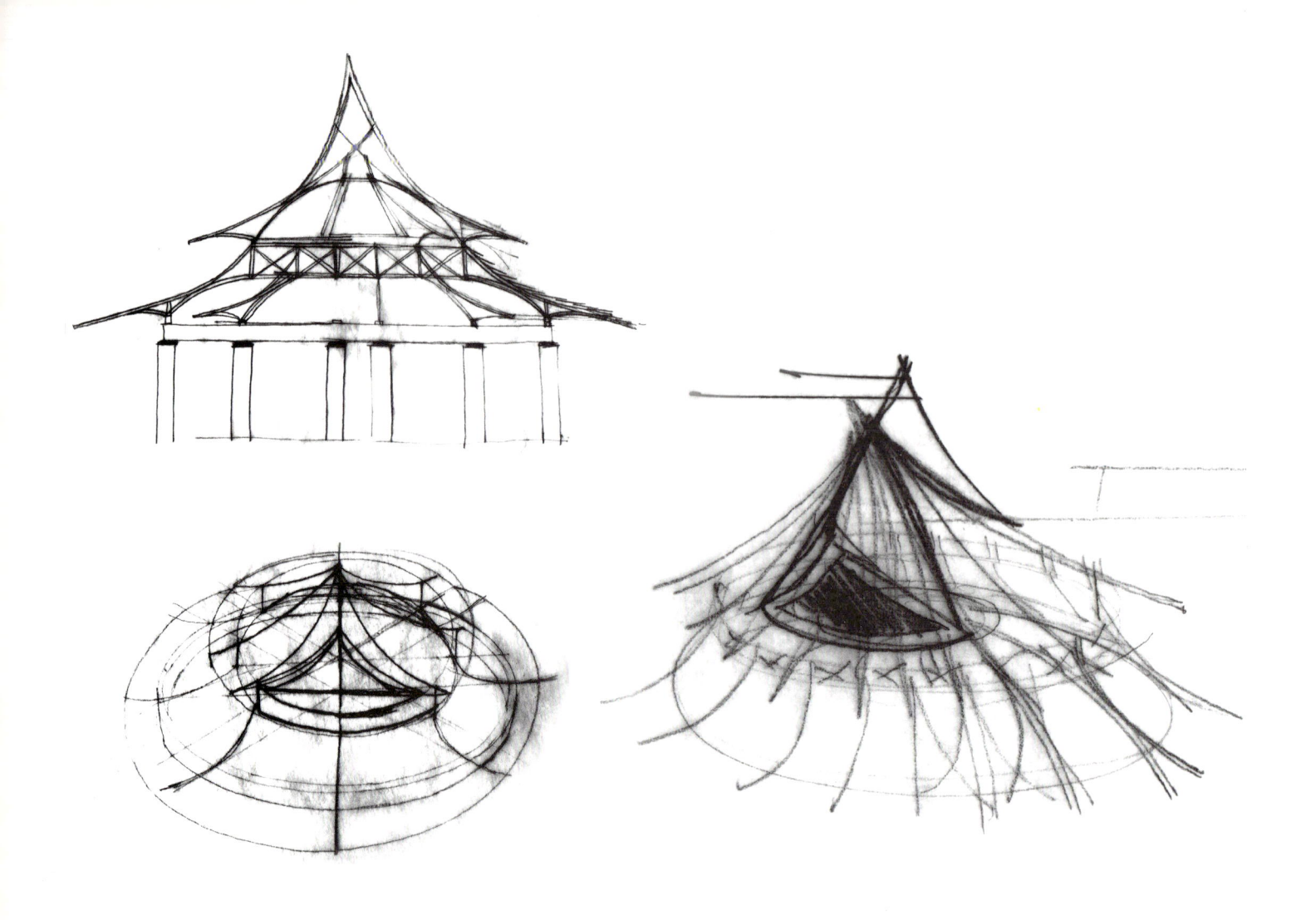

The architecture of the main huts is characterized by an eclectic style that mixes Oriental and Central American architecture and is suitable for a hot, humid climate, creating a successful fusion with the organic and curvilinear architecture of the overall design. In addition, the manaco-thatch structure is strengthened by a compression ring that articulates the two sections of each main hut. The great height that results manages to create a chimney effect that expels hot air from the interior and allows the fresh breeze to circulate through the openings. The resulting natural oasis of Casa las Olas is an example of the effective use of the characteristics of regional architecture and creates a comfortable habitat.

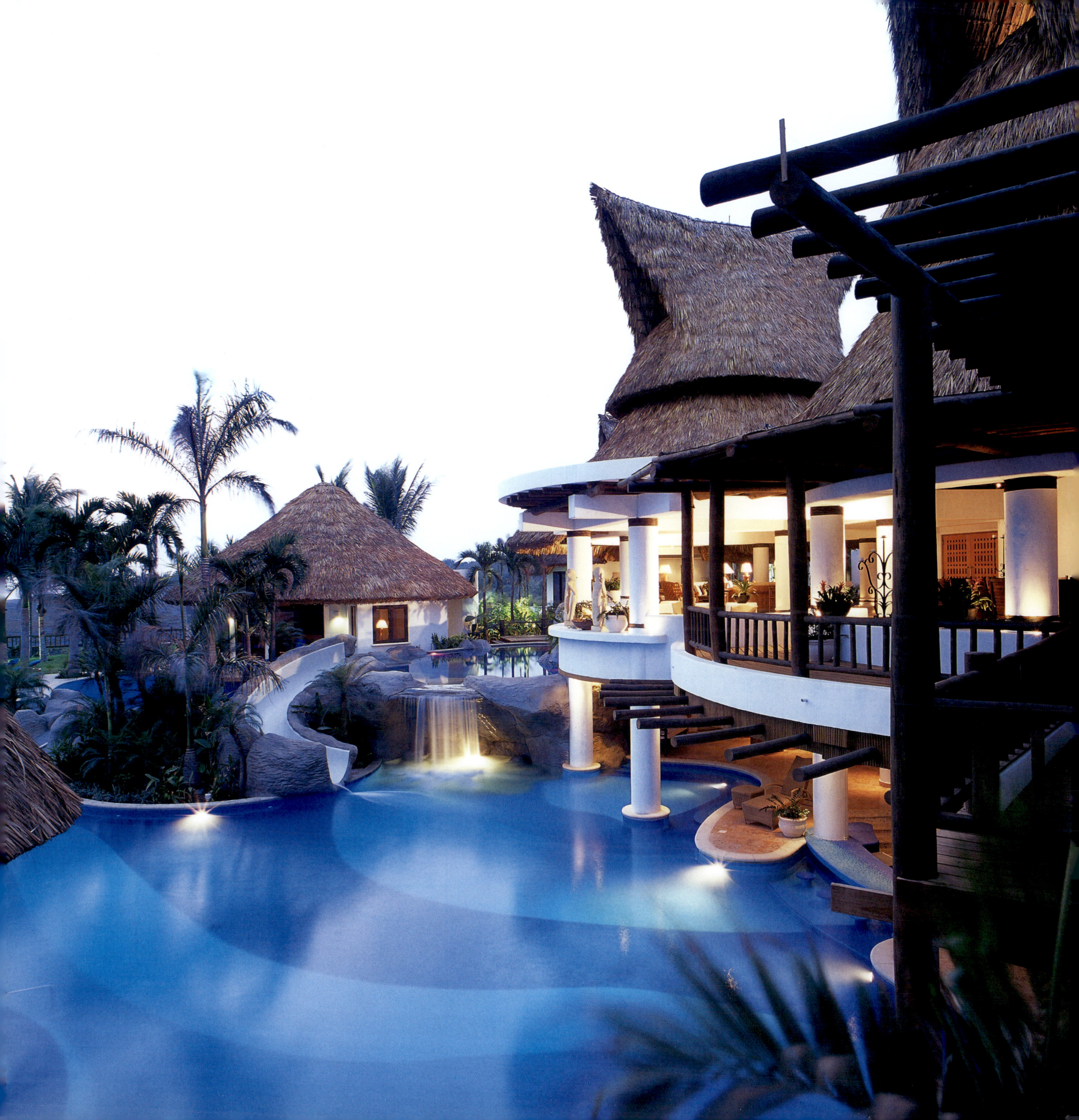

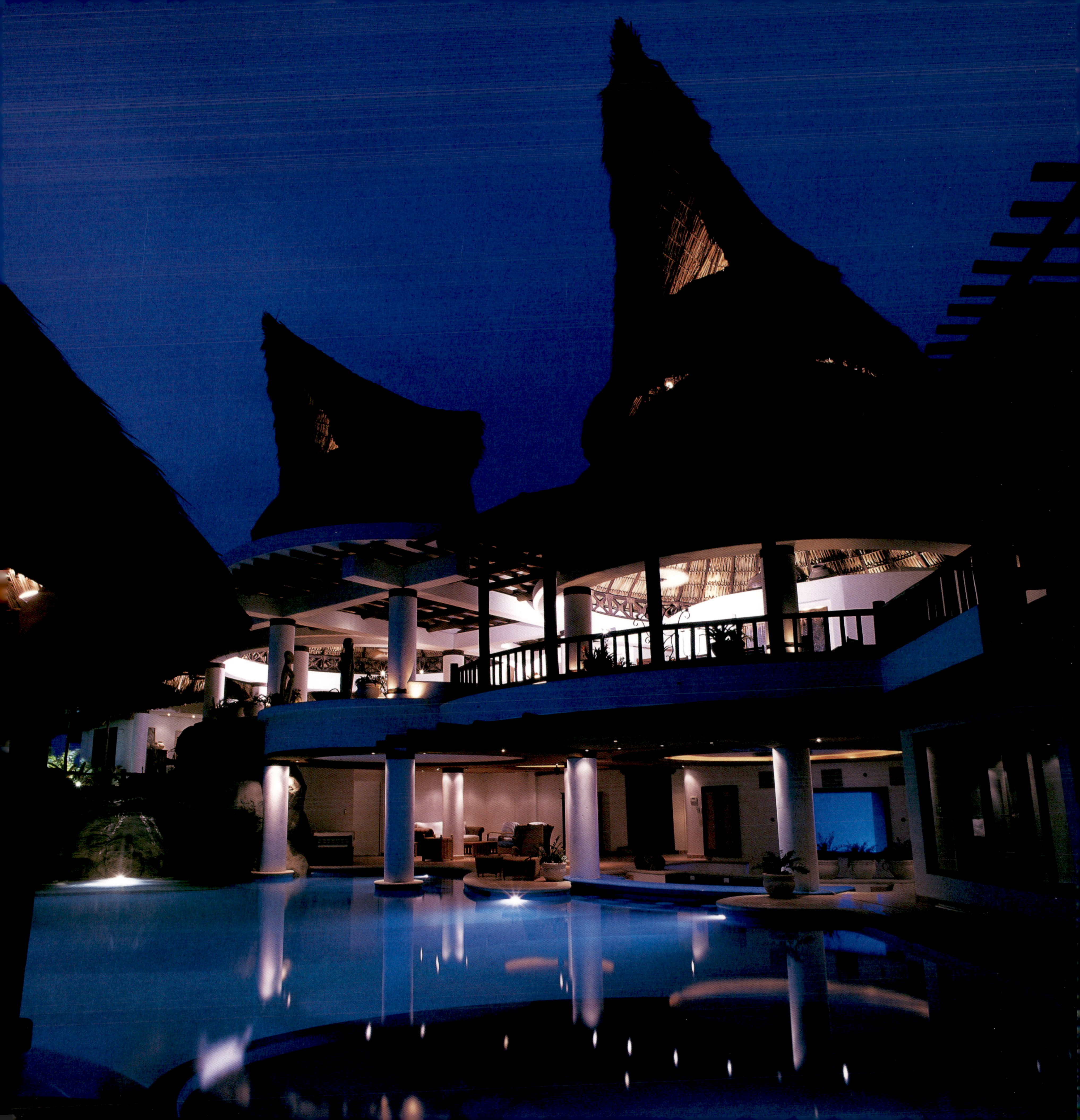

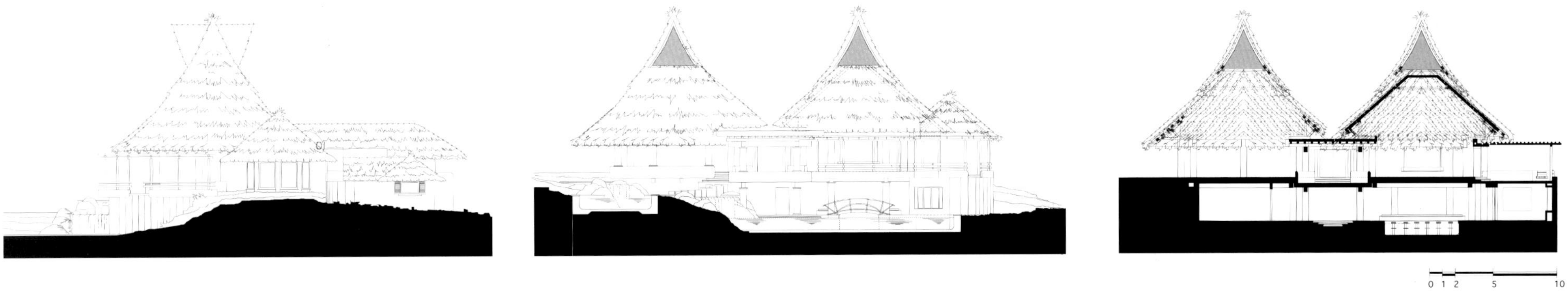
0 1 2 5 10

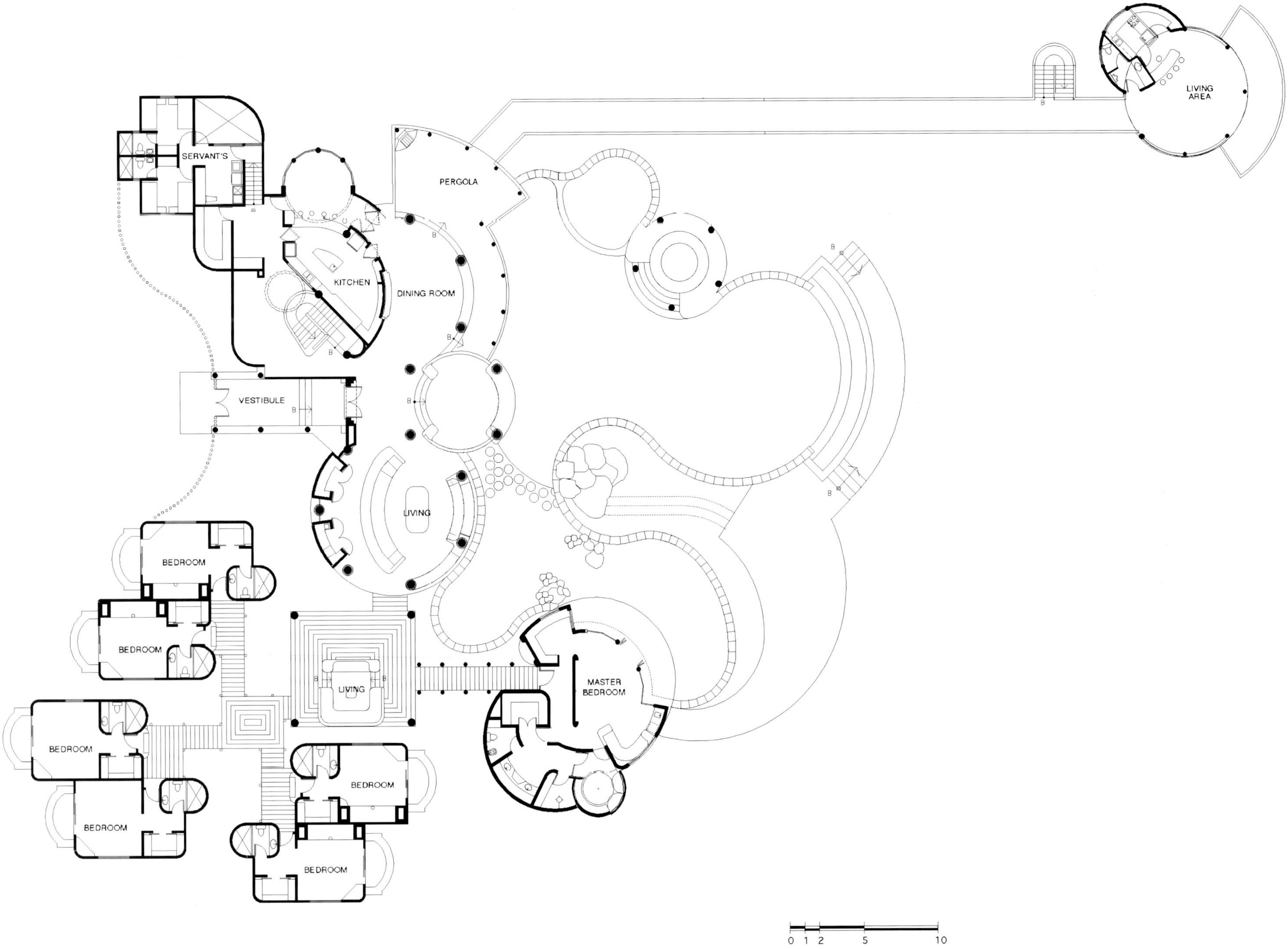
SERVANT'S
PERGOLA
KITCHEN
DINING ROOM
LIVING AREA
VESTIBULE
LIVING
BEDROOM
BEDROOM
BEDROOM
BEDROOM
BEDROOM
BEDROOM
LIVING
MASTER BEDROOM
0 1 2 5 10

Designed for the terrain of "La Luz" farm, in Puerta Parada on the outskirts of Guatemala City, and occupying a surface area of forty-five blocks, this big project consists of 249 new lots on which eight different kinds of houses were built, all of them intended to fit well into the undulating topography of the area. It is important to note that these housing sites occupy fifty percent of the terrain, while the different green areas cover thirty percent and the streets twenty percent, which creates a great visual amplitude

RESIDENCIAL LAS LUCES

and provides a setting characterized by large and pleasant green areas. In most of the houses, the design employs fired-clay bricks and a beige-colored rustic concrete block as the predominant materials. The result is a project whose overall design has a great unity and shows a coherent variety in all of its elements. Las Luces project won the *Prize for Excellence*, awarded by the Cementos Progreso firm for the period 1999-2002.

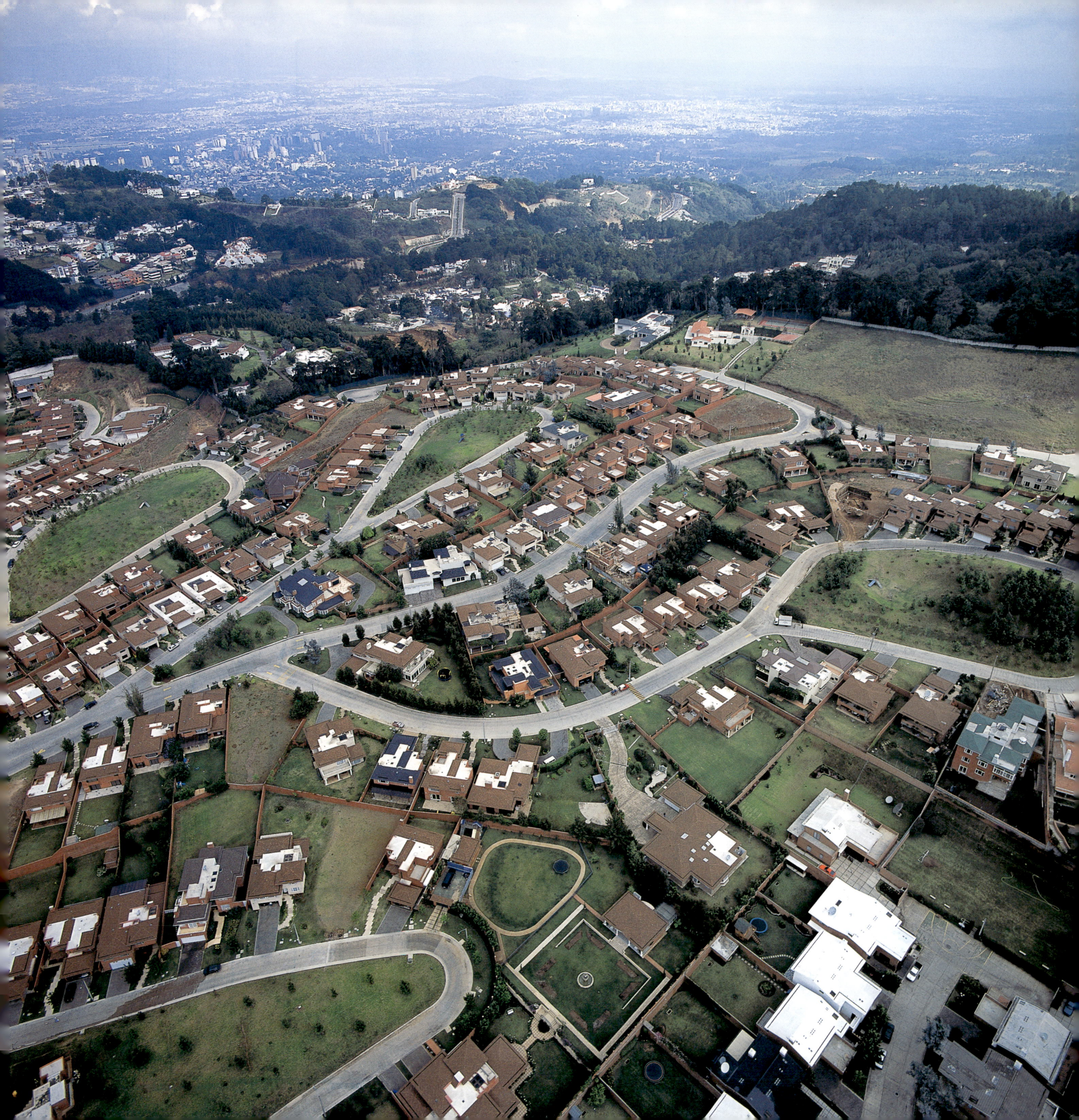

AVENIDA
LAS LUCES

N
CANCHA DE BASKETBALL
A MUXBAL
GARITA DE CONTROL
ENTRADA
AVENIDA LAS LUCES
CARRETERA INTERAMERICANA A EL SALVADOR
CANCHAS DE TENIS
CANCHA DE BASKETBALL
ESTANQUE
CASCADA
CANCHA DE PAPI-FOOTBALL
RANCHON PARA FIESTAS
PARADA DE BUSES ESCOLARES
ANFITEATRO PARA PIÑATAS
JUEGOS PARA NIÑOS
HORTENSIAS
HORTENSIAS
HORTENSIAS
HORTENSIAS
HORTENSIAS
JULIAS
PENSAMIENTOS
BEGONIAS
GARDENIAS
GARDENIAS
AZALEAS
AZALEAS
AVENIDA LAS LUCES
JAZMINES
CAMELIAS
AVENIDA LAS LUCES
AVENIDA LAS LUCES
LIRIOS
LIRIOS
LIRIOS
IRIS
IRIS
CAMELIAS
0 20 50 100 200 300

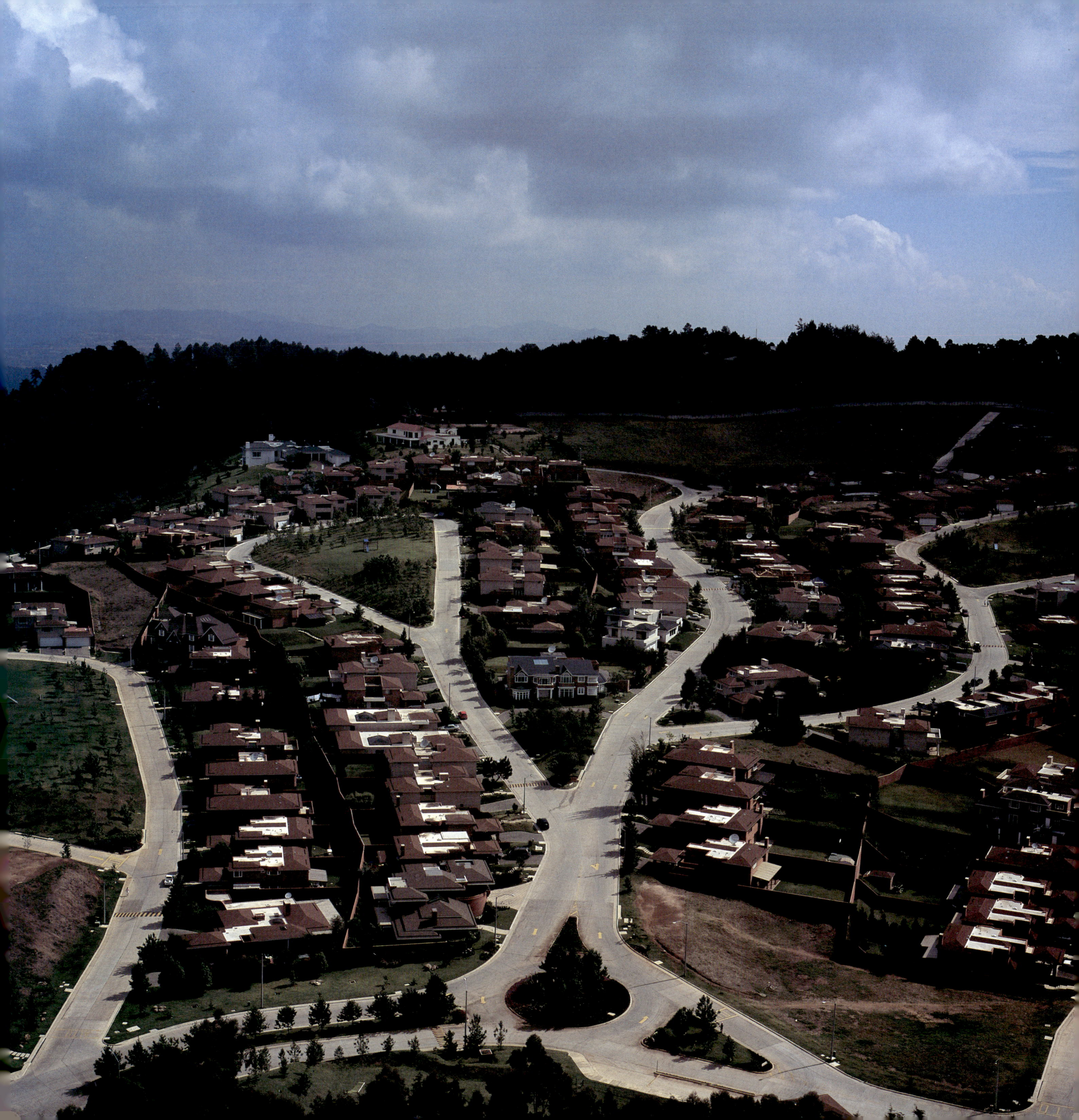

minondo&giesemann

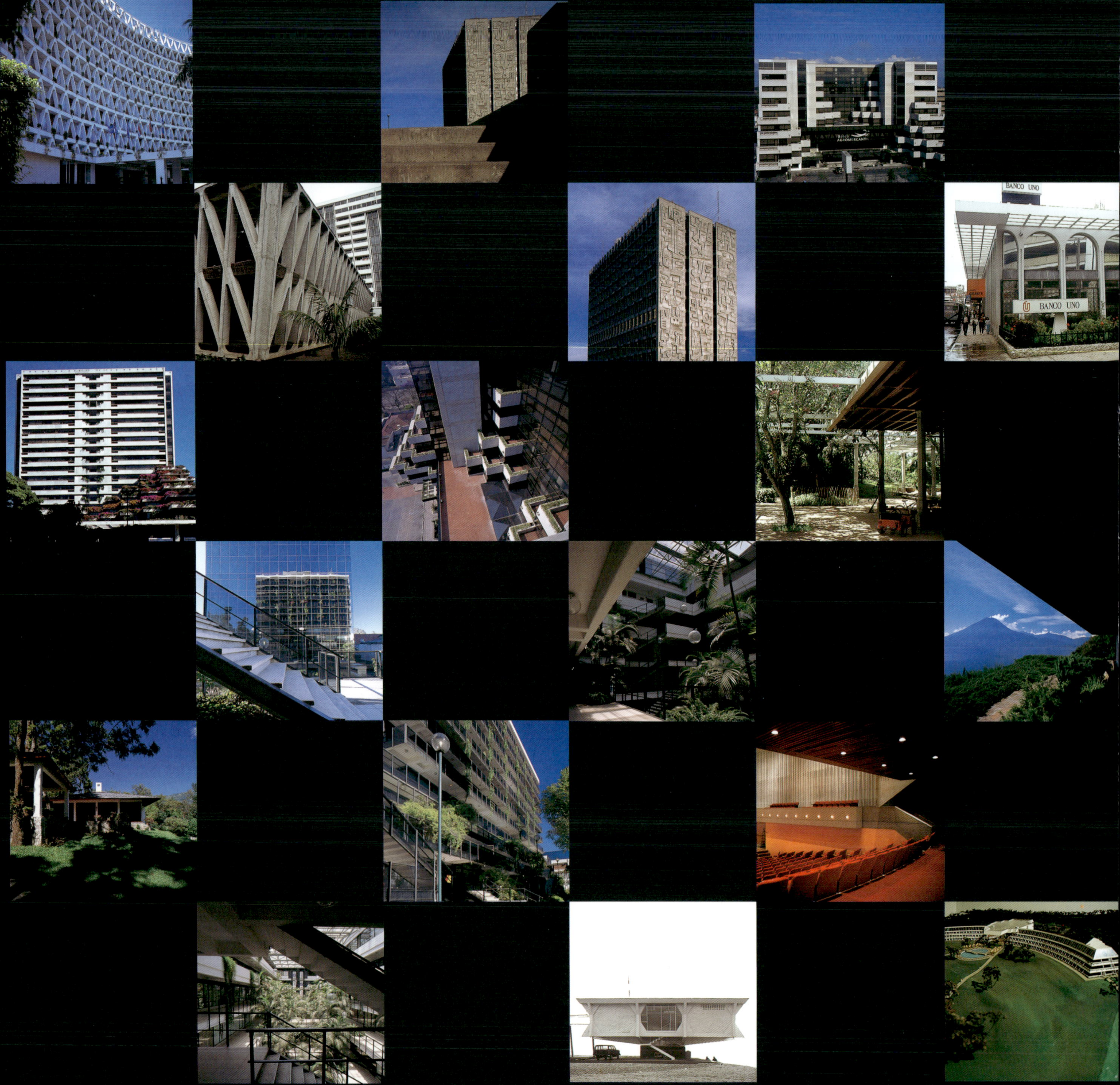
BANCO UNO
BANCO UNO

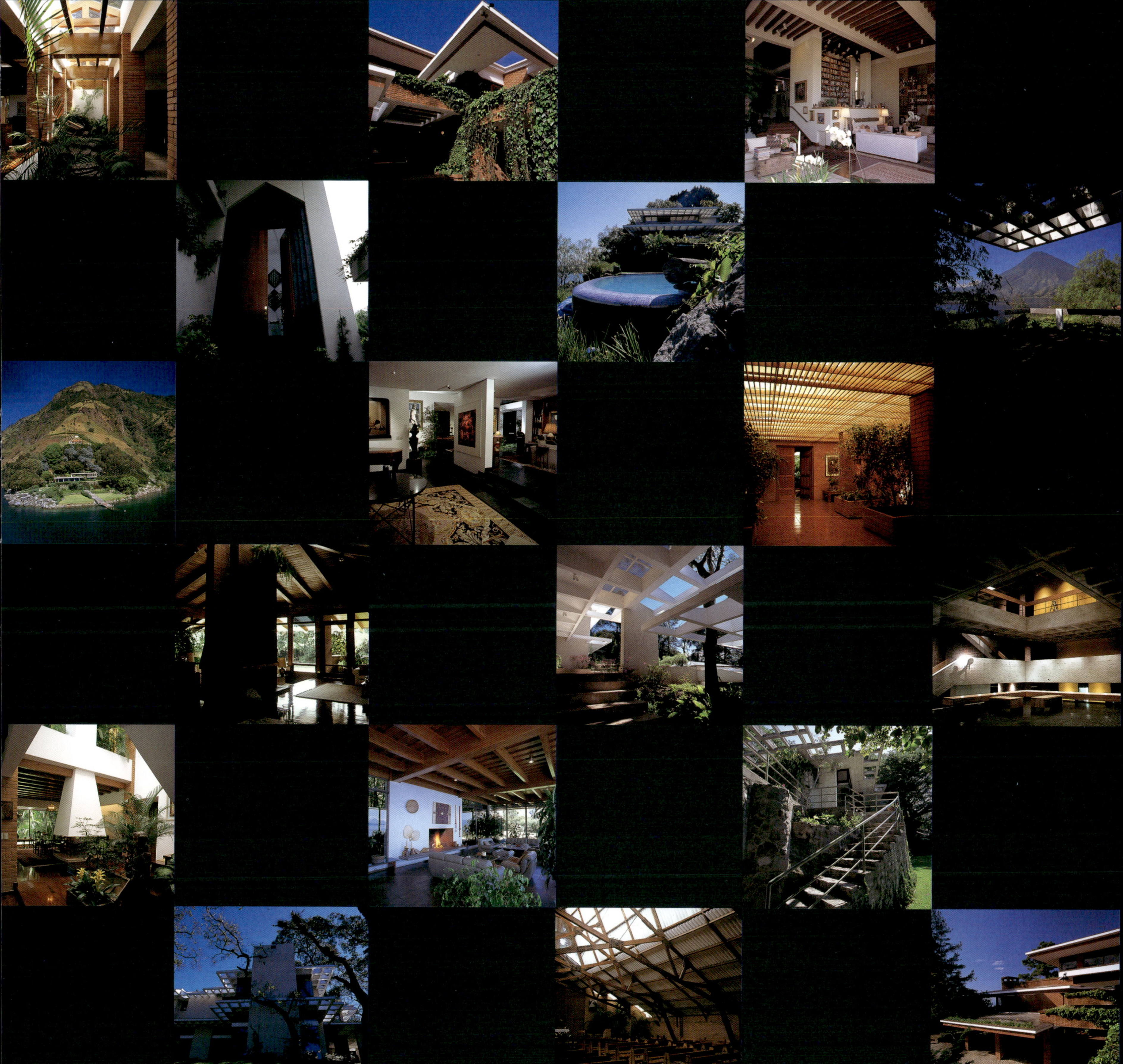

With more than sixty years of service to the public, the Banco Agromercantil has been one of the most prestigious banking institutions in Guatemala. The headquarters of this bank were located in the historic center of the city until the end of the nineteen-nineties. The neo-classical building was restored by the architect Peter Giesemann and currently represents one of the best examples of conservation in its class. In the nineteen-eighties, the executives of the bank decided to enlarge their installations by constructing new offices in the south of city, with the aim of modernizing their operations through the use of leading-edge technology. The job of designing this new corporate

BANCO AGROMERCANTIL

building was placed in the hands of Giesemann, who spent more than ten years on the project, submitting a number of proposals in response to the institution's policy of structural change and permanent reengineering. The design concept of the building that finally resulted responded to its mixed functions: the building would house the offices of the bank and offer the possibility of additional space for the offices of other companies. Under this premise, the vertical circulation was arranged so that these different functions could be independent of one another. As a result there are two pyramidal elements, one to the south and one to the north, which descend in a staggered form and give way to terraces with gardens towards the parking plaza.

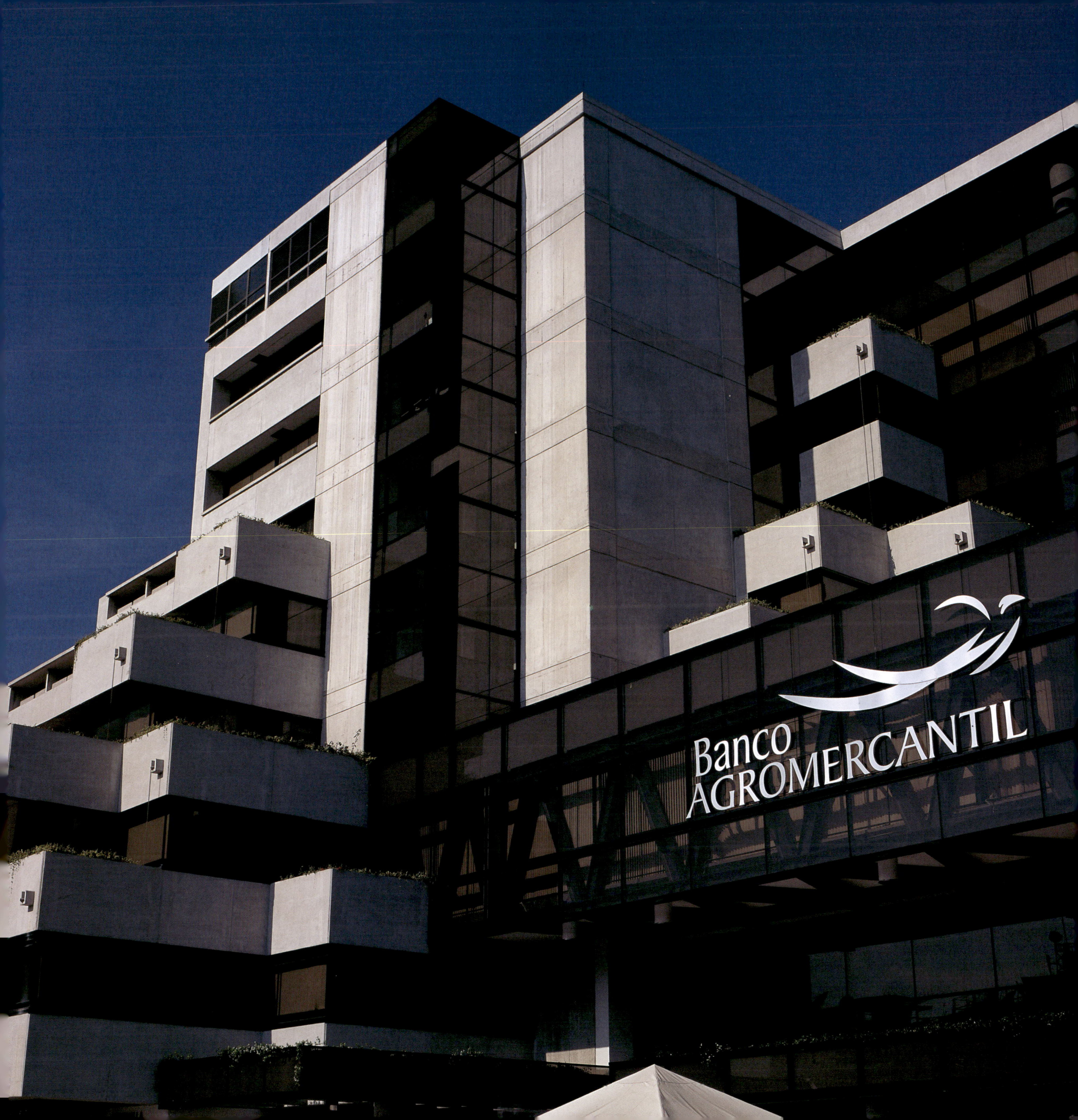
Banco
AGROMERCANTIL

On the first floor, the main lobby, three-stories-high, offers a view of the next two levels, whose perimeters are highlighted by indoor garden plots which give the space a pleasant atmosphere. Running alongside them, the safety banisters are made up of glass panels that support a light handrail, which serves to uphold the formal cleanness of the white slabs. In the exterior, the combination of dark glass and exposed concrete in the rectilinear forms of the building's volumes expresses the image of a modern institution of great solidity.

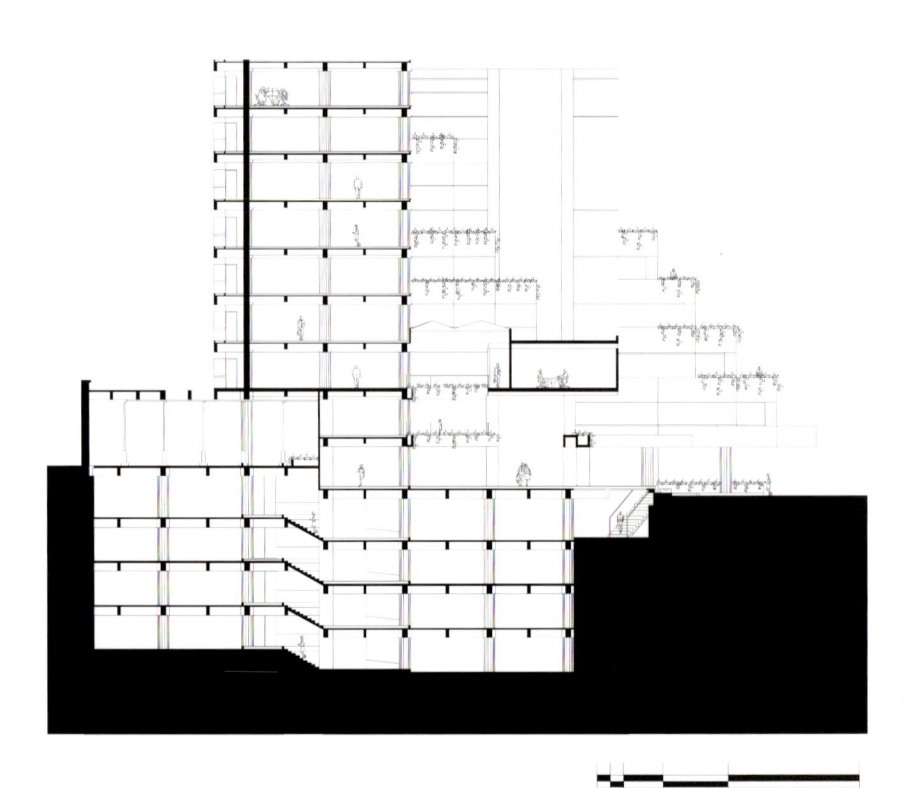

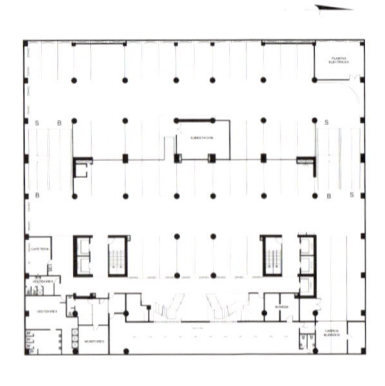

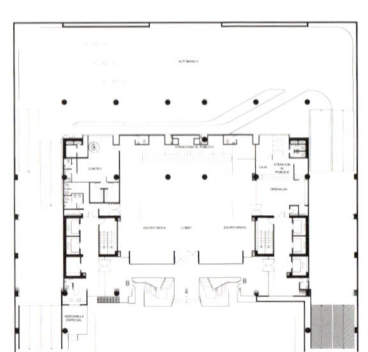

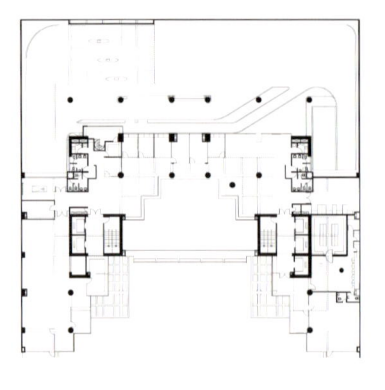

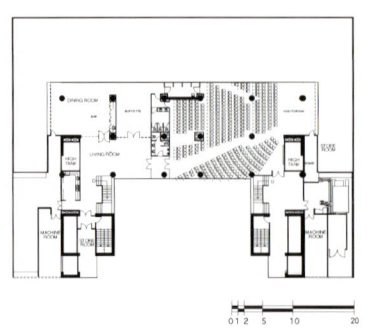

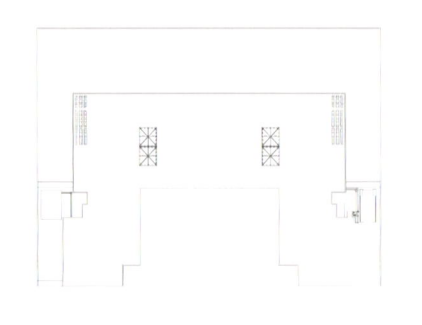

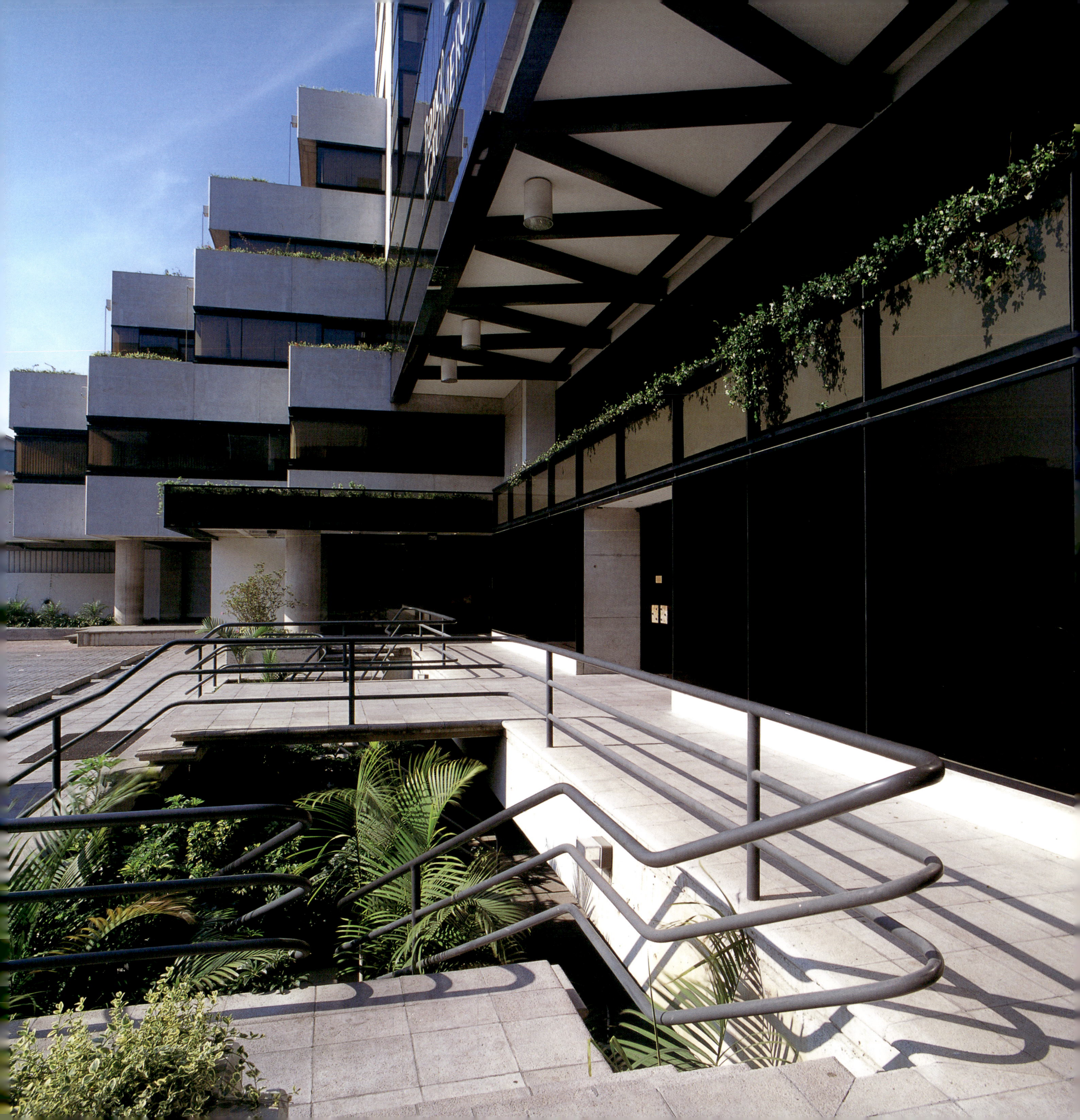

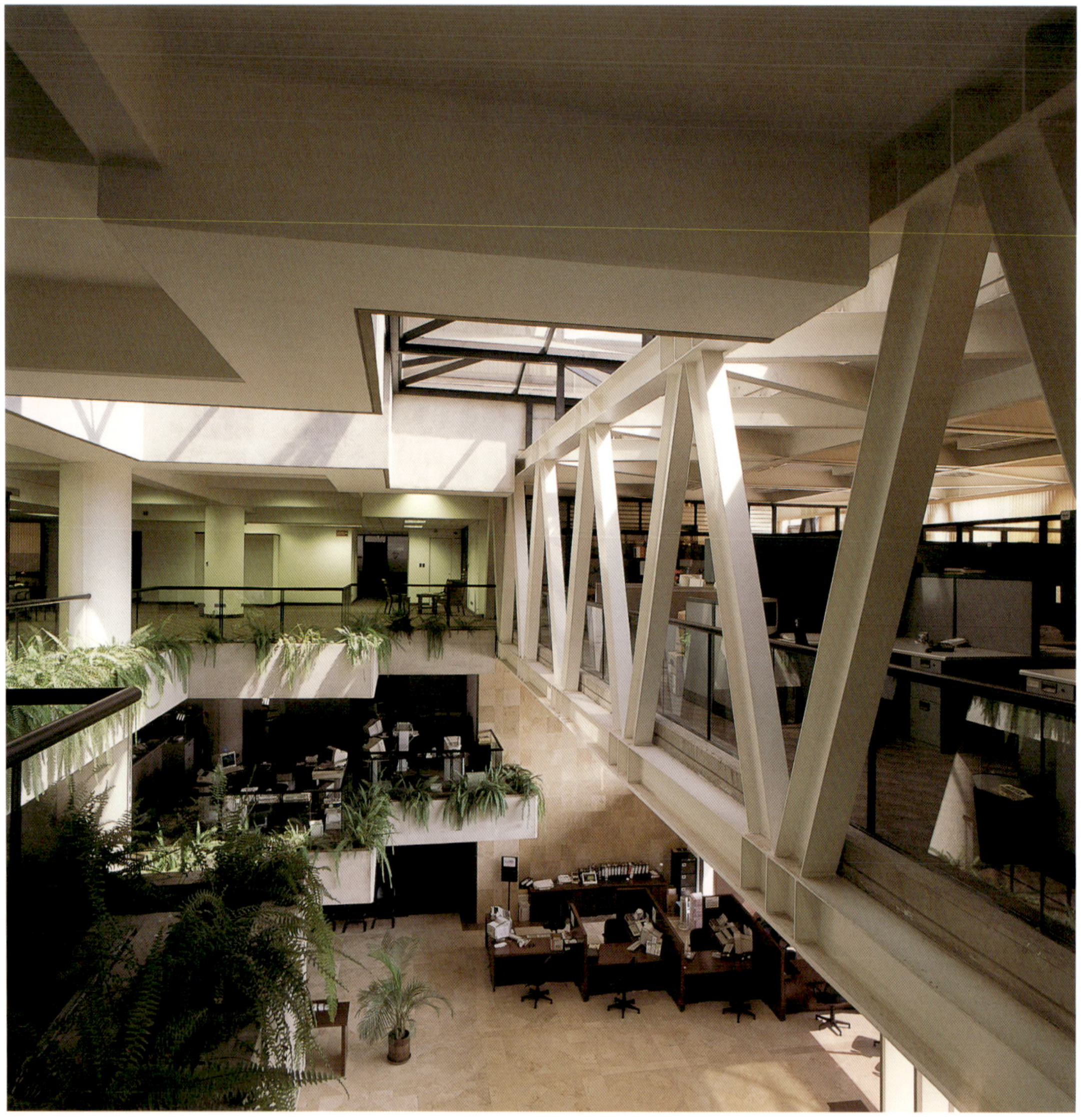

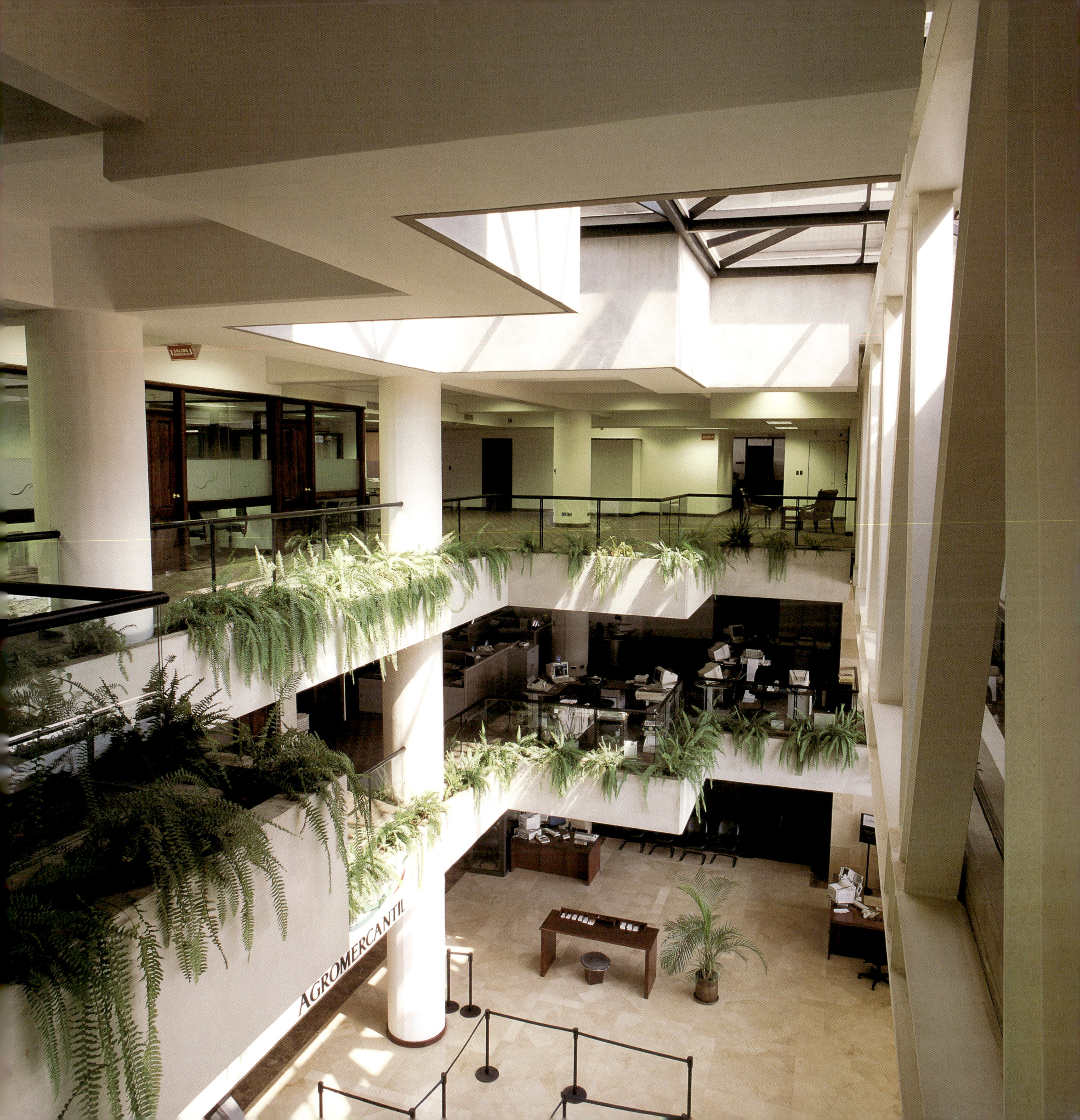
AGROMERCANTIL

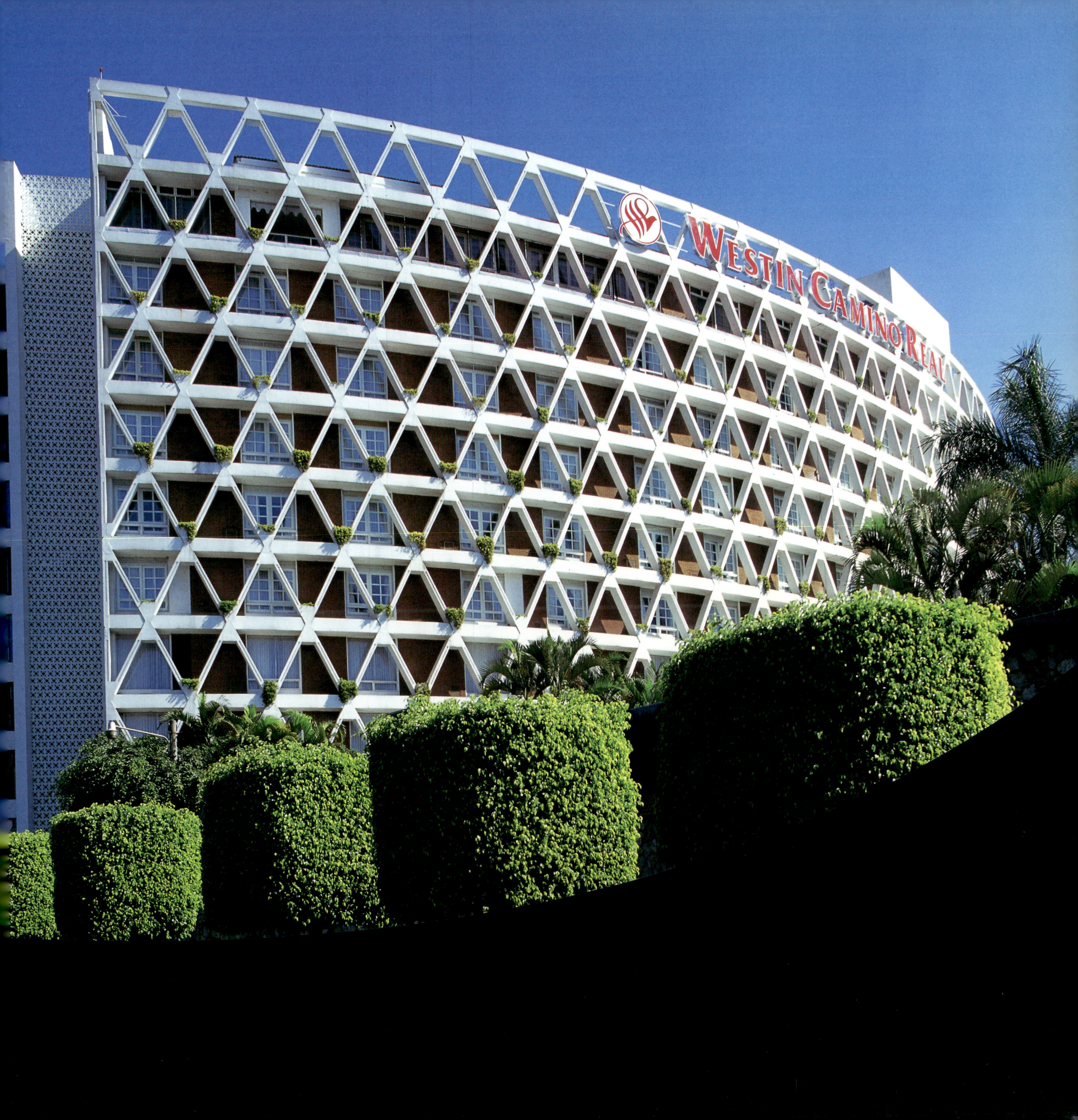
WESTIN CAMINO REAL

Set in the heart of the "Zona Viva" ("Lively District") of Guatemala City – the main center of its business, commerce and entertainment – the five-star Westin Camino Real hotel is a great example of a modern architecture which, in the course of time, has become an architectural landmark in the Guatemalan capital. Displaying a modernist tendency that is shared with other great Latin American architects, Raúl Mindondo designs an exterior structure of concrete that forms a rich geometrical pattern with a triangular base, which, in addition to its structural purposes, serves as a system of mullions in diagonal lines that provide shade for all of the rooms of the building. In the intersection of each diagonal of the outer structure, above the slabs, a number of flower beds form a system of natural points which, in combination with the brick of the walls and the clean concrete of the structure, create an inviting architectural language that shows a contemporary character, without recurring to a specific regional image. On both fronts of the curved building, the superposition of the grid plane on the flat surface, with its rhythm of vertical strips of window and brick, creates a geometric play of contrasting depths in the elevation. With four hundred rooms, tennis courts, gymnasium, spa and swimming pools, four restaurants, shopping arcade, art galleries and convention halls, the Camino Real hotel is considered to be one of the best in Central America.

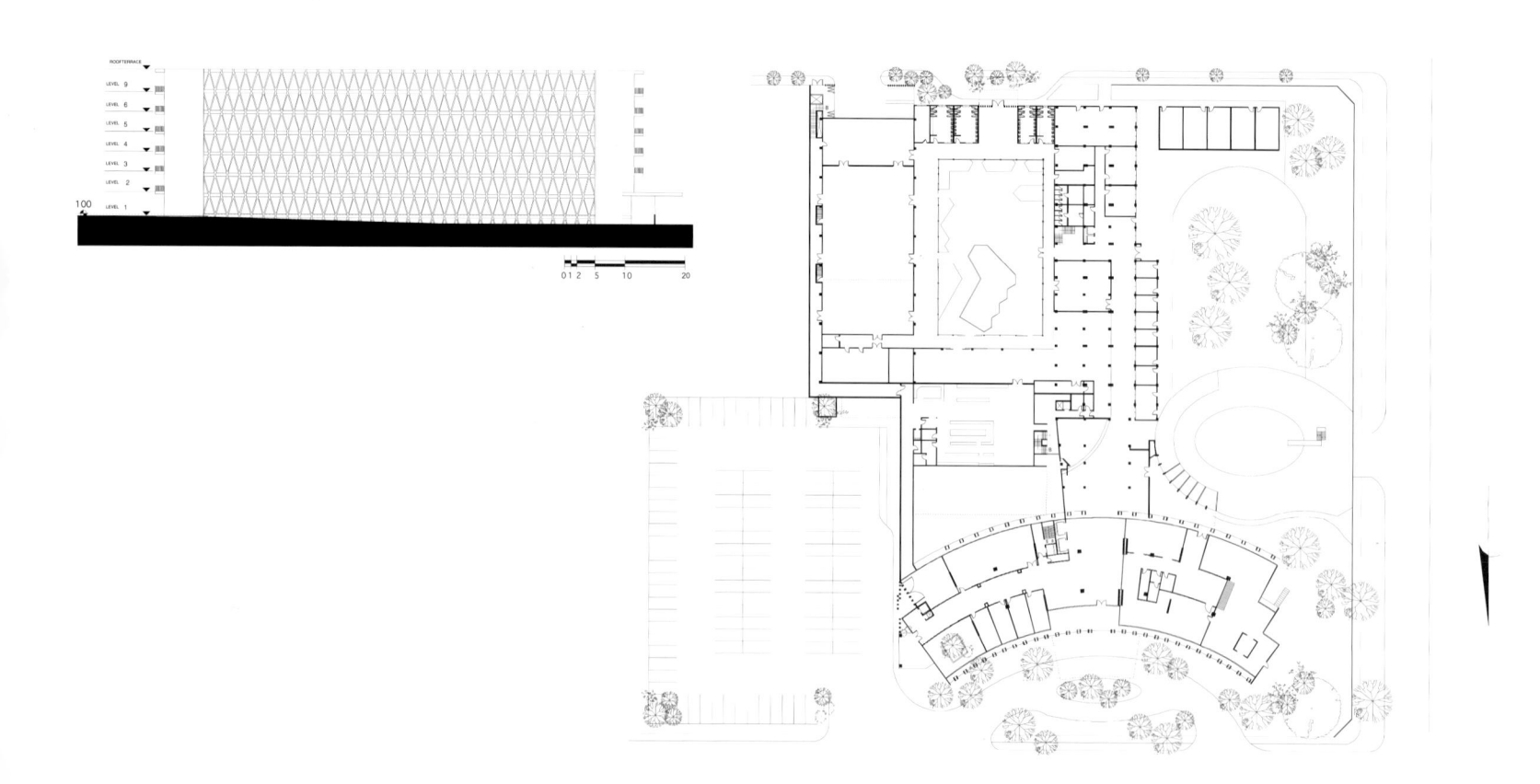

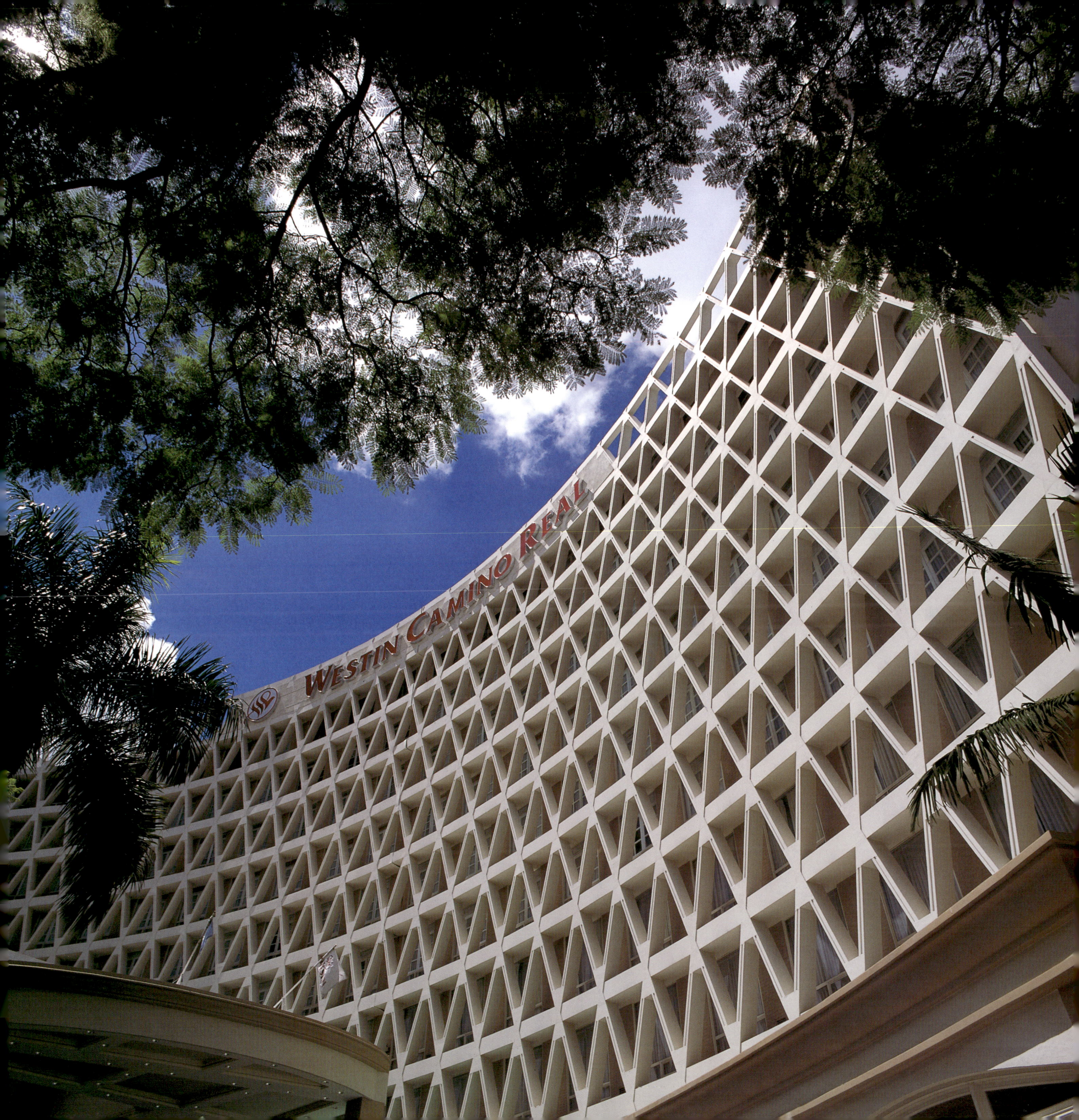
WESTIN CAMINO REAL

Without doubt one of the first mega-projects in the city, with a constructed area of more than 100,000 square meters, this complex is a magnificent example of the sound use of exposed concrete. The two great towers, which are very narrow and have a rectangular base, emerge from a plaza that is full of exuberant vegetation. At the back stands the corporate headquarters of the Pantaleón, S. A. company, which has a strong sense of solidity and tradition, as though it were hinting at the origins of this park. An elegant conjunction of pergolas and terraced gardens that

CENTRO LAS MARGARITAS

seem to be suspended in the air makes the gray of the concrete become friendly and inviting. The towers were placed lengthwise on an east-west axis, with the aim of taking maximum advantage of light and natural ventilation on the north and south fronts. The design of the façades of tower one allowed the different co-owners to intervene in the final arrangement and modify at their discretion the solid and transparent areas of the building's fenestration. The result is a mixed texture of glass, concrete and vegetation, which is asymmetrical in its context.

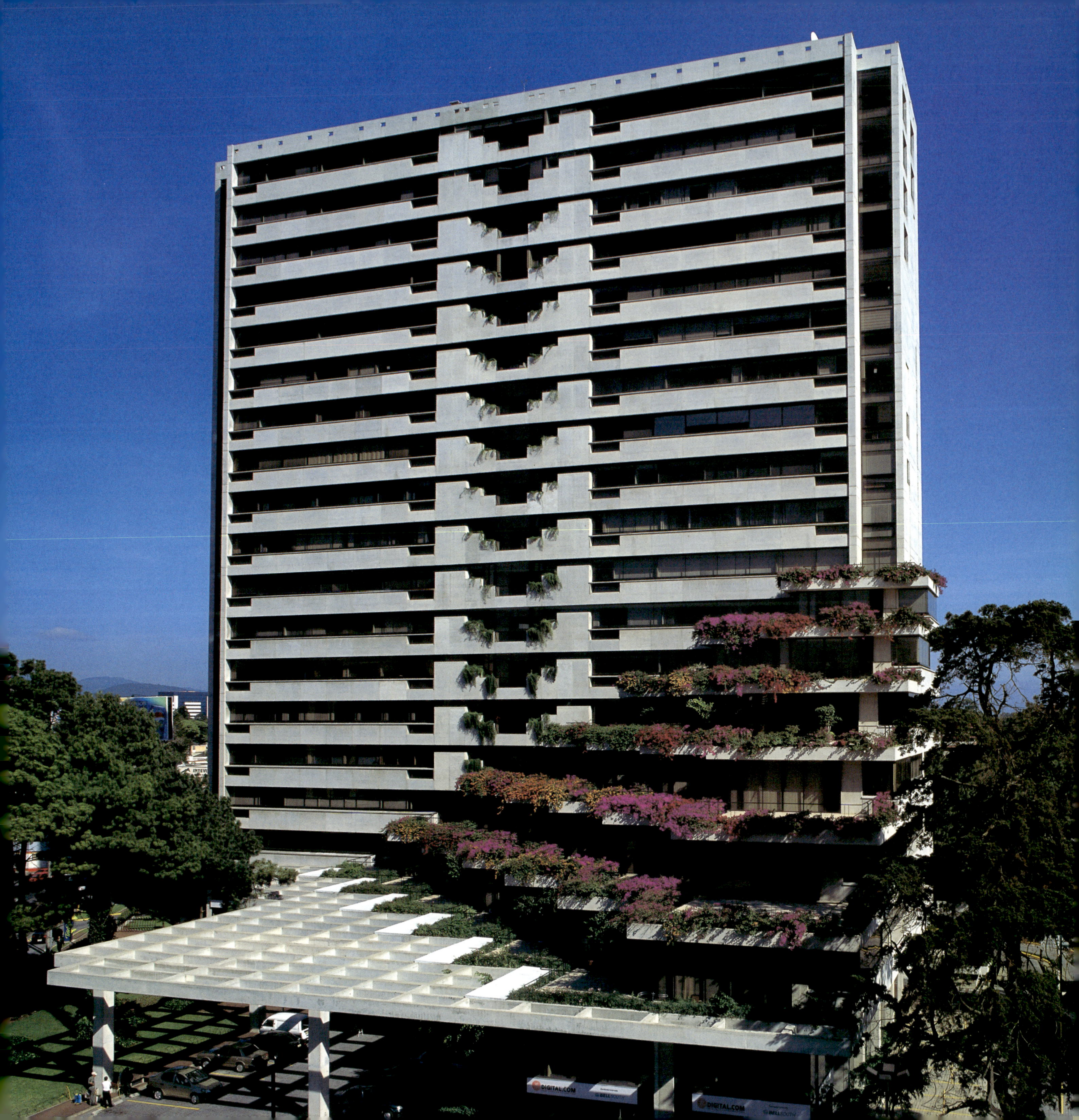
DIGITAL.COM
BELLSOUTH
DIGITAL.COM
BELLSOUTH

Tower 2, built more recently, has a front of clean, even lines. The ashlars of the windows serve as a parapet for the electrical and mechanical installations. A pyramidal volume, formed by staggered elements with terraces full of plants and flowers, adheres to the southern front, which, together with a two-story-high pergola, is harmoniously integrated into the public space of the plaza. The design of the corporate building takes the form of a block which opens to the interior. An interior tropical garden serves as an area of transit to the three floors of offices, which are arranged on an open plan. The original master plan called for three towers and a small corporate building. When the first tower and the small building were finished, around 1988, the original plan was modified and the third tower was discarded. The result of this was a better use of the free space in the plaza.

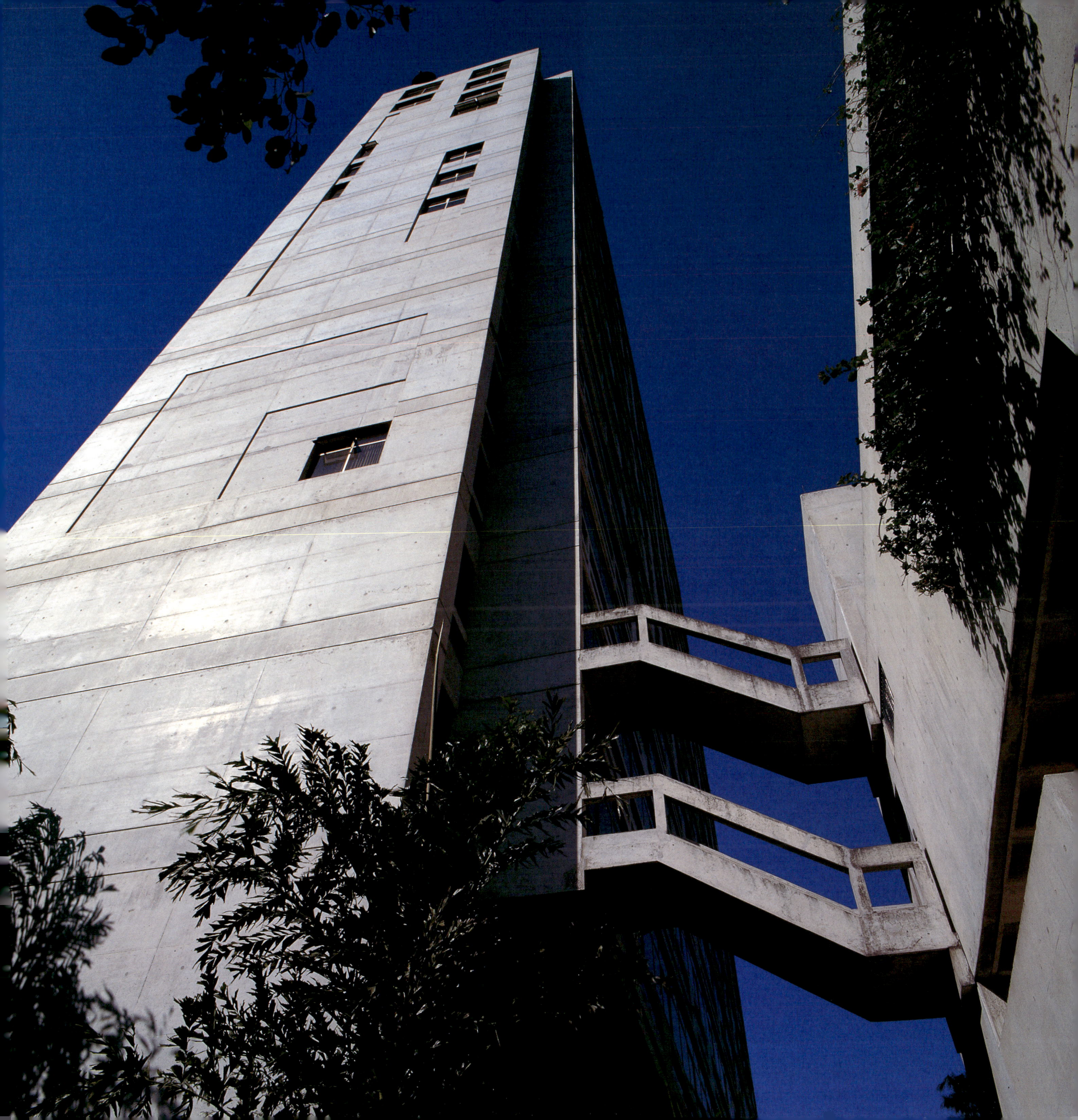

BANK
BANCO DE AMERICA CENTRAL
VISA
Plata
VISA
BANCO CUSCATLAN

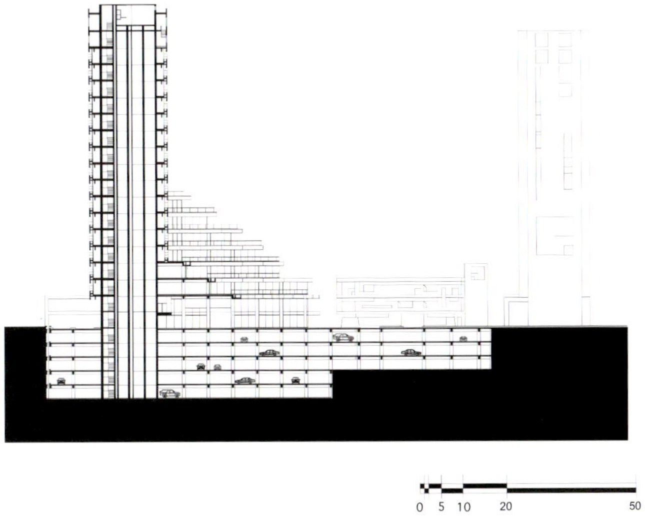
0 5 10 20 50

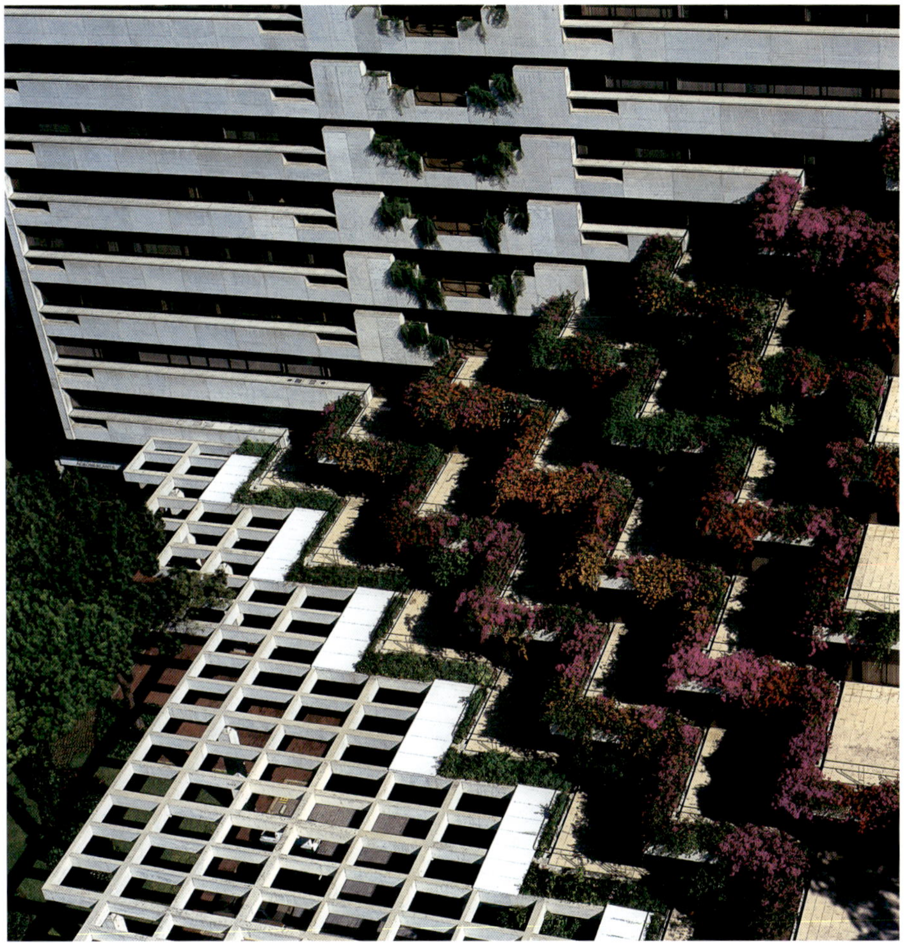

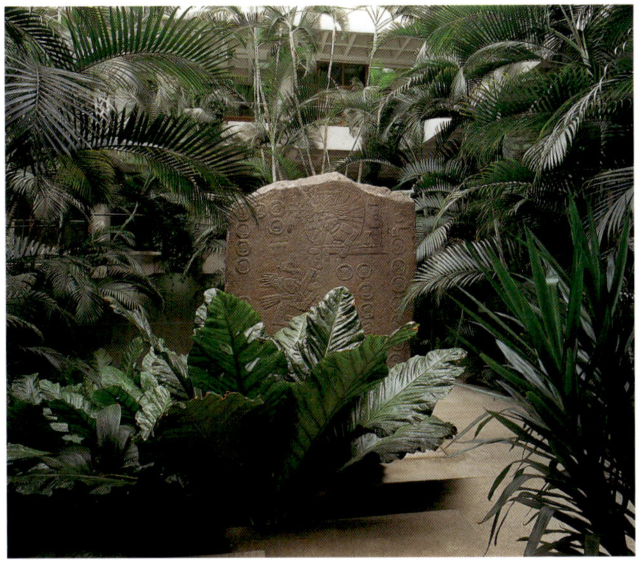

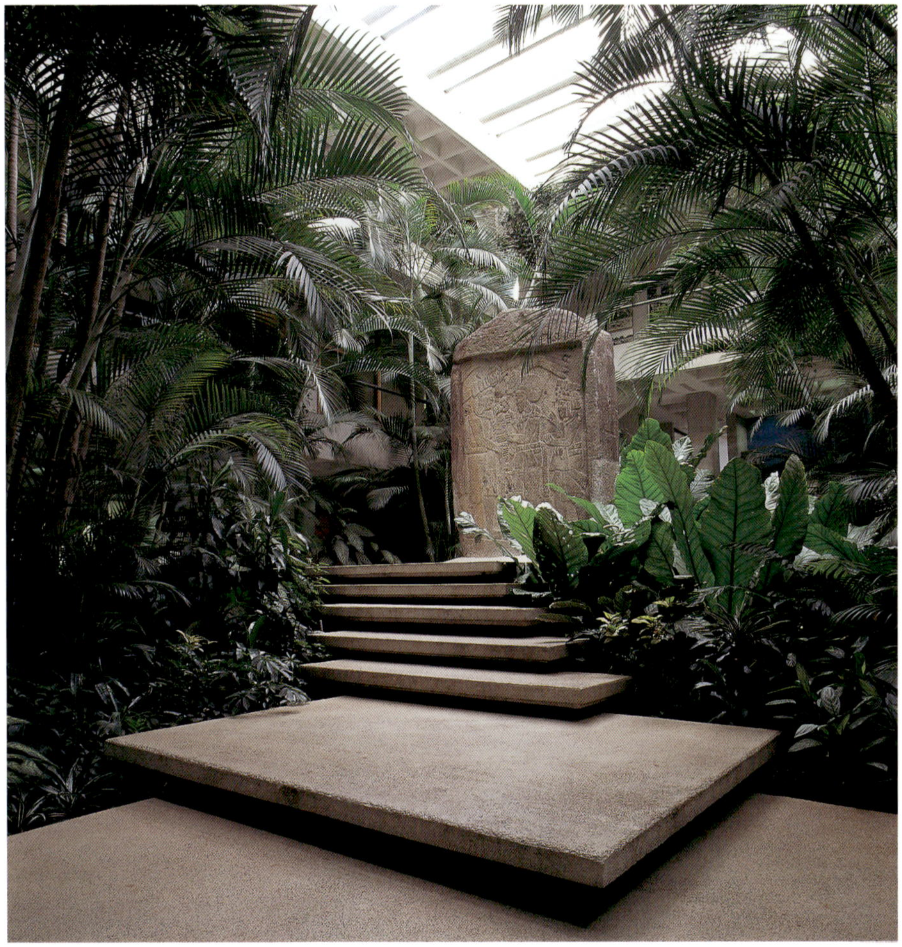

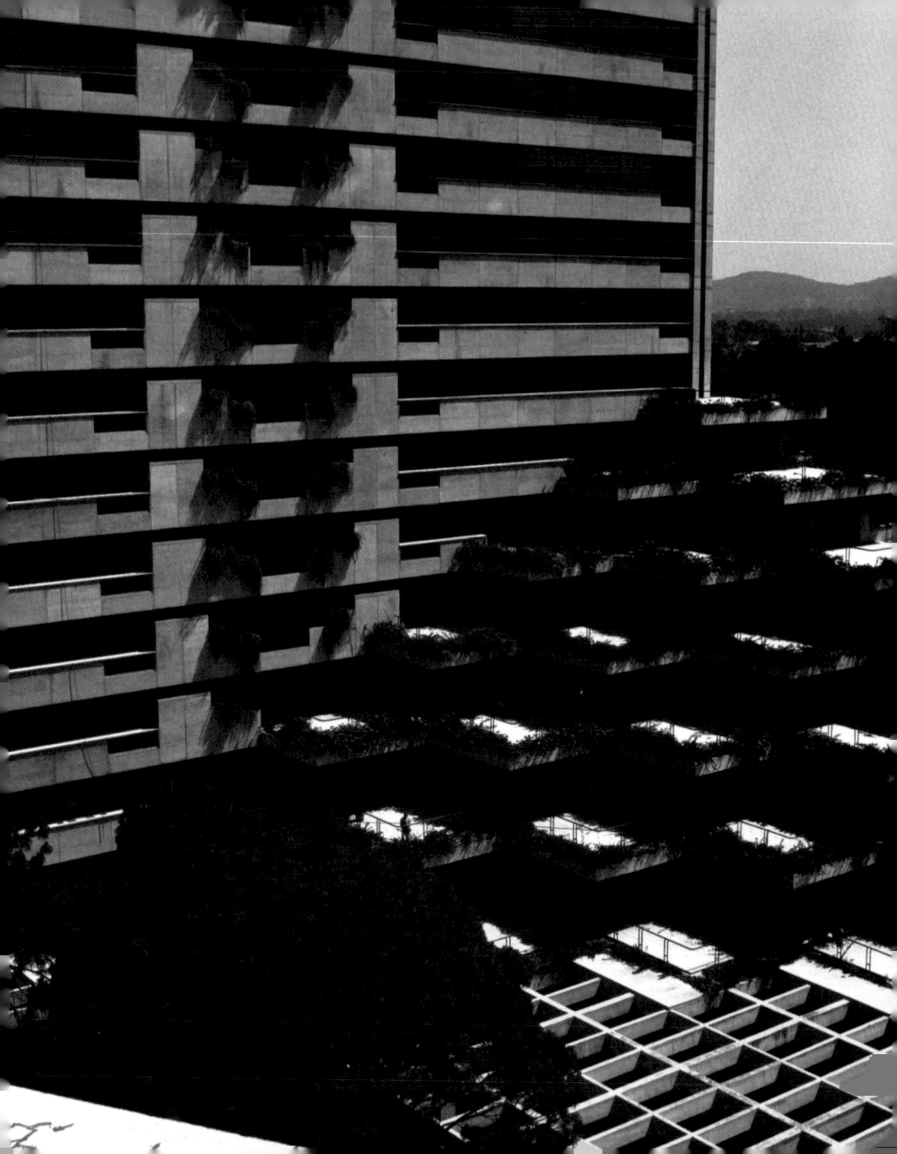

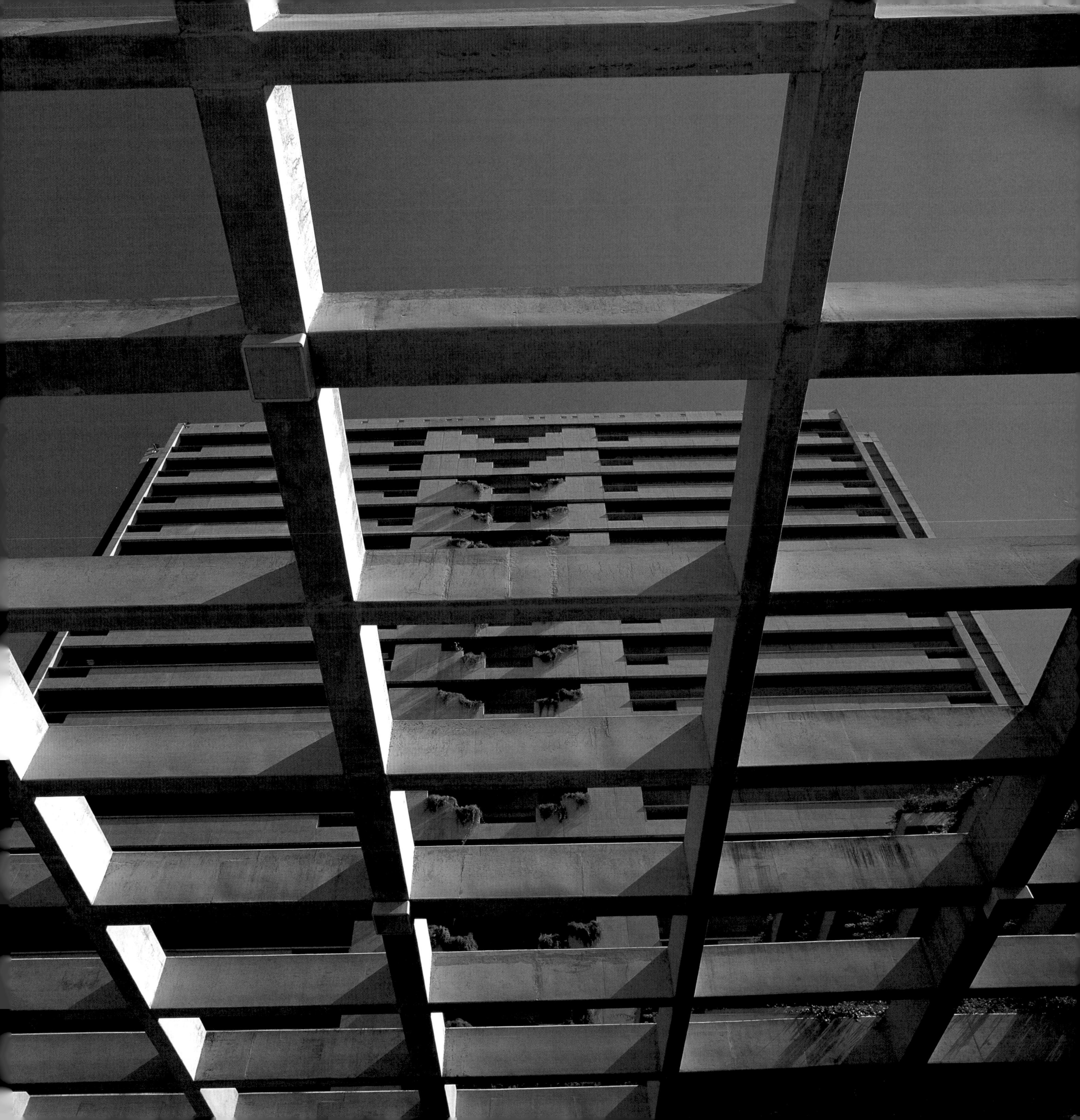

The final proposal for this building, which is the seat of the of the National Coffee-Growers Association was the result of the combined efforts of the architects Giesemann, Minondo, Montes, Porras and Castillo, among others. The key concept was to create an atrium, instead of the auditorium required by the original program. In this way, the four-story-high atrium, flooded with natural night, serves for a variety of purposes, such as art exhibitions, receptions and conferences. In addition, it establishes a visual interaction between the four floors of offices and the uppermost floor, which houses the executive offices and board room of the Association. To make use of

ANACAFÉ BUILDING

overhead light, the roof, which is supported by a large stereo-structure, makes use of "Lexan Thermoclear" polycarbonate sheets and has a chamber of air to control heat. This ingenious design for the roof provides a great amount of light for all of the floors and makes the vegetation of the interior ambit more luxuriant. The main front has a staggered surface of reflective glass, a strategy that was adopted after studying the mass of the building, which led the architects to conclude that a one-story-high entrance would not suit the final scale. With this in mind, they designed a front with a system of modules that are inset in a staggered way to create the depth suitable to the scale and which serve to gradually announce the main entrance.

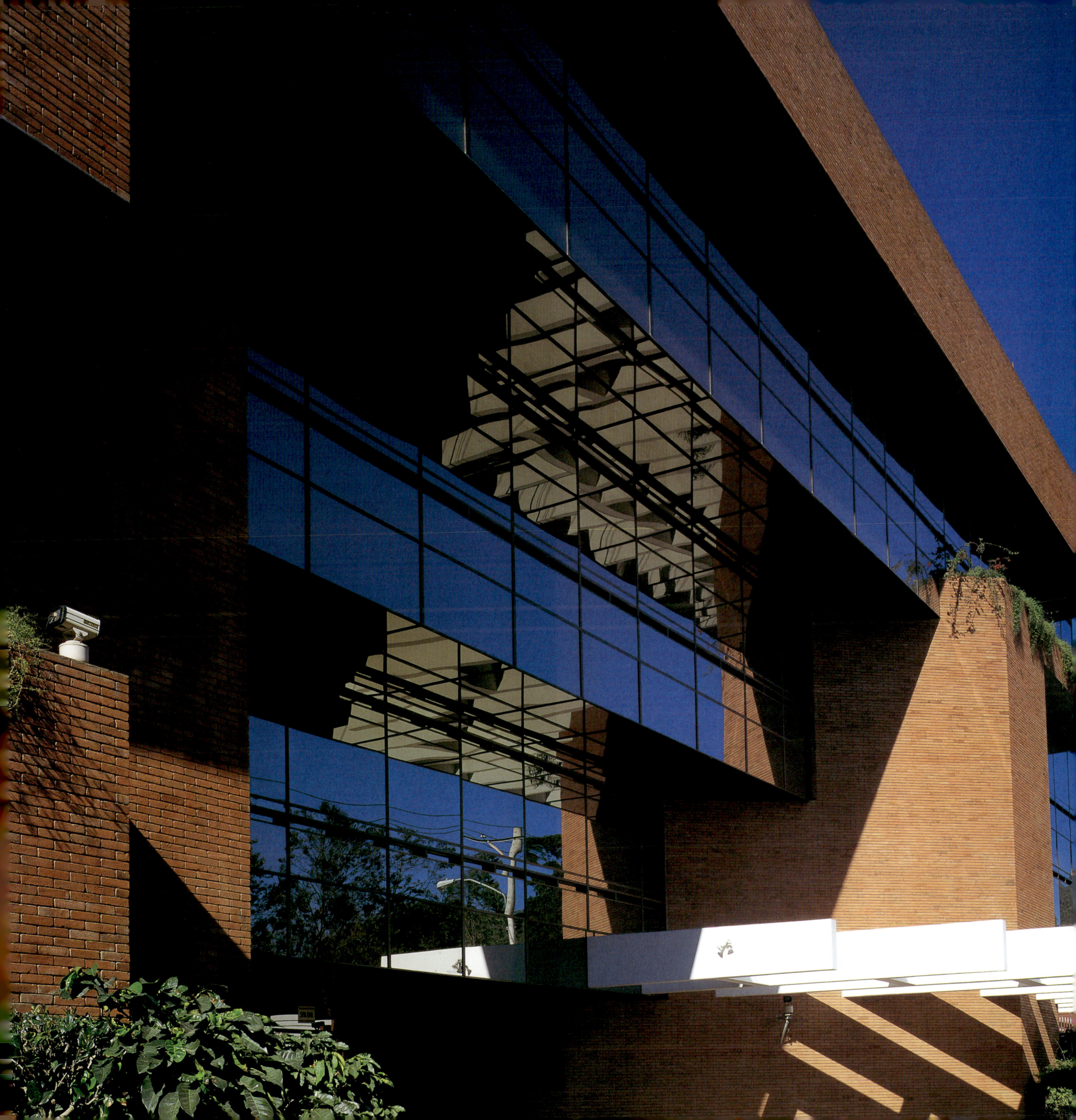

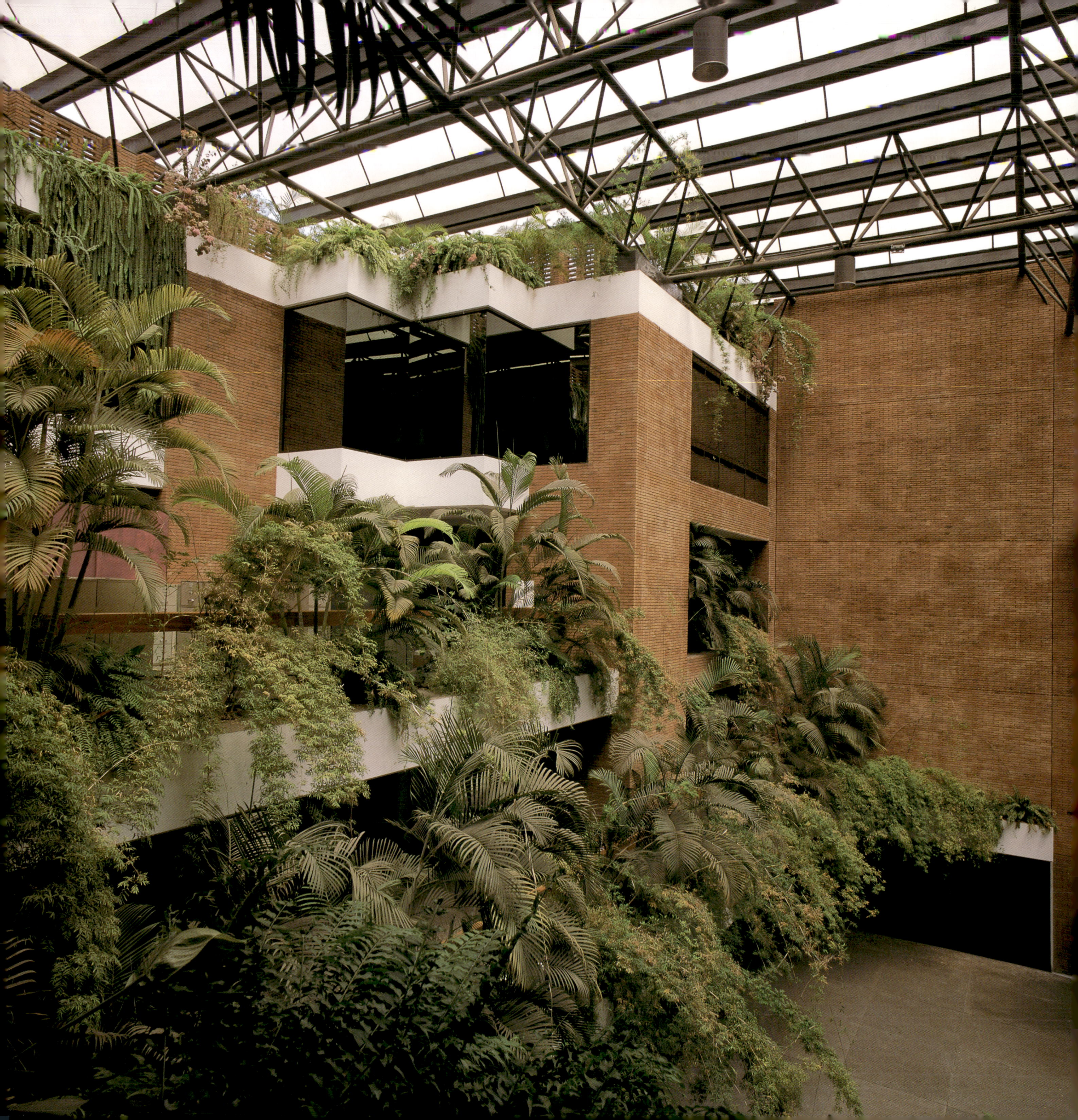

For the exterior walls, artisanal bricks from the Chimaltenango area were employed. They are placed so as to create an interesting texture that hides the concrete and provides a kind of allegorical reference to the coffee plants that rise from the soil. The brick front also suggests the solidity of this sector of the Guatemalan economy, a major source of employment for more than a century.

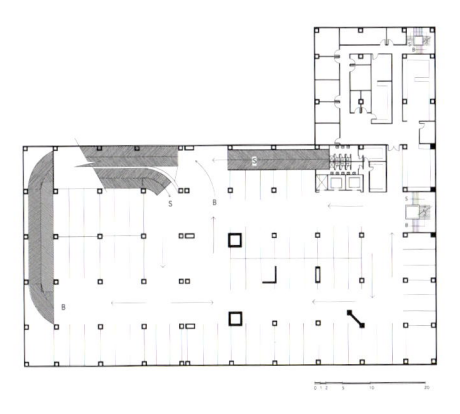

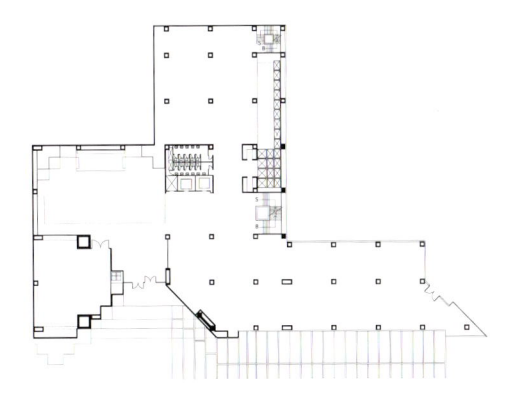

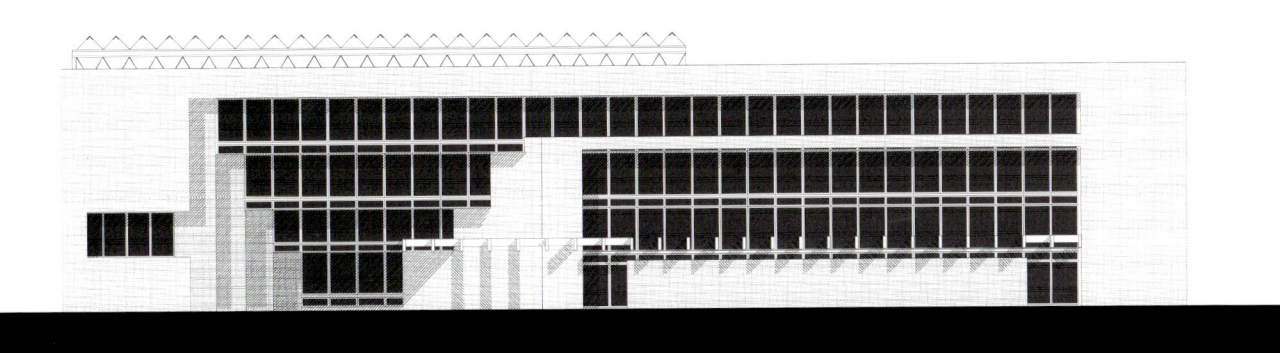

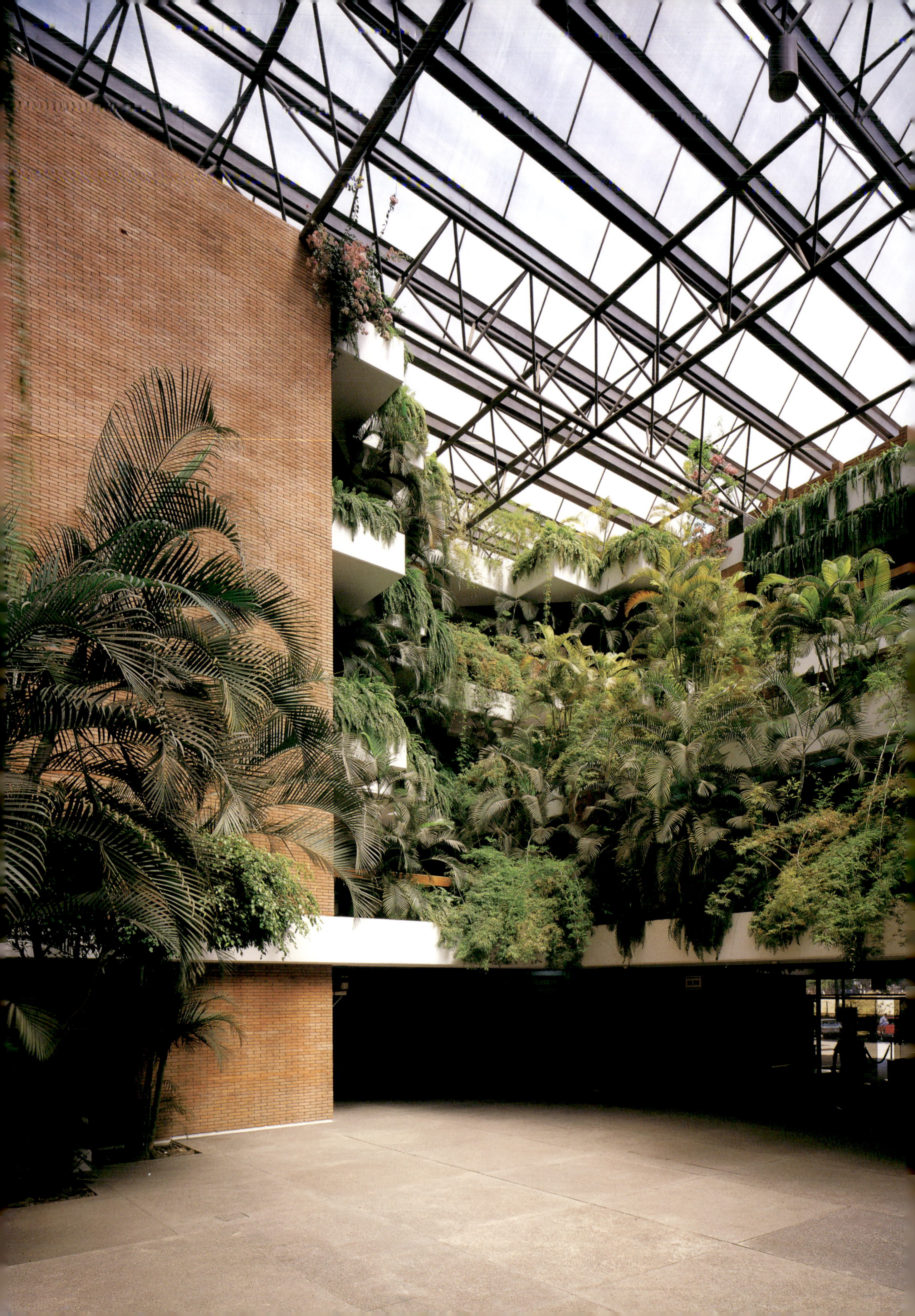

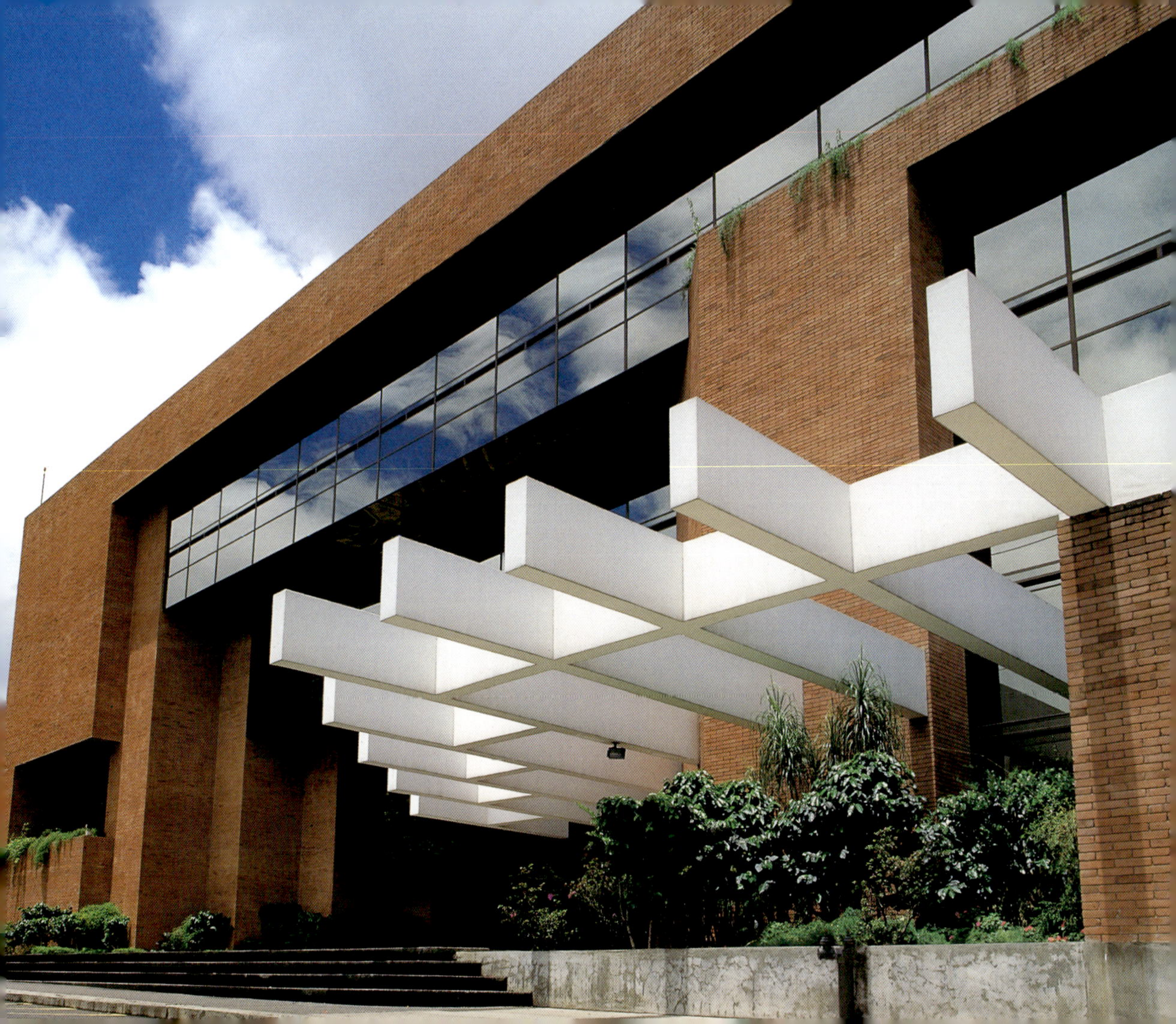

The site where the Ixchel Museum now stands lies on the grounds of the Universidad Francisco Marroquín de Guatemala, an important Guatemalan private university which agreed to provide the land for the building. After realizing several topographical studies and choosing a site with the best accessibility, the Ixchel Museum, together with the Popol Vuh Museum and the university auditorium, were included in a great cultural complex. The architectural program includes three major halls: the general gallery for temporary exhibitions; the gallery for children and youngsters; and the gallery which displays a permanent exhibition of indigenous

THE IXCHEL MUSEUM

textiles. The latter includes watercolors by the artist Carmen de Pettersen, which depict in great detail traditional daily and ceremonial Mayan clothing. Due to the predominant use of brick on the university campus, the architects decided to utilize the same material in order to establish a harmony with the existing buildings, but they took it a step further. The brick-laying pattern follows a traditional textile design from the Comalapa region, which gives great distinction to the building. The Museum is turned at a forty-five degree angle to the axis of approach, in order to provide a better perspective of its volume as one approaches.

MUSEO IXCHEL

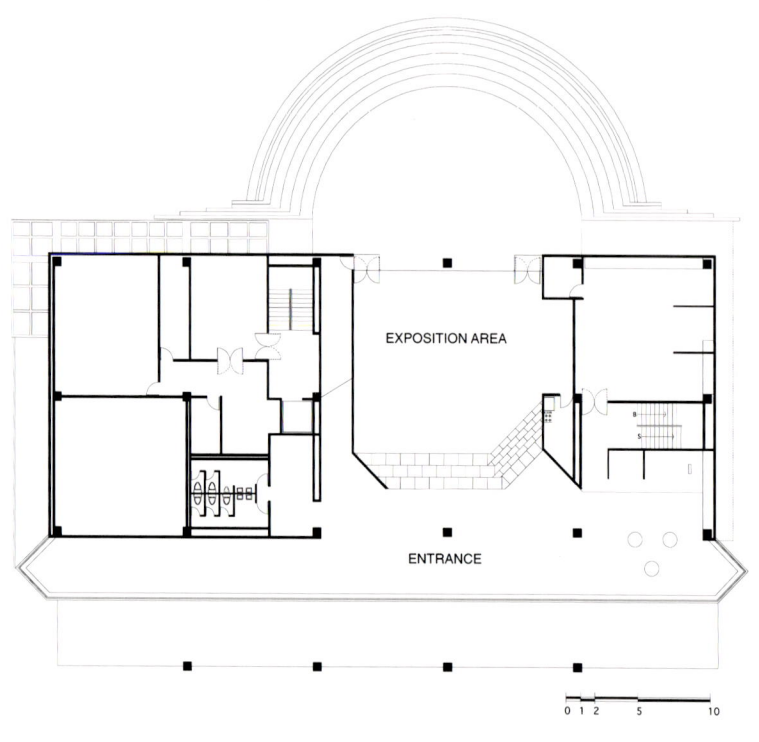

In the interior, the pyramidal skylights bathe the main atrium in natural light. Its floors are a green, unpolished marble, whose opaqueness provides a somber tone that is ideal for displaying the works of art. To walk around the exhibition in the main gallery one makes use of the surrounding ramp, which has the dual purpose of exhibiting the museum's objects of art and establishing a connection with the second level. The Museo Ixchel, with its impressive architectural design, is so skillfully integrated into the grounds of the Francisco Marroquín University that it makes the campus, as a whole, one of the most beautiful university complexes in Latin America.

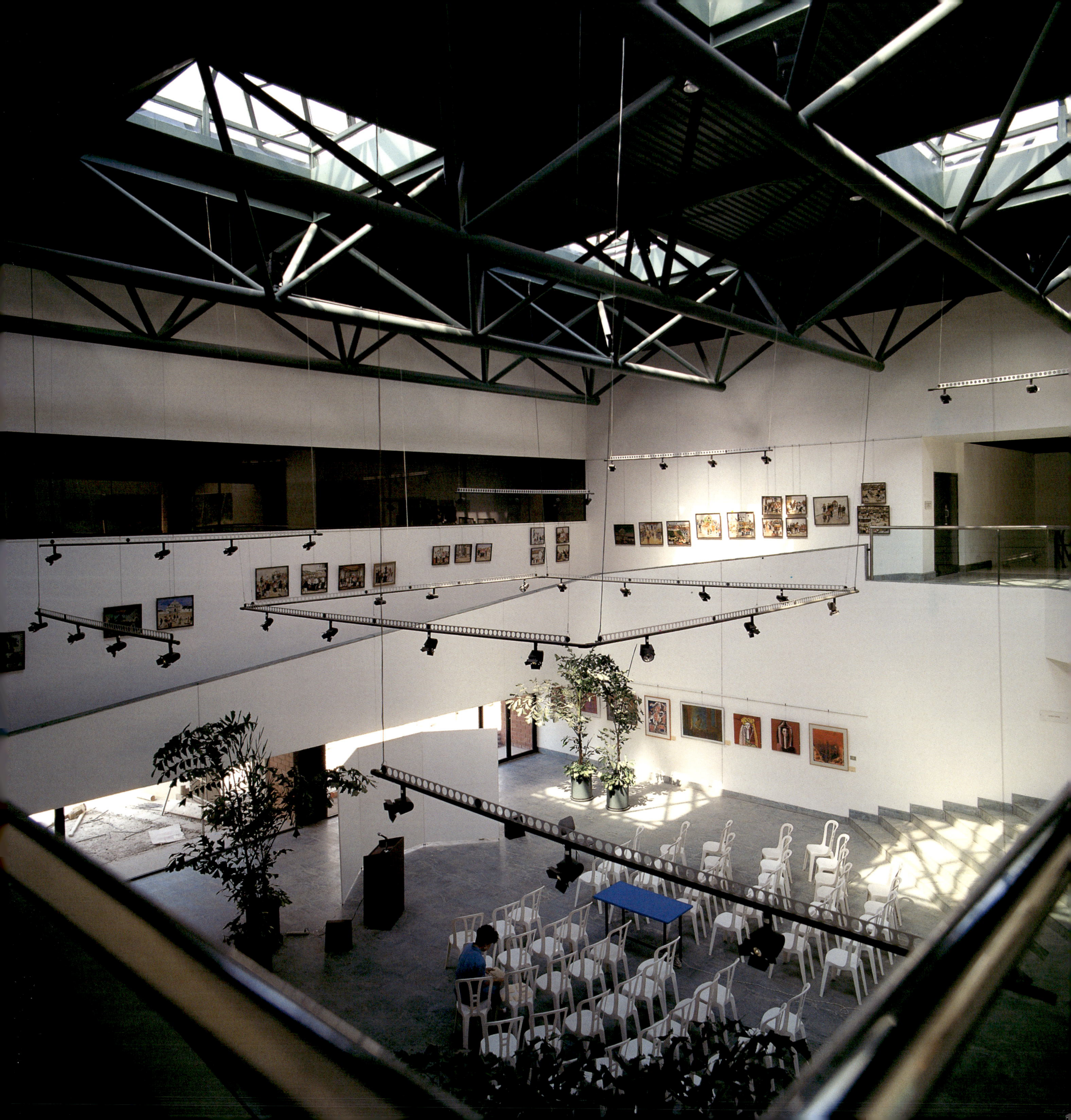

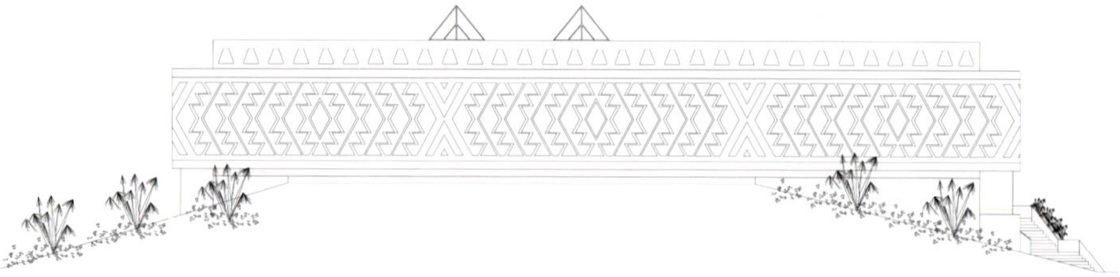

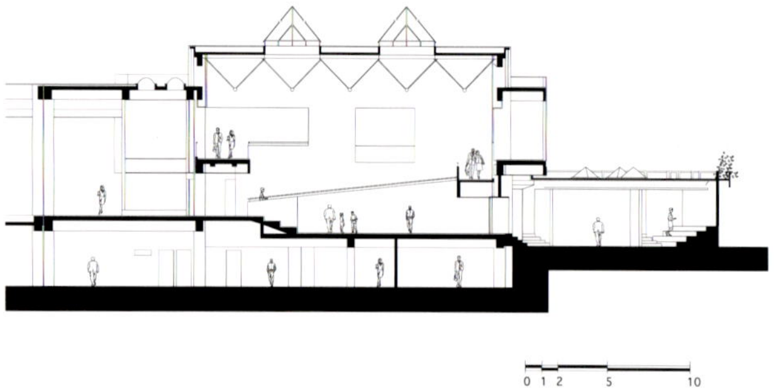
0 1 2 5 10

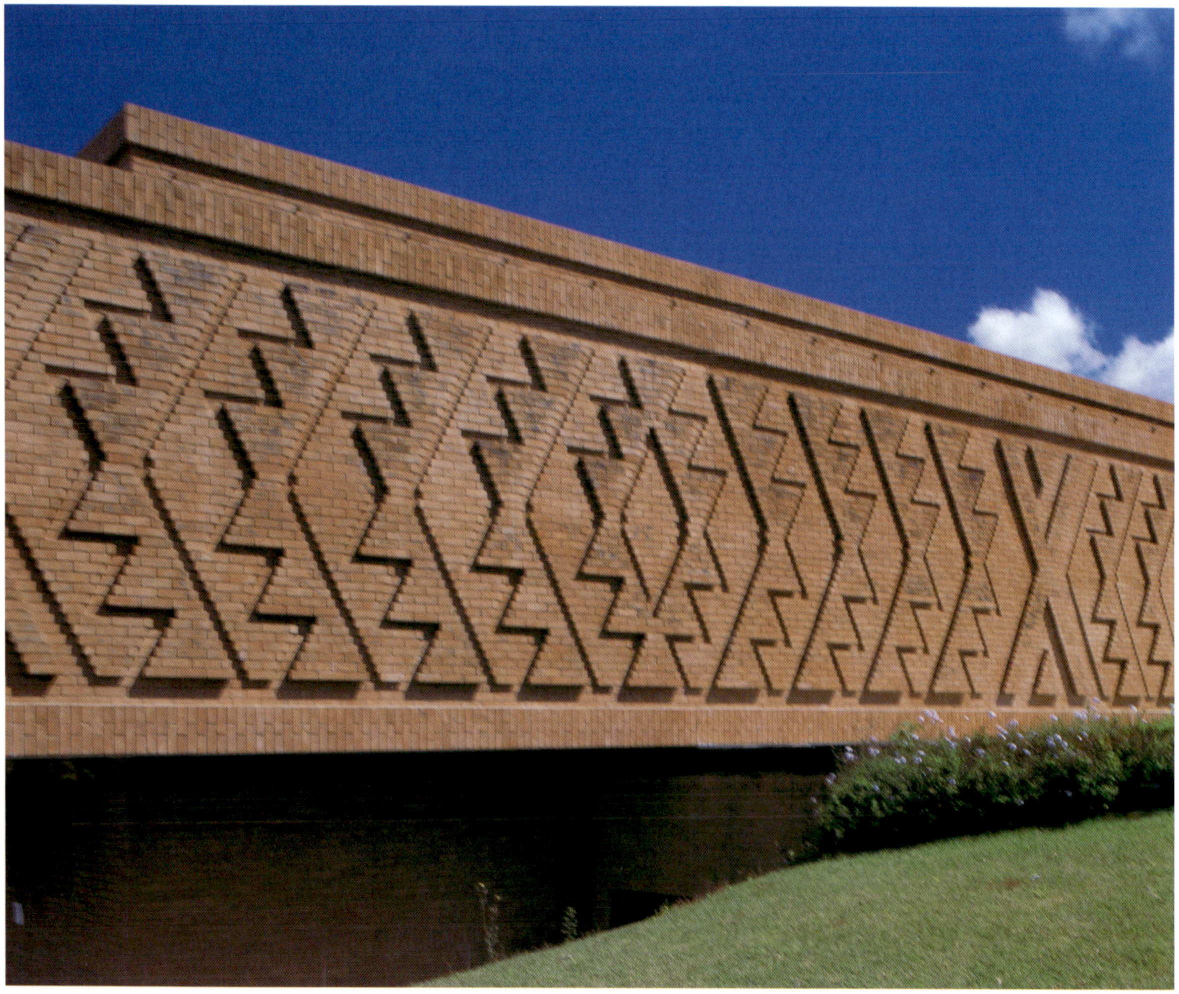

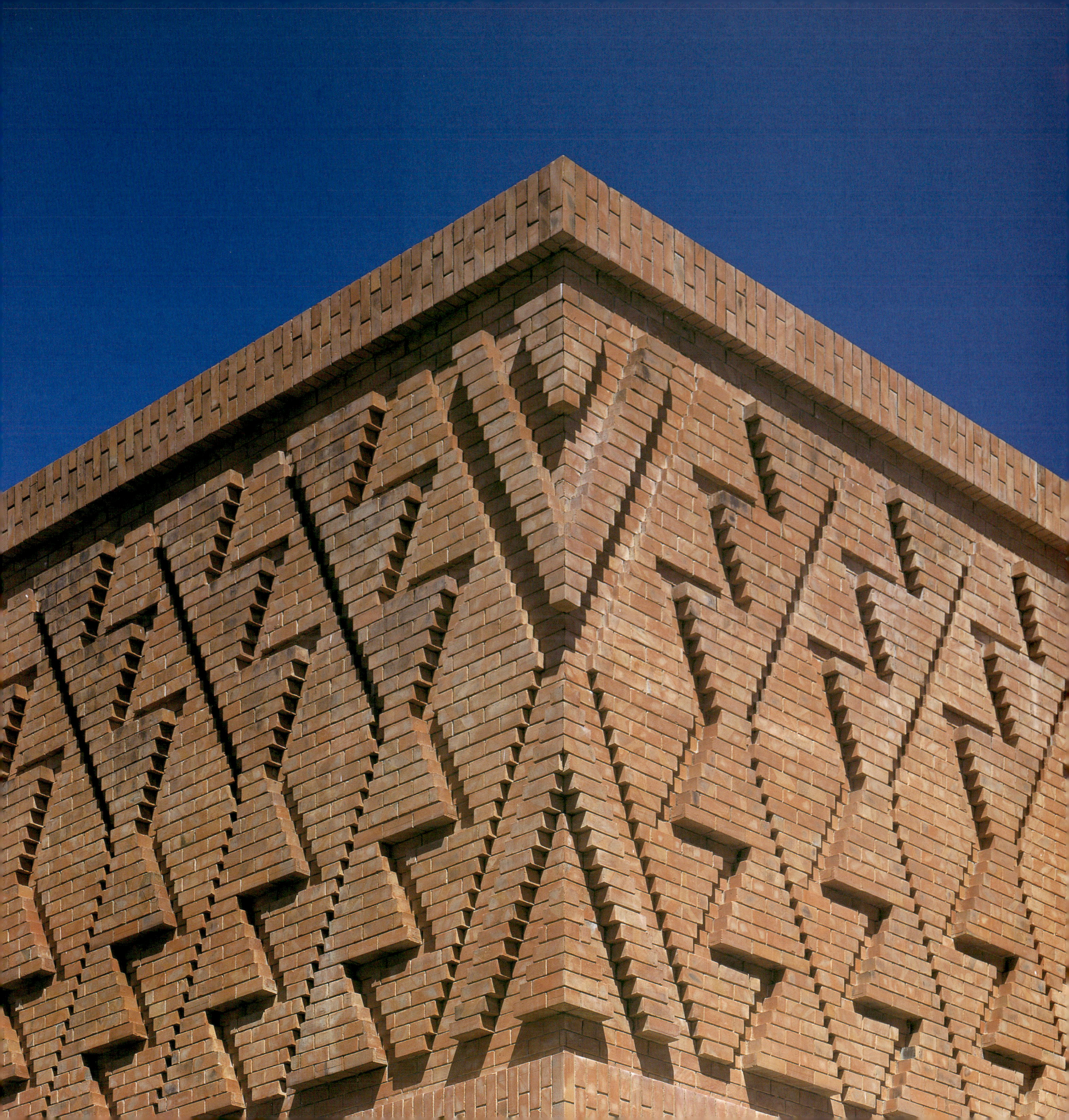

The inspiration for the design of the Tecnológico de Santa Lucía (Santa Lucía Technological Institute) is derived from the structures used for the traditional coffee-processing mills that are characteristic of the tropical architecture of Central America. Due to the high humidity and temperature of Guatemala's south coast region, this architecture provides a suitable response to the climate, while its light structures give it a cool touch and act as a protection against the bright sun. With this aim in mind, the design of this building employs superposed sloping roofs that provide additional shade to the lower roofs. This inclination also serves as a necessary protection against

TECNOLÓGICO DE SANTA LUCÍA

the heavy rainfall of the area, a circumstance which also played a role in the three and a half meter-long cantilever roofs protecting the perimetral corridors. Despite the slanting nature of tropical rainfall, these big projecting roofs manage to provide an adequate protection for the users of the building. In order to provide thermal insulation for the roofs, they were constructed with a duralite coating and ceramic tile to create a double layer of protection. They rest on double structures of metal anchored to concrete columns. The monitors in the building's roof allow hot air to be expelled by a chimney effect that creates cross-ventilation along the perimeter of the lower part.

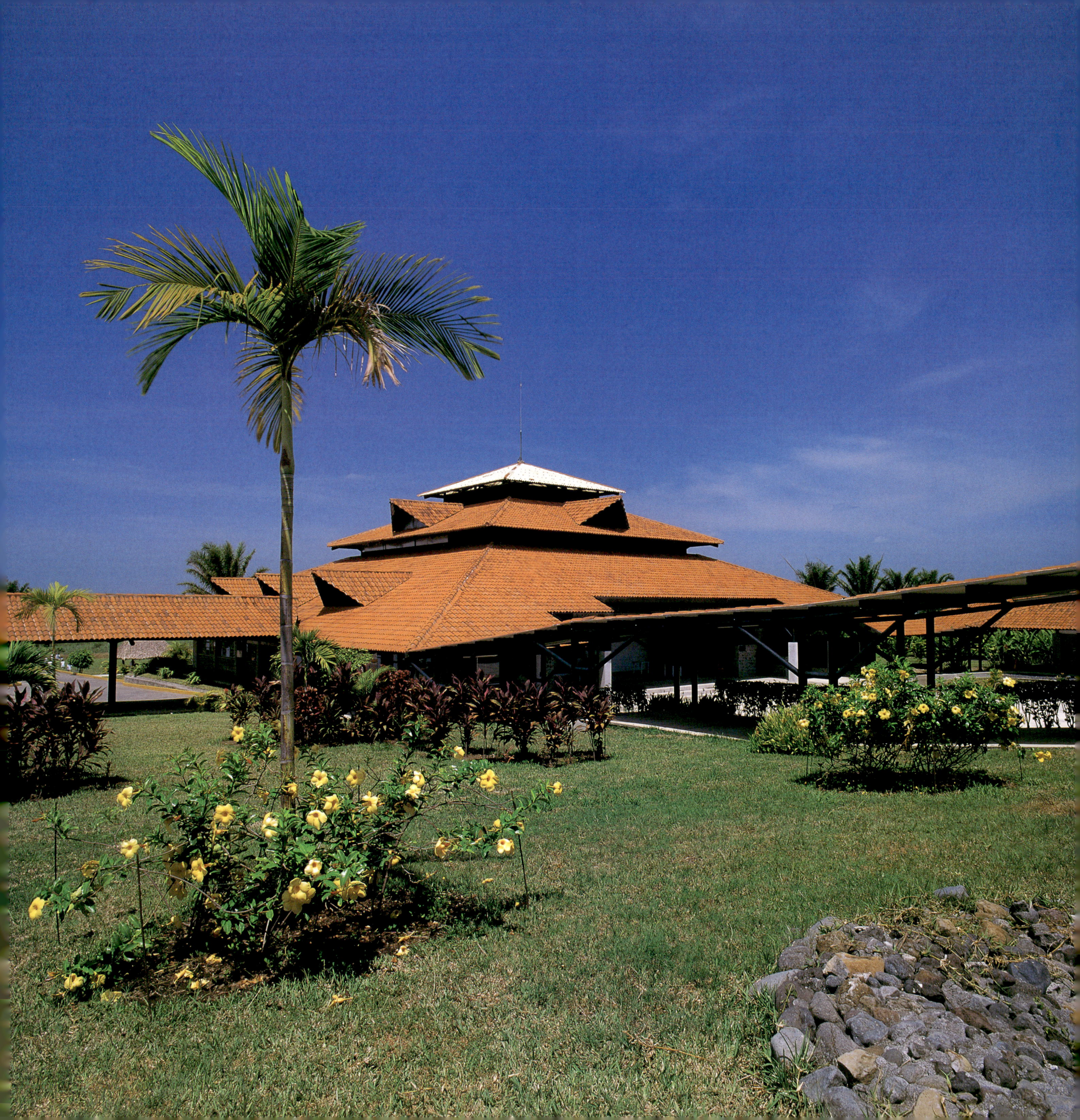

Taking advantage of the great height of the main roof, an entrance with overhead light was designed for the center of the building, which illuminates the main stairway that ascends from an interior garden. As partitions for the different lecture rooms and administrative offices, adobe-type walls were built of river stone and cement, which serve to screen off the heat of the tropical climate. In addition, the roofs have large openings in the upper part to create a flow of cross-ventilation and keep the interior spaces cool.

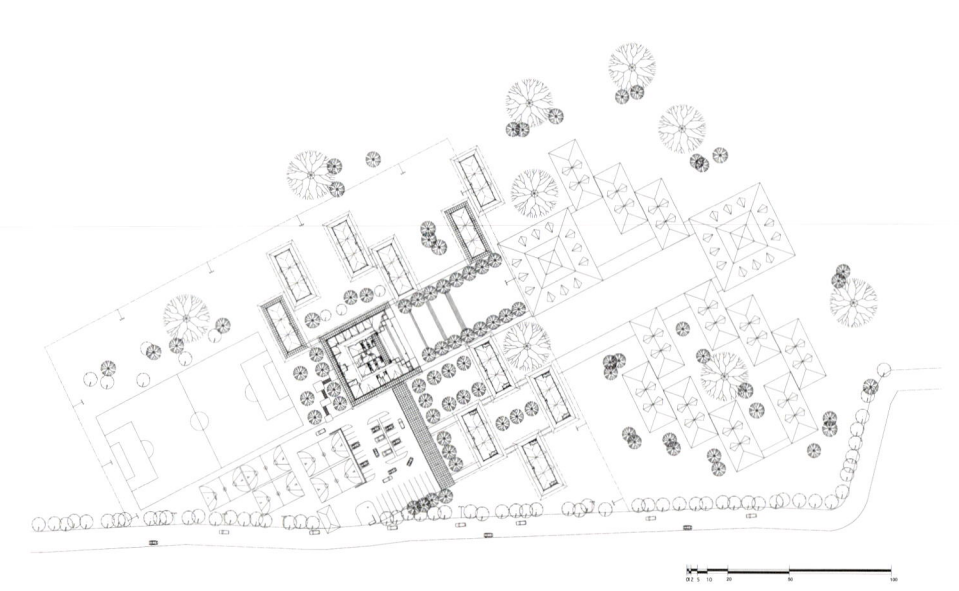

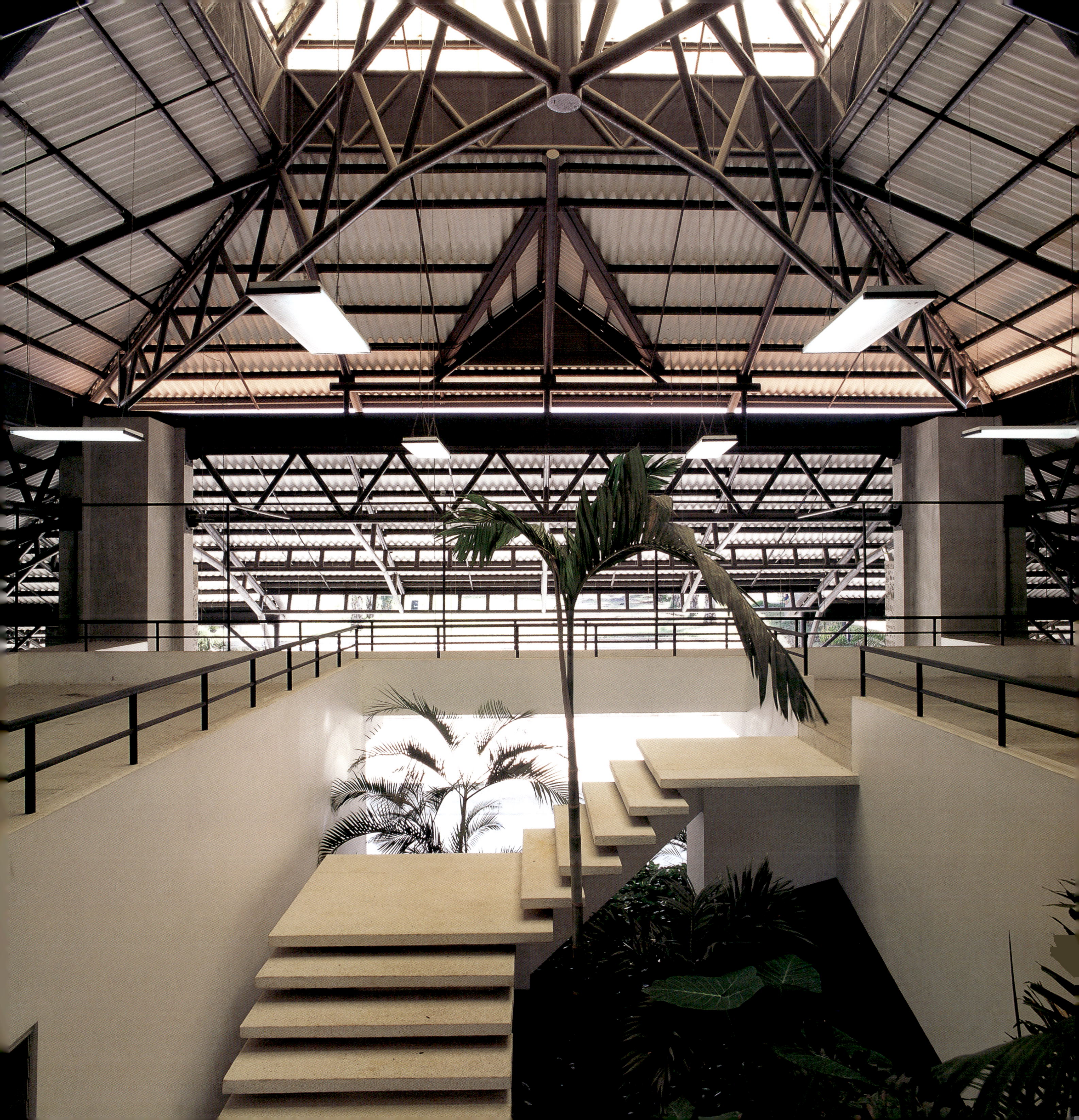

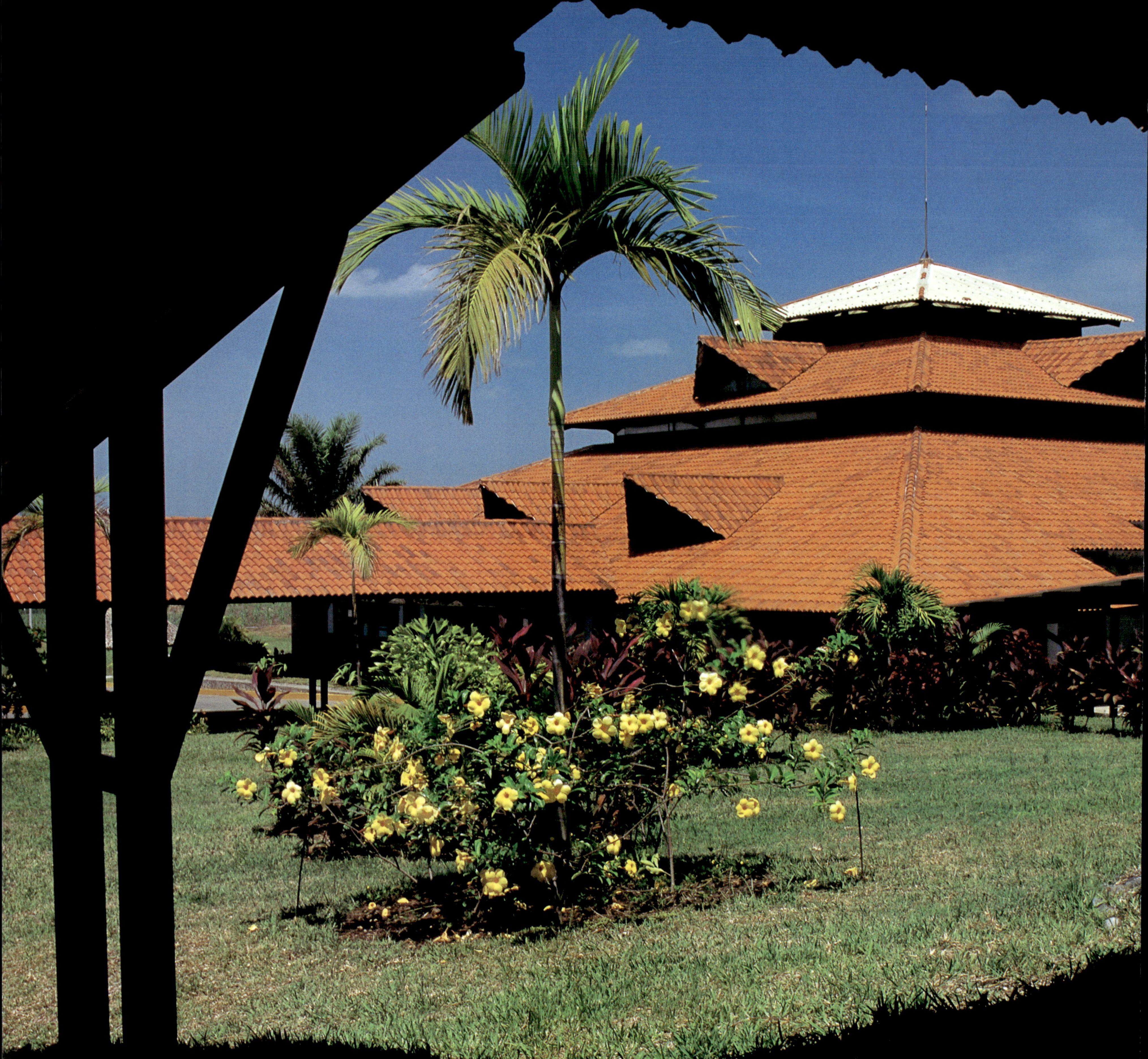

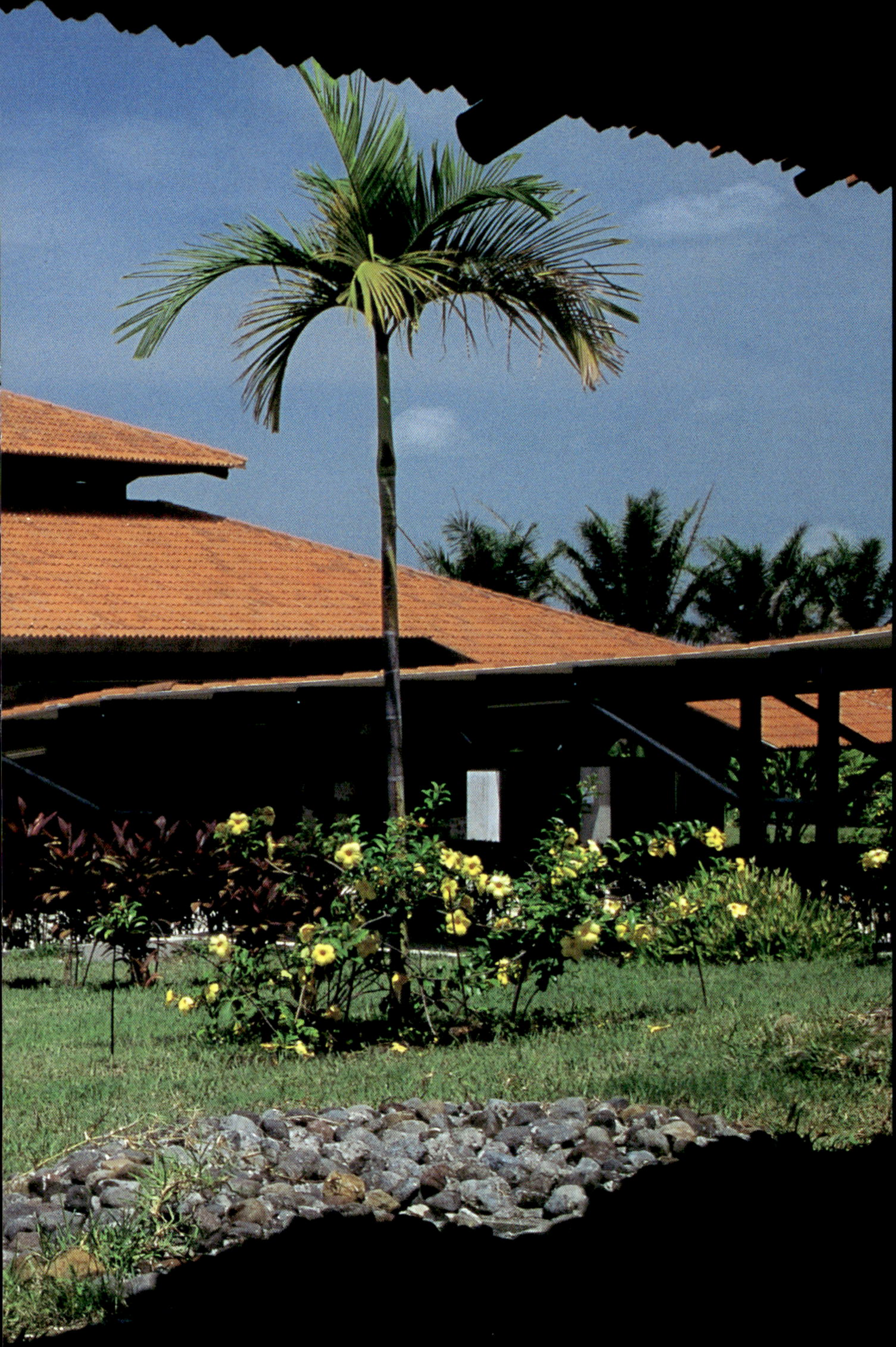

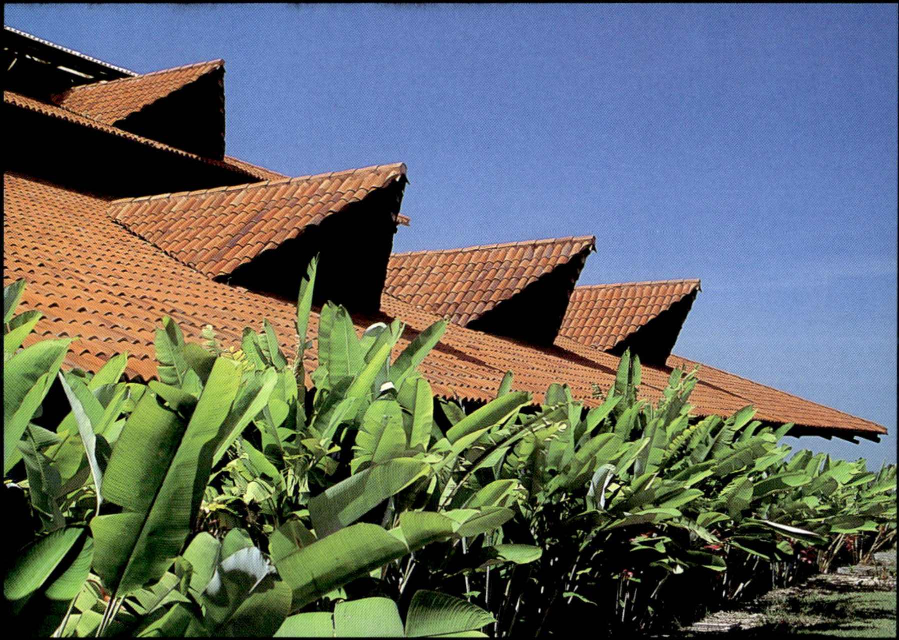

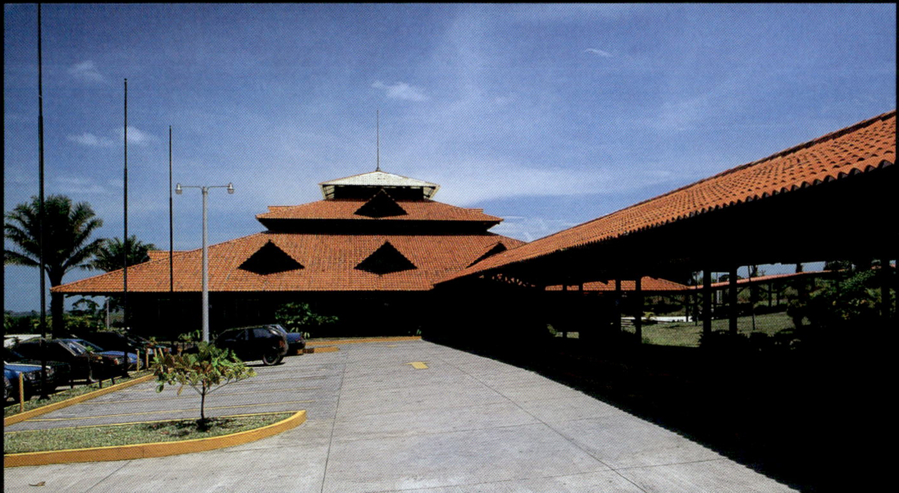

The main design concept of the Casa Cristal arises from the wish to incorporate the architecture into the natural setting and the need to house the owner's large art collection. The solution employs a modernist architectural language, of clean white volumes organized around a big two-story-high atrium which houses an interior garden. This atrium, which unites the gardens at both ends of the house, is naturally lit from a roof with a double layer of glass, which also provides the light needed to highlight the works of art that are exhibited throughout the space. slate imported

CASA CRISTAL

from South Africa was used for the interior floor, while slabs of black granite were employed in the kitchen. Casa Cristal makes use of two big window-doors that slide into the walls so that the space is completely opened and any visual obstacle towards the exterior disappears. Overlooking the atrium and illuminated by overhead light, a bridge on the second floor joins the main bedroom to the other private areas of the house, granting an additional richness to this two-story-high space.

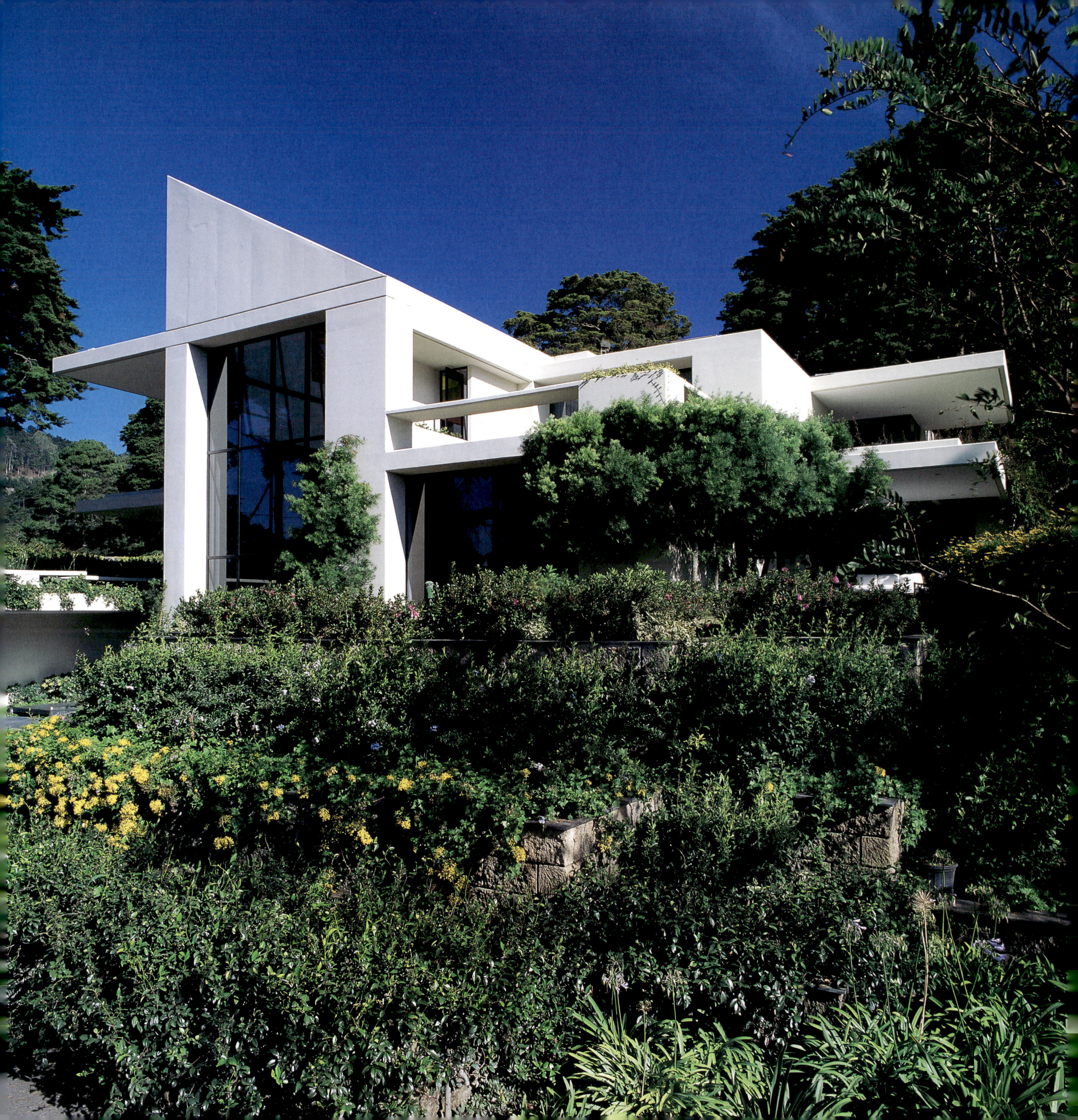

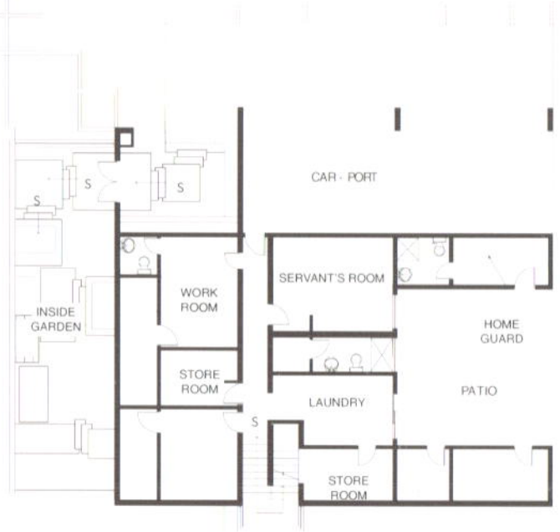

S
S
S
CAR - PORT
WORK ROOM
SERVANT'S ROOM
INSIDE GARDEN
HOME GUARD
STORE ROOM
LAUNDRY
PATIO
S
STORE ROOM

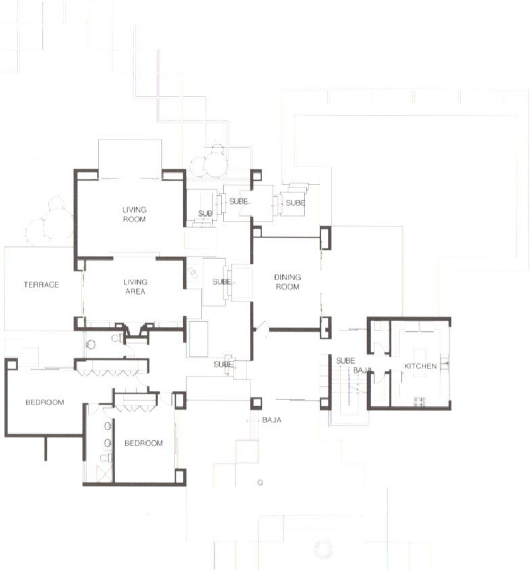

LIVING ROOM
SUB
SUBE
SUBE
TERRACE
LIVING AREA
SUBE
DINING ROOM
SUBE
SUBE
BAJA
KITCHEN
BEDROOM
BAJA
BEDROOM

TERRACE
MASTER BEDROOM
LIVING AREA
B
S
TERRACE
TERRACE
0 1 2 5 10

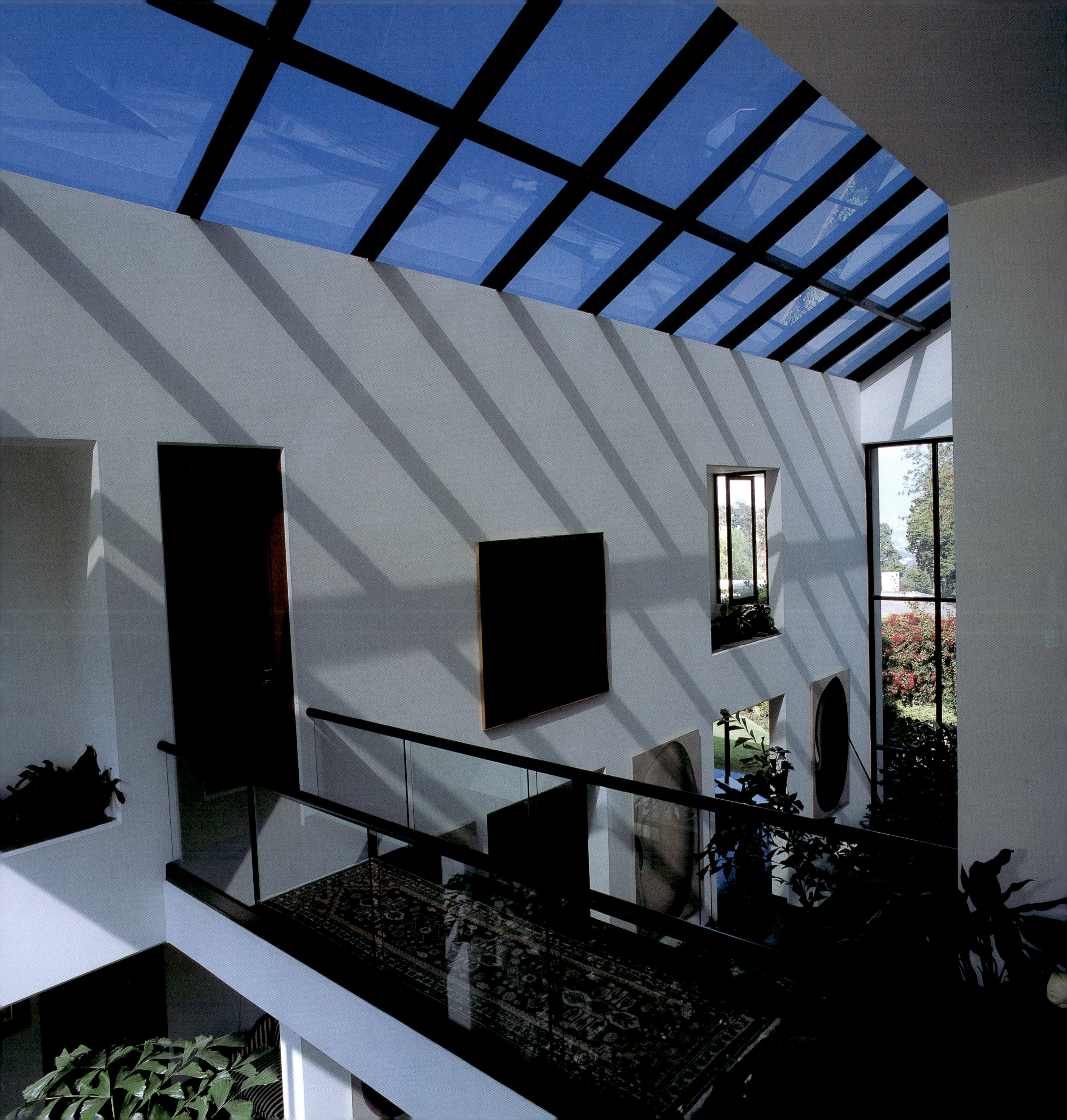

The relationship among the different areas is determined by a play of vertical planes, set at right angles, which form a sequence of spaces of a varying depth and enable the different works of art to be seen under different conditions of light and shadow, a strategy which recalls the words once uttered by Le Corbusier: "Architecture is the wise, correct and magnificent play of volumes joined together under light. Our eyes are made to see the forms under the light."

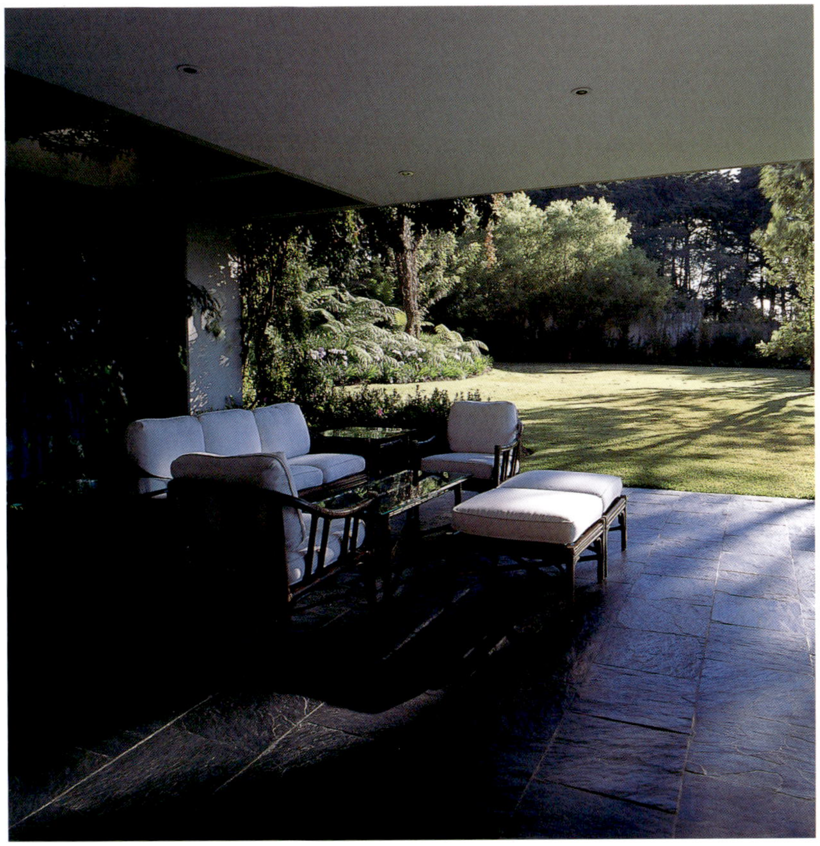

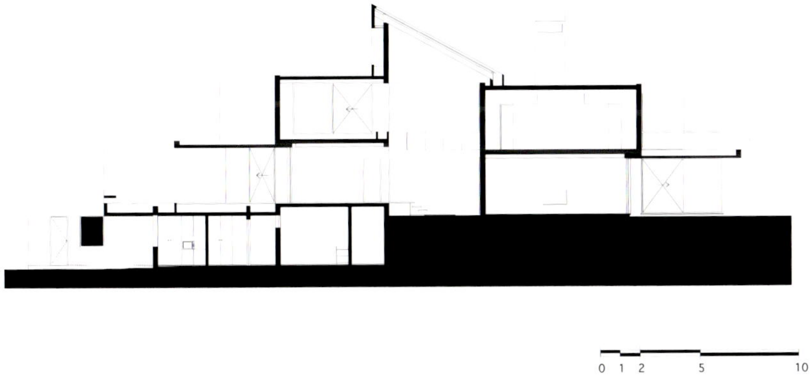
0 1 2 5 10

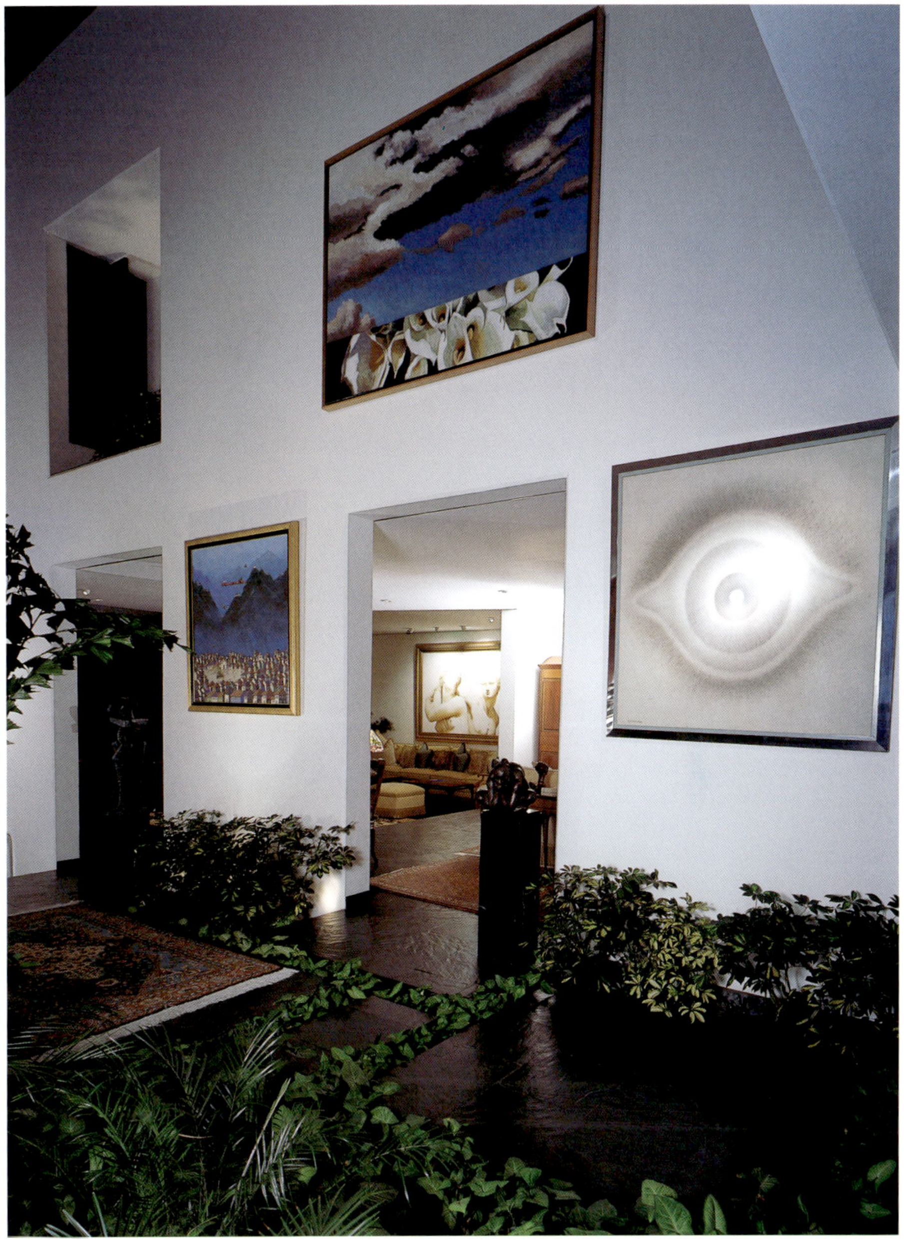

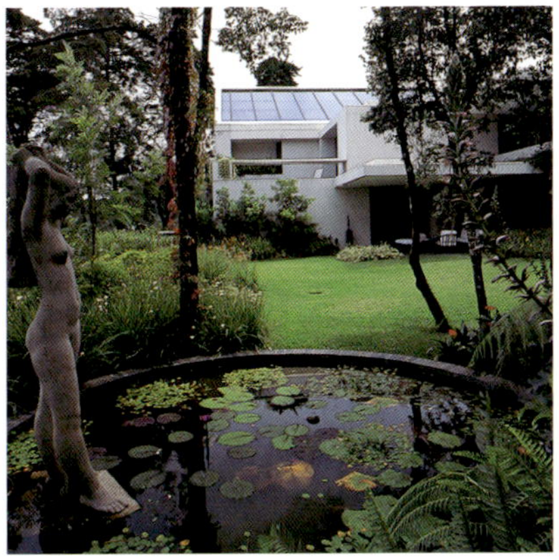

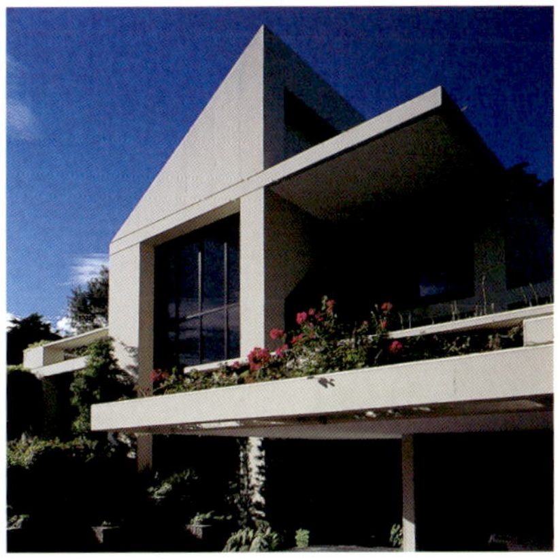

Using natural materials like stone, brick and wood, Casa Zompopero has a modest scale in comparison with the grandeur of its natural surroundings. On entering from the exterior garden, the first impression one has is of a building whose shingle roofs with large eaves extend the horizontality of its architecture to cover parts of the garden and provide shade for the interior spaces. The serenity of its horizontal forms is carried on in the interior, where the visitor enters through a vestibule, illuminated from above, whose two-story height is broken by a bridge with flower beds on either side, thus creating an interior floating garden. Encountering the same coherent use of

CASA ZOMPOPERO

materials in the interior that is found outside, one's glance is directed towards the stairs that rise to the second floor. These consist of a series of orthogonal platforms that seem to be incrusted in a great wall of brick covered by the plants that grow up out of the interior garden beneath them, which is also bathed in overhead natural light. The overall effect is that of a series of fragments of a garden, which interlace, in all parts, with the architecture of the house, creating a contrast between the smoothness of the white surfaces and rough texture of the brick adorned by plants.

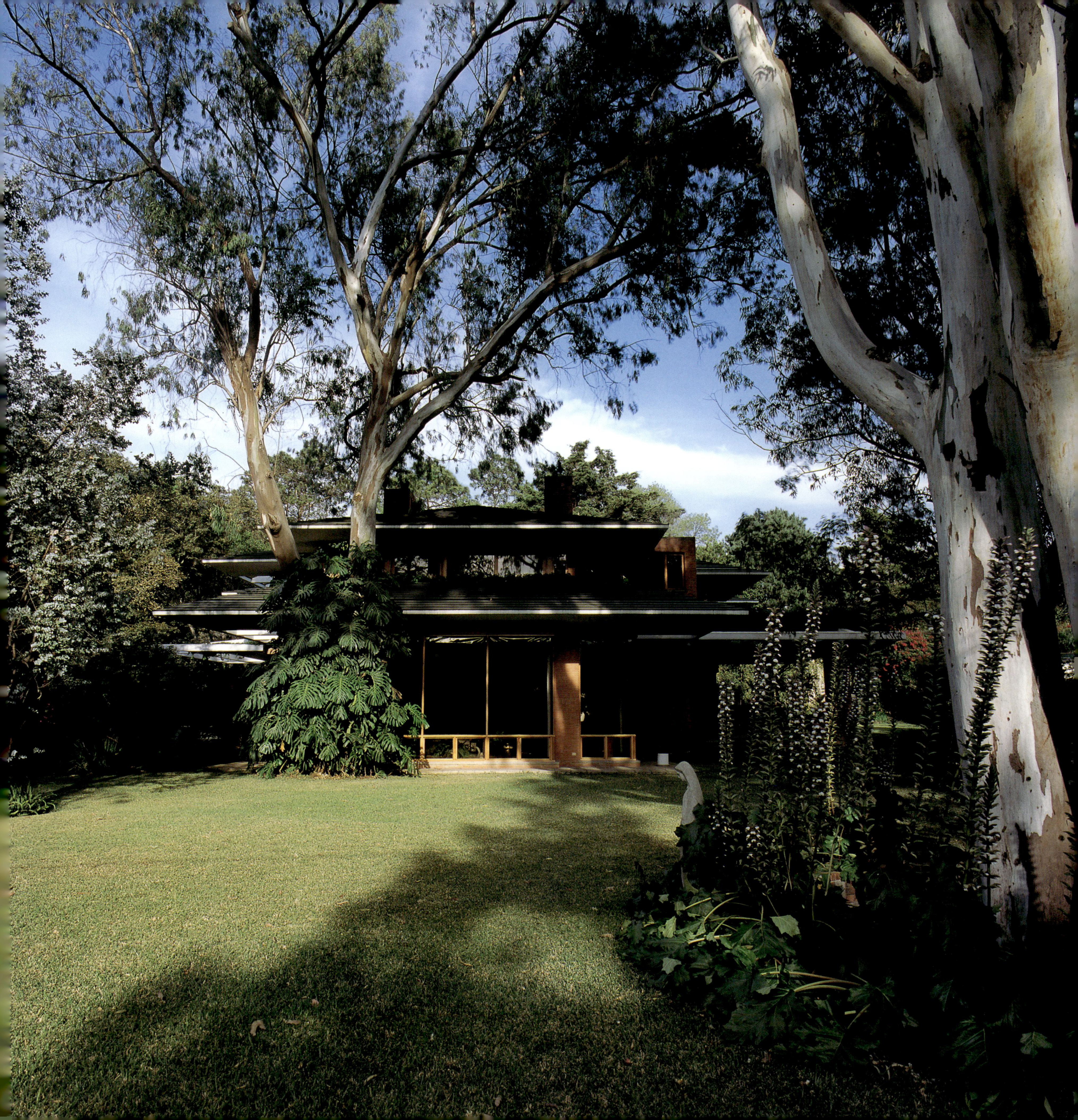

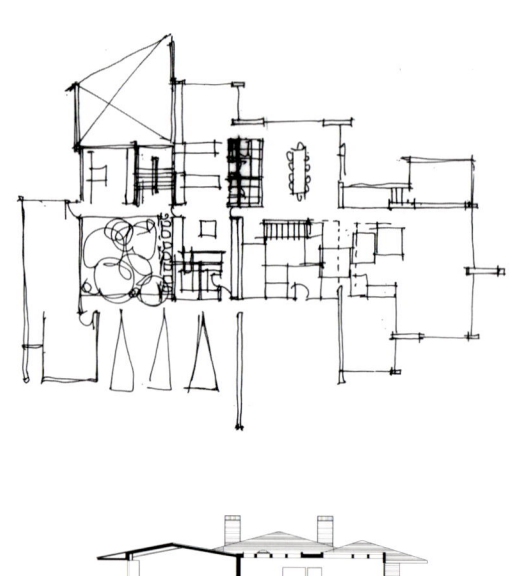

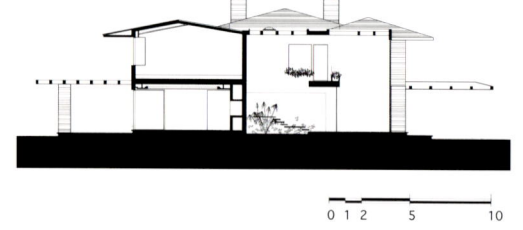

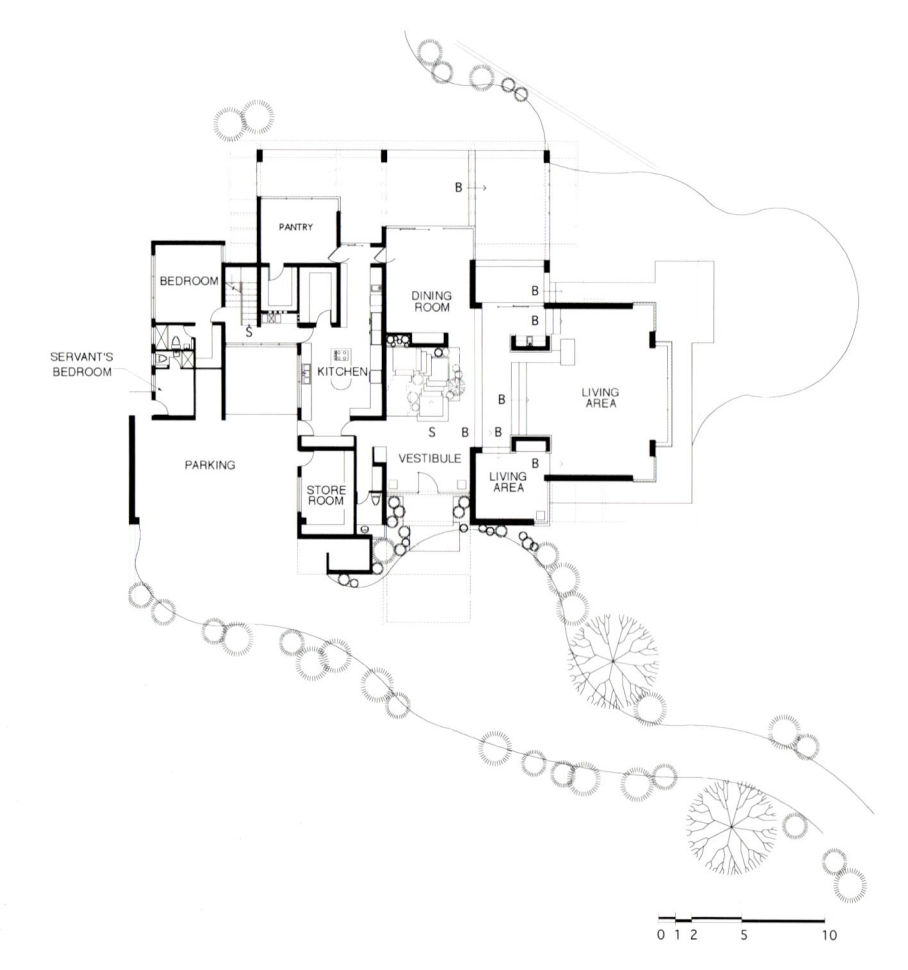

	PANTRY	
BEDROOM		DINING ROOM
SERVANT'S BEDROOM	KITCHEN	LIVING AREA
PARKING	STORE ROOM	VESTIBULE
		LIVING AREA

0 1 2   5   10

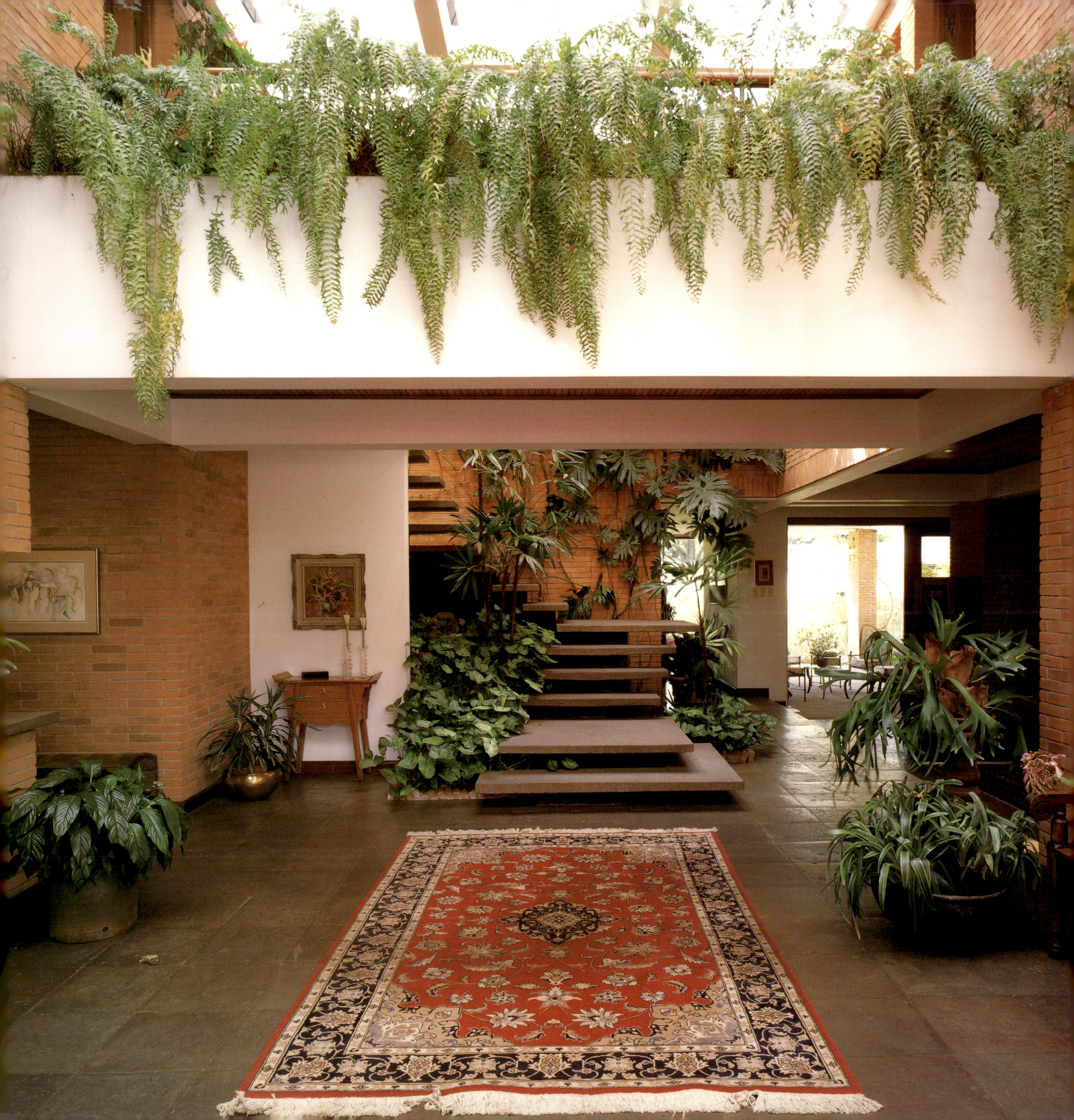

On one occasion Le Corbusier said that in architecture "the elements of the place intervene by virtue of their cubic volume, their density and the quality of their material." And in a similar context, the architecture of this house in Santa Rosalía allows the characteristics of the place where it stands to intervene in its spatial organization and formal response. Utilizing a metallic structure that stands on the terrain, the house was raised 80 centimeters above ground level, so that humidity would not significantly affect the interior ambits.

HOUSE IN SANTA ROSALÍA

The house is organized around a cross-shaped floor plan with ample windows that provide different views over the surroundings and the volcanoes named Agua (water) and Fuego (fire) on the horizon. The semi-circular-shaped breakfast room underlines the rectilinear character of the general design: it stands out from the main volume of the house to enable one to enjoy a 180 degree view of the forest outside.

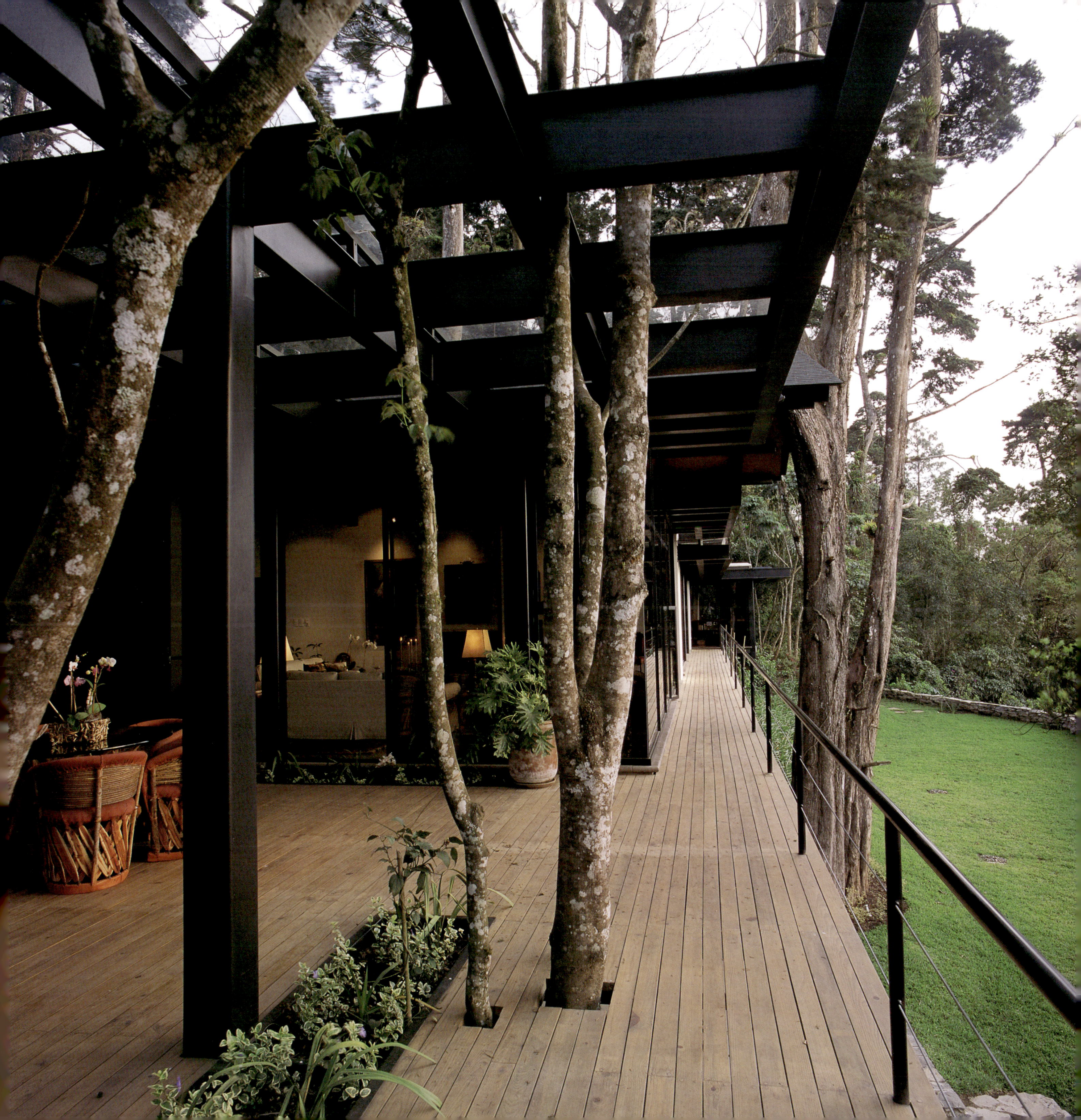

In the main entrance, an old door, which seems to float in the air, is incorporated into planes of glass, which, echoing the skylight turned at a forty-five degree angle in the roof of the vestibule, frame views of the green areas under natural light. Below this skylight in the vestibule is the main stairway, which, leading towards the lower level, intermingles with the garden and serves as a natural link between the two levels.

By raising the house up on a platform, the design obtained a space between the ground and the house which contains different installations, while the trees on the site integrate with the house to form a forest that is a hybrid of nature and architecture. This wooden deck, surrounded by a hand-rail made of tautened steel to avoid visual checks, gives way to a series of outside spaces and passageways that are protected by eaves and geometrical pergolas that give the house its contemporary character.

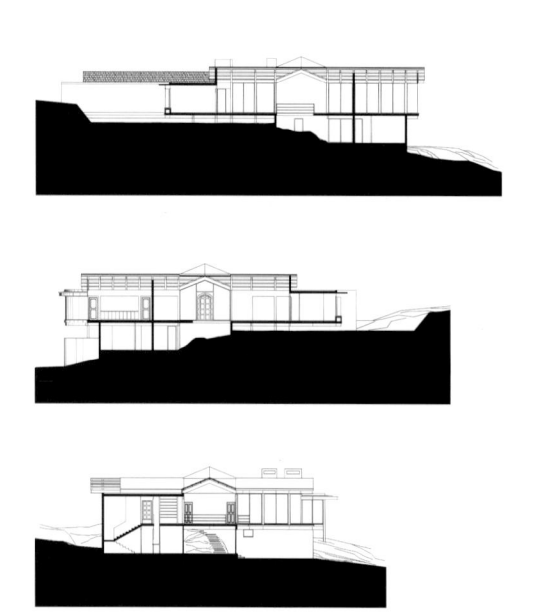

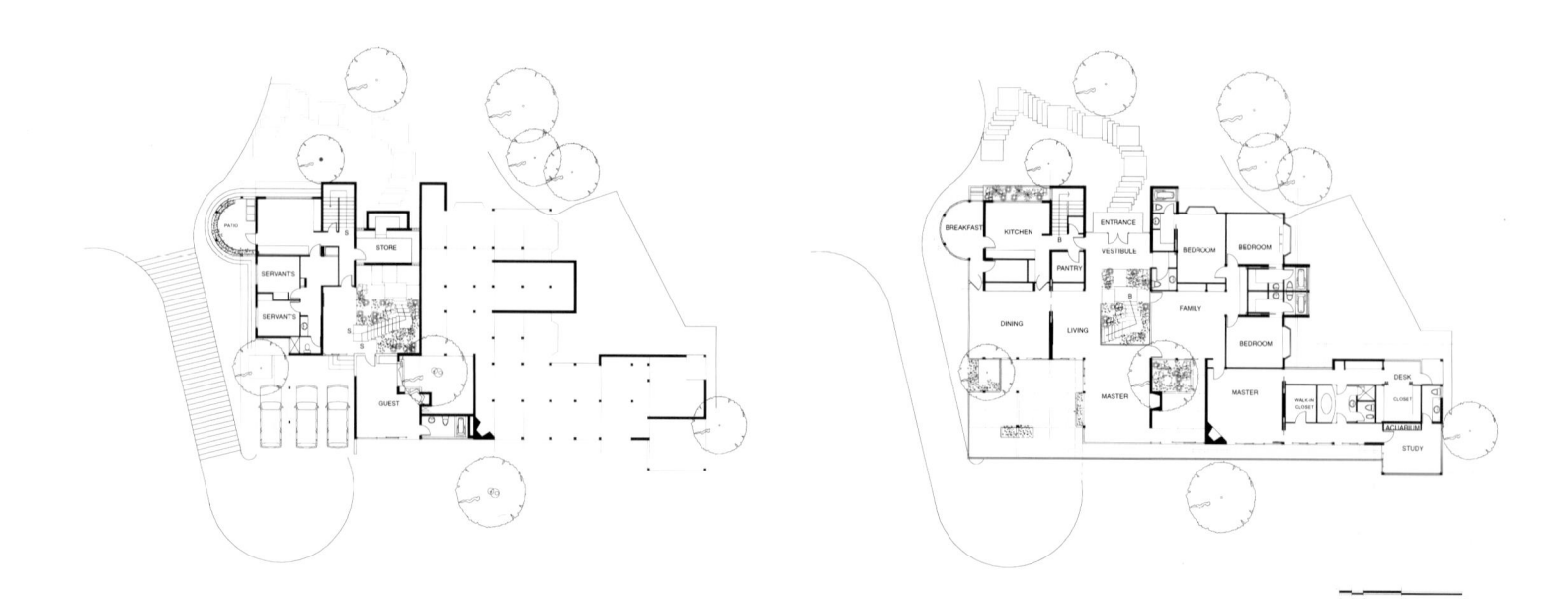

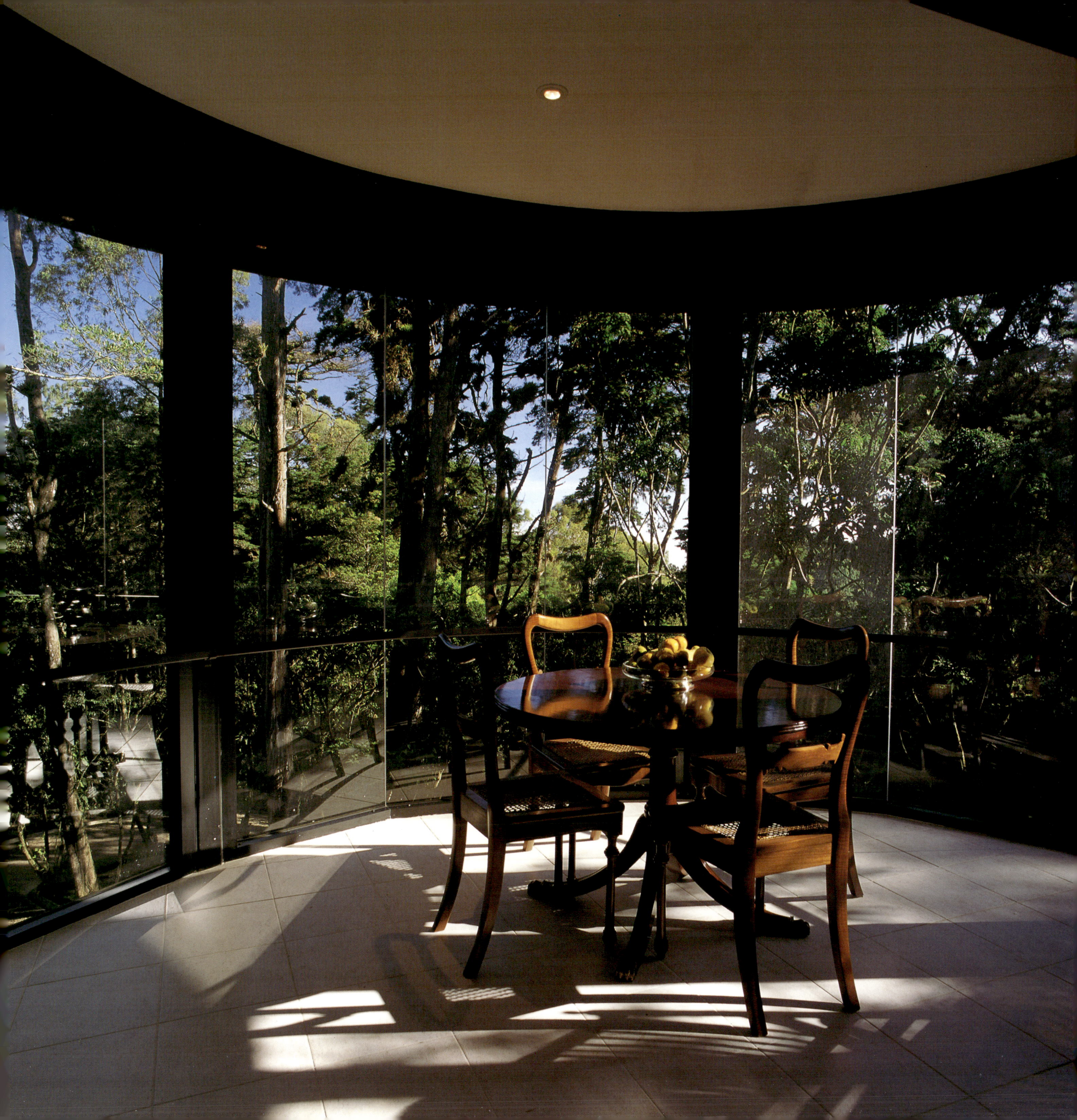

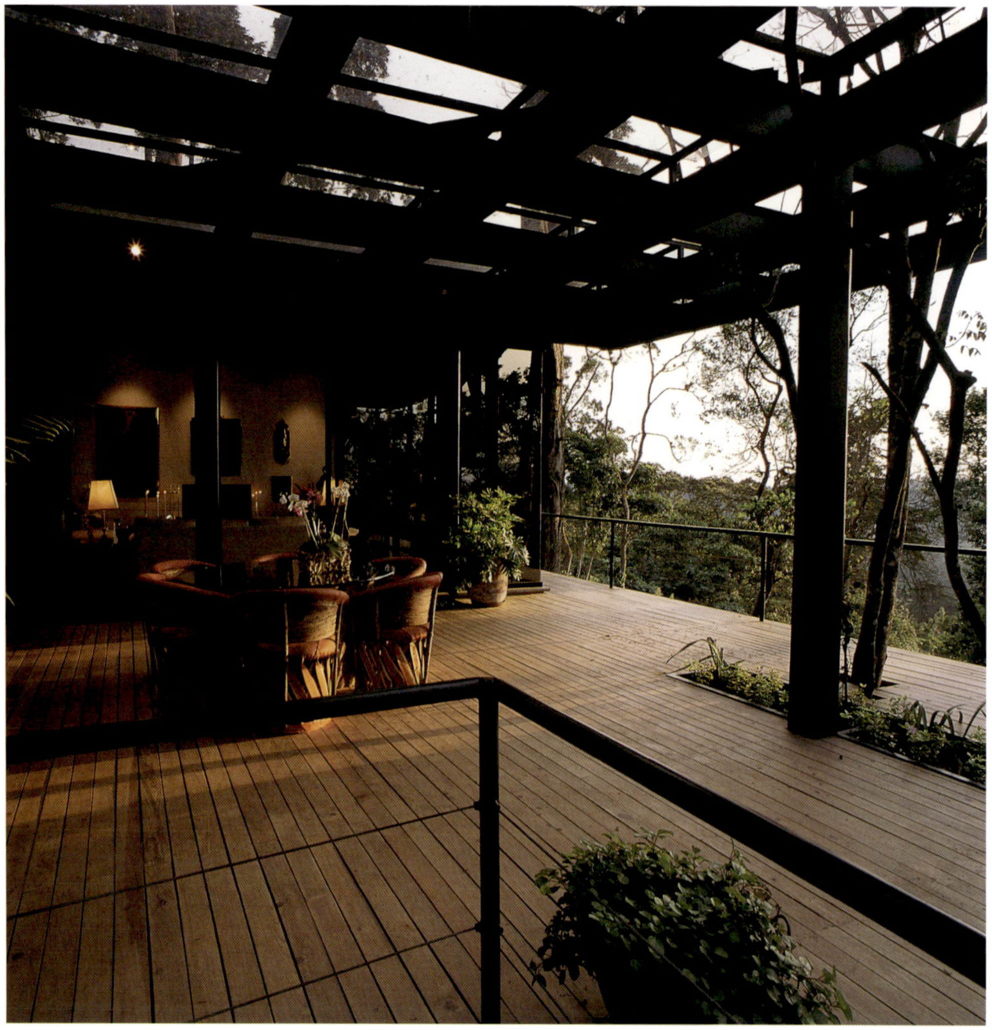

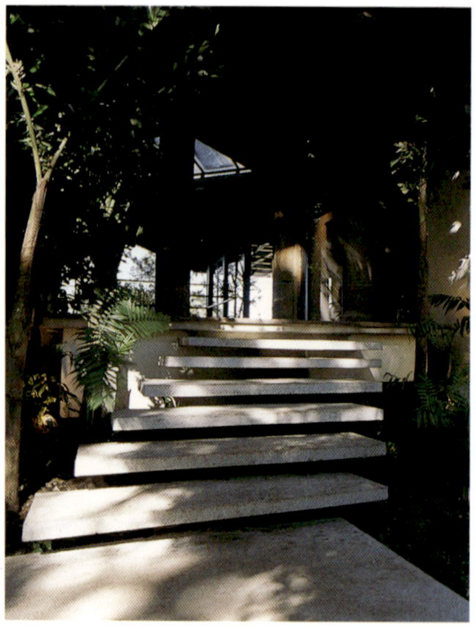

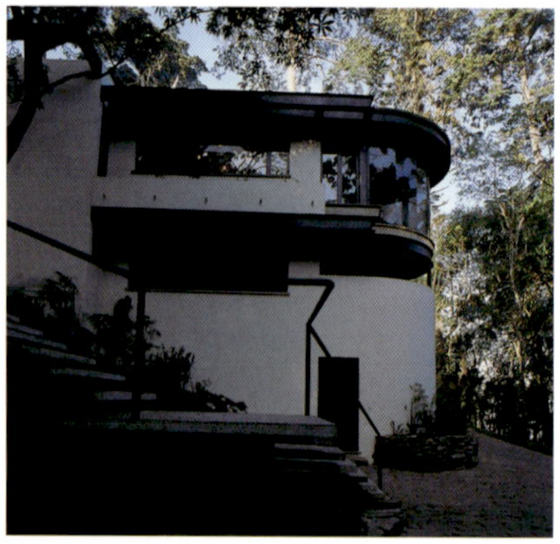

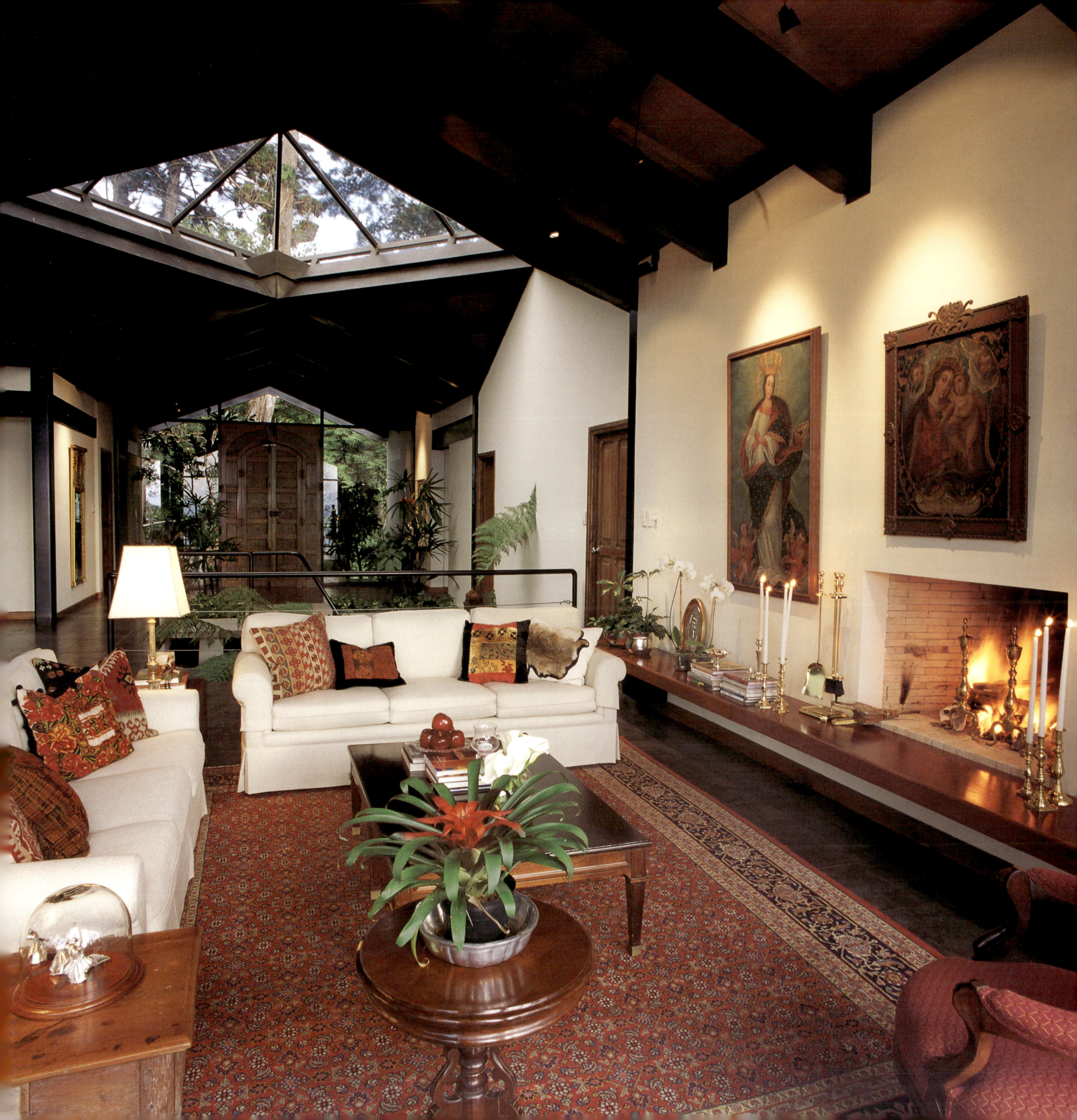

The original character of Casa Elgin is mainly due to the extensive use of pergolas in different places on its perimeter. The design intends that the pergolas, mostly made of exposed concrete, will become covered by vegetation with the passage of time and thus create organic textures of light and shade on the surfaces of the house. At the main entranceway, two of them rise up and overlap above to draw one's attention toward the entrance. The pergolas continue into the interior, crossing the entrance and ending above a flower bed in the vestibule, whose back wall

CASA ELGIN

contrasts with the exterior walls made of brick from the region of Chimaltenango. Inside, the house maintains an introverted character as it opens into a series of inner gardens that are partially covered, which prevents the different spaces of the house from seeming enclosed in themselves; instead, they retain a spatial looseness and fluidity. Saw-cut stone was employed for the interior floors so that its smooth surface may form a gentle tactile and visual contrast with the stone of the patio.

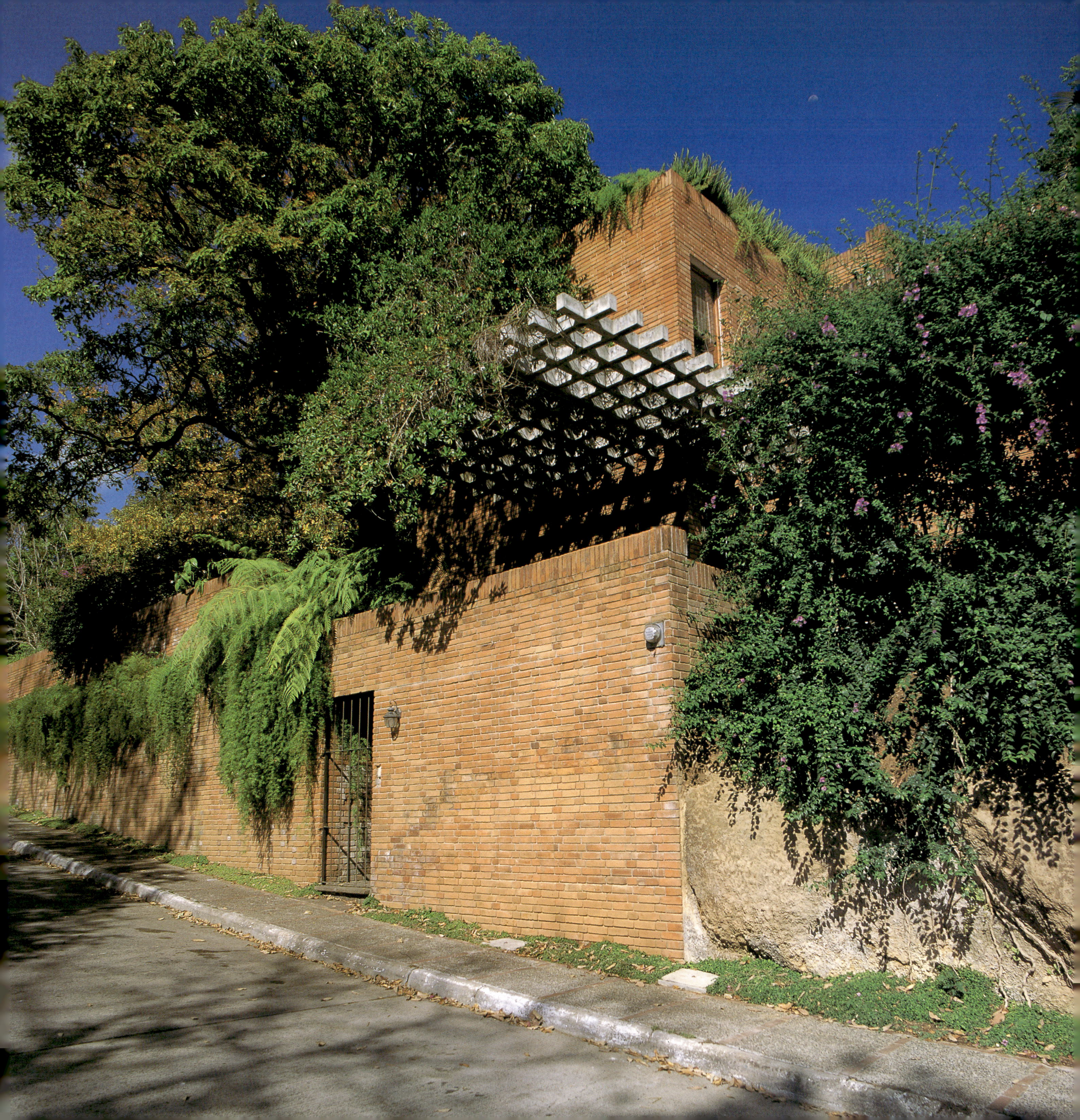

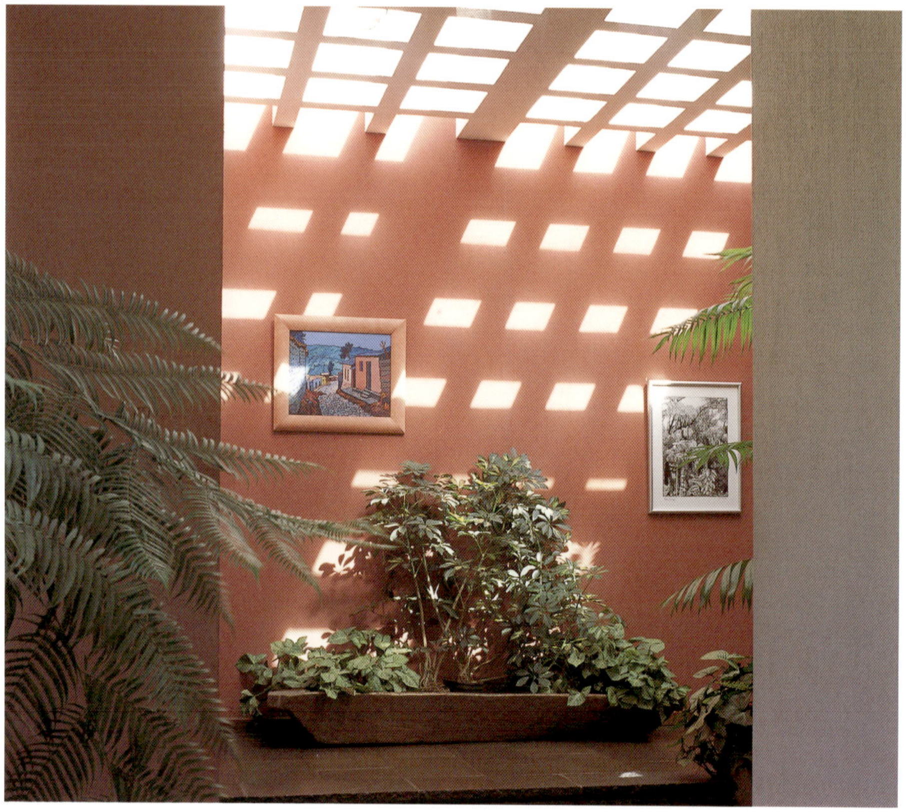

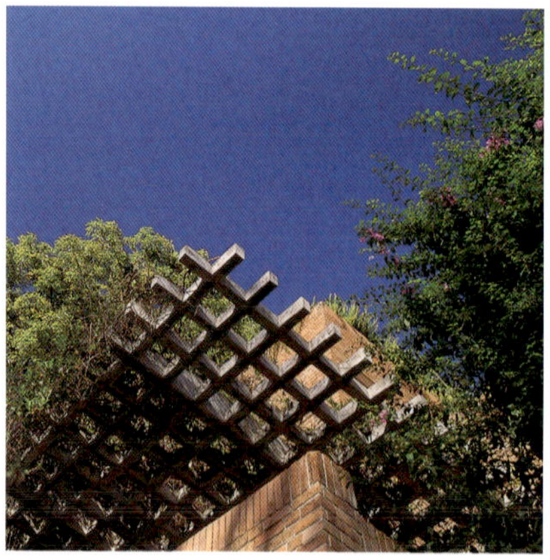

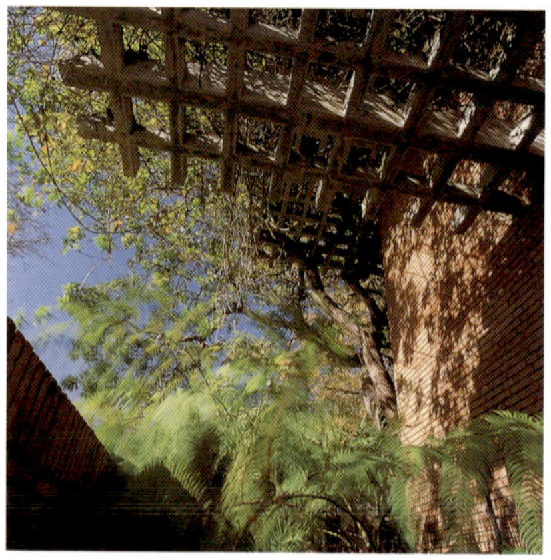

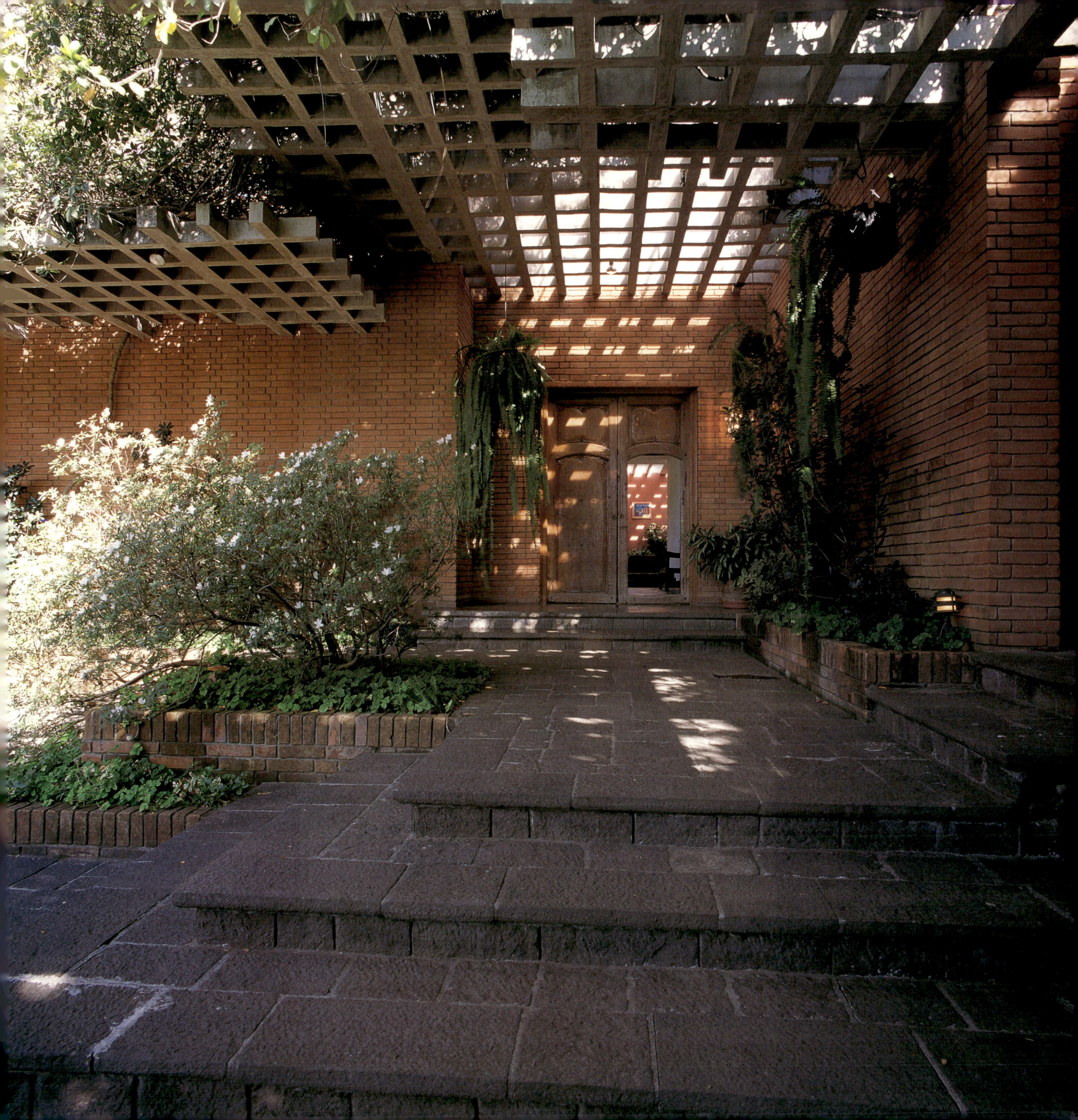

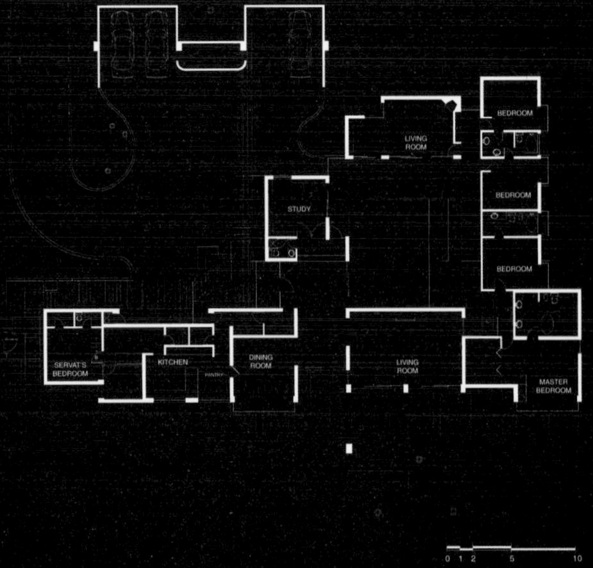
BEDROOM
LIVING ROOM
STUDY
BEDROOM
BEDROOM
SERVAT'S BEDROOM
KITCHEN
PANTRY
DINING ROOM
LIVING ROOM
MASTER BEDROOM
0 1 2 5 10

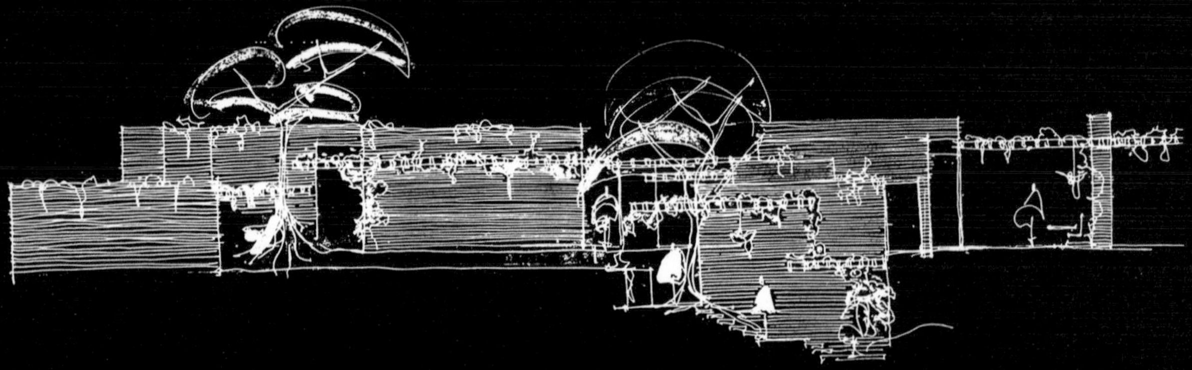

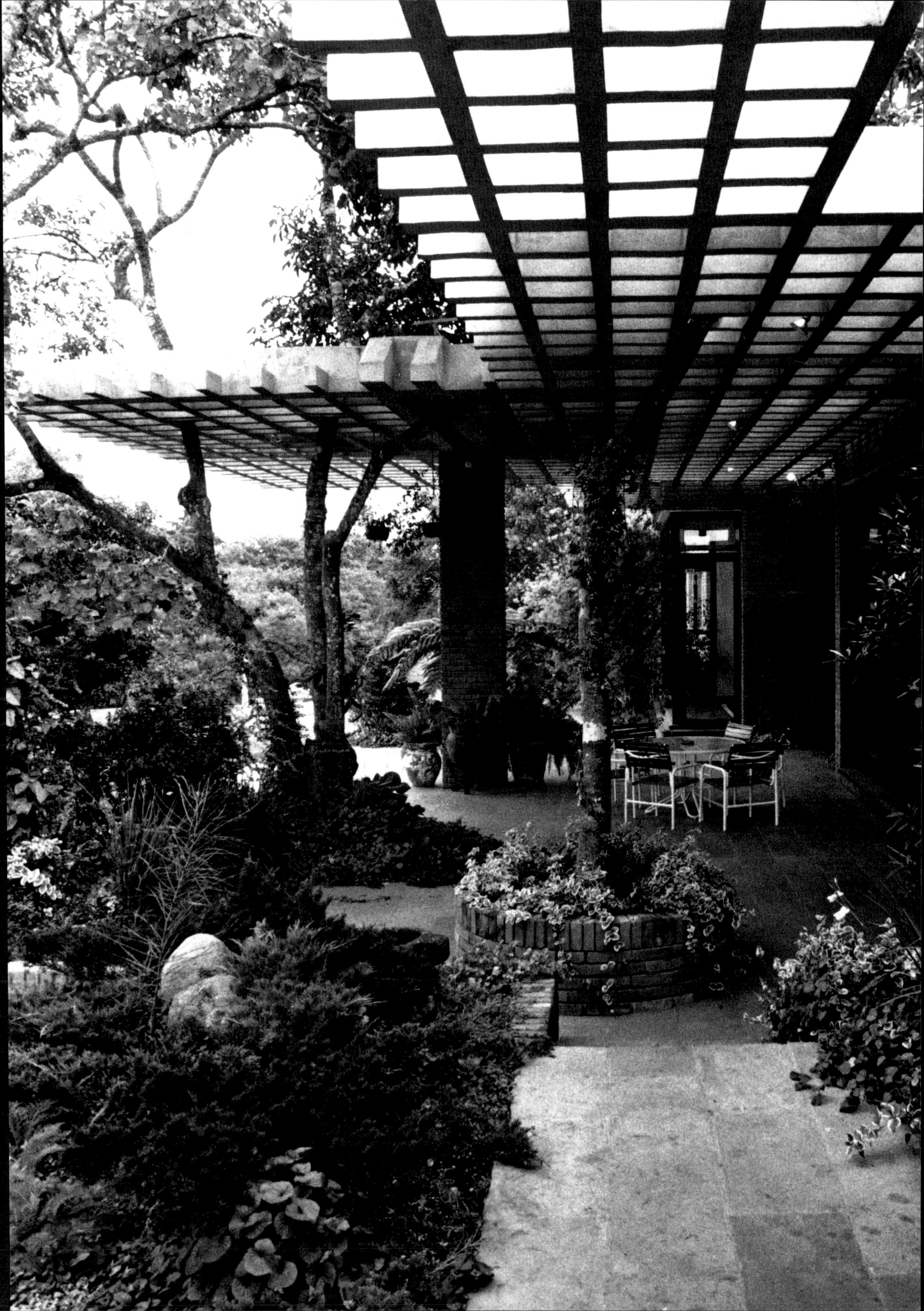

From the entrance Casa Capuchinas displays a fabulous mixture of contemporary architectural design and the use of warm materials that maintain a dialogue with the nature around it. The stone path that leads to the main entrance is covered by an elegant structure of wood that subtly incorporates a majestic tree. Within the house, the atrium with slate floors opens onto an inner garden with a stone wall that separates it from the social area. The white walls that divide the different spaces give way to a number of brick columns in order to establish a relationship both with the exterior of

CASA CAPUCHINAS

the house and an open-air leisure area at the far end, which is covered by a wooden pergola which projects a geometric grid of shadows onto the floor. The banisters of all the transit areas consist of glass panels supporting a wooden handrail which, as it floats in space, seems to merge into the clean white walls and also provides visual continuity throughout the passageways. Both the inner garden and the bridge on the second floor receive direct overhead light through a glass roof upheld by crossbeams of fine wood, repeating the contemporary-regional vocabulary that characterizes the overall design.

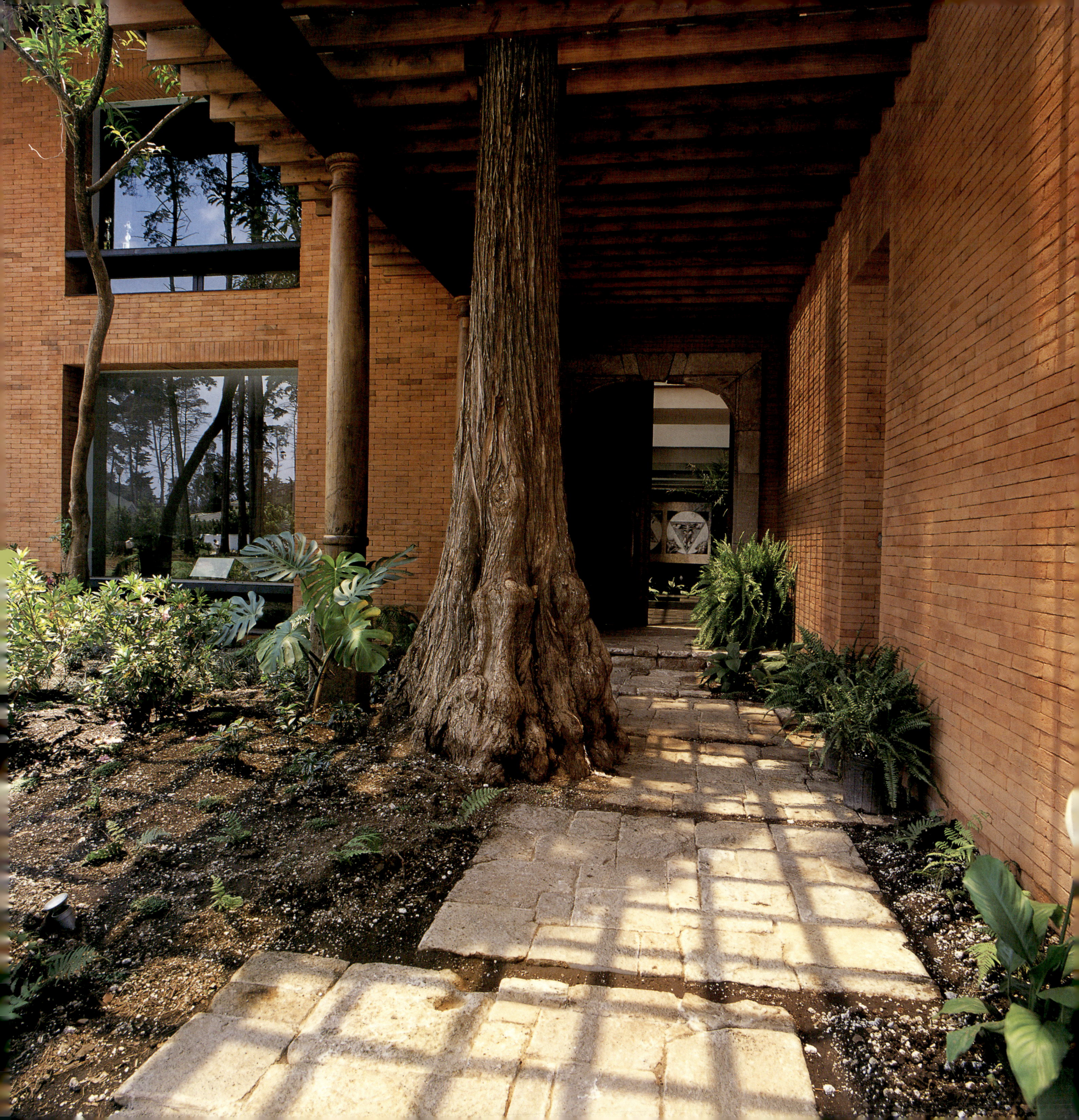

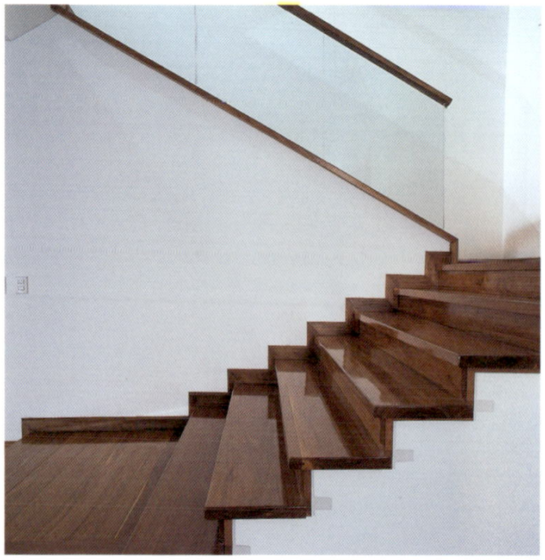

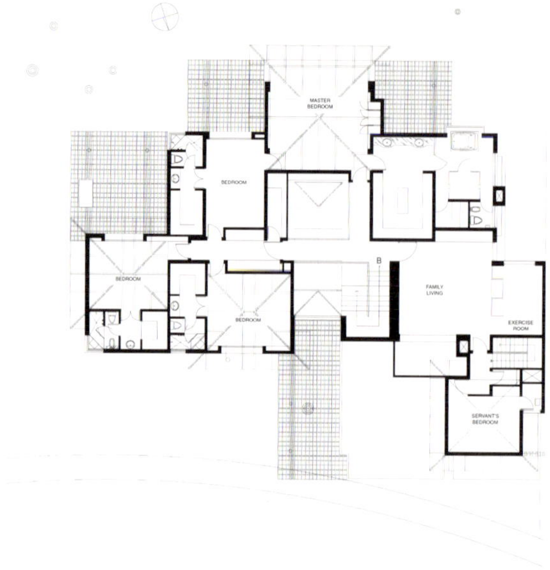

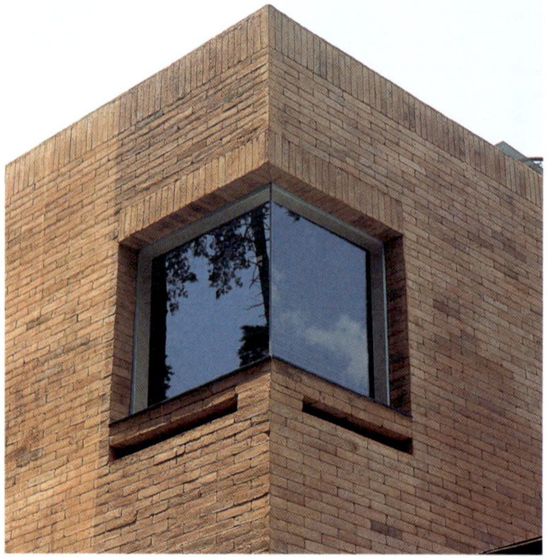

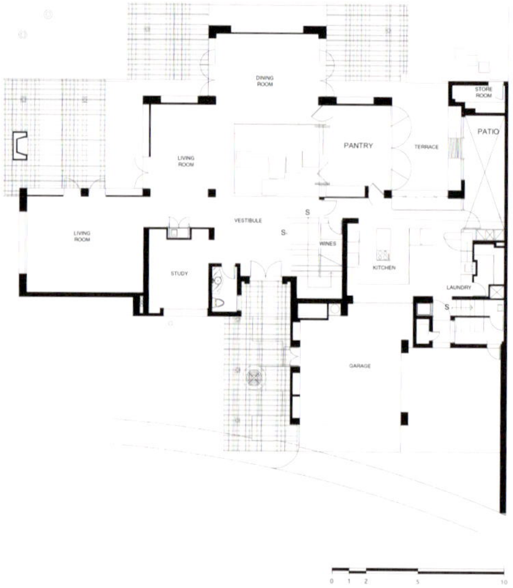

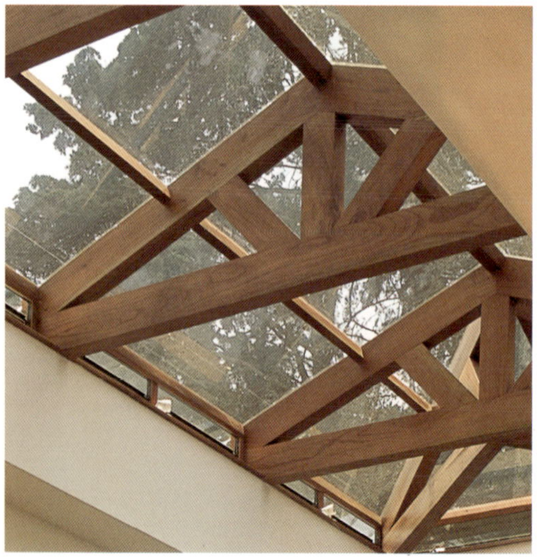

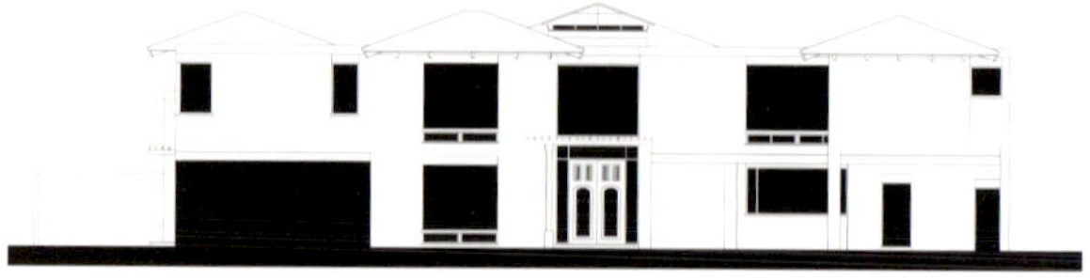

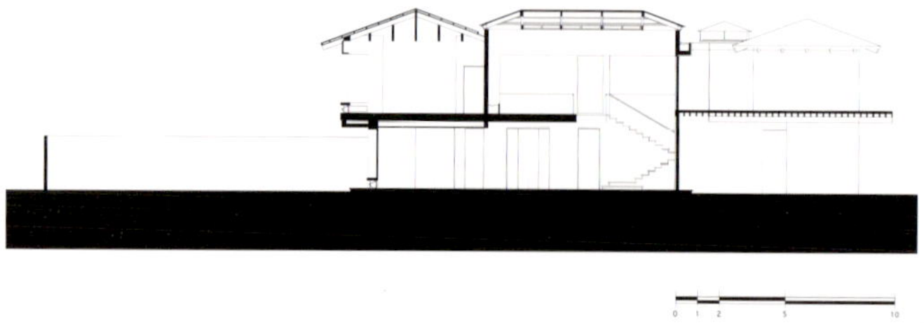

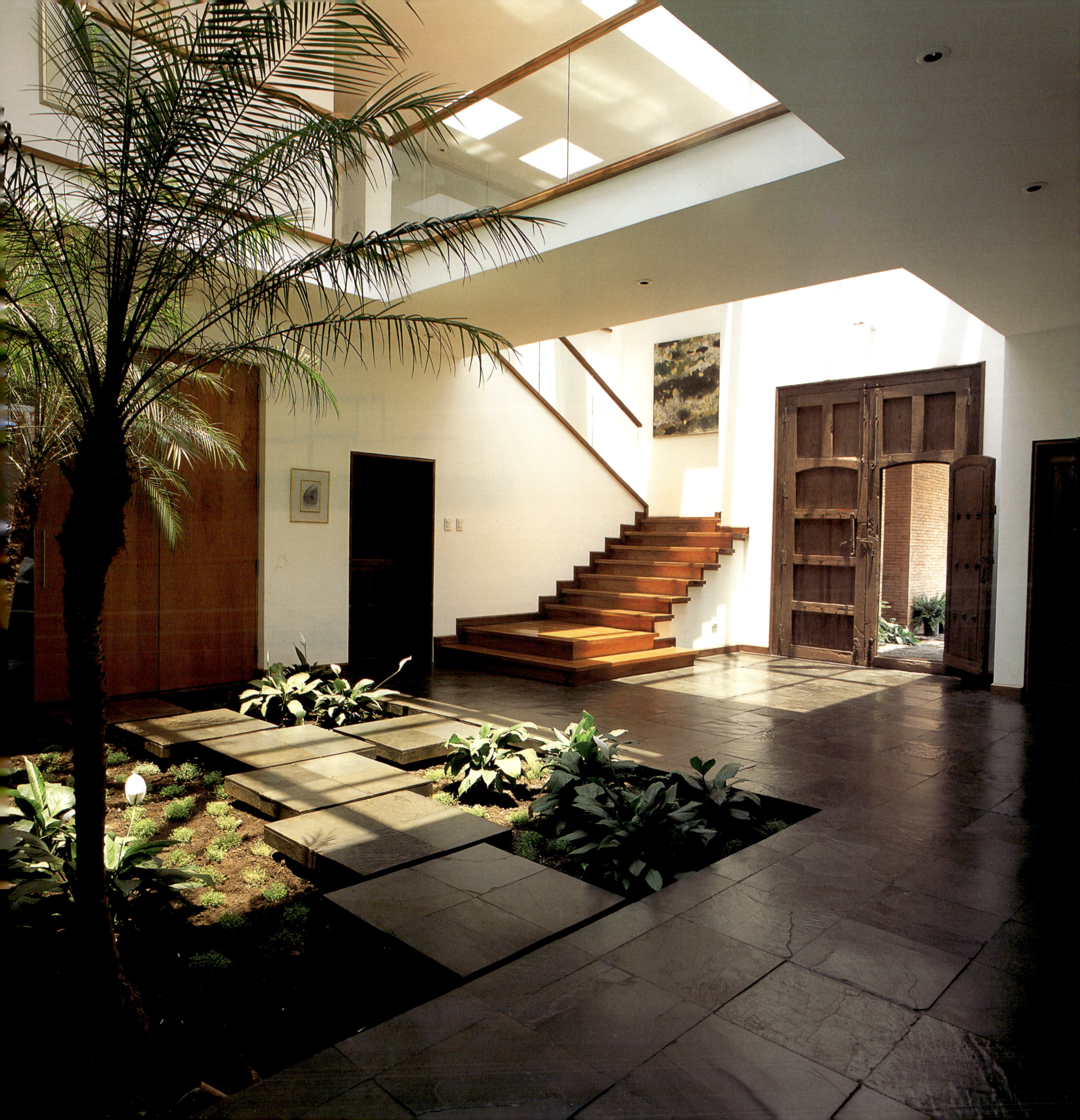

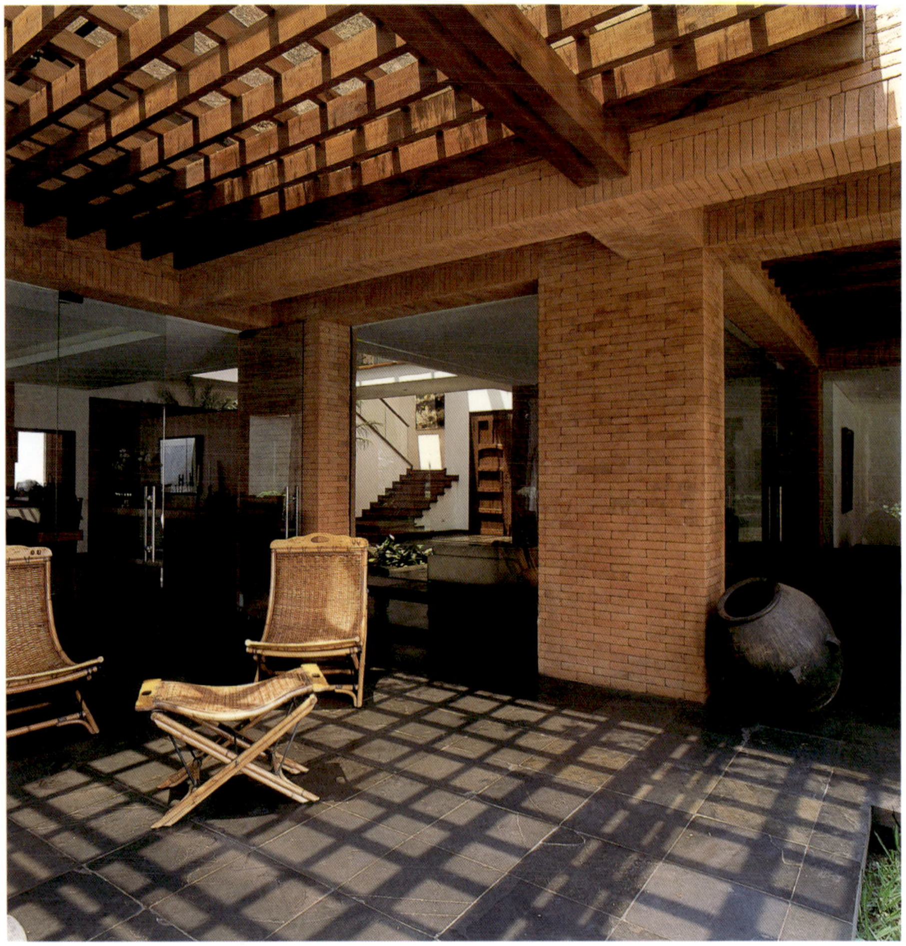

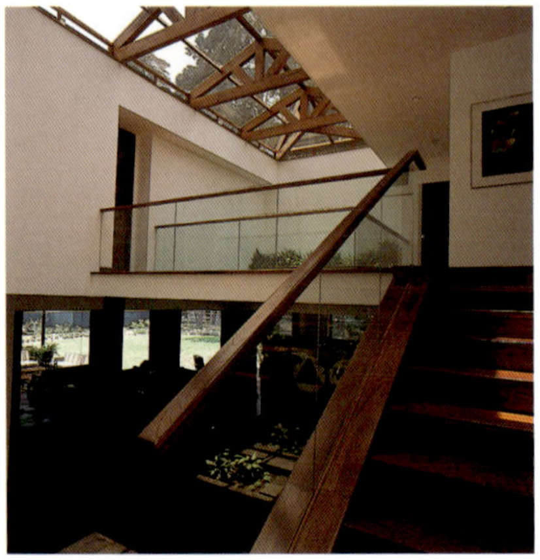

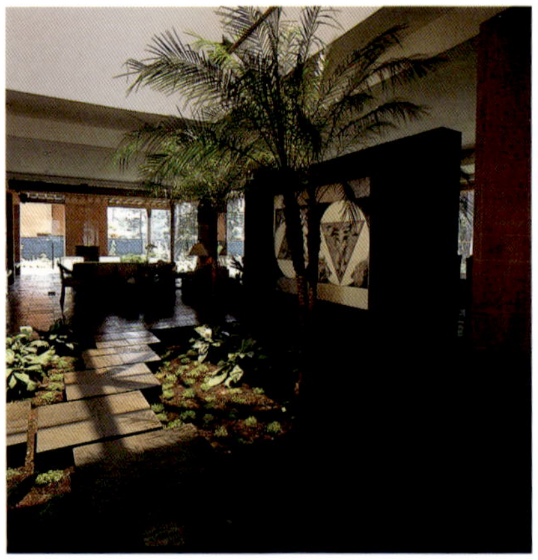

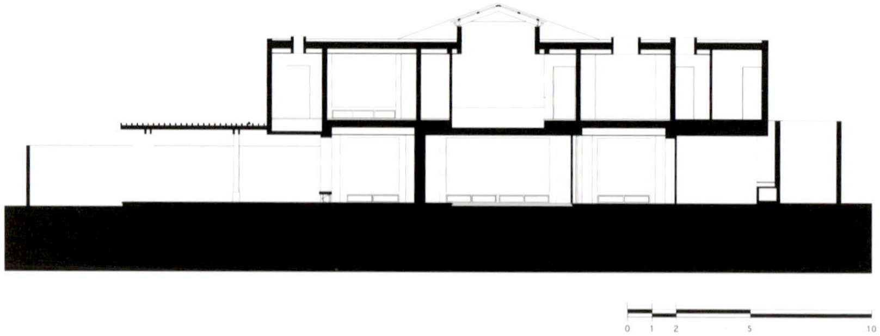

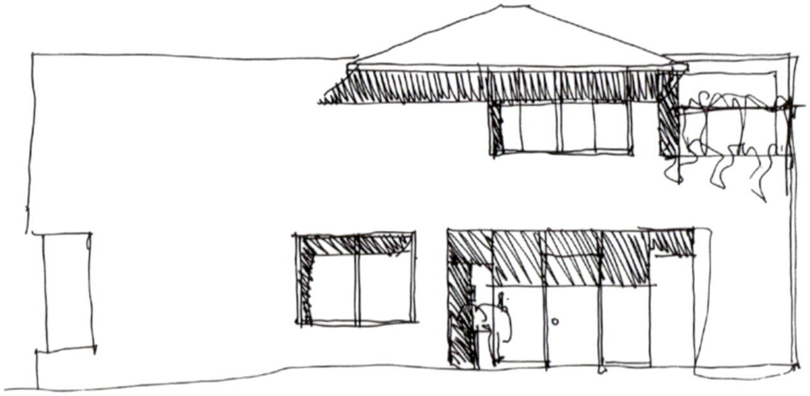

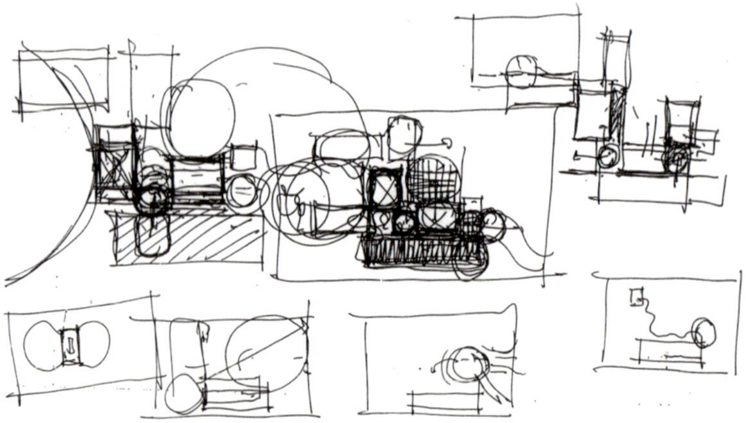

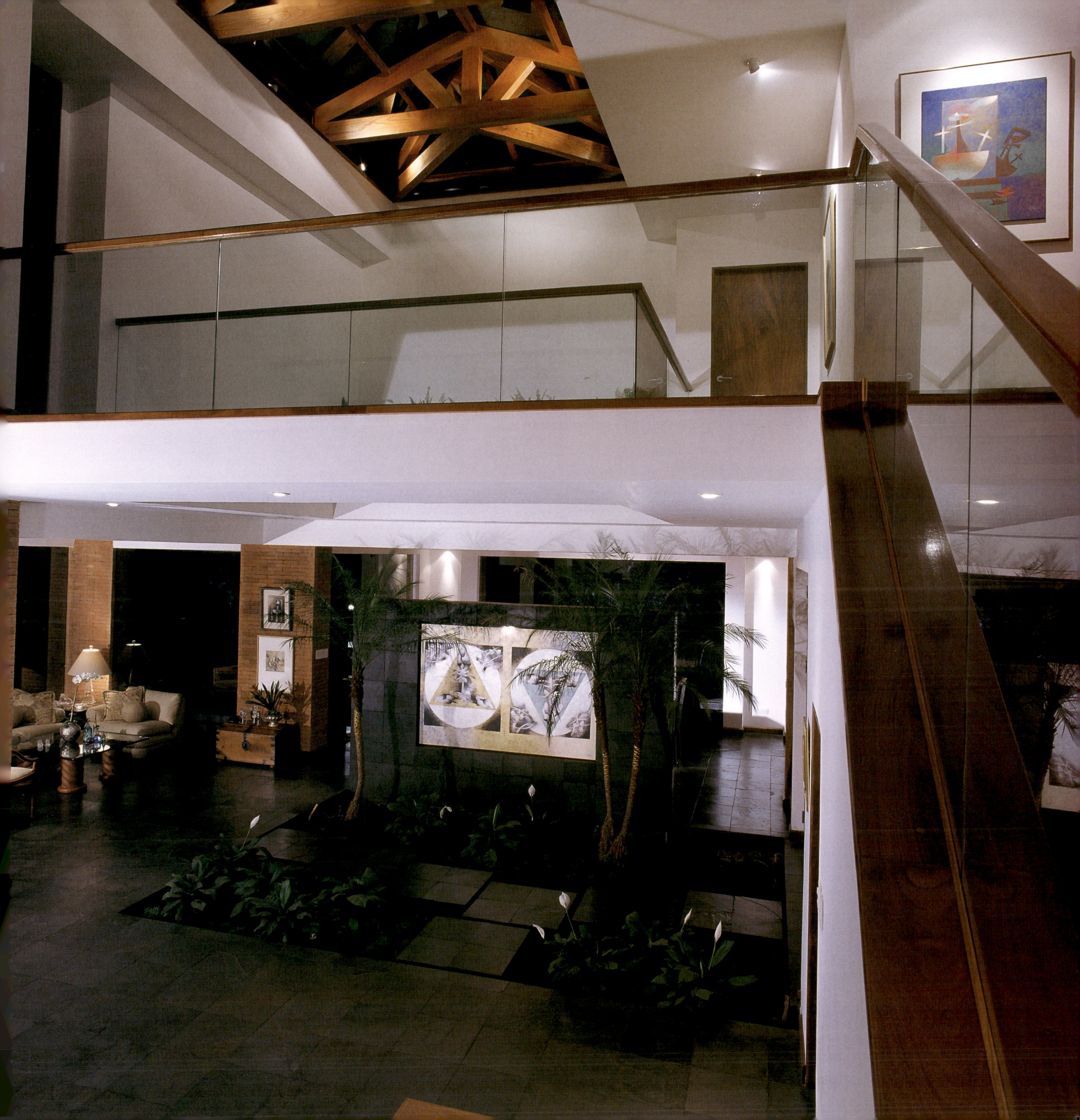

Set between two hills that face a natural lake, the site on which Casa Socorro stands was raised a meter and a half above its natural level so that the house would obtain vistas of the lake and avoid a direct connection with the street which separates the lake from the grounds. Thus, the design allows all of the ambits to enjoy views towards this body of water and the tall cypresses in the surroundings. Toward this end a glass pyramid was placed in the center of the house, which allows one to see the crowns of the cypresses outside, while, at the same time, it gives light and emphasis to the inner patio from which the different areas of the house radiate. Running through the inner

CASA SOCORRO

garden at the end of the main axis of circulation, a fountain bathes the smooth stones of the wall with water, creating a touch of nature. When the two moveable glass panels that divide the living room from the dining room are opened, the spatial permeability between their ambits is complete. In addition, a special feature of Casa Socorro is that the design allows all of the interior spaces to open onto the natural surroundings. This erases barriers between the interior and the exterior and forms an architectural mesh that takes full advantage of the surrounding vegetation and gardens.

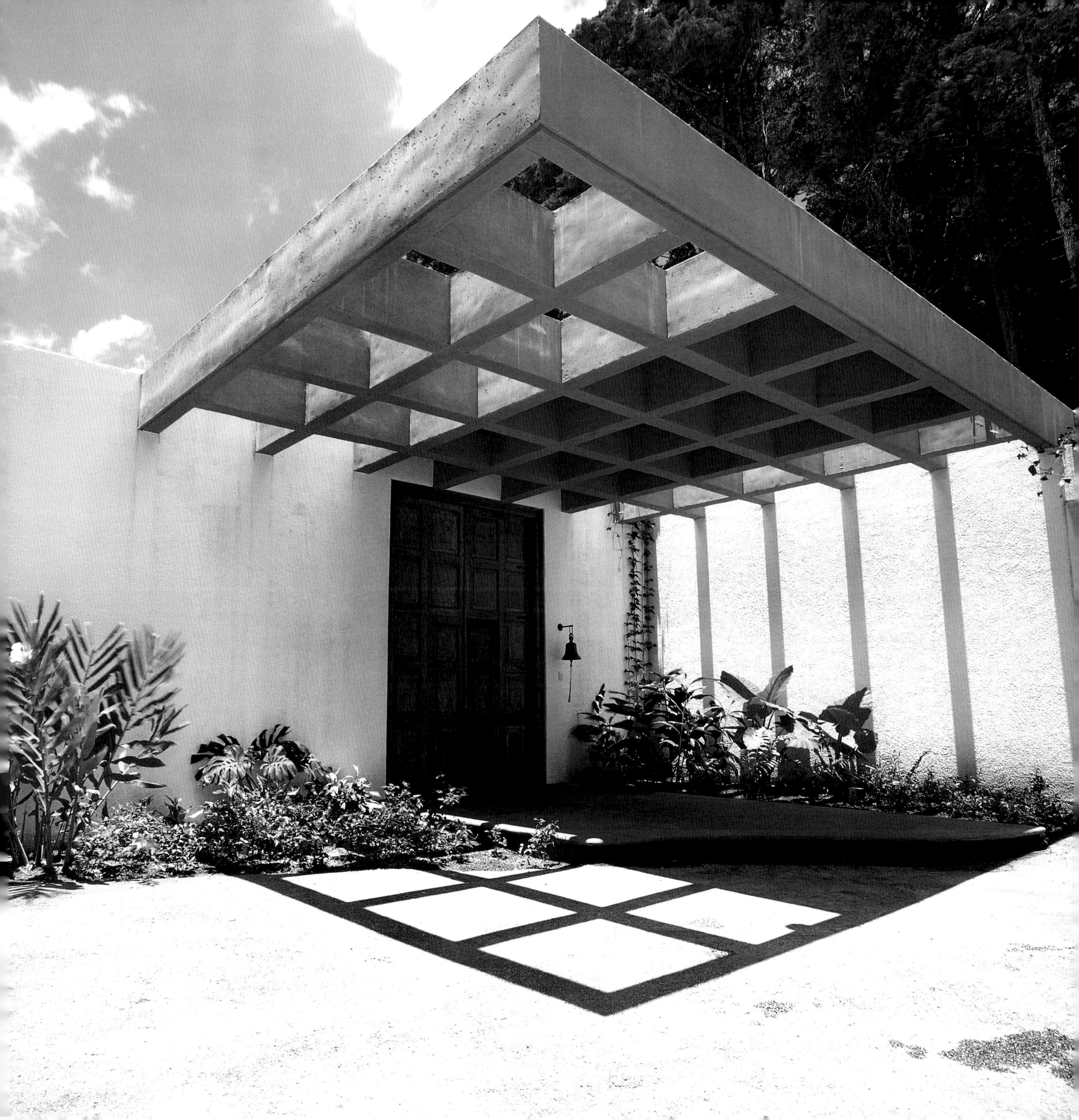

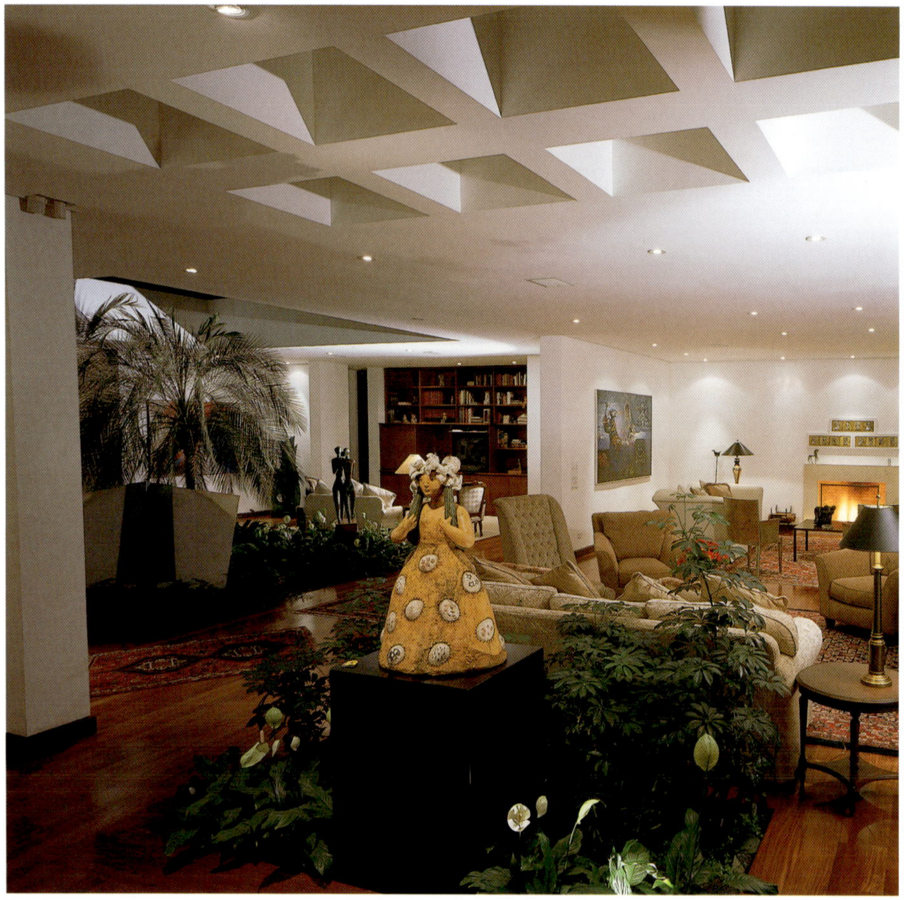

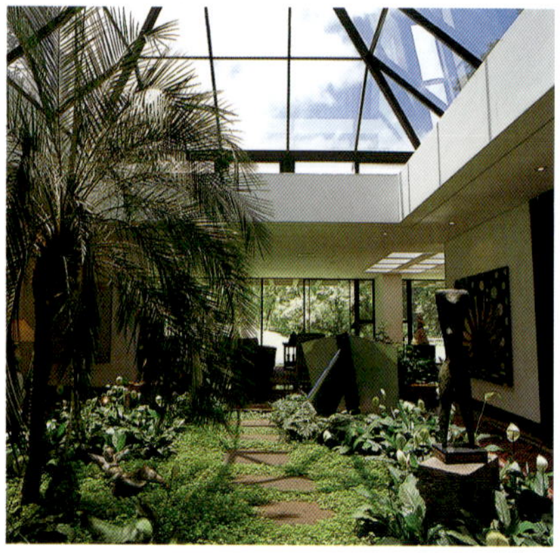

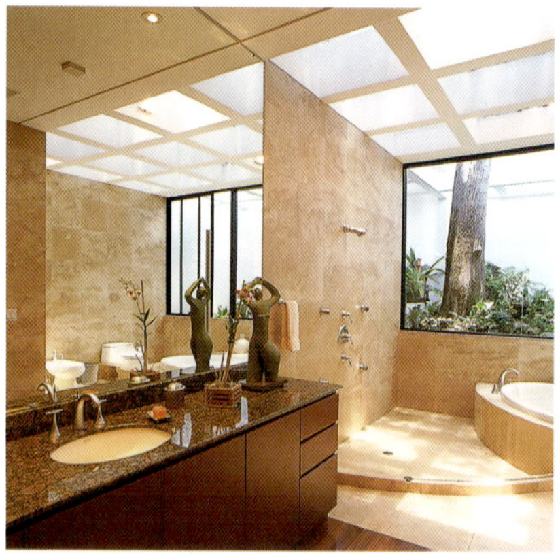

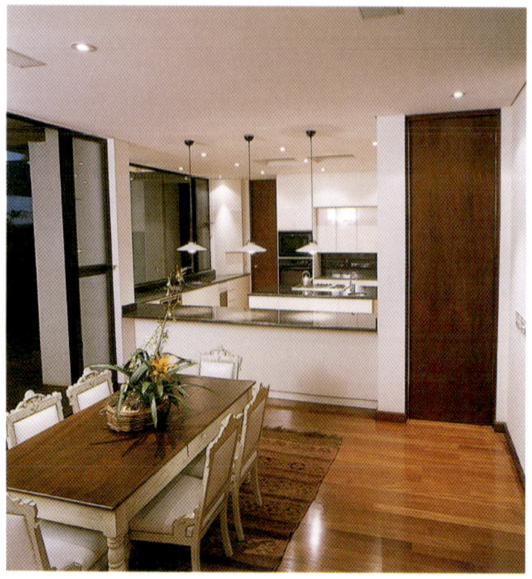

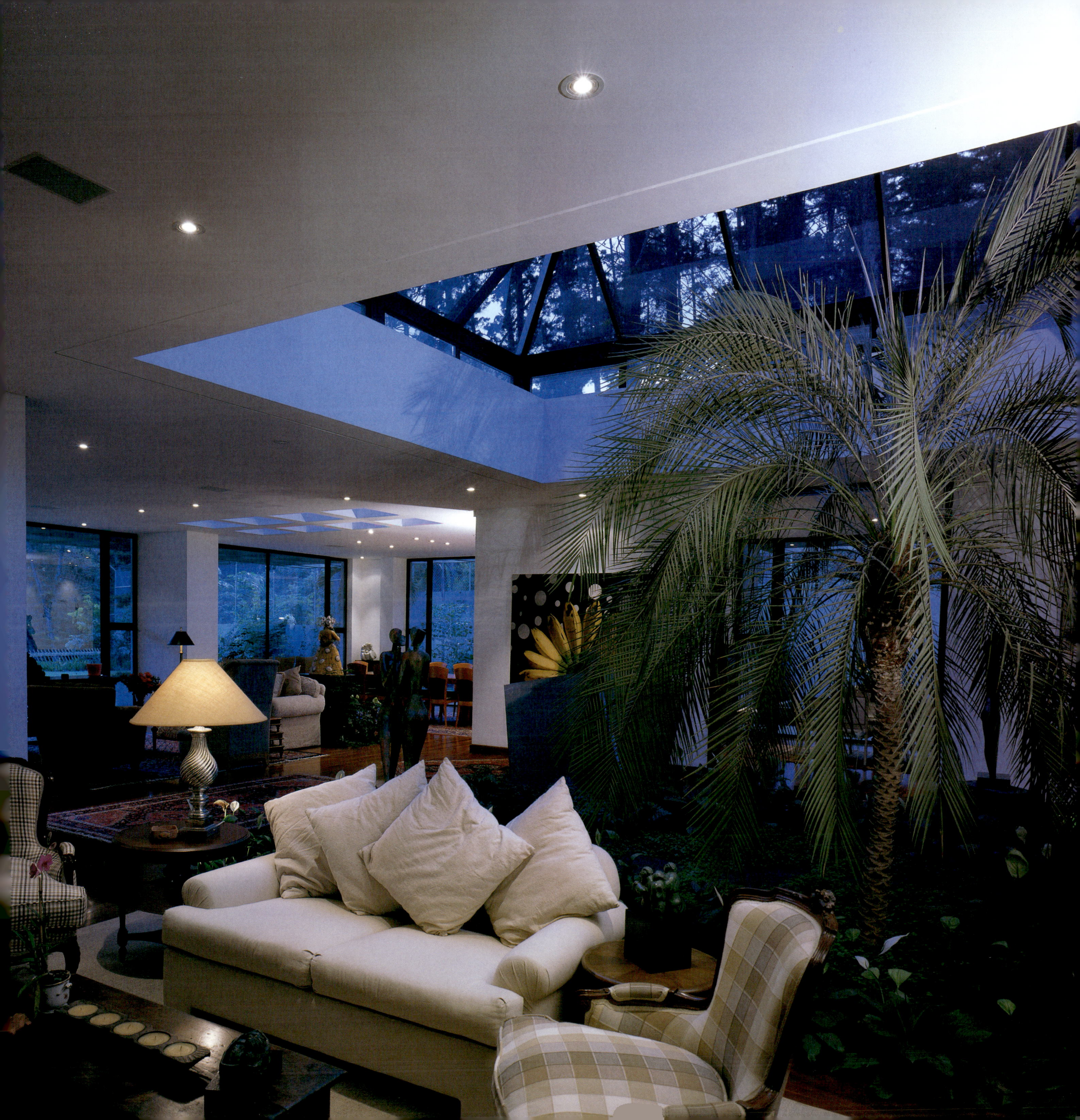

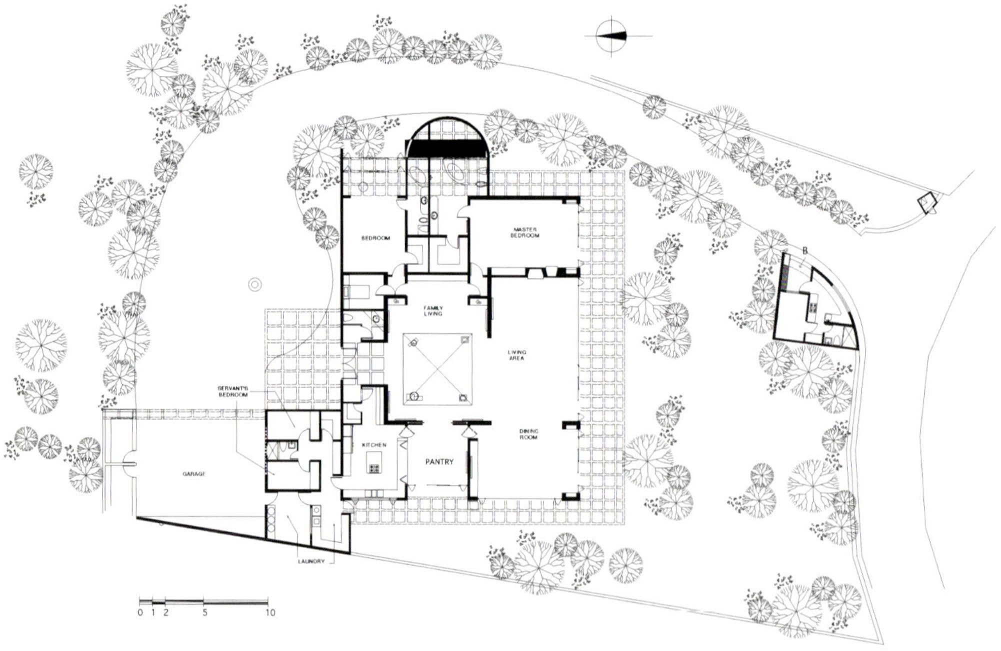
BEDROOM
MASTER BEDROOM
FAMILY LIVING
LIVING AREA
SERVANT'S BEDROOM
KITCHEN
PANTRY
DINING ROOM
GARAGE
LAUNDRY
0 1 2 5 10

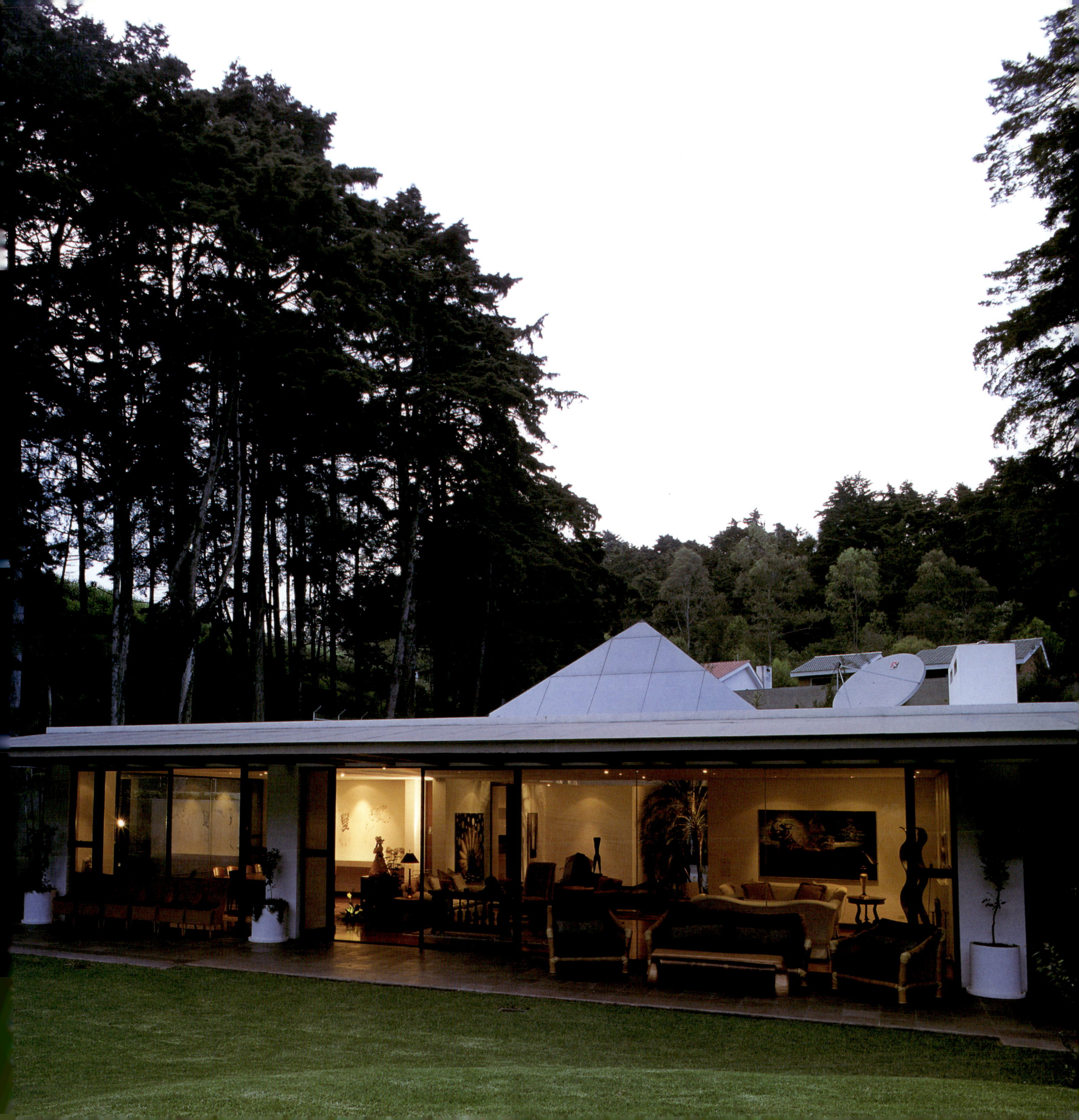

The interior spaces of the Casa del Naranjo ("Orange Tree House") are grouped in a parallel along a central axis of circulation, which joins the main entrance at one end to the main hall at the other. Due to the slightly sloping terrain, the central passageway gradually descends along three levels to wind up in the family room, with a view of the main chimney as a backdrop. From the outside, the ordering of the spaces along this axis has a legible form, since this main spine is covered by a flat roof, while the areas that branch out from it have one-slope

CASA DEL NARANJO

roofs, upheld by wooden structures that are reminiscent of traditional crossbeams. The main hall contains three different ambits: musical, social and working, while the family lounge, surrounded by bedrooms, is separated from the dining room by a bell chimney which provides a needed warmth, due to the cold climate of the region where the house stands. On the other end, the family lounge frames the view of the outside garden through large windows and a sloping glass roof that faces south to take advantage of the warmth and light of the sun.

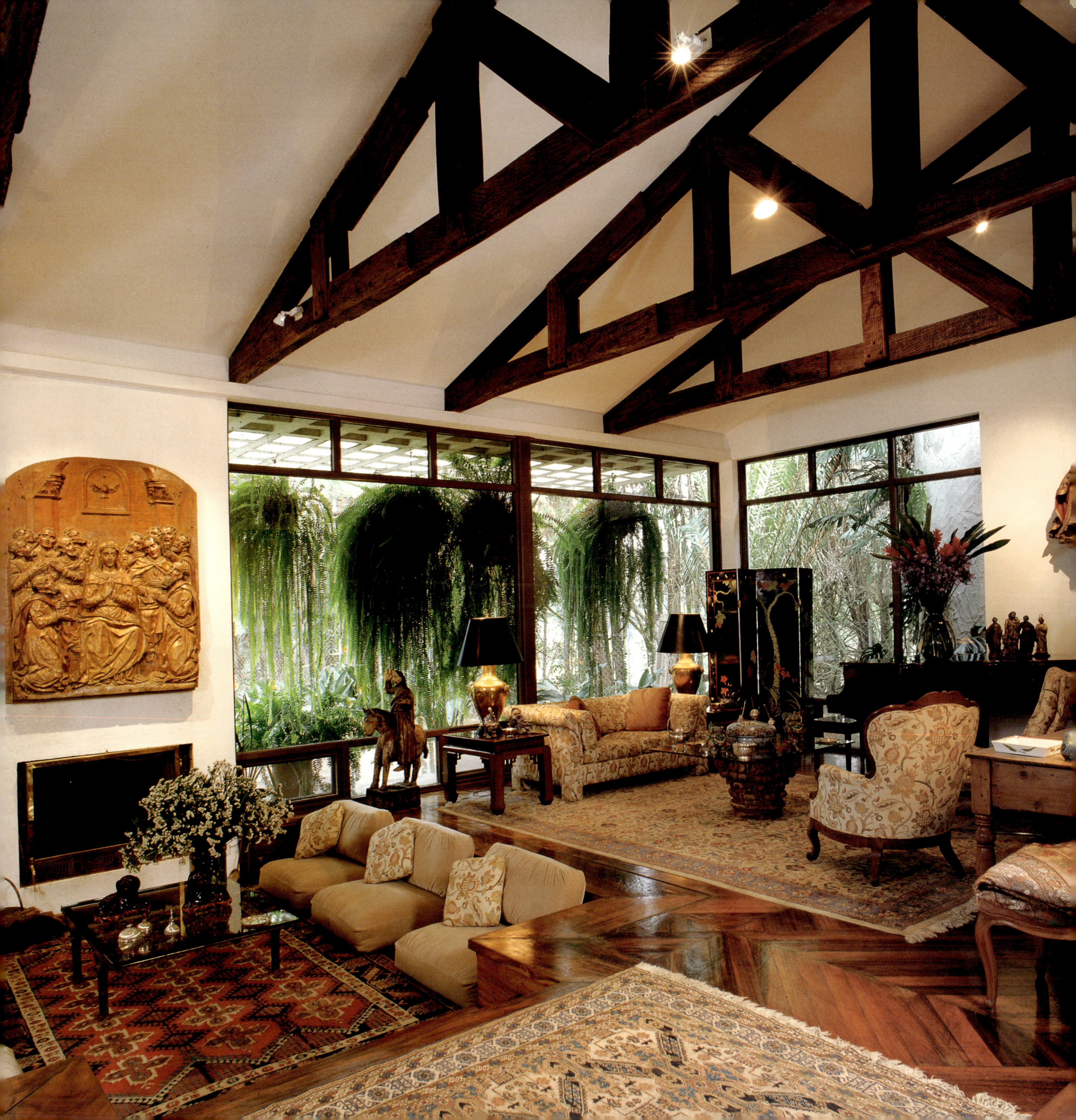

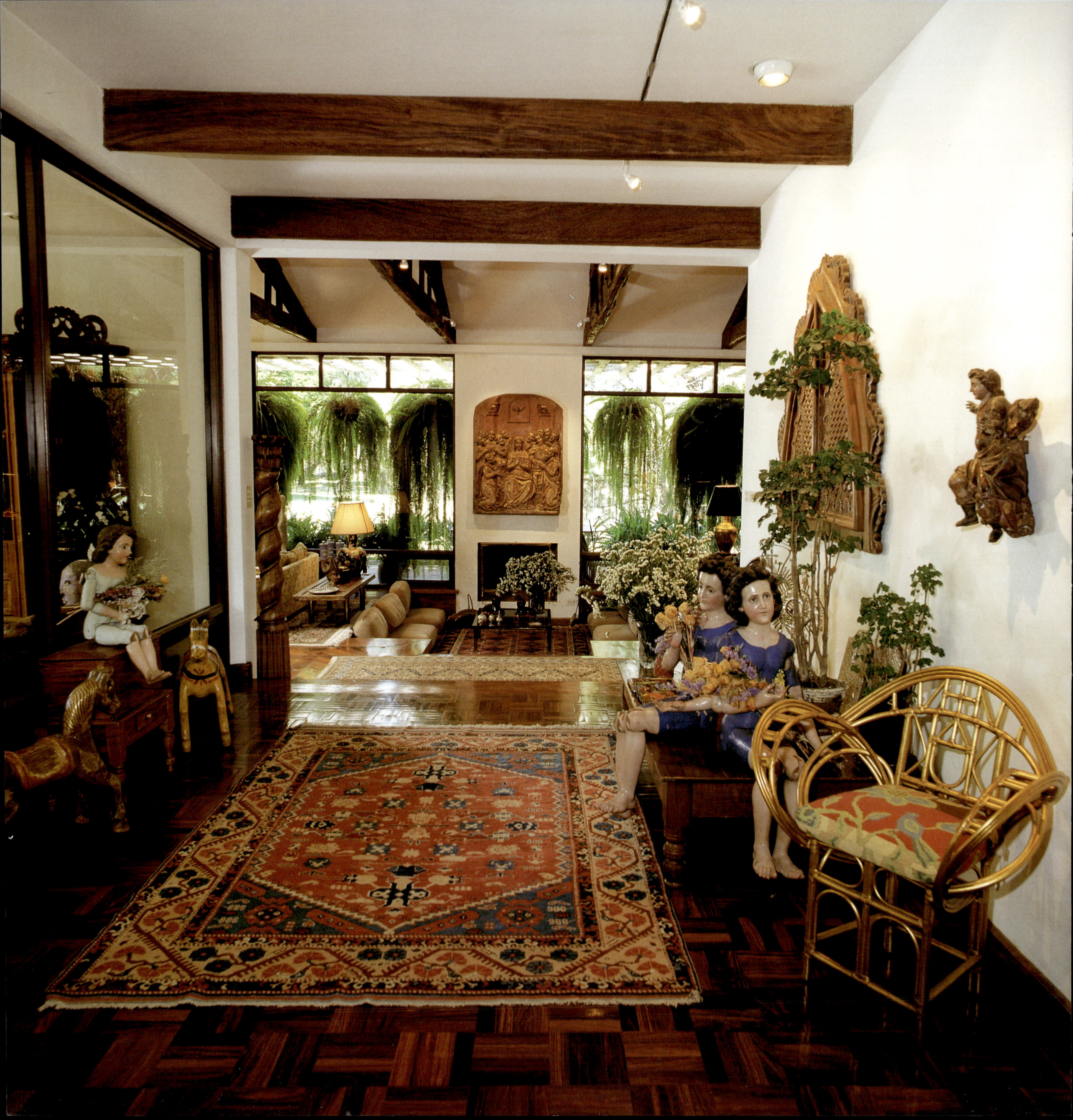

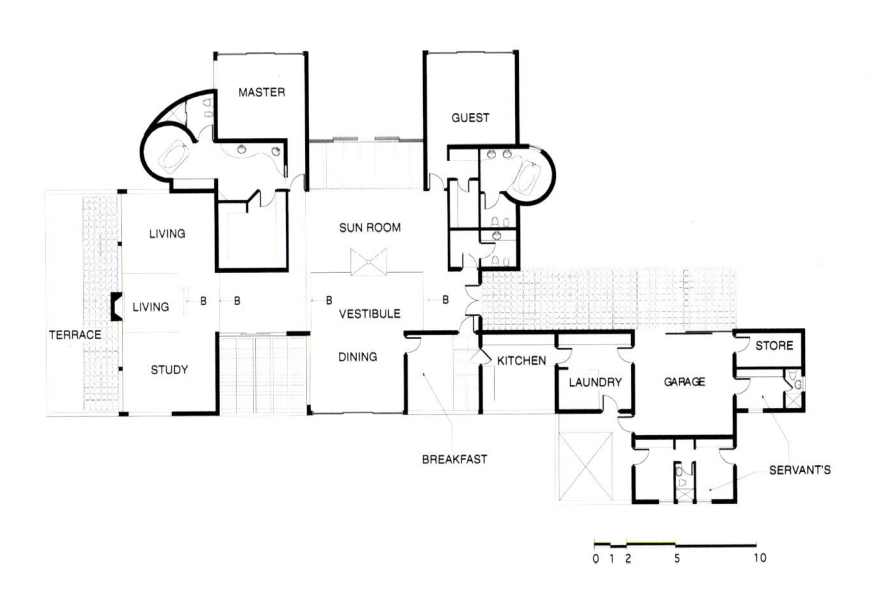

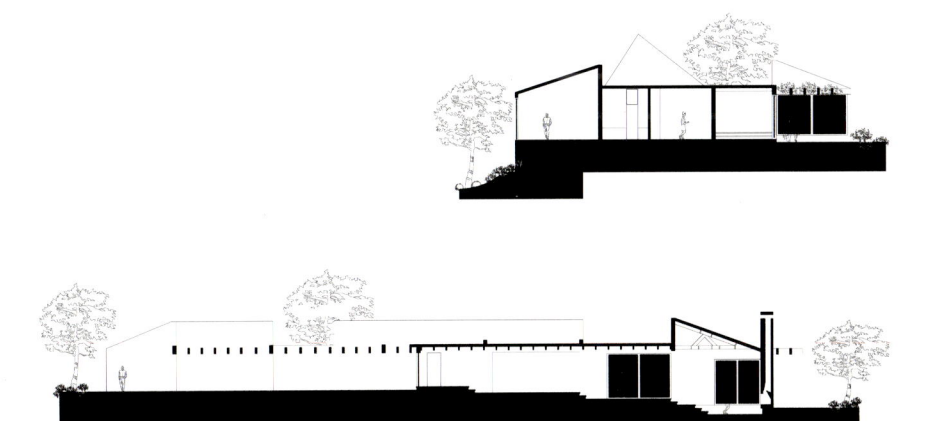

The simplicity of the spatial arrangement and the quality of the materials employed give Casa del Naranjo a restrained and comfortable elegance that takes advantage of both the topographical and climatic features of the terrain.

The overall lines of the floor plan and elevation of Casa Lomas del Bosque ("Forest Hills House"), designed for a sculptress and painter, reveal a contemporary touch. The main front is articulated by a strip of glass that frames the entrance doors and divides the front into two brick planes that respond to their geometry. It creates a sense of depth that seems to push the entrance slightly inwards, giving it emphasis and revealing some aspects of the interior at the same time. On entering the three-story-high vestibule, covered by a bubble skylight, one's attention is drawn towards

CASA LOMAS DEL BOSQUE

a bridge on the second floor that leads to the private areas. The ceilings within the four-sided inclined roofs which cover the main areas are lined with tongue-and-groove strips of wood, creating a clean series of vaults that define the spaces beneath them. The floor plan enables the main spaces on the first floor to communicate with one another in a diagonal way and thus maintain a continuous perspective without visual blocks. In the exterior, the floor of black slate imported from South Africa aptly combines with the warm terracotta of the brick walls.

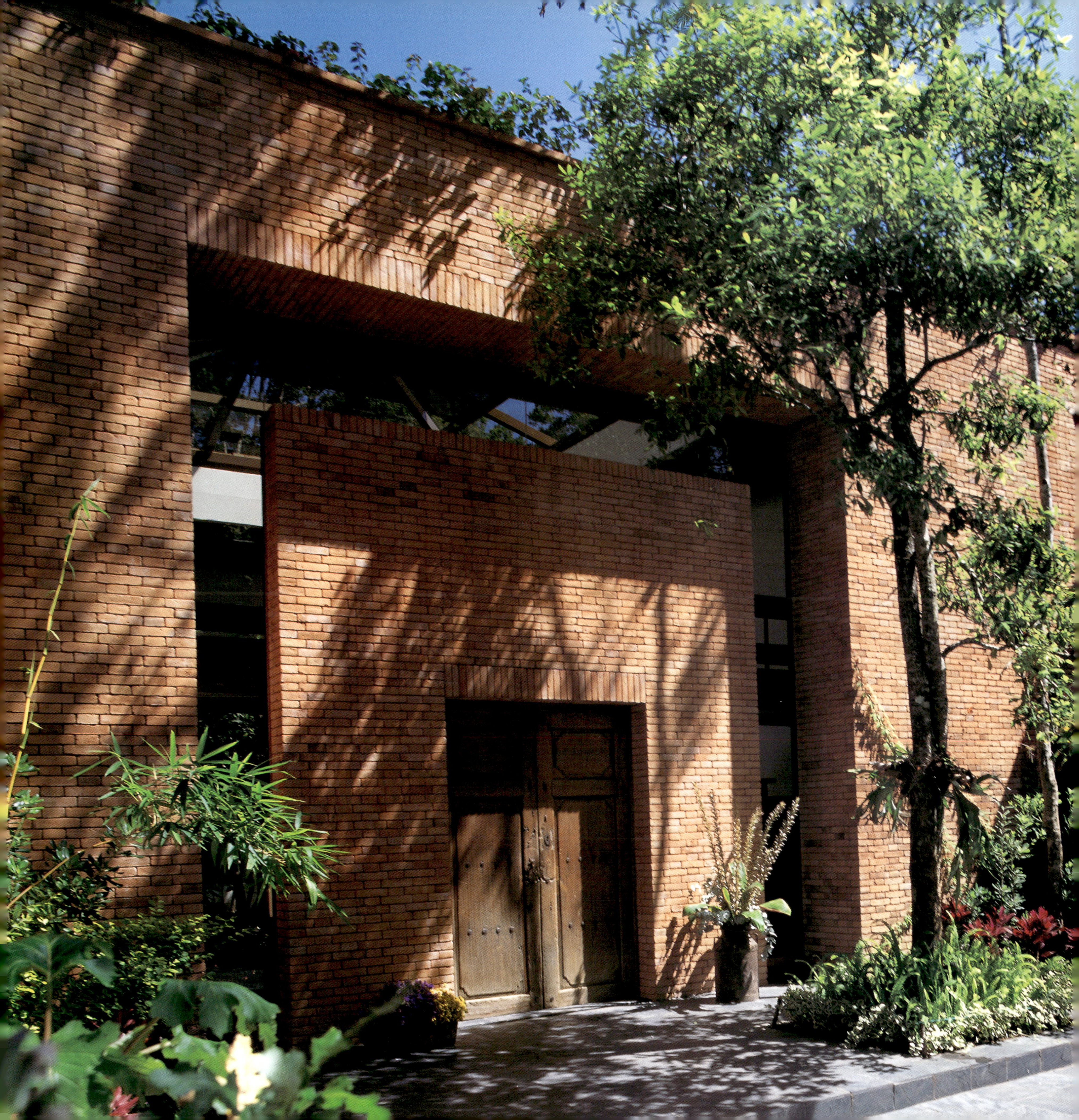

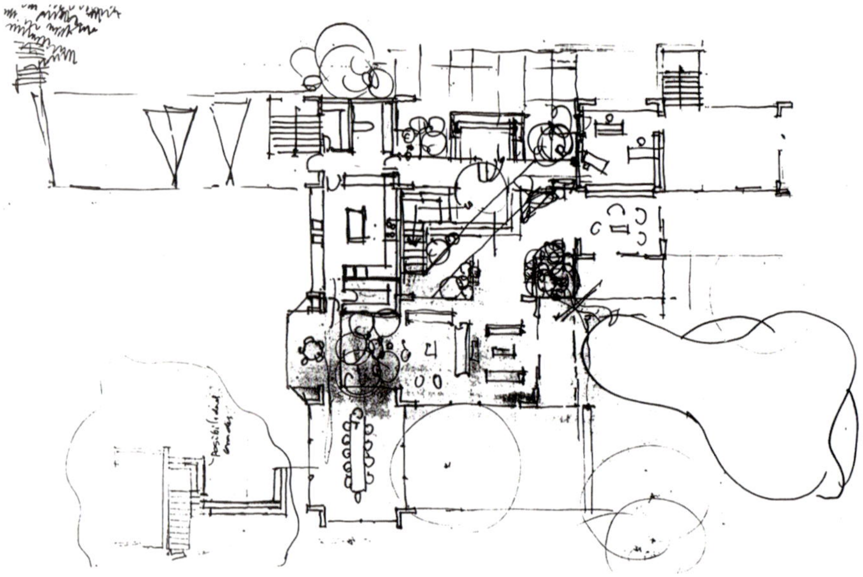

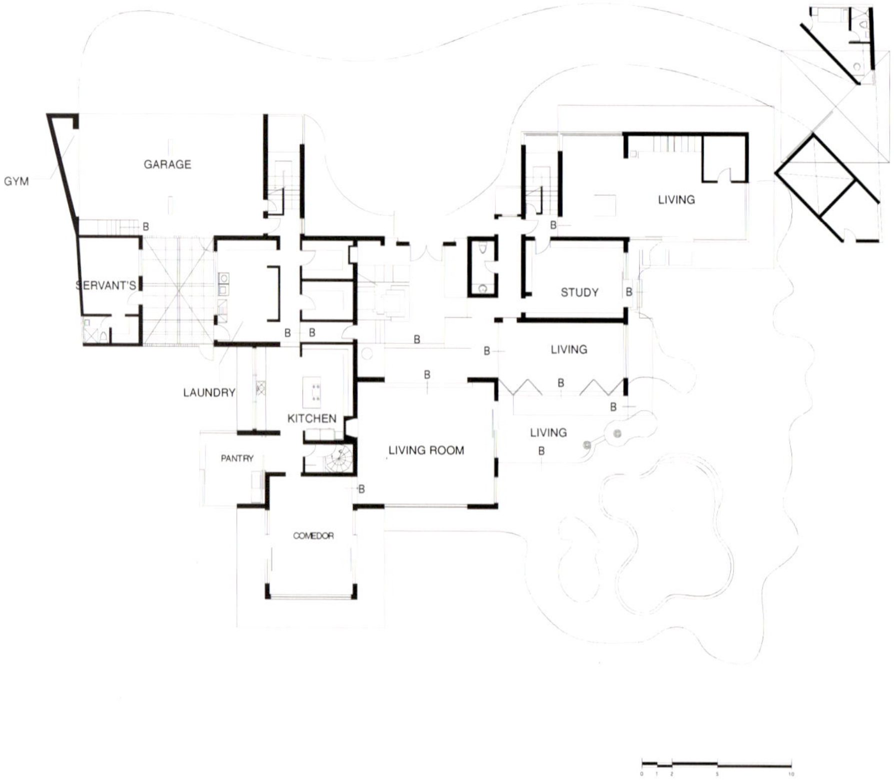
GYM
GARAGE
SERVANT'S
LAUNDRY
KITCHEN
PANTRY
COMEDOR
LIVING ROOM
LIVING
STUDY
LIVING
LIVING

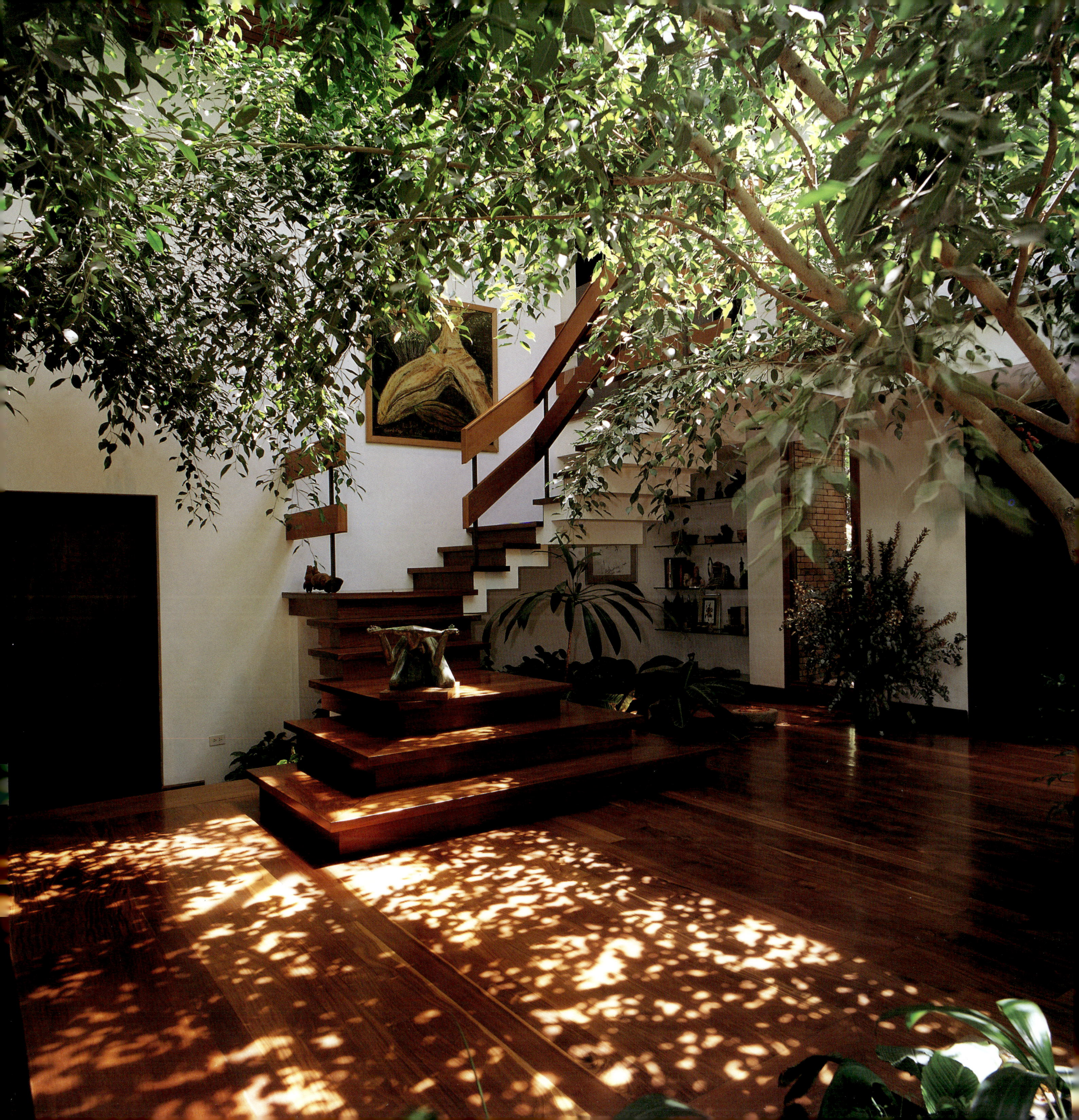

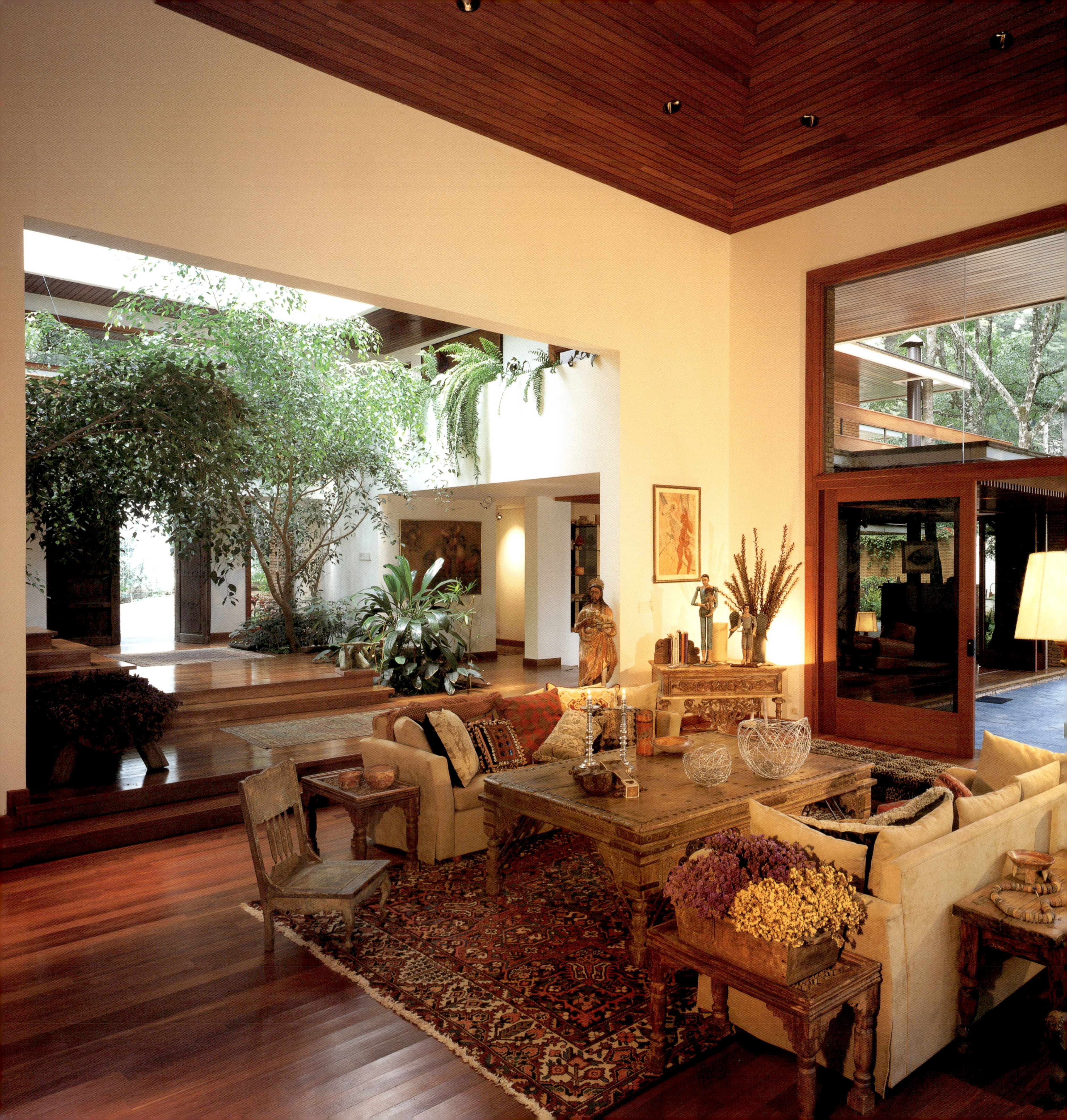

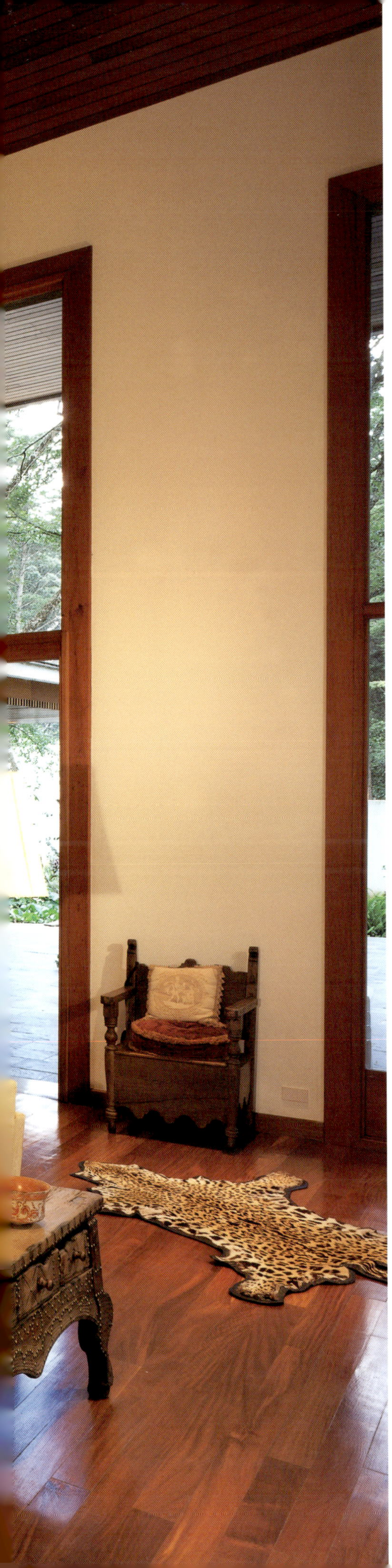

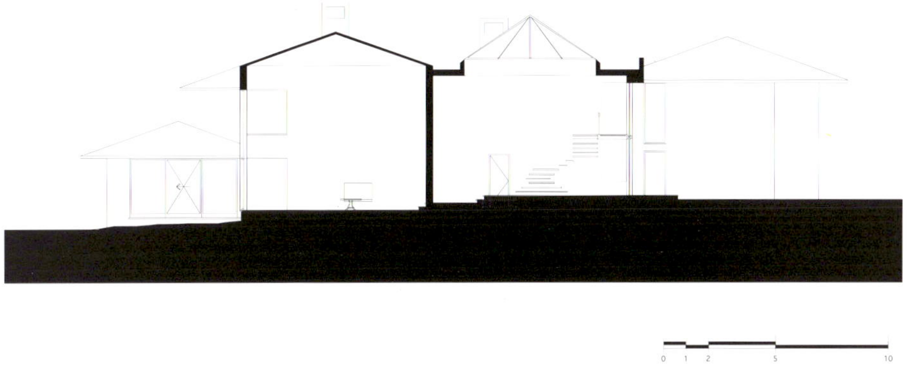
0 1 2 5 10

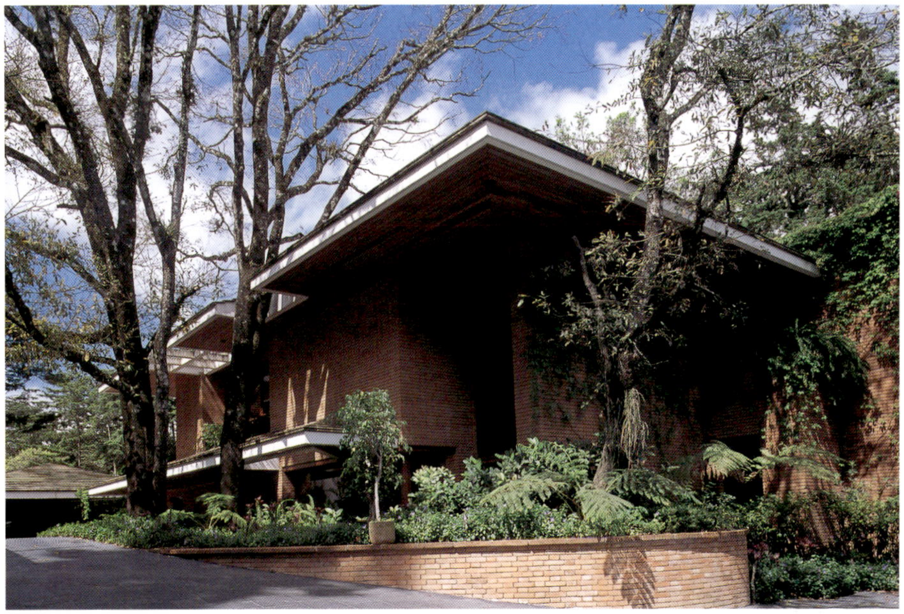

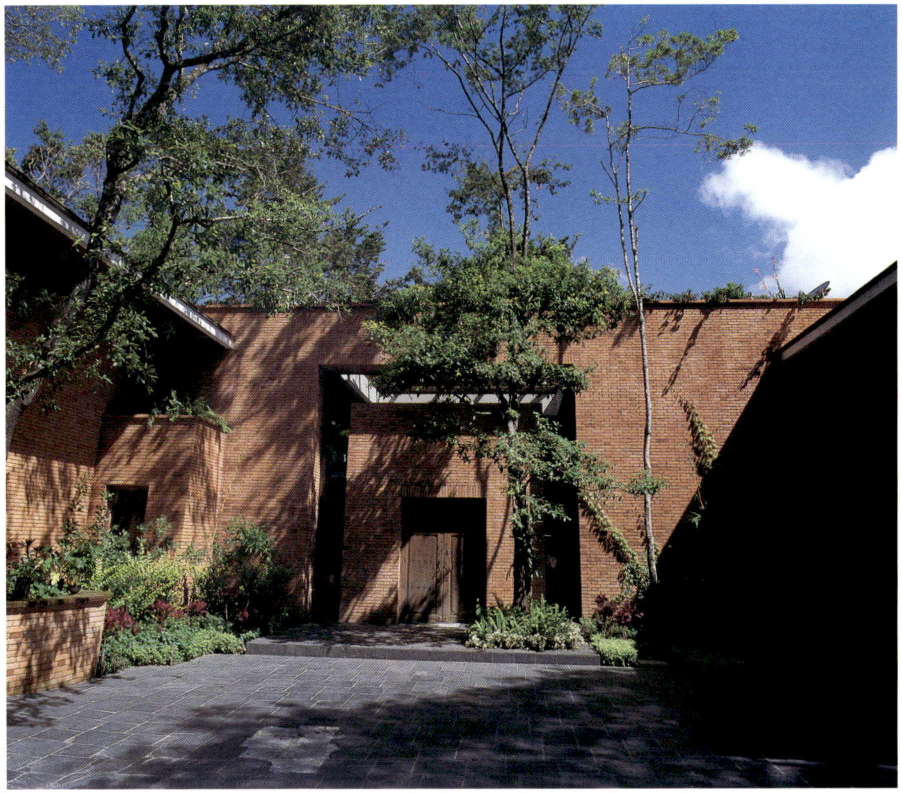

The challenge of constructing Casa de las Rocas ("House of the Rocks") had to do with the difficult terrain – the summit of a hill on a peninsula of Atitlán Lake. When the water level rises, the rocky terrain on which this house is situated becomes completely surrounded by water, a natural effect that had to be taken advantage of when considering the possible views. Designed as though it were emerging from the very rocks, the house makes us recall the words of Frank Lloyd Wright, who said that even buildings are "the children of the earth and the sun." Architect Giesemann utilized the rock formation so that it would serve to unite the first and second floors, digging out stairs in the stone to form a link between the building and its

CASA DE LAS ROCAS

natural setting. The chimney in the main room echoes this gesture. It is made up of a big rock on the site, which has a natural hole that was hollowed out to function as a flue, resulting in a piece that is reminiscent of the crater of a volcano. The hall, dining room and kitchen, adjacent to the chimney, are directly connected to a patio protected by projecting concrete pergolas, which affords a panoramic view of the lake and the San Pedro volcano. Incorporating the trees on the site, the white walls interlace with other rocks to form the different spaces of the house, some of which are also covered by pergolas that embrace the branches of the trees, as though to suggest a noble respect for the natural setting.

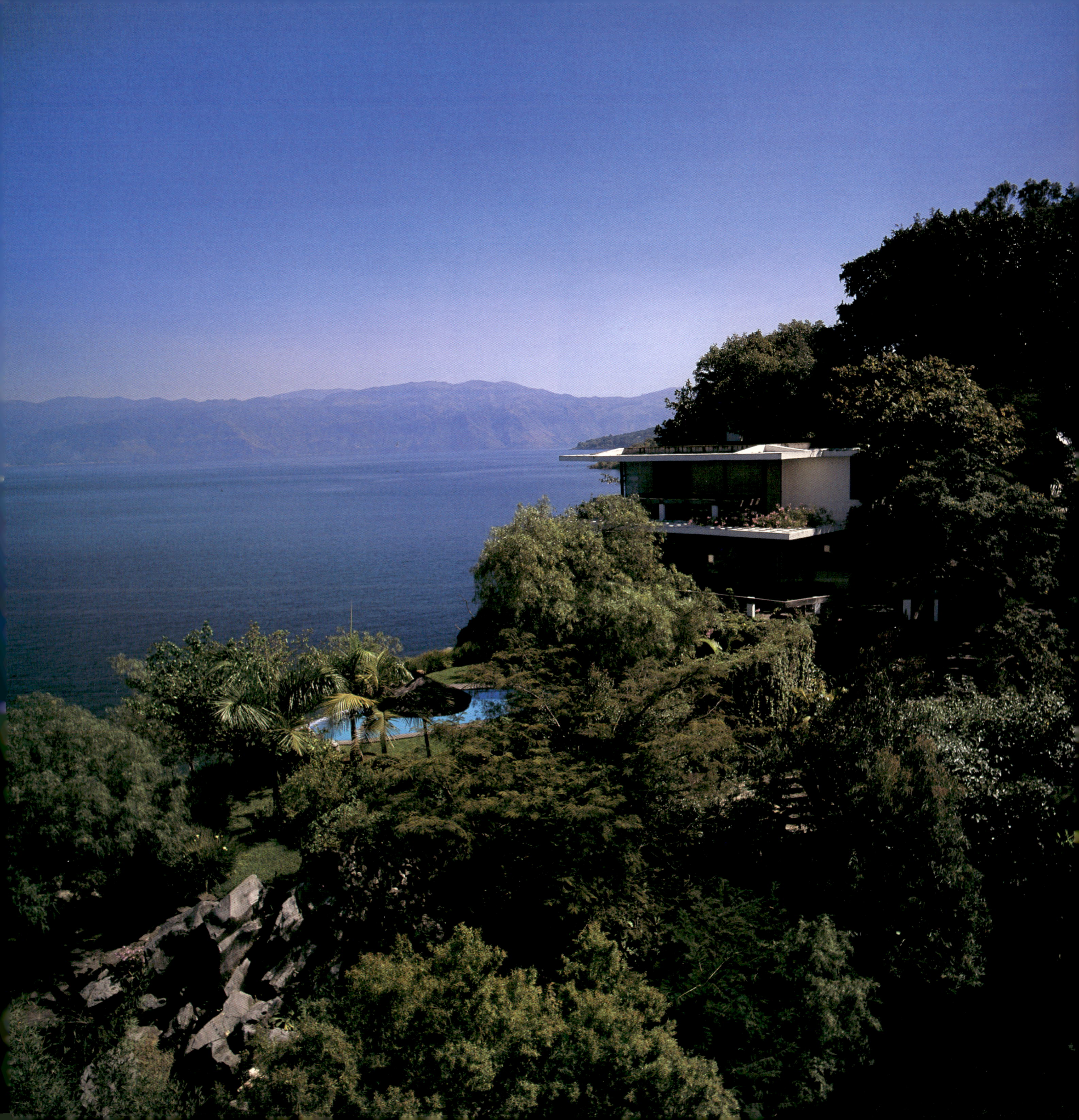

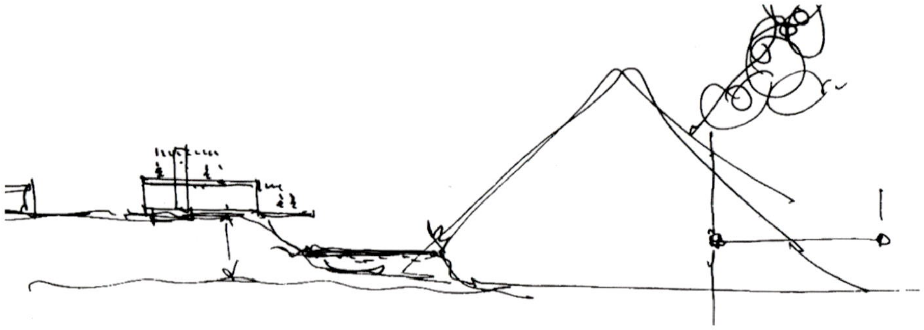

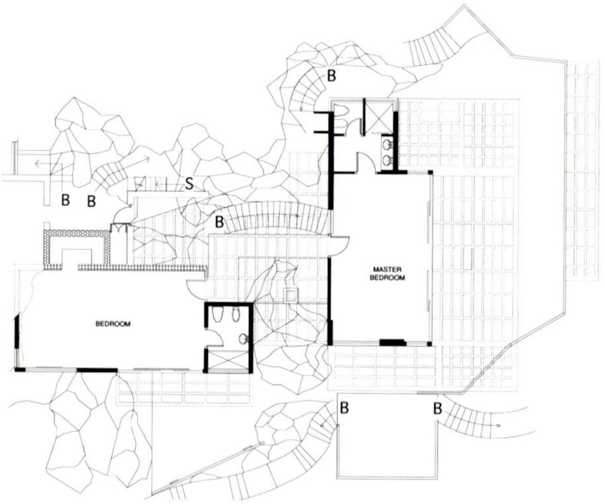
B
B
B
S
B
MASTER BEDROOM
BEDROOM
B
B

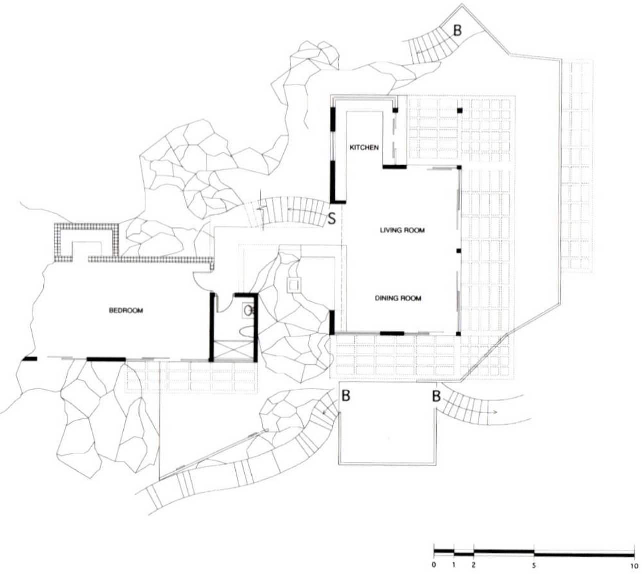
B
KITCHEN
S
LIVING ROOM
BEDROOM
DINING ROOM
B
B
0 1 2 5 10

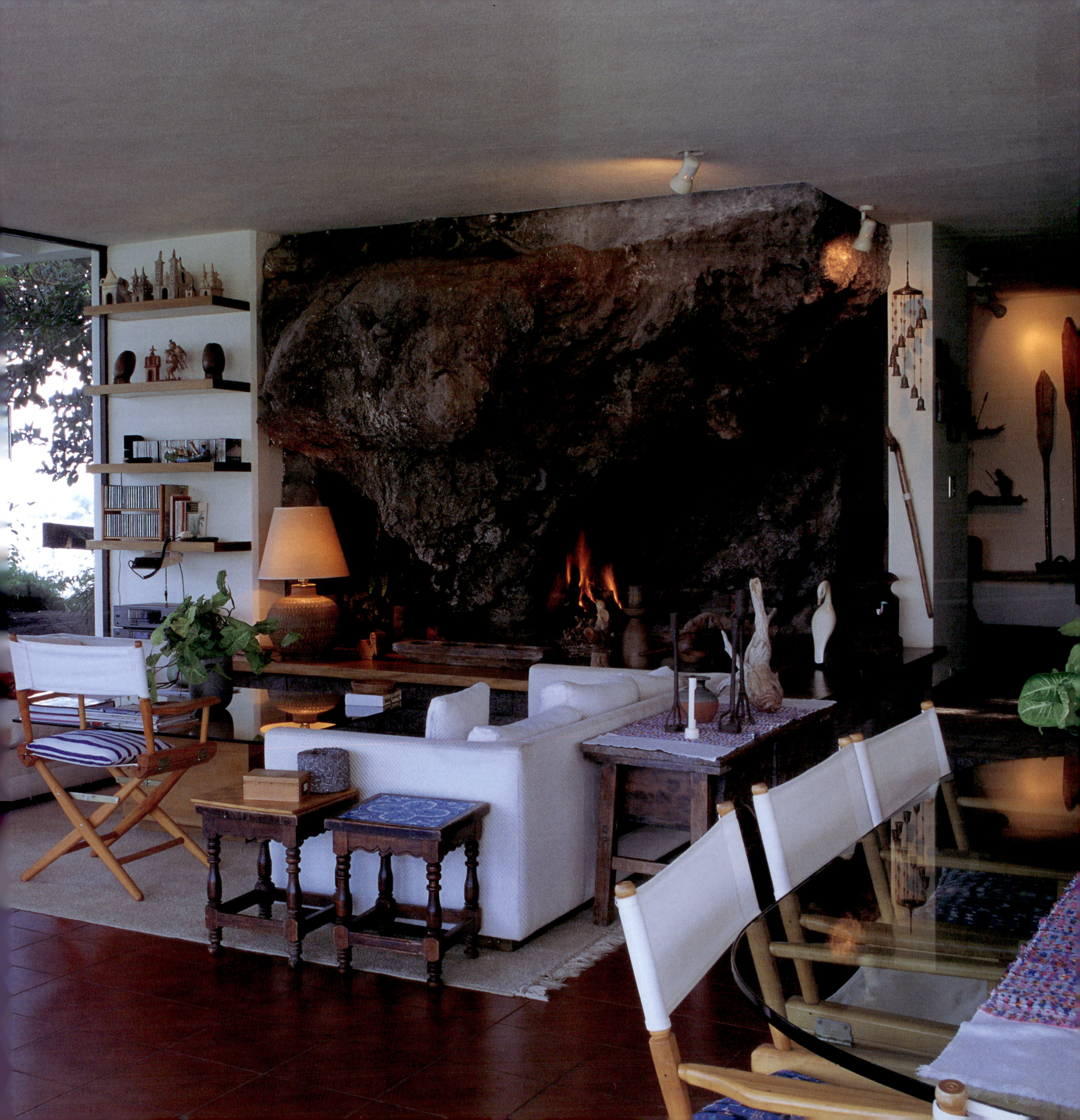

Located in Santa Catarina Palopó, on the shores of Atitlán Lake, Casa Soc-Kmoló continues with Gieseman & Minondo's concept of incorporating the rocks found on the terrain into the architectonic design. On climbing the stone steps to the level of the house, a number of pergolas in exposed concrete, supported by columns clad in the local stone, invite one to enter a terrace which unifies all of the exterior spaces. The main house is found at one end of the terrace: it contains the different social areas, which seem to emerge from nature, a suggestion reinforced by an exposed rock that is used as a

CASA SOC-KMOLÓ

division between the living room and the master bedroom. Here, by the side of the bedroom, skylights dapple the rocks that form its walls with natural light. Behind one of the rocks is found the main bathroom, where a space for the shower, illuminated by natural light, was dug out of the same stone, a detail that integrates the two ambits of the master bedroom. On the other end of the patio there are four bungalows with a kitchenette for every two modules, which gives them a certain autonomy.

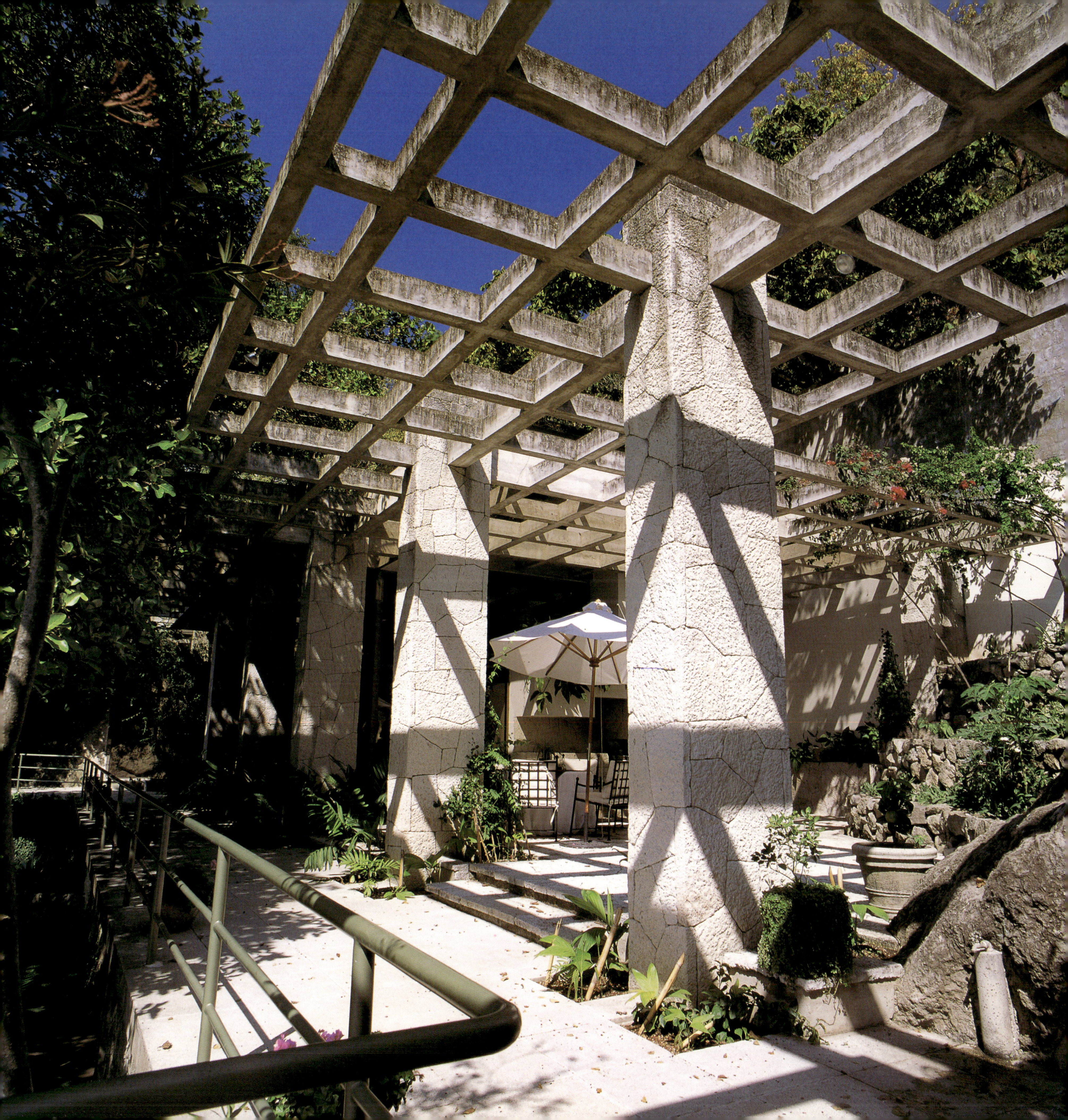

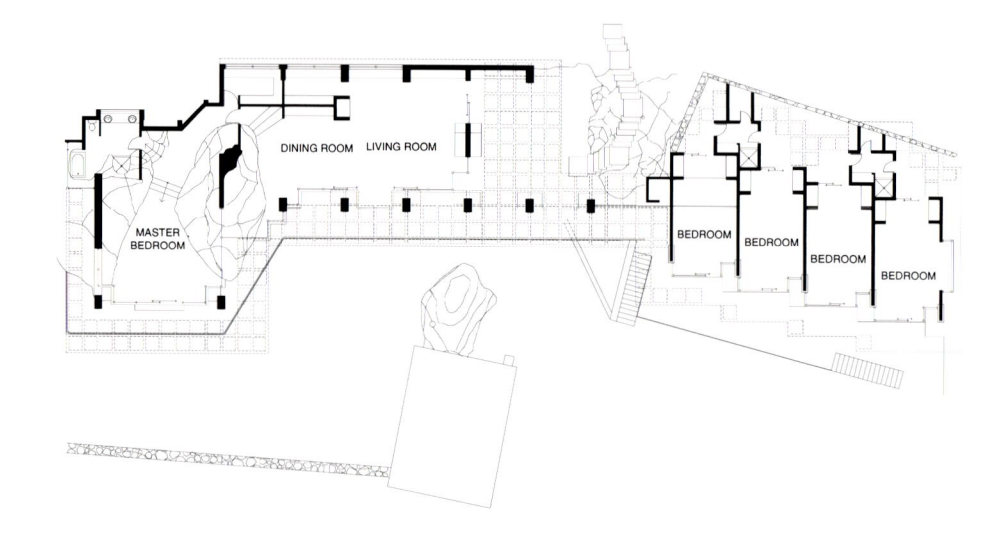

Utilizing big glass windows, whose corner joins are stripped clean to allow for the widest possible view, the architectural language of Casa Soc-Kmoló achieves an impeccable synthesis of the dialectic between contemporary materials and the natural resources of the site.

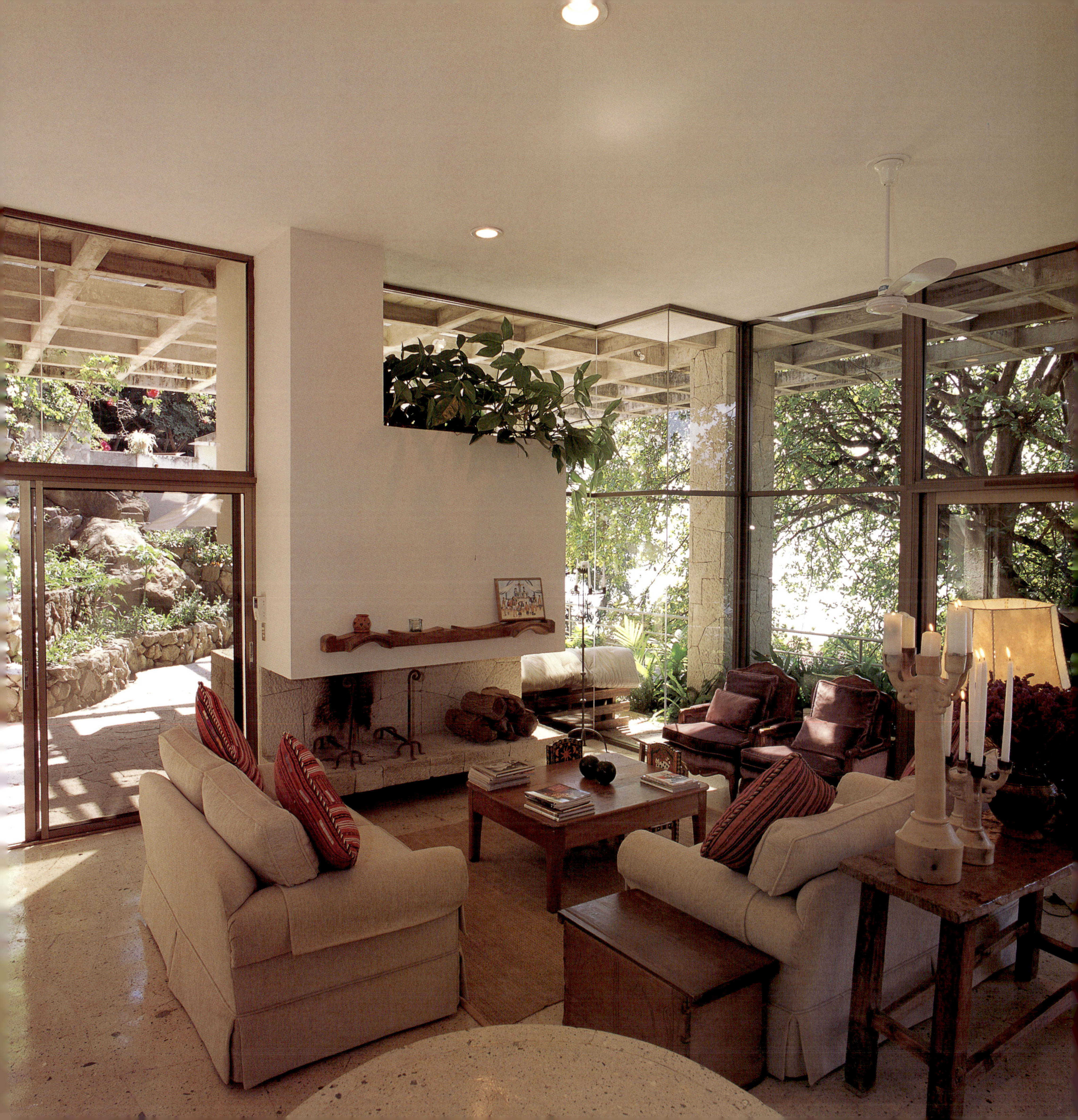

building the houses. A dry river bed that runs through the site was paved with stones to create a road that connects with all the houses and the units were spread around the terrain in way that allows each house to enjoy optimum views of the lake and the volcanoes in the background. Toward this end, the axis of each house was turned to face the shores of the lake, giving an organic character to its position, while a series

PROYECTO JUNCAYÁ

of geometrical pergolas create a grid of shadows that provides a common theme for the different volumes and gives a strong unity to the whole complex. A number of retaining walls were built to adapt the project to the topography. Made of local stone, they give a regional air to the complex. With shingle roofs, and interiors and windows of cypress wood, the spaces within each house are organized around a chimney which provides warmth for all of the social spaces. The corner joins of the windows which look out to the lake were left bare in order to give a lighter character to the general volume and remove visual obstructions to the beautiful vistas.

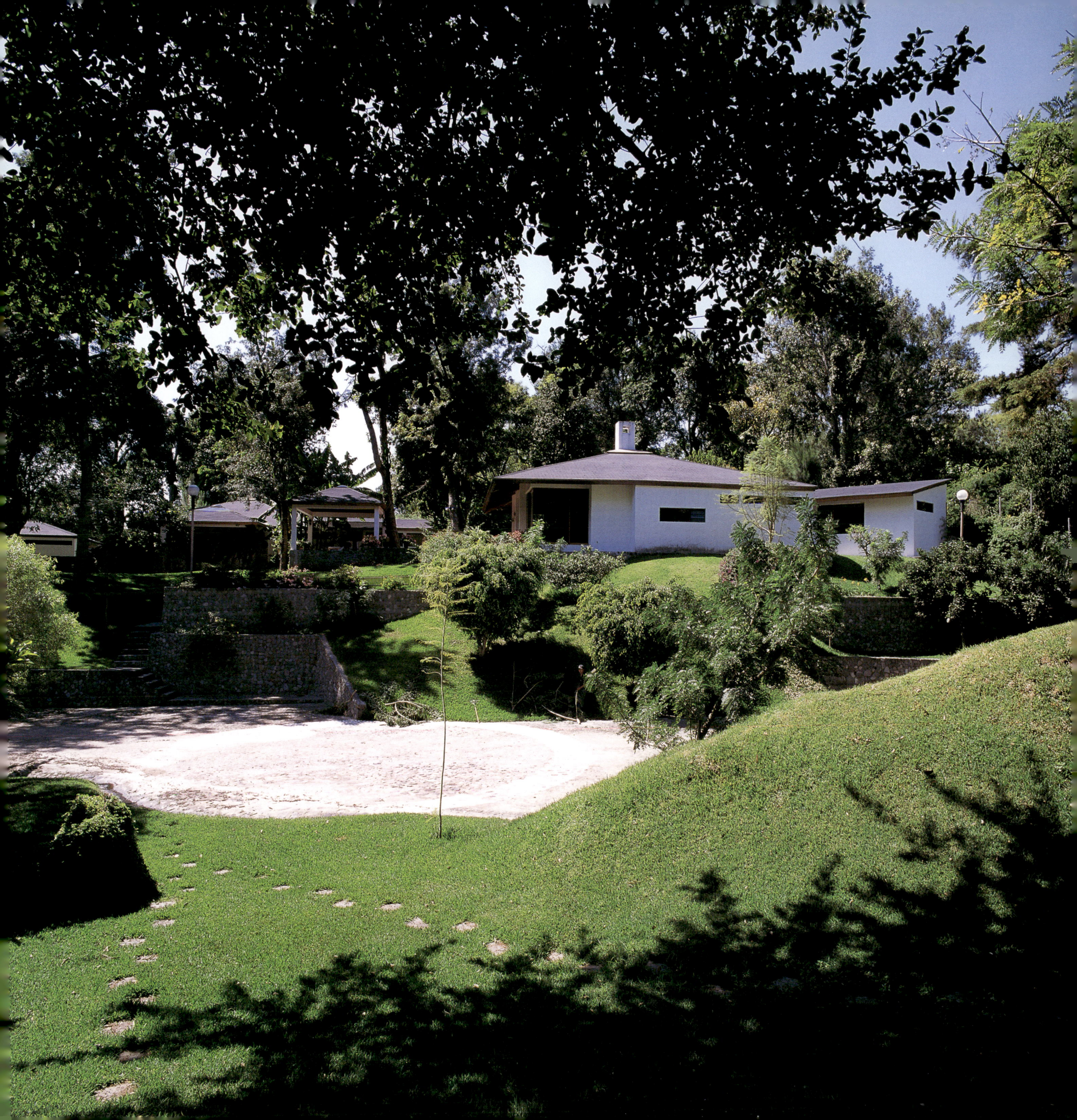

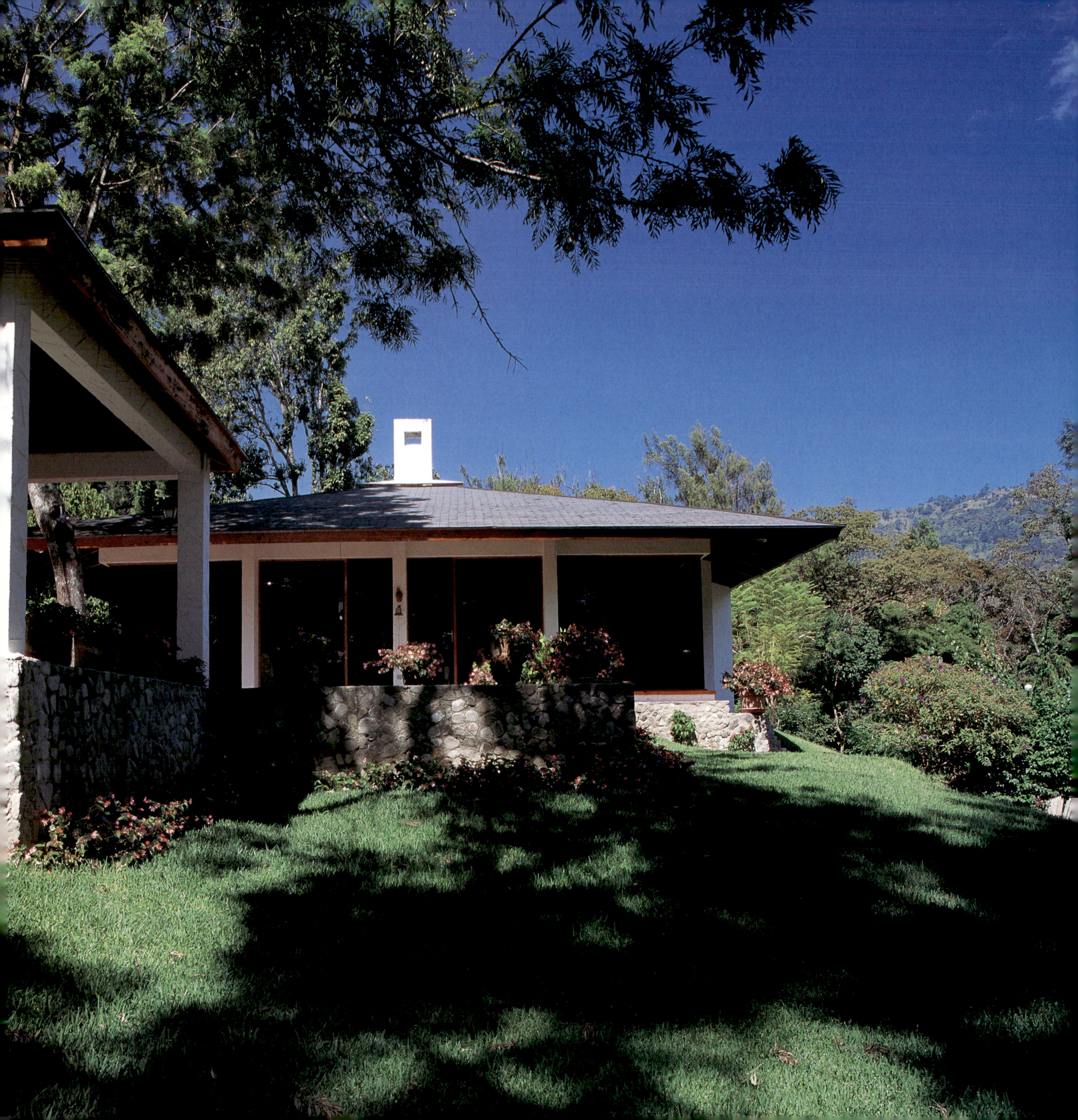

LAGO DE
ATITLAN

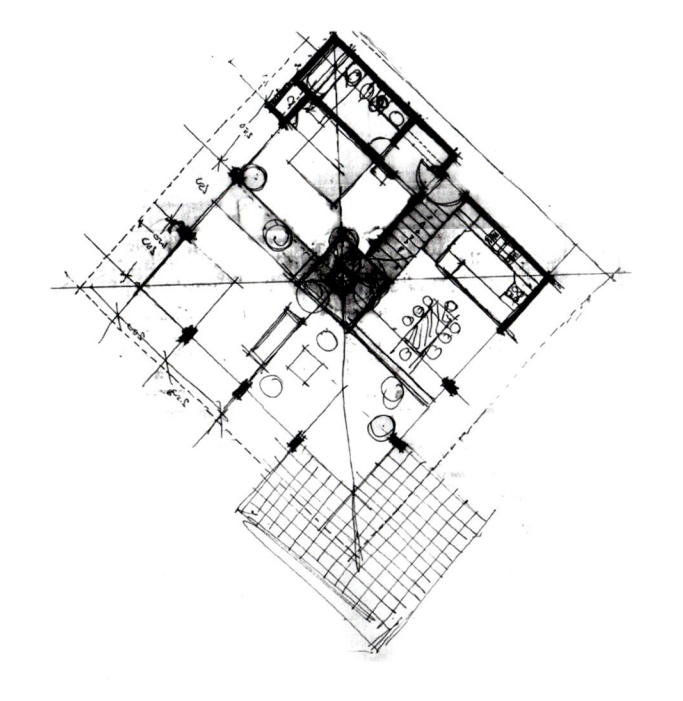

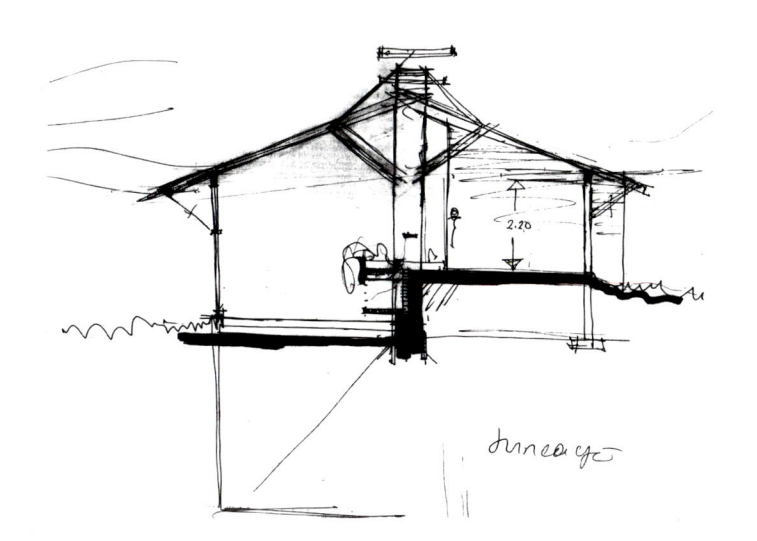

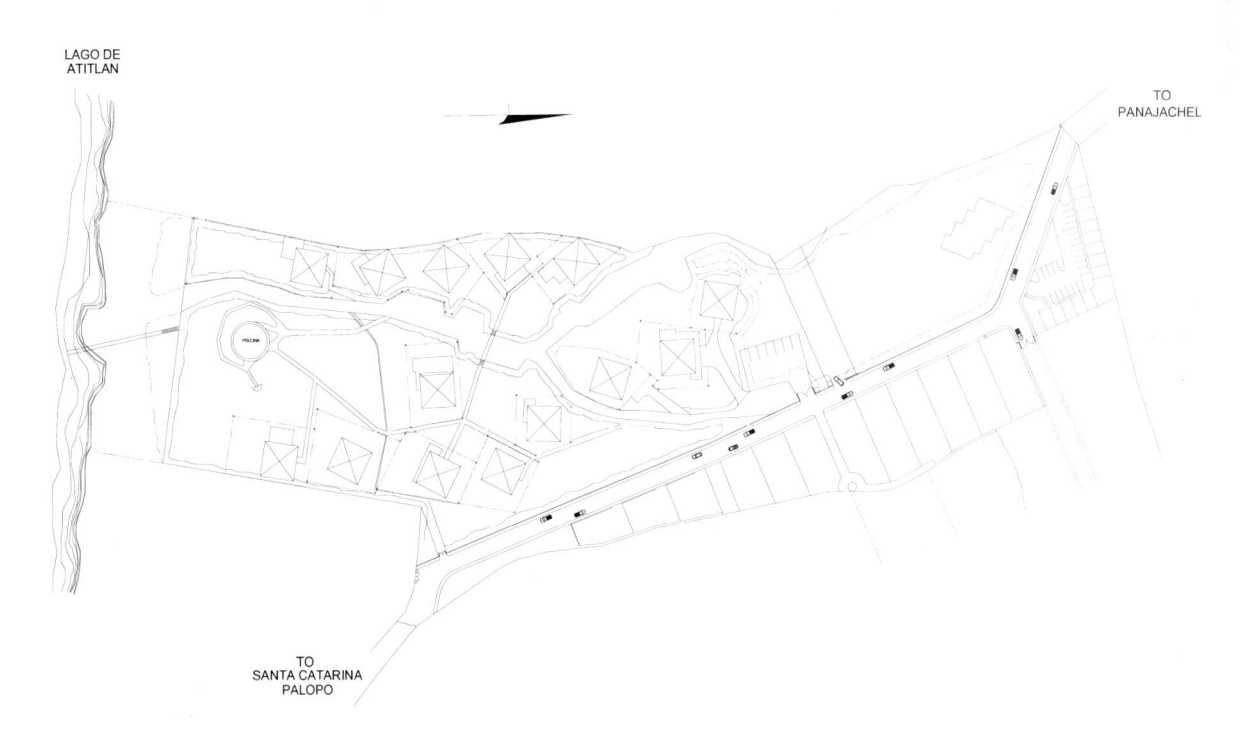

TO
PANAJACHEL

TO
SANTA CATARINA
PALOPO

seisarquitectos

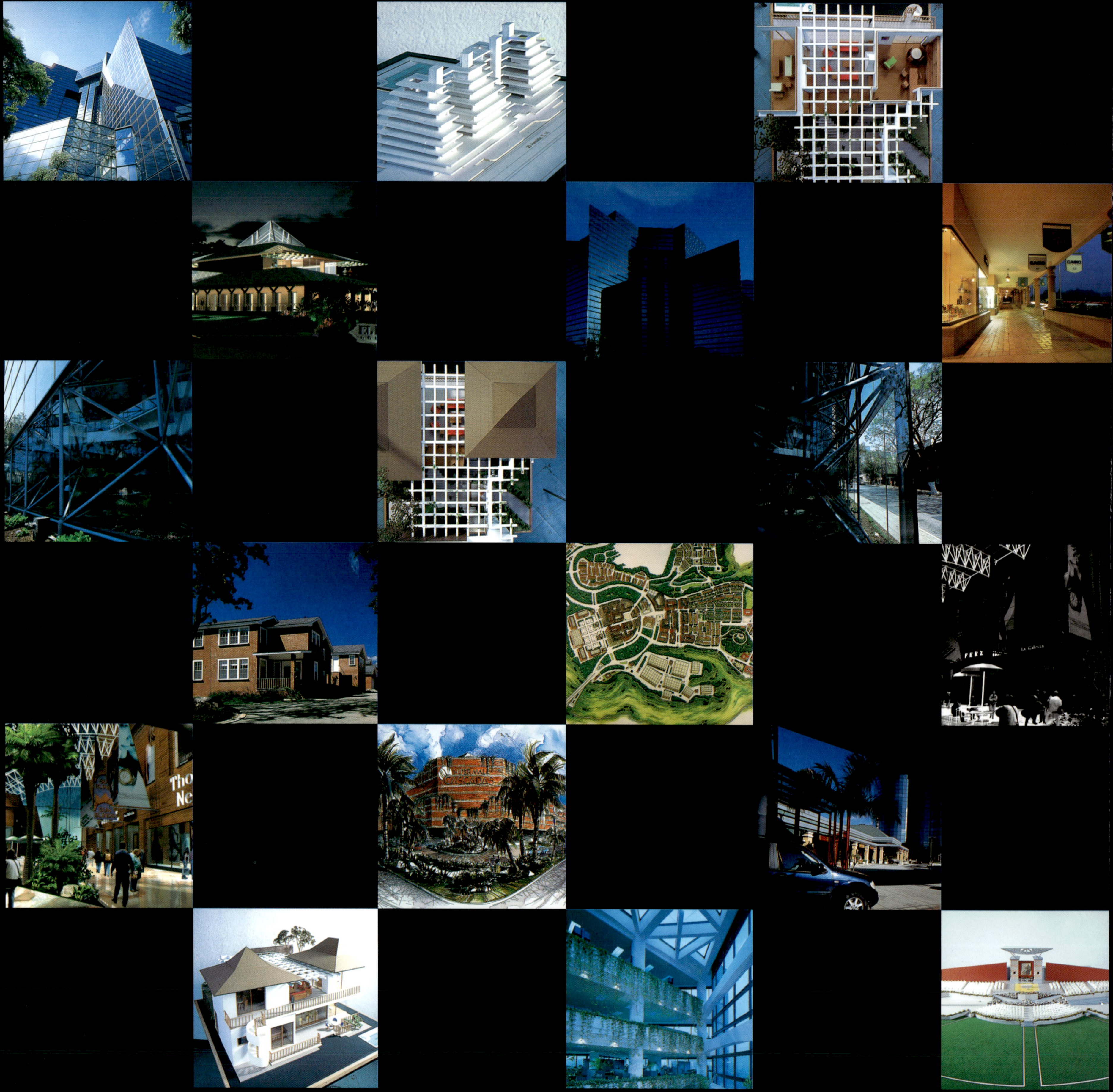

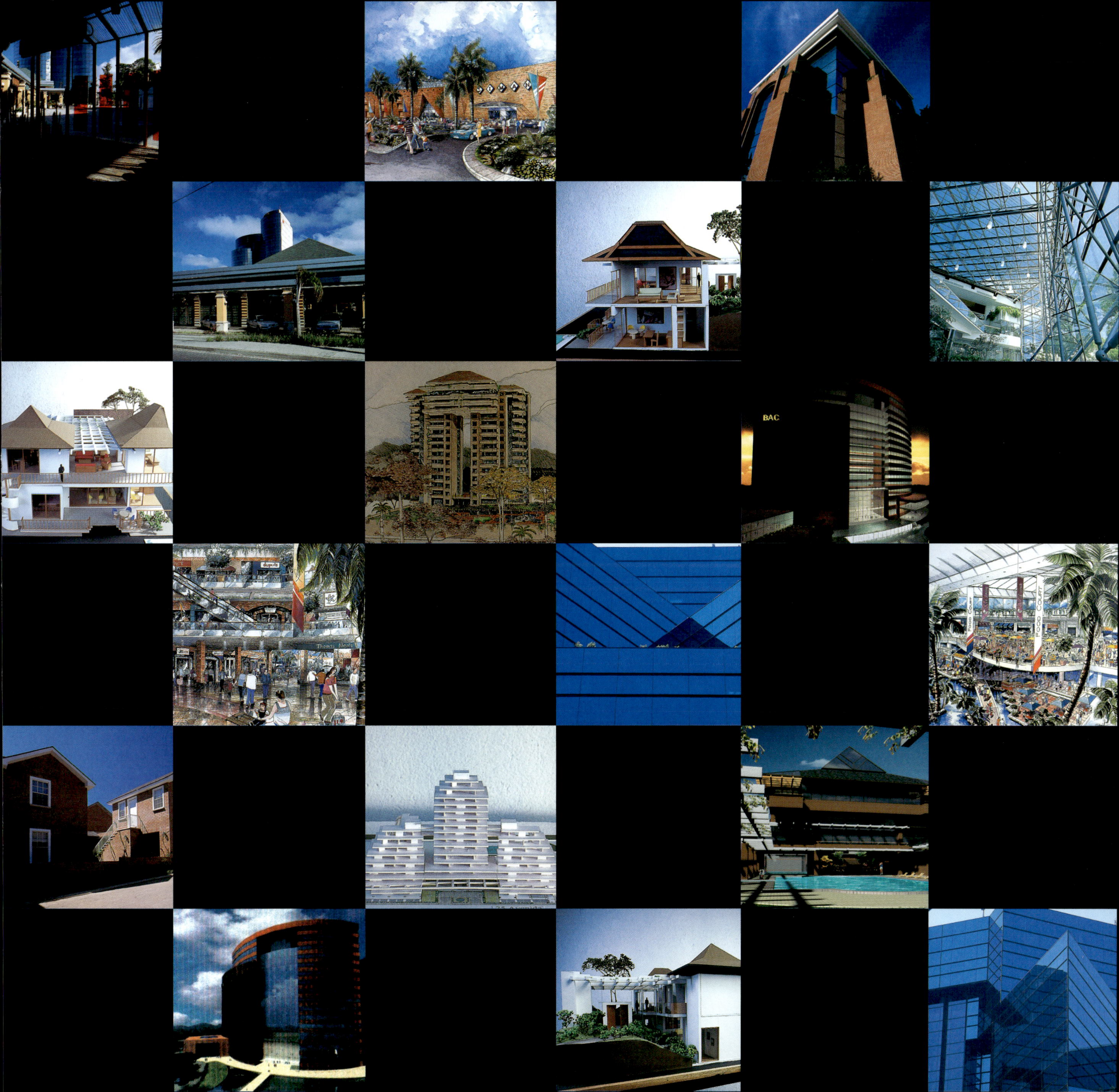
BAC

Minondo & Giesemann and Solares & Lara. Few buildings have the high impact of this singular work: its design surprises, from whatever angle you look at it. Situated in the "Zona Viva" of Guatemala City, Atlantis is an urban landmark that resembles a crystal monument by virtue of its broken forms that are sculpturally combined, creating multiple effects of light and shadow and different reflections of the blue sky on its surface. Completely clad in a reflective double glazing, Atlantis has a siphon-type system of

ATLANTIS BUILDING
solares & lara / minondo & giesemann

ventilation, which creates an effective natural ventilation through a number of strategically-placed apertures that evacuate hot air. Novel and daring concepts were harmoniously incorporated into the design of every aspect of the building, obtaining, as a result, a clean and dynamic architecture that reflects contemporary design trends. The building has five basement floors and 19 floors above street level. Its towers, turned at a 45 degree angle to the line of the street, and the terraces set on different levels create a set of salients that grant great originality to the overall form.

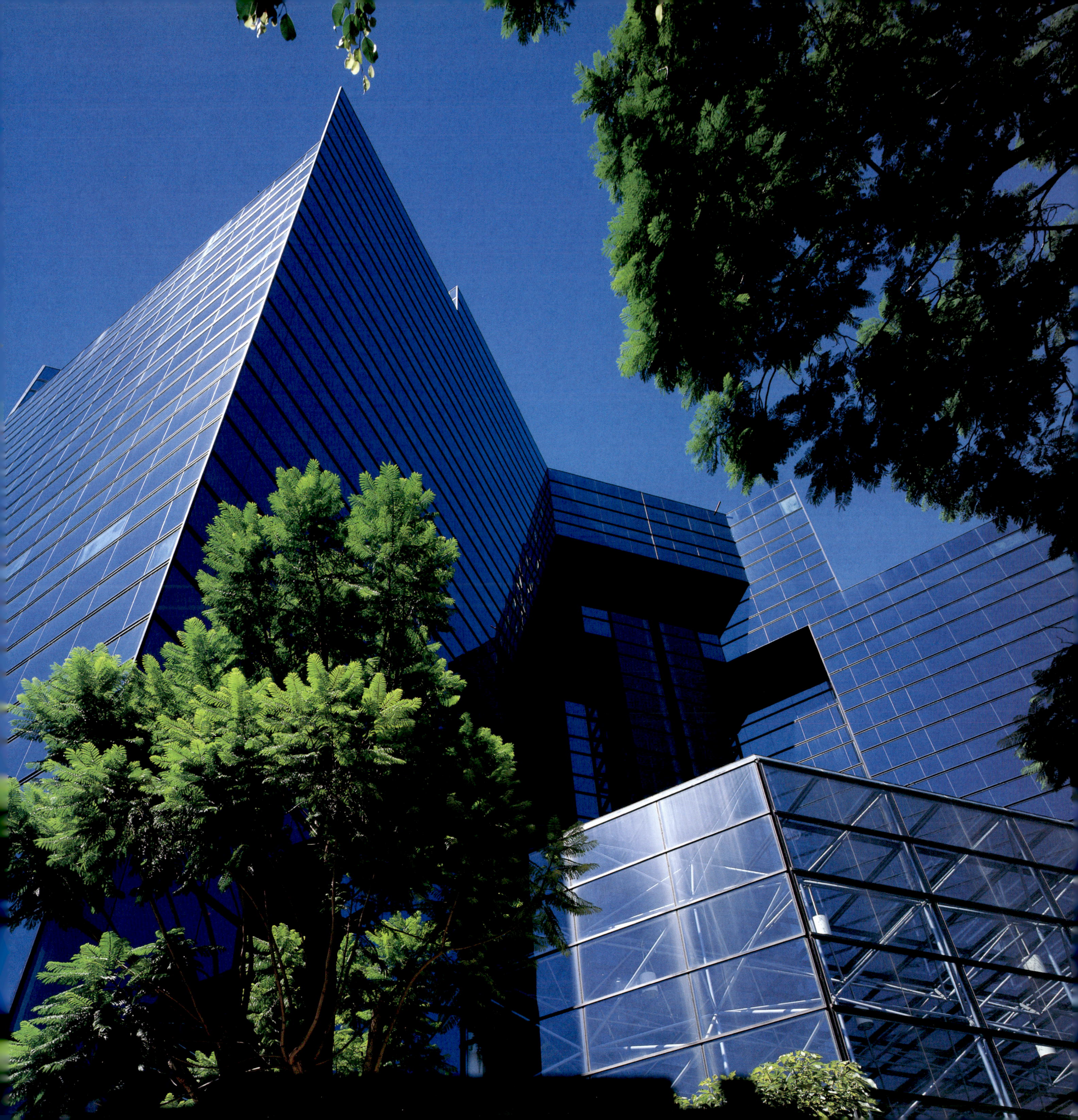

A good example of the leading-edge technology which has been applied to the building is found in the spatial stereostructure that covers the central atrium: it enables the tempered glass roof to span wide spaces between the columns without undue stresses, despite the weight of the structure. In addition, the curtain wall contains a nearly imperceptible strip of ventilation in the usual system of anchoring, while the window supports were later put on the market as a new product line by the U.S. company that fabricated it for the building. Atlantis is one of the first structures in Central America to incorporate the concept of the "intelligent building": it counts upon a totally-computerized central monitoring system to reduce the risk of accidents and hazardous situations.

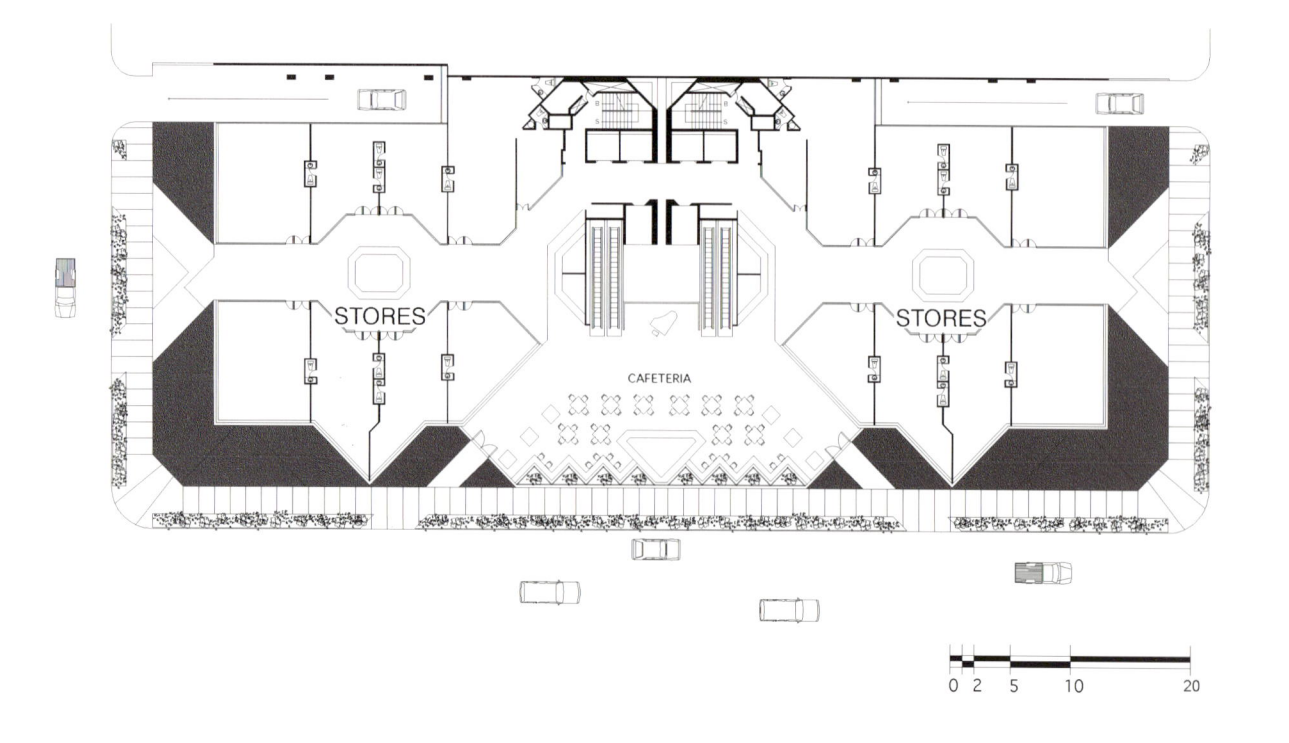

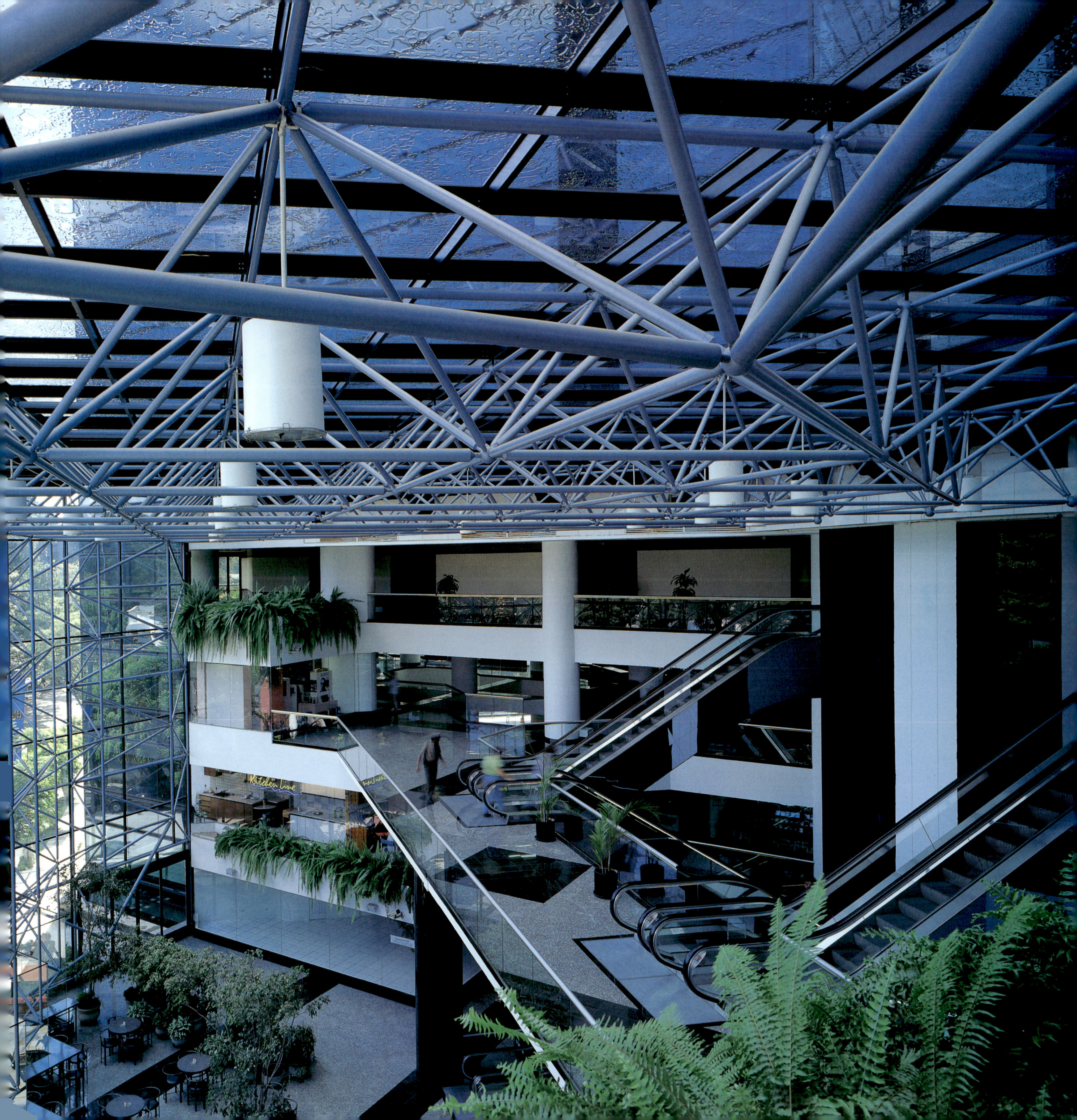
Kitchen Line

Kitchen Line

OFFICES OFFICES

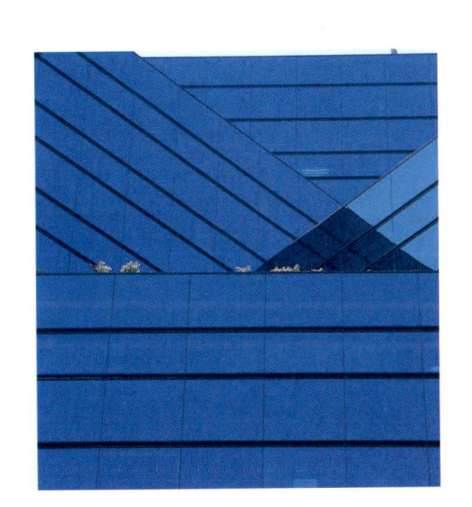

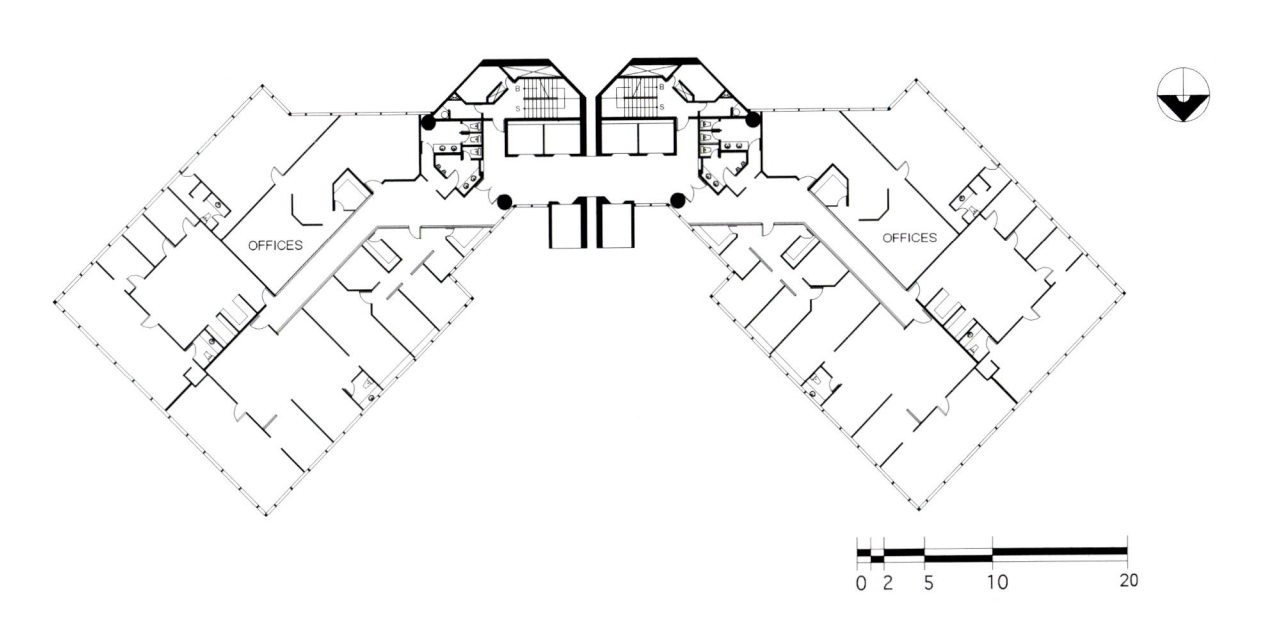

0 2 5 10 20

the brick bastions open spaces for other garden areas, whose vegetation will eventually cover part of the walls. The original design of the building consists of a solid base that seems to vanish as it rises, while the solidity of the brick in the harsh surface gives way to the green glass that completes its covering. The latter material was chosen to reflect the color of the forest that surrounds the building and also to provide climatic protection.

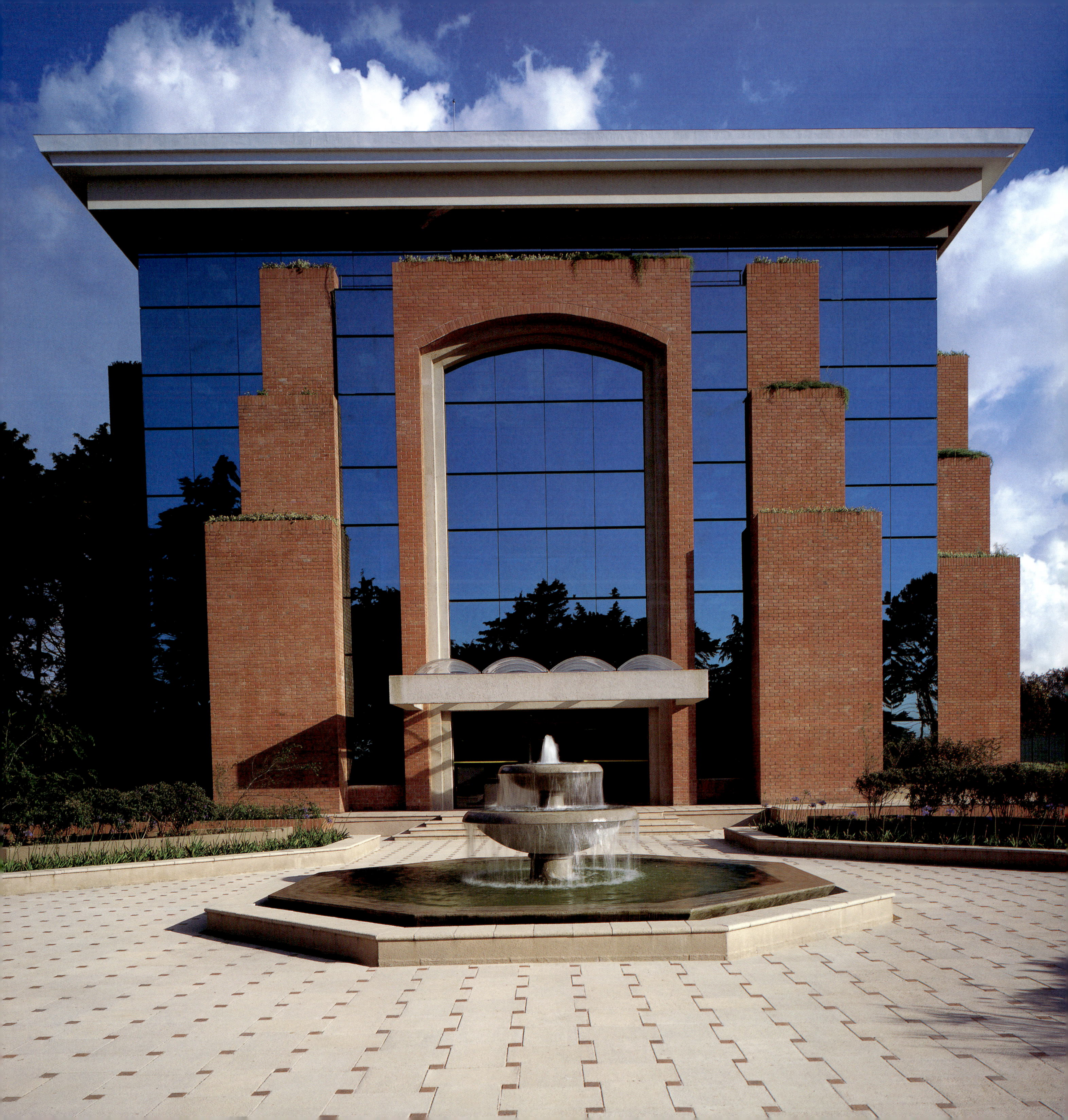

In addition, the roof was covered with an asphalt shingle of the same color that harmonizes with the crowns of the trees and gives it a fresher appearance. Originally intended to be a corporate headquarters, the interior spaces of the Cervecería building are flexible enough to permit subdivisions into smaller units for other kinds of offices. In mechanical terms, the building has a water purification system that enables it to recycle 45% of the water it uses and an emergency electricity plant that keeps the building functioning when there are power cuts. Due to the climate of the region in which it is located, it was not necessary to include air-conditioning, but its efficient natural ventilation acts like a chimney, evacuating the hot air that forms in its interior.

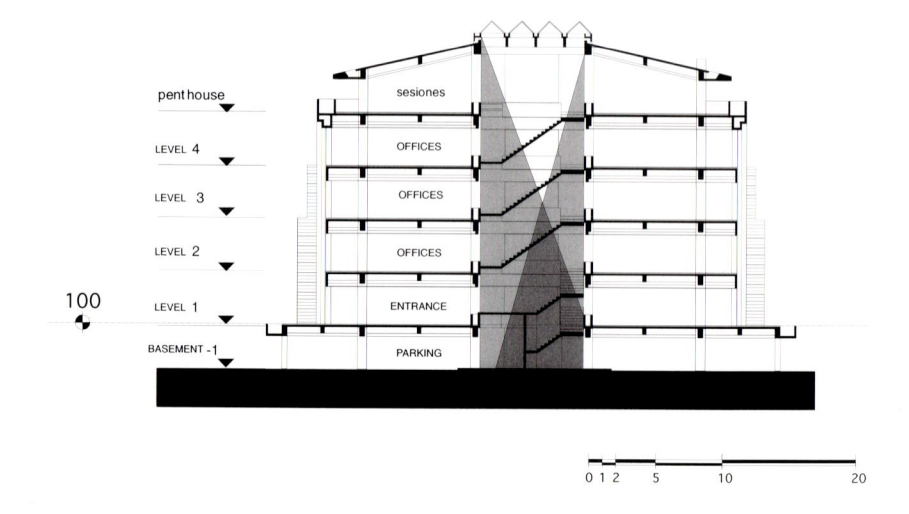

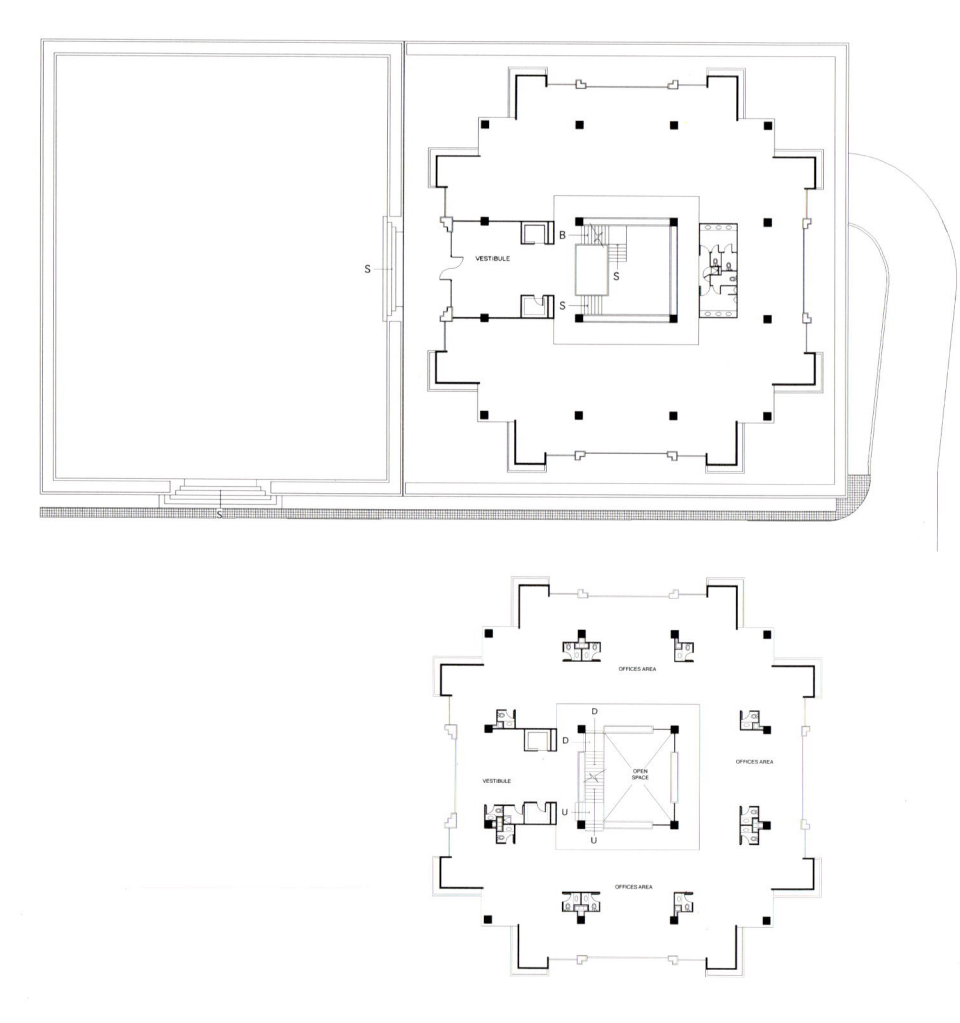

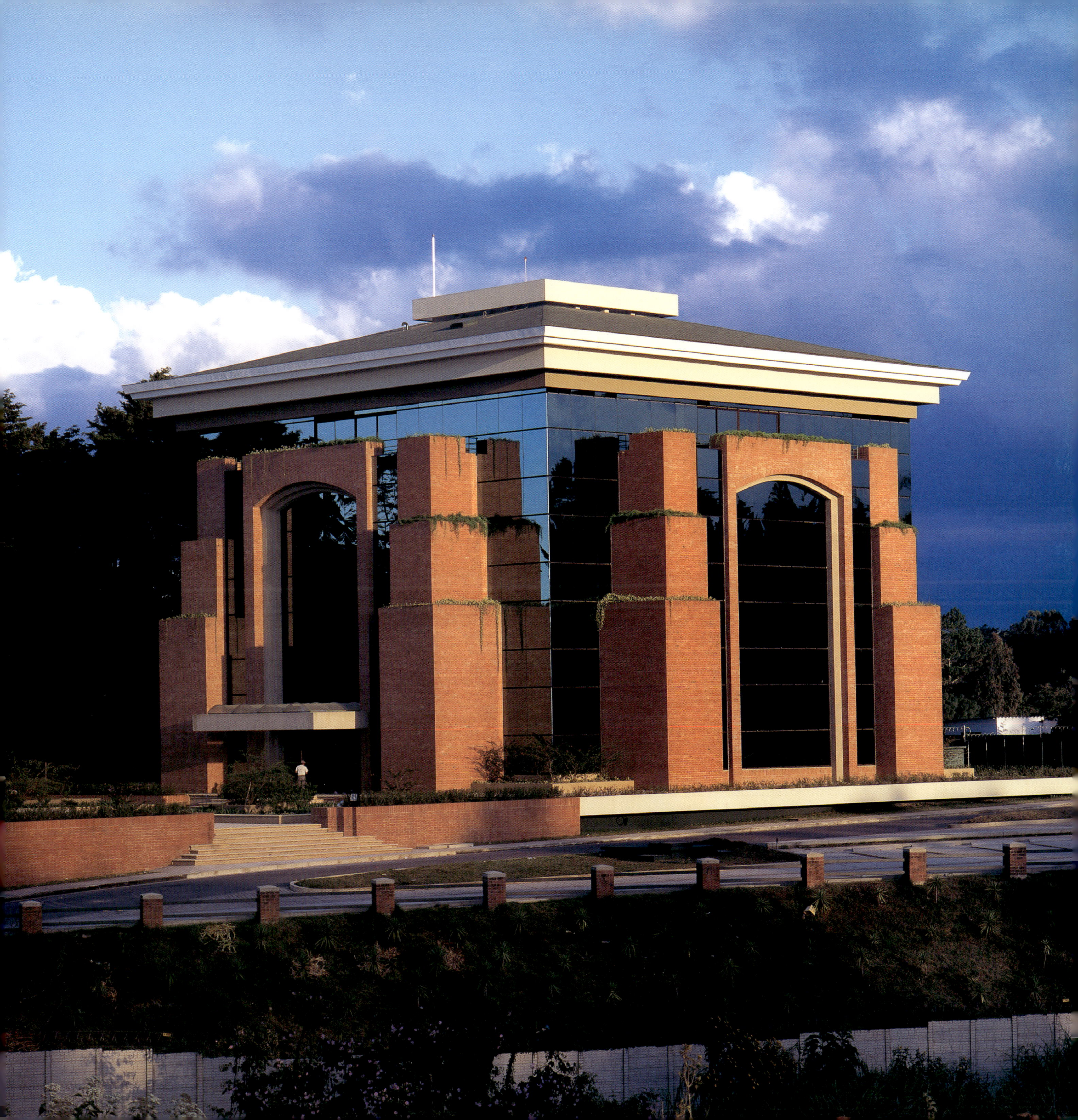

Built on a road that will be the main artery of this big new development on the outskirts of Guatemala City, Calle Real Condado Concepción represents the introduction of an urban touch to an eminently rural zone. With the idea of creating an avenue in which pedestrians will have priority over cars, the original concept of the master plan shows the influence of the theories of the "New Urbanism", which is based on the ideal of making different aspects of city life more human. The Calle Real Concepción consists of a linear-shaped building with ten store premises set along a wide corridor with flower beds between the columns of the

CALLE REAL CONDADO CONCEPCIÓN

portico. It is flanked, on both ends, by two-story buildings, one currently occupied by an Italian restaurant and the other by an art gallery. Decorative bricks were used in the floors of the corridor to form different designs that give it a special character, while the names of the different stores are shown through a system of banners, which harmonize with the restrained nature of the architecture. With a structure of concrete and steel and tile roofs, the building employs an architectural language characterized by a repeated use of cornices, moldings, capitals and hammered concrete details that reflects the post-modernist concepts of its design.

Illumination is provided by lamps manufactured in the city of Antigua Guatemala that are a reinterpretation of the traditional street-lamps of colonial architecture. When the project as a whole is completed, the urban sense of the complex will become more pronounced, since the pedestrian traffic that flows through the different shops will become bigger and bigger as the district grows.

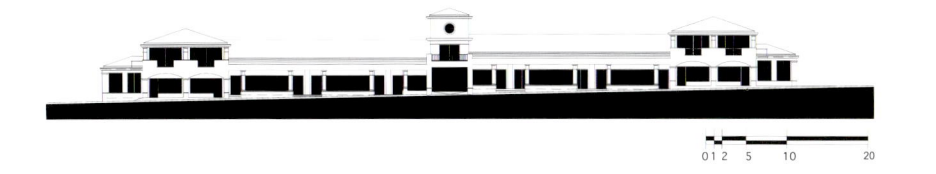

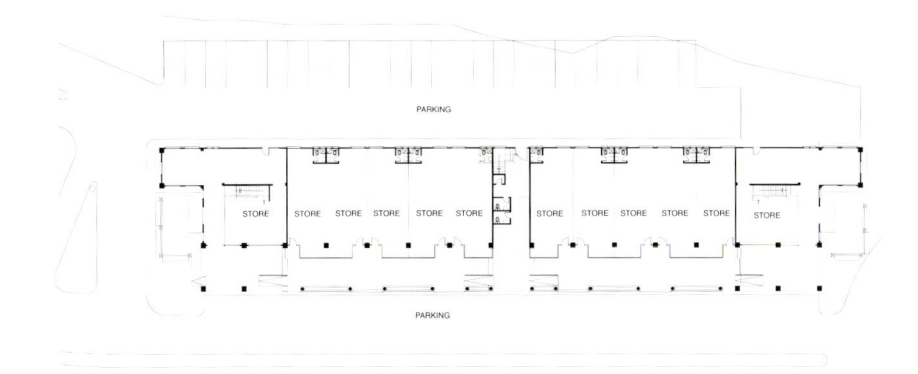

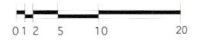

of the most important locations in Guatemala City, the Plaza de los Próceres, the project developed a series of conceptual ideas and different alternatives. Some time later, the Mercedes Benz automobile company installed a café for its clients in its show rooms. This café, which was run by the entrepreneur Emilio Méndez, became the main focus of the project, which gave rise to the idea of including similar cafés in the show rooms of other car dealers. Today, Plaza Obelisco (Obelisk Plaza) has become a major attraction

PLAZA OBELISCO
tinoco & porras

for the young people of the city. The structure of the buildings had to have a relatively modest cost, since the shopping center is intended to operate for only fifteen years. In addition, it was necessary to design a structure that could be erected quickly, so that the participating businesses would be able to display their products as soon as possible. The design concept is based on an architecture that uses concrete columns with a steel structure that can be dismantled, asphalt shingle roofs and decorative brick In the passageways, which was used for the first time in a random pattern of diverse colors.

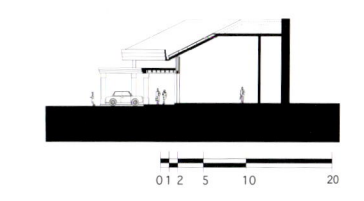

Moldings and capitals were used in the car parks and passageways to give the shopping center a warmer image, while the fronts oriented towards the two highways outside – the Avenida Reforma and the Boulevard los Próceres – employ a great deal of glass to reflect the passing cars, thus giving the building a modern character that is suitable to its functions.

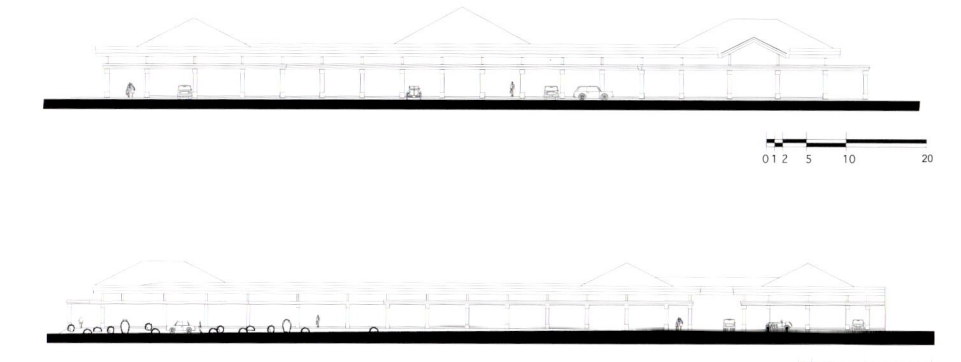

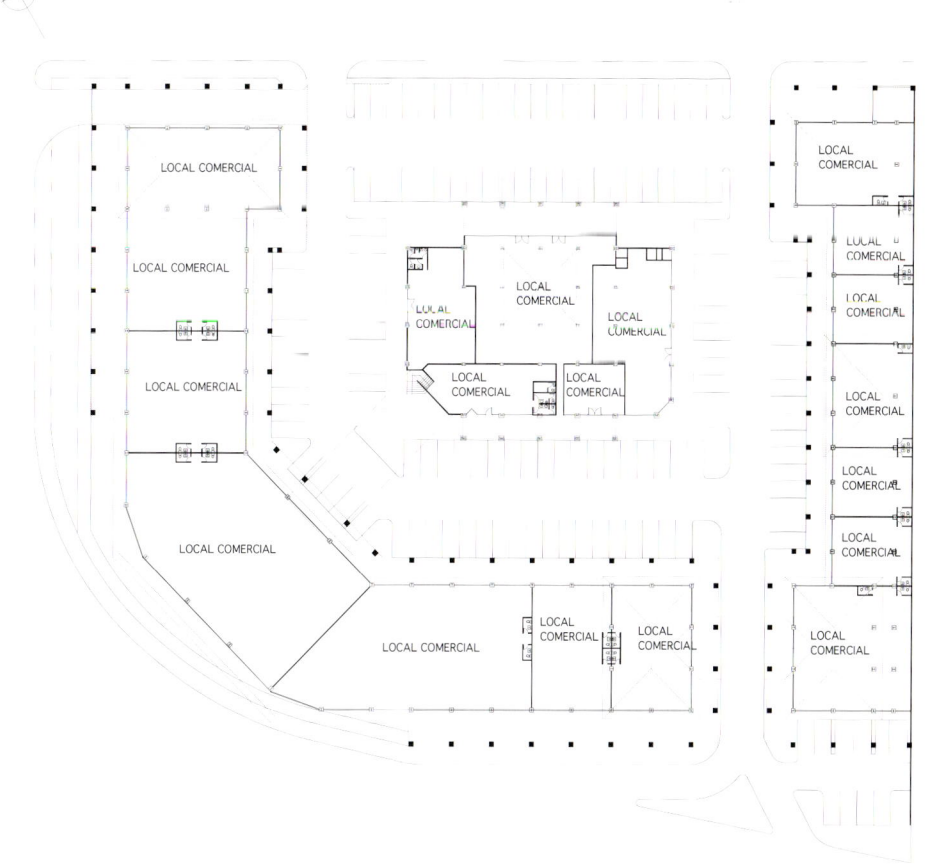

seisarquitectos/workinprogress

EL RECREO GOLF CLUB
Guatemala

Winner of First Prize in the Design Contest for the Club

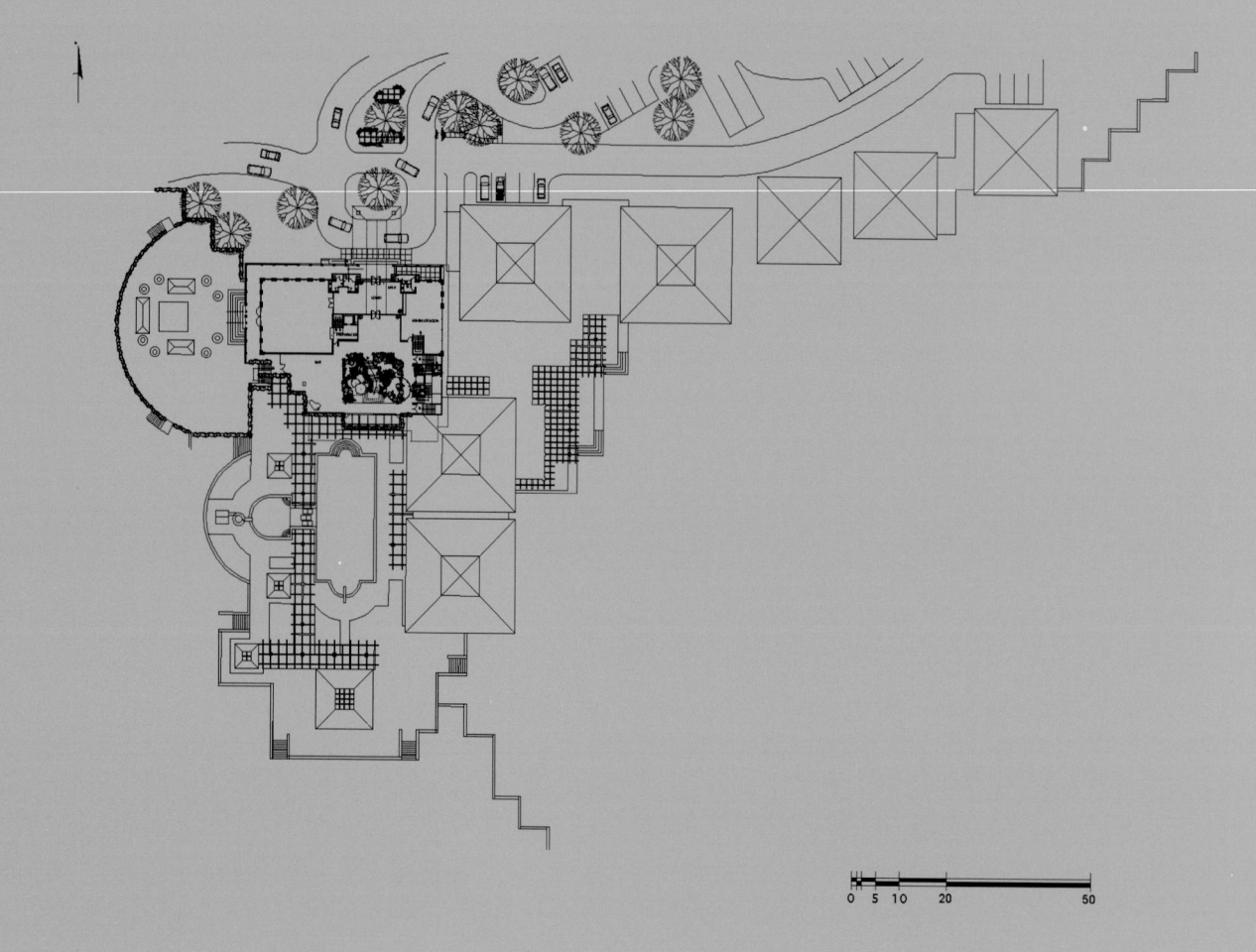

Based on the geographical location, the topography of the place, the environmental setting and the landscape that surrounds it, the design concept for the architecture of El Recreo Golf Club establishes a link with the vernacular architecture of the estate-owners' houses of the coffee plantations of the region in which it is situated. The ample corridors and the extended eaves protect the different areas of circulation, while the large four-sided sloping roofs provide a regional touch, without detriment to the very comfortable and luxurious interior ambits. The efficient distribution of spaces in the interior results in a play of forms and volumes that are seen from the outside; each with a majestic and seignorial character. As a starting point, the lobby leads the member to the dressing rooms in a direct and private way, welcoming him at the same time to the swimming pool and outdoor recreation areas through the exuberant vegetation of the central garden. From here, the member who has not come for sports, and his guests as well, easily reach the bar or the dining room on the upper floor, where they can enjoy views of the lake, the forest and the golf course. In addition, the recreational areas are clearly separated from each other by screens of trees and gardens on different levels, which create a visual and acoustic protection. The golf club and the caddies shack, as well as the garage for the carts, are strategically placed in order to provide a quick and unobtrusive service. The design proposal allows for the effective functioning of the club's infrastructure of service, so that members and their guests may take full advantage of all the comforts and facilities of the installations. Finally, the architectural design offers the possibility of the building an area of squash courts and a hall for social events in a subsequent stage of development. There are also plans for a structure made up of columns and pergolas that will support a light, transparent roof for the swimming pools.

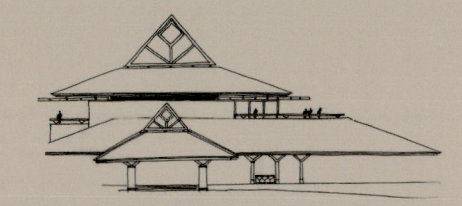

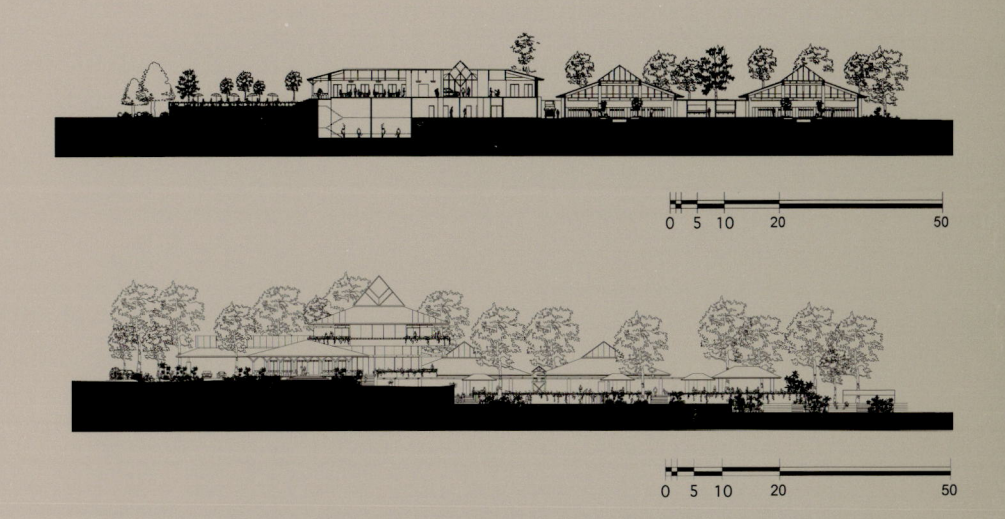

BANCO AGRÍCOLA
El Salvador

Project that won First Prize in the International competition sponsored by the Banco Agrícola of El Salvador.

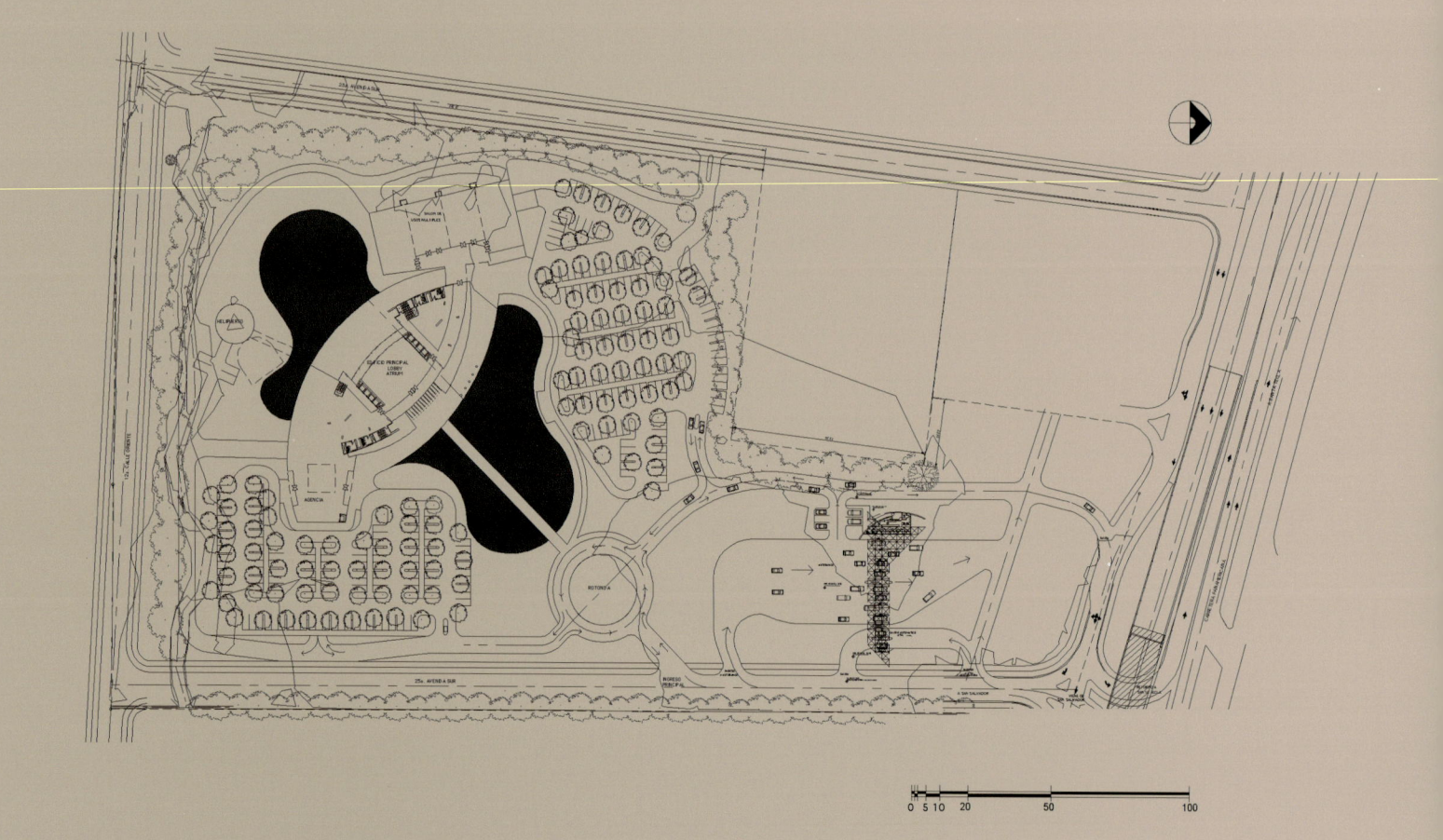

Without question the most outstanding private bank in Central America, the Banco Agrícola Comercial has, in a matter of years, won an international recognition for its efficient management and ambitious plans. In March, 1999, the executives of the bank organized a competition for the design of its new corporate headquarters in Nueva San Salvador. As a result, local and foreign firms submitted their proposals in July of that year and the first prize was awarded to the firm Seis Arquitectos S.A. The architectural proposal was elaborated on the basis of the institution's requirements and, for that reason, took into account its location and access, the neighborhood setting and landscape, climate and exposure to sunlight, among other factors. The design concept sought to establish a relationship between the institution, the future building and a vernacular symbol of Salvador. In this way, the ogival-shaped petal of the national flower became the matrix which inspired the floor plan of the main building. As the written description of the project points out, "the resulting volume is impressive, majestic, symbolic and, at the same time, very efficient for the distribution of the different spaces which the program requires." In fact, the curvilinear form softens the block and makes it more natural, integrating the building into the green areas and the artificial lake that surround it.

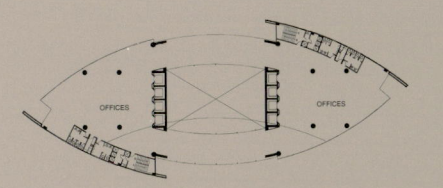

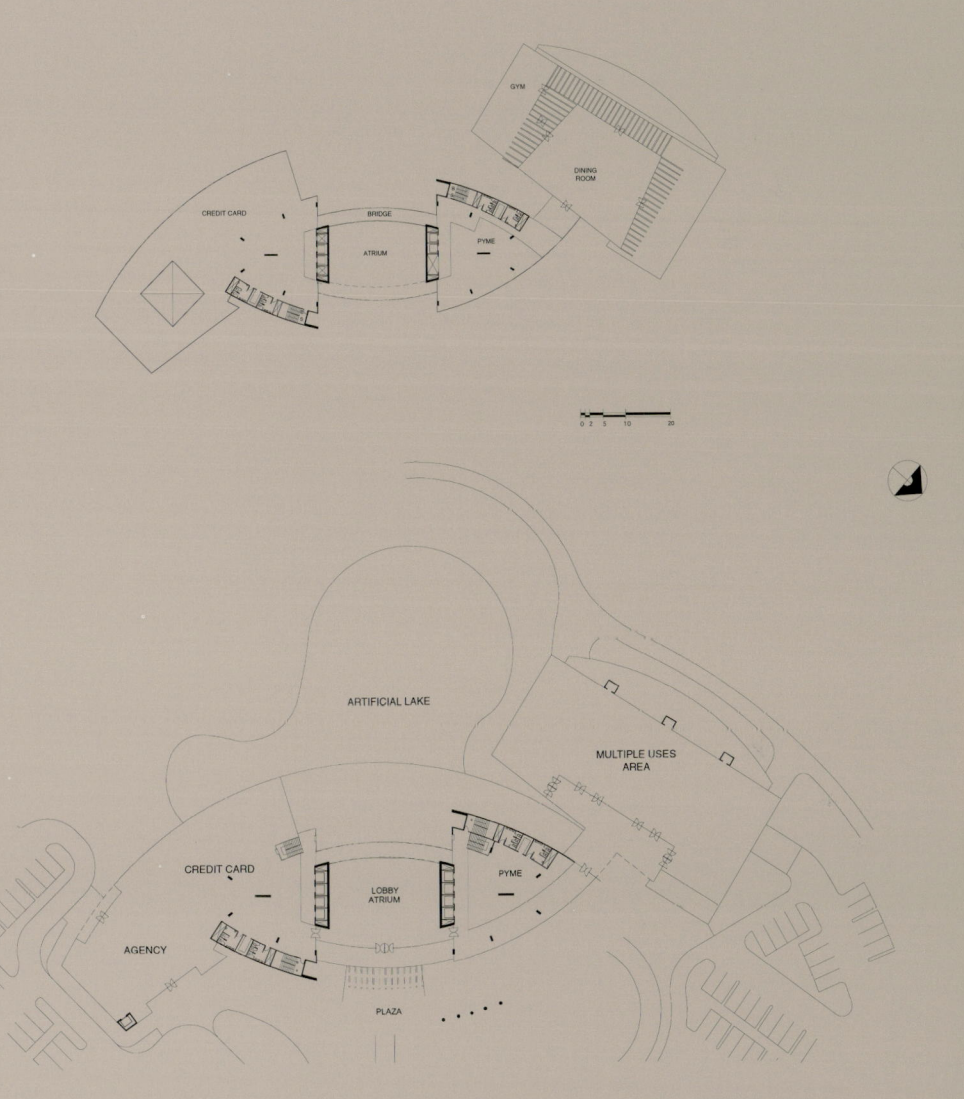

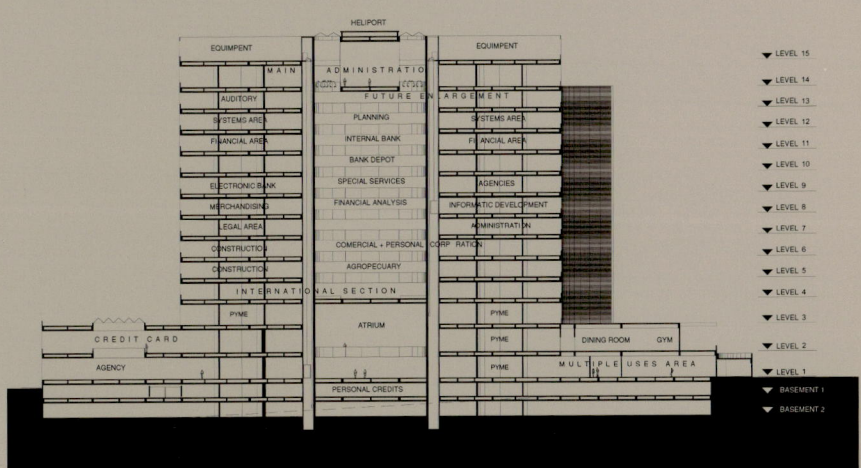

LAS CASCADAS HYPERMALL
El Salvador

The Hypermall will be developed in the city of San Salvador, on the road to Ciudad Merliot, on a site which is known as El Espino. This Hypermall will be focused around a supermarket which, in contrast with the usual design of supermalls, will have a portico on its main front. This portico will be covered by a series a white canvases stretched over stainless steel tensors and posts. Instead of having a solid, closed front, as is customary in these kinds of shopping centers, the arcade and the adjacent commercial premises will provide a free and easy communication between the public areas of the shopping center and the different stores, which will stimulate a lively social activity in that area. In addition to the outside premises and the supermarket, the Hipermall will have a closed indoor mall with shops of different types and an area of restaurants or "foodcourt", which will also be covered by stretched white canvases. Parking for this shopping center will consist of one ground-level car park, with trees to provide shade and a green area, and an additional car park in the basement. In the latter a number of trees will be planted, whose foliage will ascend to the upper level, thus providing a strong touch of nature.

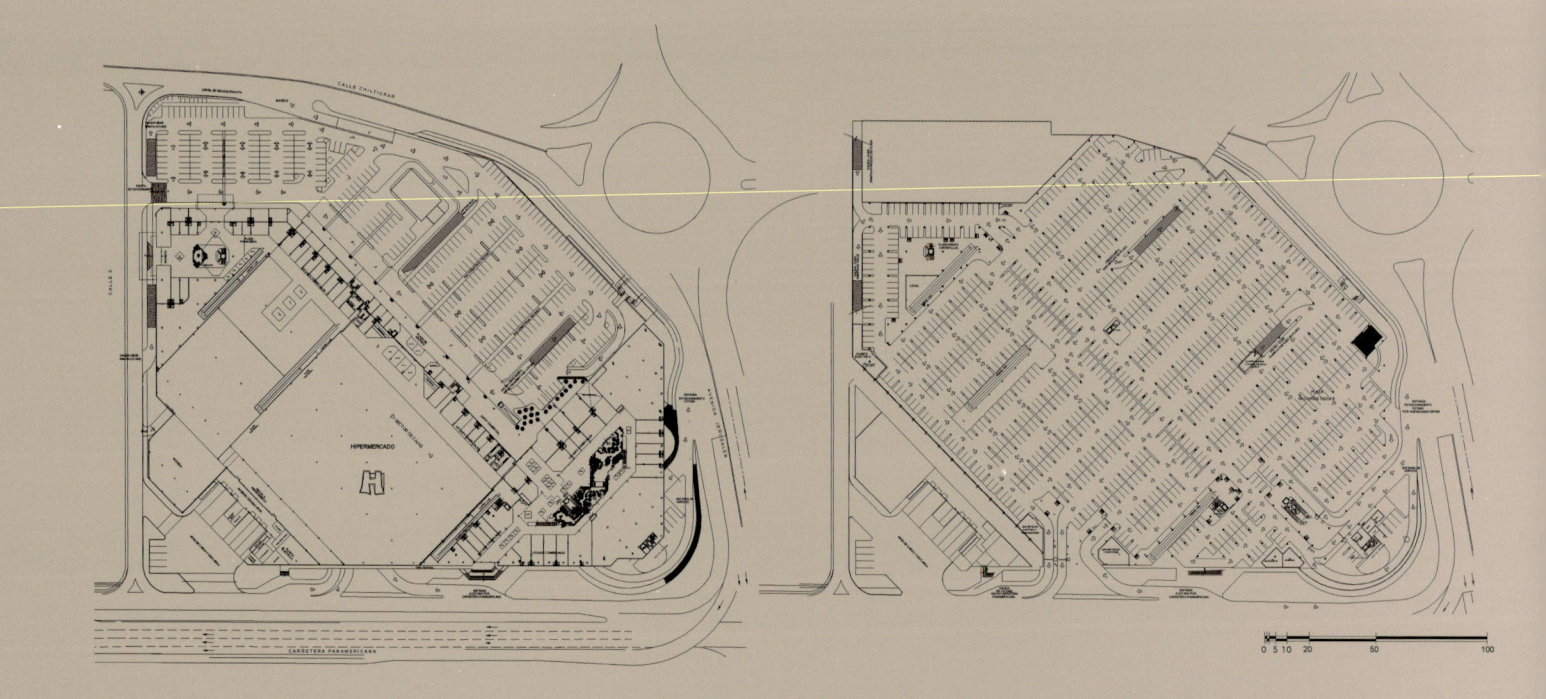

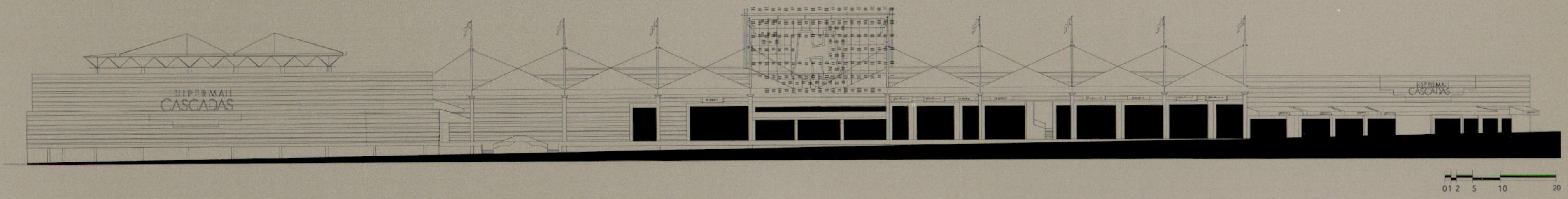
HIPERMALL
CASCADAS
01 2 5 10 20

01 2 5 10 20

HIPER MALL
CASCADAS

ESCALÓN APARTMENTS
El Salvador

The fundamental characteristic of this residential tower complex, which will be built in the capital city of El Salvador, is the system of vertical circulation, which consists of a series of elevators that will directly link the lobby to each apartment and to the penthouse area in the uppermost floors. In addition to these elevators, it will have a service elevator for each two units. All of the apartments will also have terraces with flower beds, from which one will be able to enjoy a fabulous view of the city of San Salvador, since the tower will stand one of the highest points of the capital. The design seeks to give the building a residential character, both in its form and its spatial distribution. It will also have a gymnasium, tennis courts and subterranean car parks. Echoing the atmosphere of its setting, the top of the tower will climax in a series of staggered roofs that will give a special character to this luxury apartment complex.

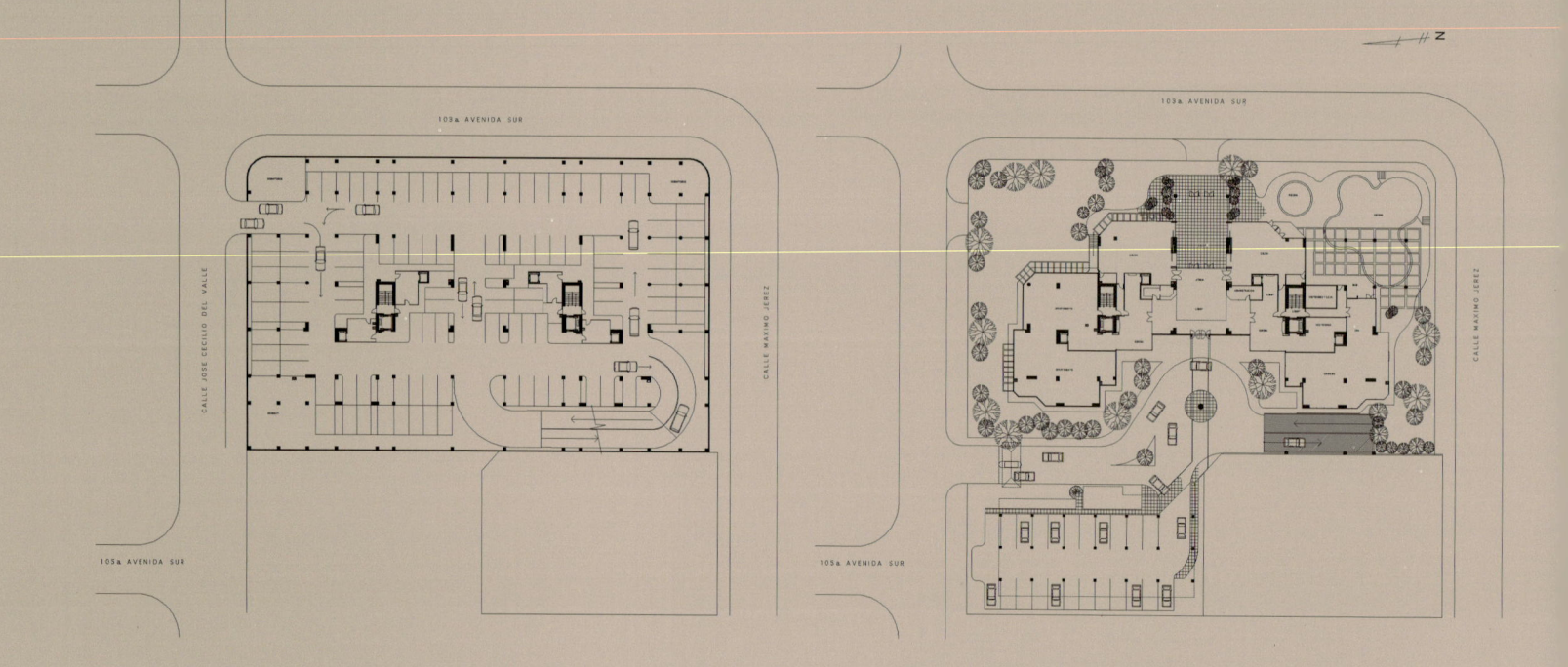

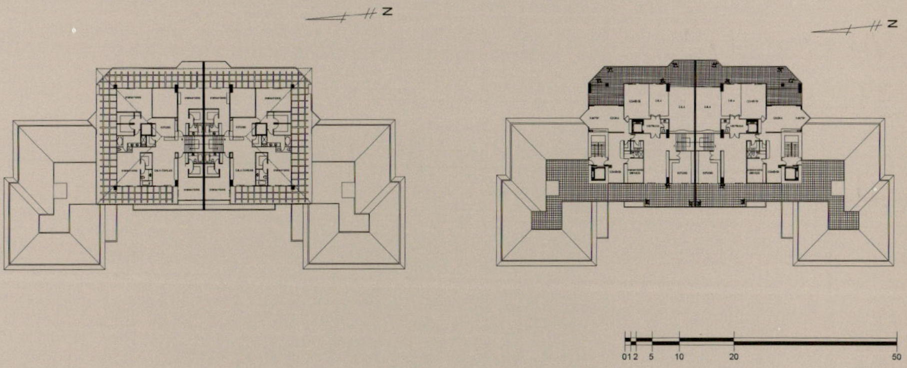
N
012
5
10
20
50

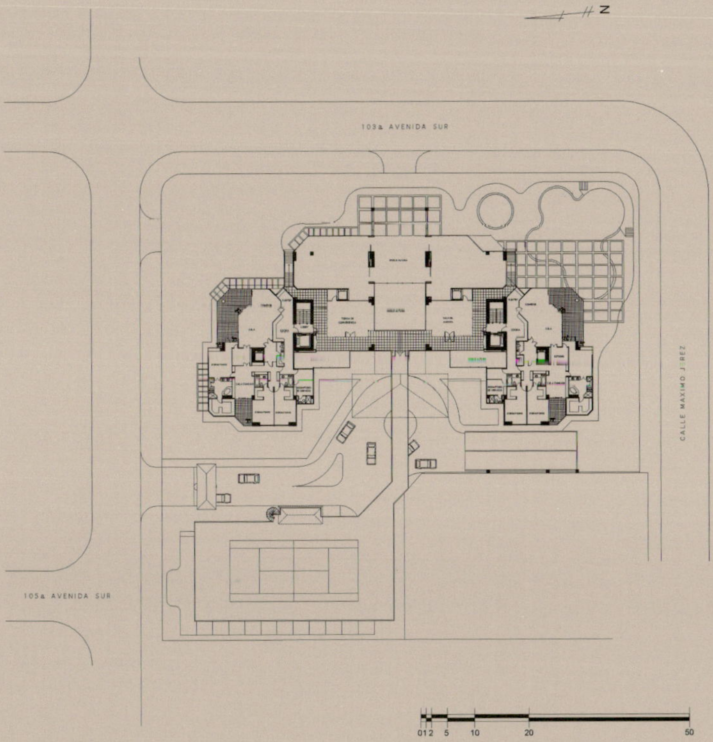
N
103a AVENIDA SUR
CALLE MAXIMO JEREZ
105a AVENIDA SUR
012
5
10
20
50

GALERÍAS MIRAFLORES SHOPPING CENTER
Guatemala

Situated on the Calzada Roosevelt, the Miraflores shopping center is divided into three main blocks: the main shopping mall, a multiplex cinema with 16 salons and commercial premises. In the original design only one end of the shopping mall was clearly visible from the main street, due to the orientation of the latter. In order to make the mall more prominent, it was decided to turn the front of this volume towards the street, so that it would more clearly stand out from its physical surroundings and face the movement of vehicles and pedestrians. With the idea of maintaining a clear unity in the design, this same inclination will be utilized in the elevation, giving more dynamism to some of the volumes in the exterior of the complex, which will be clad in a two-toned brick. To give it a unique character and not alter the architecture of the exteriors, a system of triangular pennants was designed, which will serve to signpost the different stores that will occupy this important shopping center.

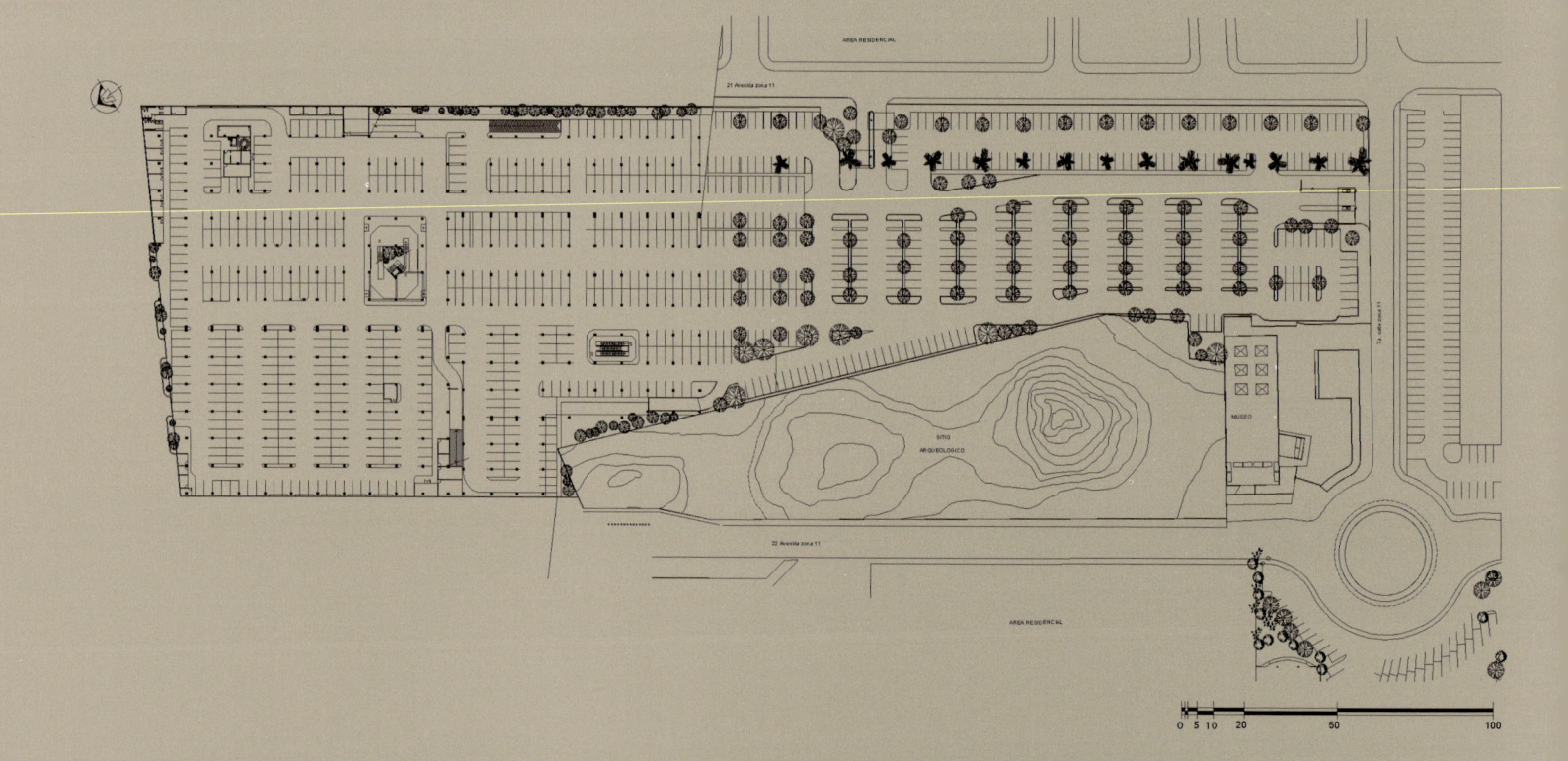

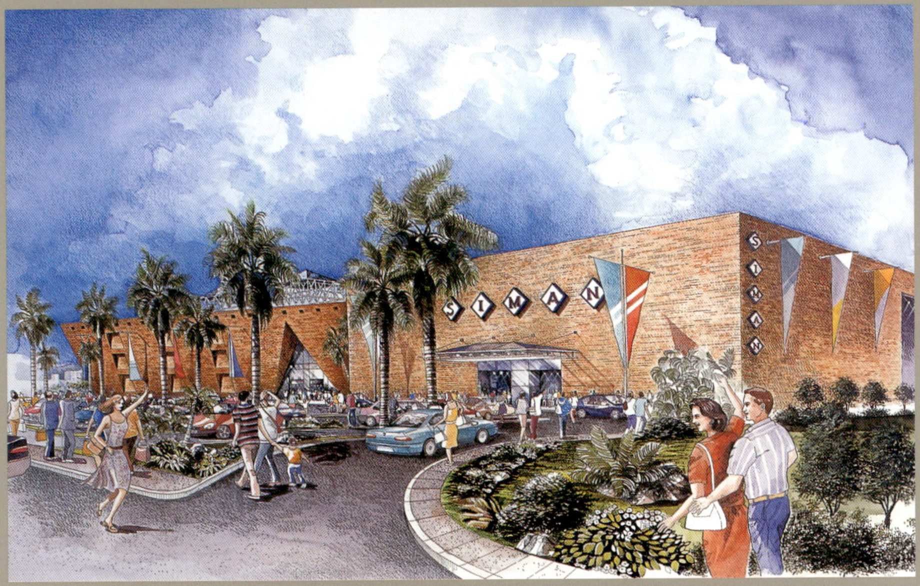

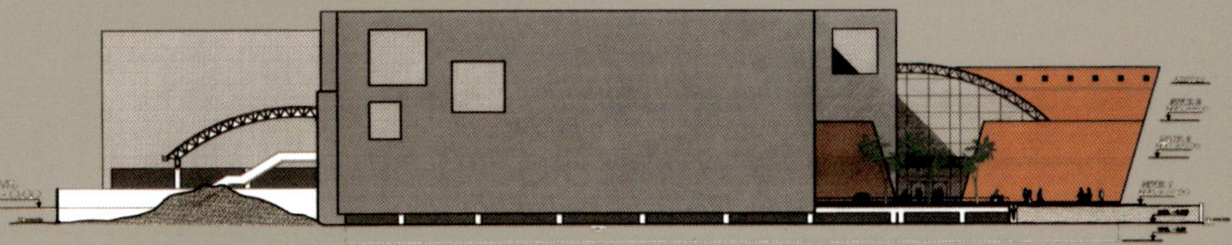

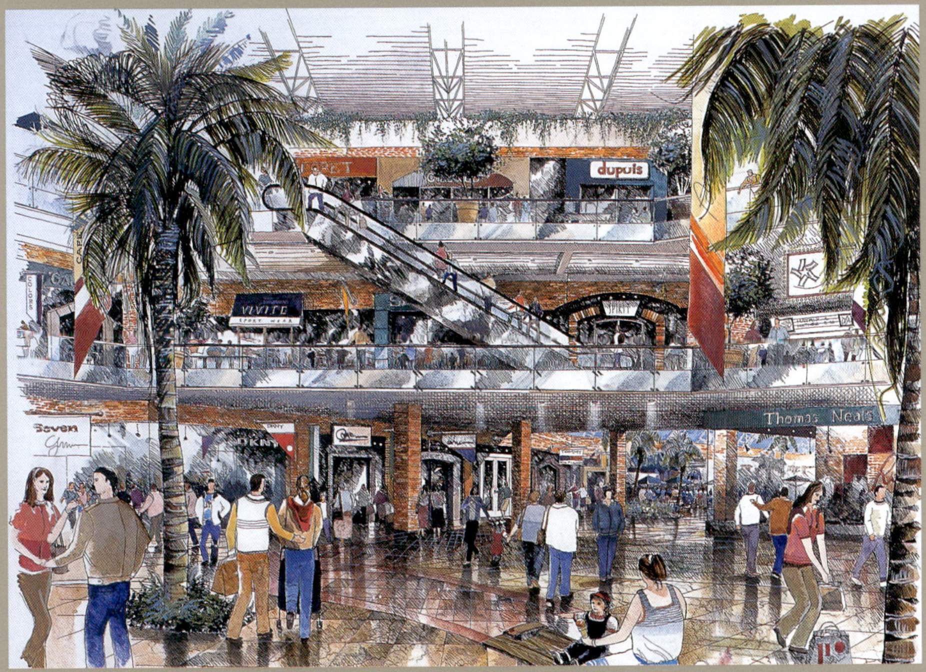
dupuis

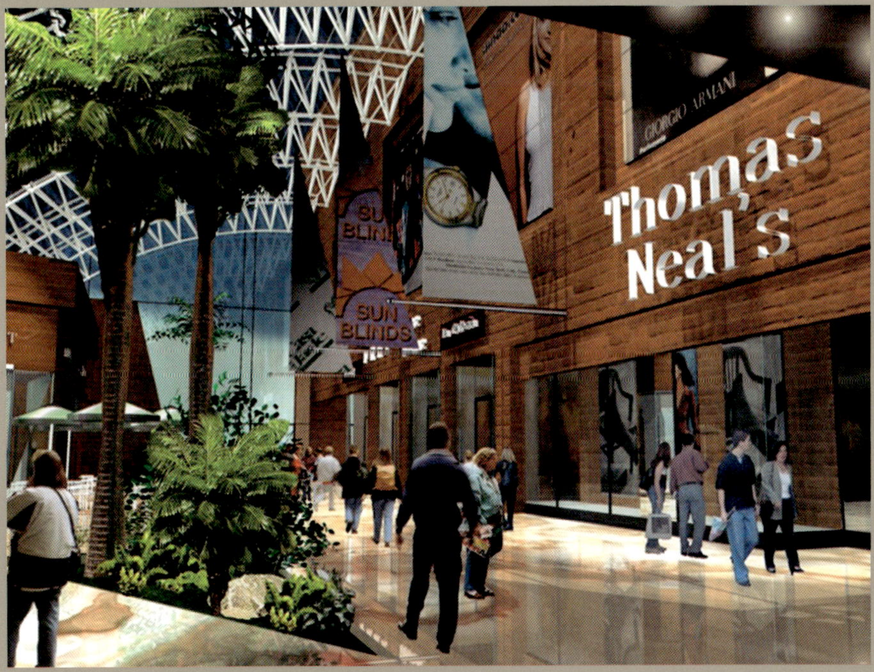
Thomas Neal's
GIORGIO ARMANI
SUN BLINDS

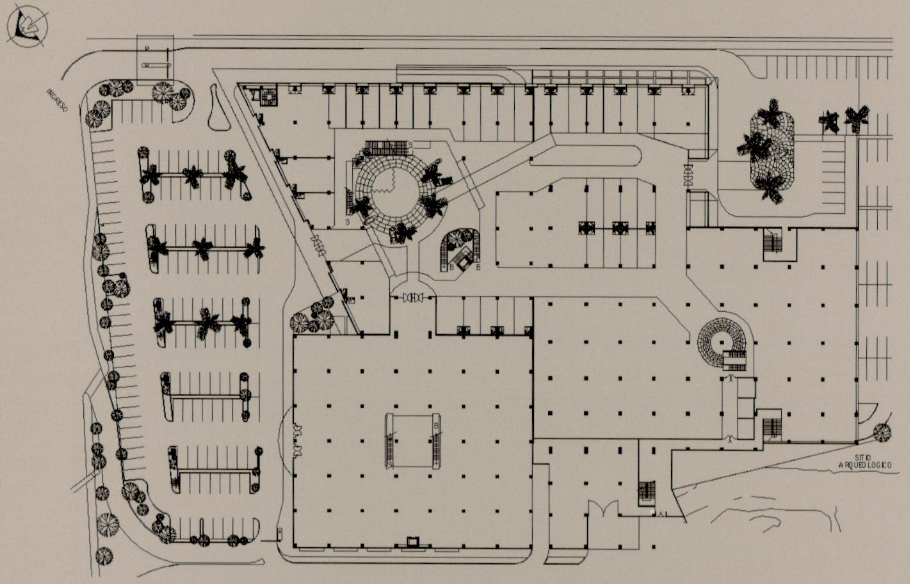
SITIO ARQUEOLOGICO

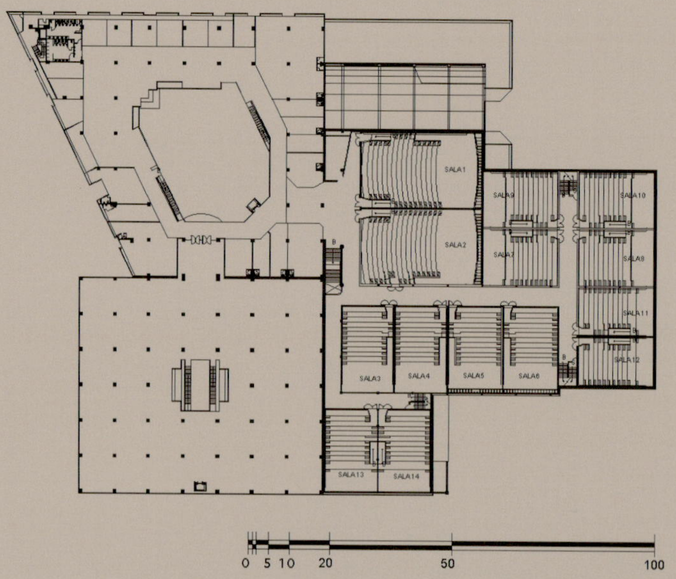
SALA1
SALA2
SALA3
SALA4
SALA5
SALA6
SALA7
SALA8
SALA9
SALA10
SALA11
SALA12
SALA13
SALA14
0 5 10 20 50 100

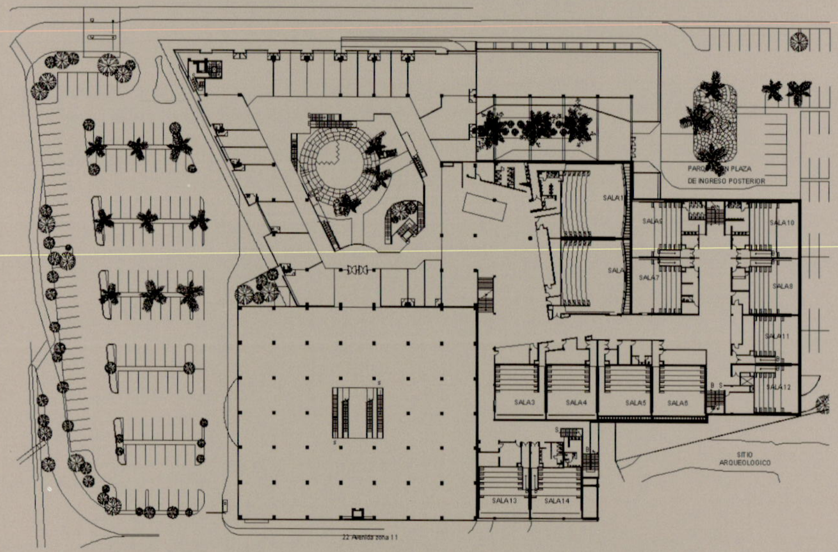
SALA3
SALA4
SALA5
SALA6
SALA10
SALA11
SALA12
SALA13
SALA14
SITIO ARQUEOLOGICO

La Galería

NUEVA CIUDAD DE LOS ALTOS IN XELA
Guatemala

Based on some of the criteria of the "New Urbanism", as well as an original concept of the Seis Arquitectos group, this project (whose name may be roughly translated as "The New City on the Heights") has as its objective the creation of a city made up of neighborhoods with a Latin American character and with certain vernacular elements pertaining to the Guatemalan high plains region. The master plan for this city foresees the creation of five districts: four devoted to housing and organized into neighborhoods and one for the use of the Rafael Landívar University. The culture that characterizes the traditional way of life will be emphasized through a harmonious integration of the residential, educational, commercial and recreational sectors, creating a system of streets, promenades, plazas and pedestrian paths which pay special attention to the conservation of the natural environment of the setting. In addition, a system of co-ownership is proposed for the legal framework, in order to obtain a better administration and maintenance of the different neighborhoods. In this context, the master plan foresees the creation of a city center that will be located in the university sector and be made up of the central plaza, principal church, conference center, public offices and buildings of mixed use.

NUEVA CIUDAD DEL NARANJO
Guatemala city

The master plan for this city is unique in Guatemala. Located in the northwestern part of this city, the tableland on which it is built still conserves the shade trees of the coffee plantation that once stood there. The promoters of the scheme wish to conserve this natural setting and offer housing that will improve the quality of neighborhood life. The aim is to create a city whose inhabitants have opportunities to get to know one another, that is, the antithesis of the big city of today. The design foresees the integration of vernacular elements of the architecture and urbanism found in Latin American cities with an up-to-date infrastructure of technology. Pedestrian circulation is given priority. Its inhabitants will only need to walk a few blocks to reach their places of work, shopping and recreation. All of the neighborhoods have plazas, built in a colonial or early-republican style, reminiscent of those which typify the cities of the region. These plazas, in turn, constitute the meeting points for civic, administrative, religious, educational and commercial activities. The master plan was based on an "S"-shaped boulevard designed by the architect Antonio Prada. The plan includes a code which regulates the respective prominence given to streets, avenues, boulevards, promenades and peripheral roads. A great respect for the conservation of nature is evident. The streets become promenades shaded by existing trees and newly-planted ones, which at the same time serve to link the plazas and large green areas. The code also sets forth a language for the architecture of the buildings, which encourages harmonious architectural proportions and regulates the use of construction materials and textures, among other things, with the main objective of achieving an architecture that will never lose its timeliness. The influence of the Neo-Urbanism of the Corea Valle Valle, Inc. firm is evident in the elaboration of the design concept. The pooling of ideas that determined the master plan began on June 11, 1998, with an intensive planning session which involved urban planners, architects and other professionals; specialists in housing, business and marketing; public officials; and ordinary residents of Guatemala City.

PEDREGAL DEL NARANJO

CASA SANTA ELENA
El Salvador

The special topography of the terrain of Casa Santa Elena, in the city of San Salvador, presents a challenge in terms of access to this project, since the summit of the site on which it will be built is eight meters above the street level. Toward this end, a street was developed which will skirt the hill to reach the parking and security area, which is set back from the house and will have a heliport on its roof. The architectural language used in the design of this house has certain oriental characteristics. This is seen in the four-sided sloping roof of wood and shingle, whose cross-section shows three separate inclinations, the eave being the lowest part. In order to create a dramatic sequence for the approach to the house, the client asked the architects to leave a considerable distance between the garage and the main entrance. To approach the house, the visitor will walk along a path surrounded by vegetation that passes a waterfall, a bridge and a wooded area before reaching the main front, which will consist of a big sheet of glass that divides the exterior garden from the interior one. This transparency establishes a visual continuity between the gardens, while the vista terminates in a cascade of water at the back.

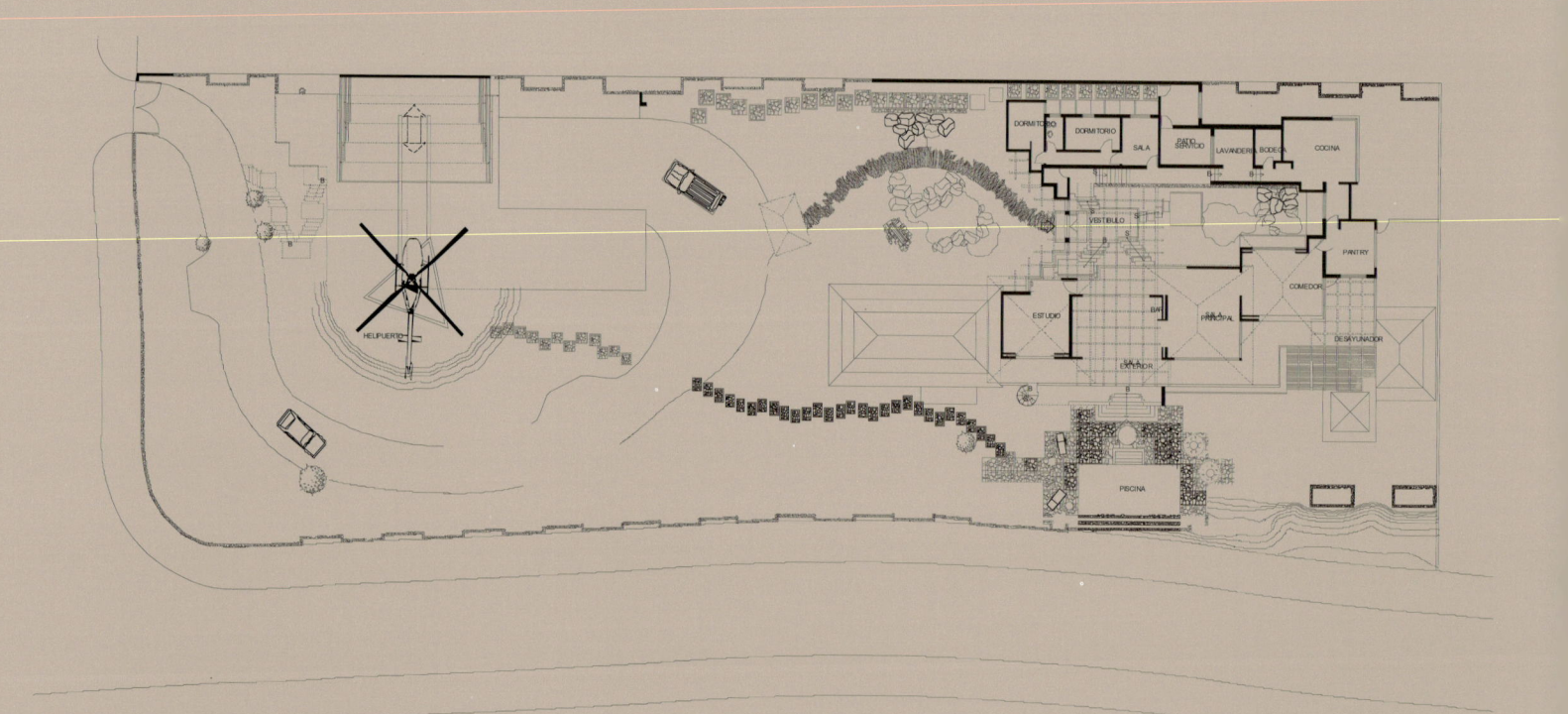

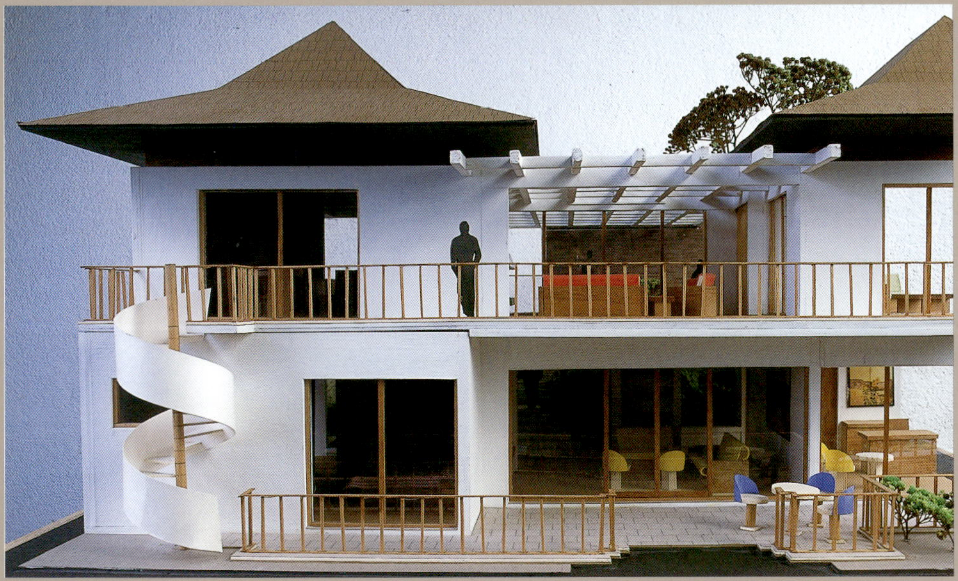

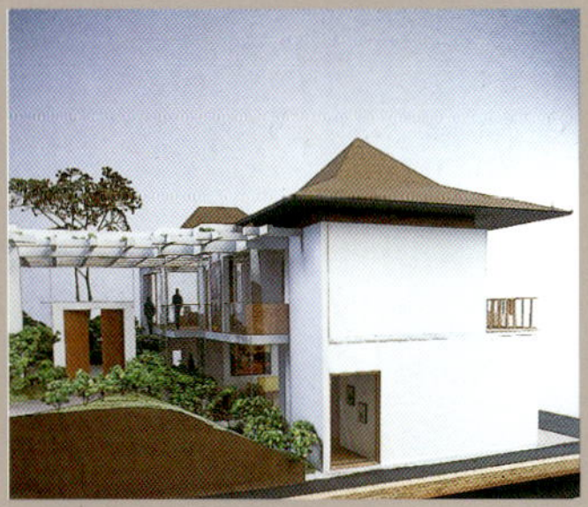

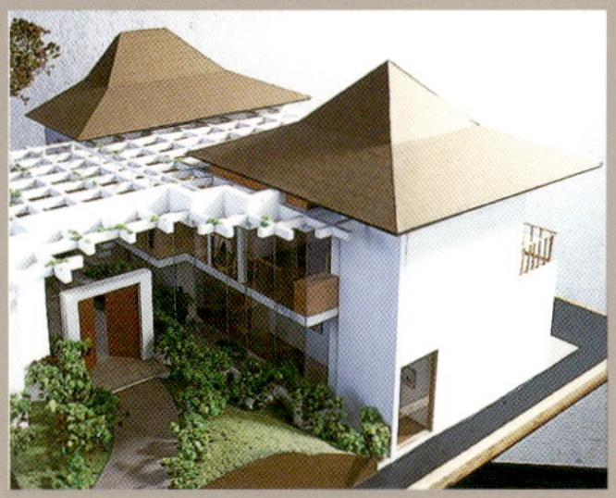

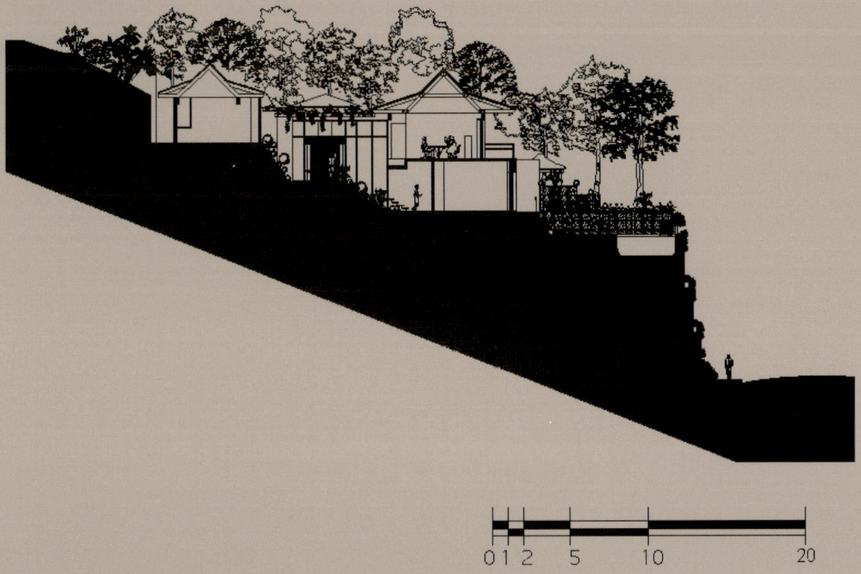
0 1 2 5 10 20

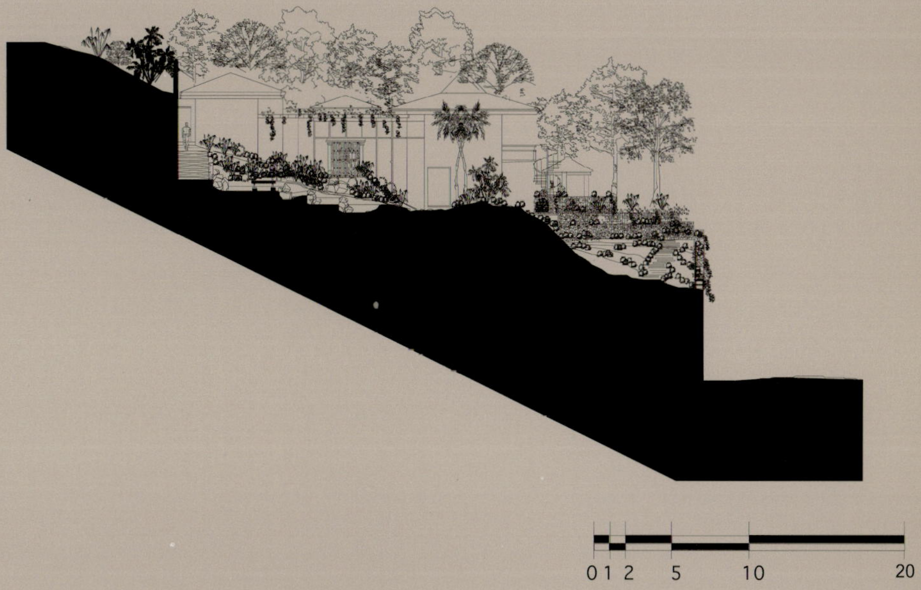
0 1 2 5 10 20

HARCARMEL
Guatemala

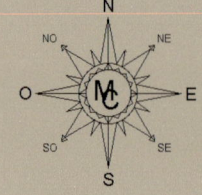

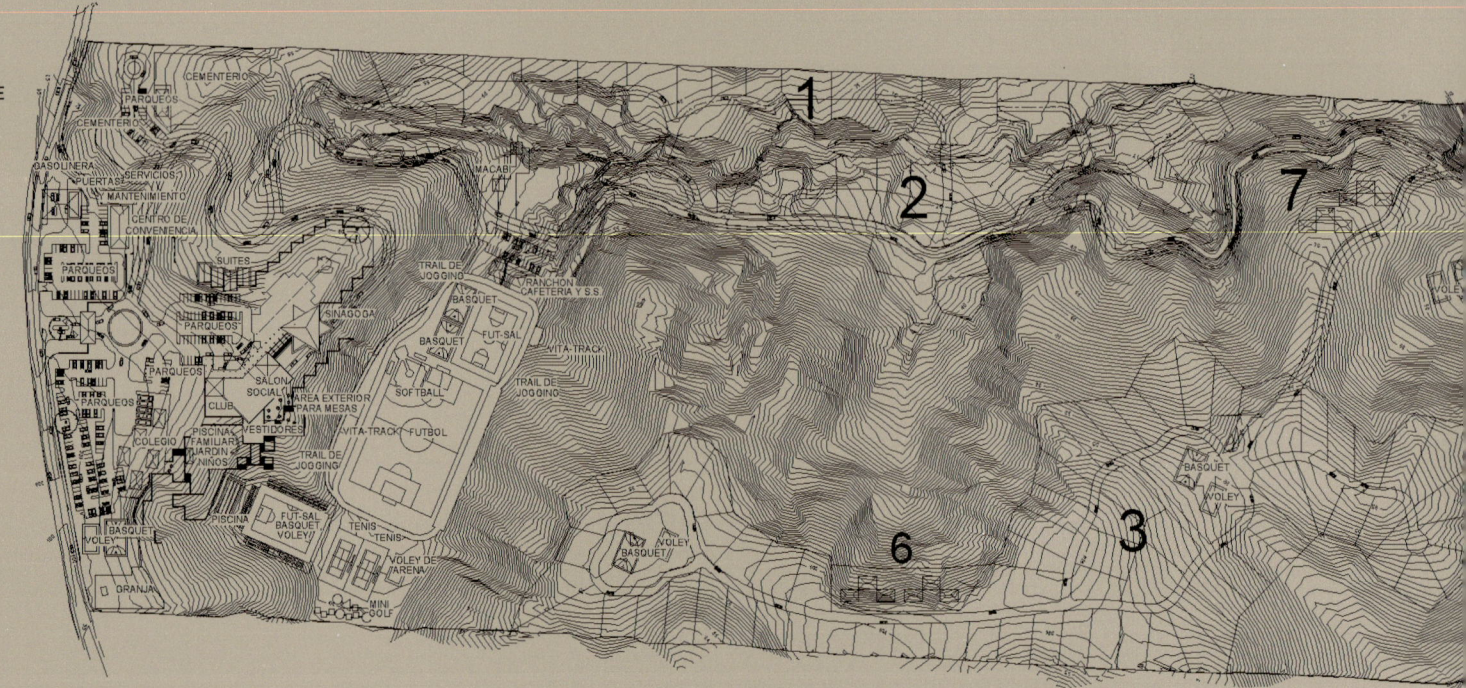

Harcarmel, which means "Mount Carmel" in Hebrew, is an urban development devoted to housing a Jewish community in Guatemala. The future complex will include residential areas, a religious temple, a social hall, a school, the Maccabee Club for youngsters, sports areas and, possibl, a cemetery built in accordance with Jewish religious norms. Located between the municipalities of Fraijanes and San José Pinula, Harcarmel covers an area of 83 blocks. It has a rather undulating terrain, with several streams: two of them contain a number of beautiful natural springs. During the first stage, an access road will be built towards the first hollow, which, because of its topographical characteristics, serves as the location for the sports fields and the social club. Thus, advantage is taken of the flattest areas on the terrain, which are protected from the north wind. The urban planning responds to the special topographical features of the land and provides building lots with a surface area of approximately 600 square meters which are suitable for either country houses or more formal ones. Given these conditions, the development of the urban complex is based on a system of nodes that will take shape as the lots become occupied. The design of private houses will not be governed by common norms, but the character of community buildings will based on the traditional architecture of Jerusalem, utilizing buttresses, cupolas and stones of the same color in a reinterpretation of the buildings of that ancient city.

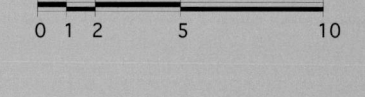

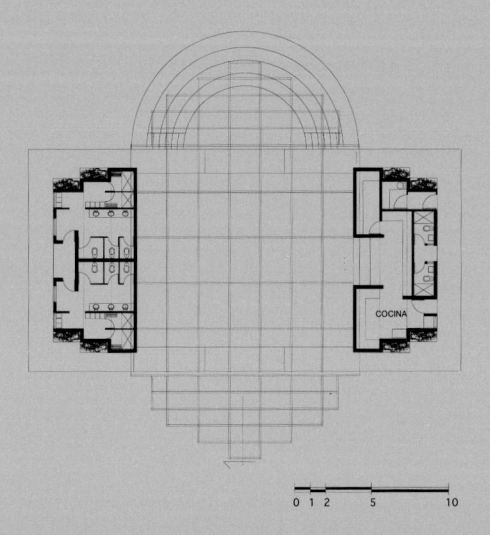

FLOR DE CAMPO
Palín

Flor de Campo, in Palín, is a master plan for urban development located to the south of Guatemala City and based on the model of the American suburbs. When the designers were organizing the spaces to be used, which included soil studies of the area that would be occupied, they ran into a difficulty. It was discovered that the terrain on which it will be developed is made up of very marshy land and thus the construction might be affected by the existing water table. To solve this problem a series of lakes will be created in the areas of housing, in order to drain the water from the marsh and thus lower the freatic level to a more suitable depth, a strategy that will also embellish the natural landscape of the urban development. In addition to housing, Palín will have industrial, sports and entertainment sectors, which will turn this big project into one of the most ambitious and complete urban developments in Guatemala.

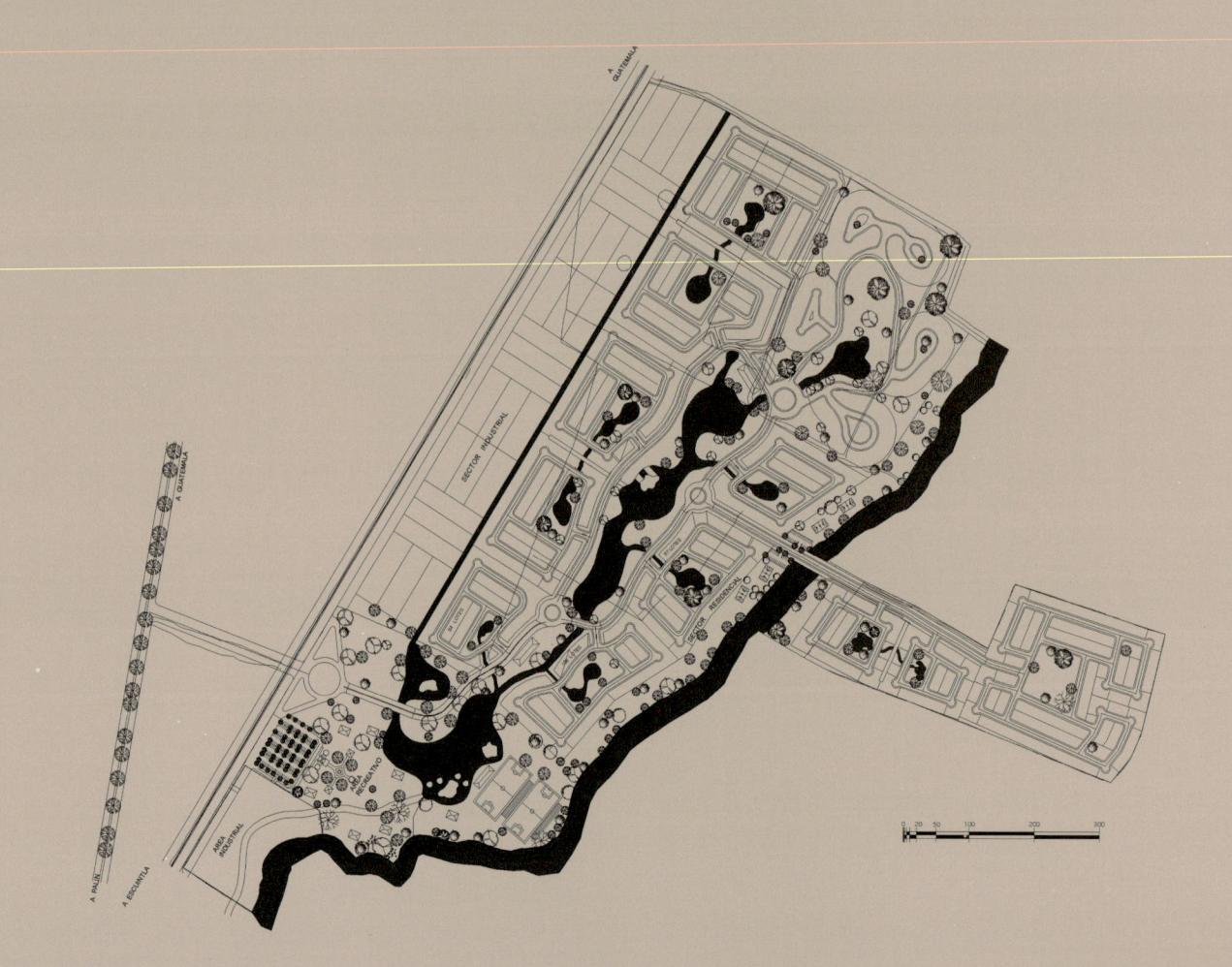

ROOSEVELT PYRAMIDS
Guatemala

This project will be located on the Calzada Roosevelt, which is one of the most important shopping districts in Guatemala City. Standing close to the famous Tikal Futura shopping center, hotel and convention center, The "Pirámides Roosevelt" project will be linked to Tikal Futura by an underground car park and pedestrian and vehicular links on the second level. In conjunction with Tikal Futura, the pyramids will establish a great complex devoted to a mixture of architectural uses that include offices, shops and apartments. Designed to be constructed in three stages, the project will have a car park that will service Tikal Futura as well as its three towers. The pyramidal form of the towers responds to an architectural language that is also meant to establish a visual identification with Tikal Futura.

technical information

solares&lara

PROJECT: BANCO INTERNACIONAL
Architectural design	:	SOLARES & LARA
Collaboratoring Architect	:	JUAN PABLO ROSALES
Structural design	:	ENGS. JUAN JOSÉ HERMOSILLA - EDUARDO LEÓN
Hydraulic design	:	ENG. ARTURO PAZOS
Electrical design	:	ENG. JOSÉ LUIS RODRÍGUEZ - TELECTRO
Builder	:	ITURBIDE and TORUÑO
Air conditioning	:	ENG. GUSTAVO ORTIZ
Development	:	JUAN CARLOS CASTELLÓN
Collaborator	:	ABRAHAM PUR
Date	:	1996

PROJECT: BANCO DE OCCIDENTE
Architectural design	:	ADOLFO LAU & ASOCIADOS and SOLARES & LARA
Structural design	:	ENGS. JUAN JOSÉ HERMOSILLA - EDUARDO LEÓN
Hydraulic design	:	ARCHILA y RIVERA
Electrical design	:	ENG. SAMUEL ROSALES
Builder	:	ITURBIDE and TORUÑO
Air conditioning	:	ENG. GUSTAVO ORTIZ
Development	:	JUAN CARLOS CASTELLÓN
Date	:	1999

PROJECT: BANCO SCI
Architectural design	:	SOLARES & LARA
Structural design	:	ENGS. JUAN JOSÉ HERMOSILLA - EDUARDO LEÓN
Hydraulic design	:	ARCHILA y RIVERA
Electrical design	:	TELECTRO - SISTEC
Builder	:	ITURBIDE and TORUÑO
Collaborator	:	JORGE GAITÁN
Date	:	1990

PROJECT: L'EXCELLENCE
Architectural design	:	SOLARES & LARA
Structural design	:	ENG. HÉCTOR MONZÓN
Hydraulic design	:	ENG. ARTURO PAZOS
Electrical design	:	TELECTRO, S. A.
Builder	:	ISA
Collaborator	:	ROBERTO AYALA, JORGE GAITÁN ABRAHAM PUR and CARLOS SOLARES
Date	:	1997

PROJECT: MURANO CENTRE
Architectural design	:	SOLARES & LARA
Structural design	:	ENG. HÉCTOR MONZÓN
Hydraulic design	:	ARCHILA and RIVERA
Electrical design	:	TELECTRO, S. A.
Builder	:	ISA
Collaborator	:	CARLOS SOLARES
Date	:	1993

PROJECT: TIFFANY
Architectural design	:	SOLARES & LARA
Structural design	:	ENGS. JUAN JOSÉ HERMOSILLA - EDUARDO LEÓN
Hydraulic design	:	ENG. MANUEL ARCHILA
Electrical design	:	ENG. MANUEL ARCHILA
Builder	:	ENG. JUAN MINI, ENG. ROLANDO GÁLVEZ
Developer	:	ARCHILA and RIVERA CO. LTDA.
Collaborator	:	ABRAHAM PUR
Date	:	1992

PROJECT: PLAZA G&T
Architectural design	:	SOLARES & LARA and ARCH. HÉCTOR SANTAMARINA
Structural design	:	ENGS. JUAN JOSÉ HERMOSILLA - EDUARDO LEÓN
Hydraulic design	:	ENG. MANUEL ARCHILA
Electrical design	:	SISTEC
Builder	:	ENG. JUAN MINI
Collaborating Architects	:	HÉCTOR SANTAMARINA and ABRAHAM PUR
Development	:	ENG. MANUEL ARCHILA
Air conditioning	:	ENG. GUSTAVO ORTIZ
Date	:	1997

PROJECT: BANCO REFORMADOR
Architectural design	:	SOLARES & LARA
Structural design	:	ENG. HÉCTOR MONZÓN
Hydraulic design	:	ENG. ARTURO PAZOS
Electrical design	:	SISTEC
Builder	:	CASTAÑEDA and MOLINA
Development	:	ABRAHAM PUR
Collaborator	:	LUIS PEDRO ARROYAVE
Date	:	1997

PROJECT: CANTABRIA
Architectural design	:	SOLARES & LARA
Structural design	:	ENG. RONY SARMIENTO
Hydraulic design	:	ARCHILA and RIVERA CO. LTDA.
Electrical design	:	ARCHILA and RIVERA CO. LTDA.
Builder	:	ISA
Collaborator	:	CARLOS SOLARES
Date	:	1994

PROJECT: LAS LUCES
Architectural design	:	SOLARES & LARA
Structural design	:	ENG. ÓSCAR AGUIRRE
Hydraulic design	:	ENG. MANUEL ARCHILA
Electrical design	:	INSTALECTRA
Builder	:	C. V. G.
Urban Development	:	ENG. MANUEL ARCHILA
Collaborator	:	ROBERTO AYALA, JORGE GAITÁN, ABRAHAM PUR and CARLOS SOLARES
Date	:	1998

Winner of the Prize for Excellence for the period 1999-2002 in the competition sponsored by the Cementos Progreso firm.

technicalinformation

PROJECT: VILLAS DEL PACíFICO
Architectural design	:	SOLARES & LARA and JORGE MARIO VALDEZ
Structural design	:	INVERMAYA
Sanitary installations	:	INVERMAYA
Electrical design	:	ENG. RODRIGO COFIÑO
Builder	:	INVERMAYA
Development	:	FORMAS S. A.
Date	:	1994

minondo&giesemann

PROJECT: MUSEO IXCHEL
Architectural design	:	ARCHTS. VÍCTOR COHEN, AUGUSTO DE LEÓN, PETER GIESEMANN, ADOLFO LAU Y GUILLERMO PEMUELLER
Structural design	:	ENG. JOAQUÍN LOTTMAN
Hydraulic design	:	ARQUISISTEMAS, S. A.
Electrical design	:	TELECTRO, S. A.
Builder	:	MONTES, PORRAS & SOLER
Date	:	1987

PROJECT: ANACAFÉ
Architectural design	:	ARCHTS. EDUARDO CASTILLO, MINONDO & GIESEMANN, MONTES & PORRAS
Structural design	:	DR. HÉCTOR MONZÓN DESPANG
Hydraulic design	:	ENG. MARIO PÉREZ
Electrical design	:	ENG. RUDY CIFUENTES
Builder	:	AICSA
General Coordination	:	CARLOS CASTELLANOS
Date	:	1989

PROJECT: JUNCAYÁ
Architectural design	:	MINONDO & GIESEMANN
Structural design	:	ENG. SIGFRIDO ARRIVILLAGA
Hydraulic design	:	HOLZHEU & HERNÁNDEZ
Electrical design	:	LESLIE DRUMMOND
Builder	:	HOLZHEU & HERNÁNDEZ
Date	:	1995

PROJECT: HOTEL WESTIN CAMINO REAL
Architectural design	:	ARCH. RAÚL MINONDO
Structural design	:	ENG. JUAN JOSÉ HERMOSILLA
Date	:	1965/68

PROJECT: TECNOLÓGICO DE SANTA LUCÍA
Architectural design	:	MINONDO & GIESEMANN
Structural design	:	DR. HÉCTOR MONZÓN DESPANG
Hydraulic design	:	ENG. MARIO PÉREZ
Electrical design	:	ENG. RUDY CIFUENTES
Builder	:	CASTAÑEDA & MOLINA
Date	:	1998

PROJECT: BANCO AGROMERCANTIL
Architectural design	:	ARCH. PETER GIESEMANN
Structural design	:	DR. HÉCTOR MONZÓN DESPANG
Hydraulic design	:	ENG. MARIO PÉREZ
Electrical design	:	SALNARS & DÍAZ
Builder	:	ICONSA
General Coordination	:	CARLOS CASTELLANOS
Date	:	1997

PROJECT: CENTRO GERENCIAL LAS MARGARITAS
Architectural design	:	MINONDO & GIESEMANN
Structural design	:	DR. HÉCTOR MONZÓN DESPANG
Hydraulic design	:	ENG. MARIO PÉREZ
Electrical design	:	ENG. RUDY CIFUENTES
Builder	:	ICONSA
Date	:	1985/98

tinoco&porras

PROJECT: PLAZA OBELISCO
Architectural design	:	TINOCO & PORRAS
Structural design	:	ACEROS ARQUITECTÓNICOS, S. A.
Hidraulic design	:	ENG. JULIO SANTOLINO B.
Builder	:	ARCH. ANTONIO GUIROLA
Date	:	1997

seisarquitectos

PROJECT: BANCO AGRÍCOLA DE EL SALVADOR
Architectural design	:	SEIS ARQUITECTOS
Builder	:	AICSA
General Coordination	:	CARLOS CASTELLANOS
Date	:	1999

First Prize in the International Competition sponsored by the Banco Agrícola

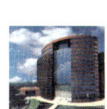

technical information

PRE-PROJECT: EL RECREO – CASA CLUB 
Architectural design : SEIS ARQUITECTOS
General Coordination : CARLOS CASTELLANOS
Date : 2000
Project awarded First Prize in Design Competition

PROJECT: CERVECERÍA CENTROAMERICANA CORPORATE BUILDING 
Architectural design : SOLARES & LARA and TINOCO & PORRAS
Structural design : ENG. JUAN JOSÉ HERMOSILLA
Hydraulic design : ENG. JULIO SANTOLINO B.
Electrical design : INSTELECTRA, S. A.
Builder : ITURBIDE & TORUÑO
Collaborator : ABRAHAM PUR
Date : 1998

PROJECT: ATLANTIS BUILDING 
Architectural design : MINONDO & GIESEMANN and SOLARES & LARA
Structural design : ENG. JUAN JOSÉ HERMOSILLA
Hydraulic design : ARCHILA RIVERA, CÍA. LTDA.
Electrical design : SISTEC, S. A.
Builder : ENG. HÉCTOR CRUZ
General Coordination : CARLOS CASTELLANOS
Date : 1992

PROJECT: MASTER PLAN, CONDADO CONCEPCIÓN 
Architectural design : SOLARES & LARA and TINOCO & PORRAS
Date : 1995

PROJECT: CALLE REAL CONCEPCIÓN 
Architectural design : SEIS ARQUITECTOS
Structural design : ENG. EDUARDO MONZÓN
Hydraulic design : ENG. EDUARDO MONZÓN
Electrical design : ENG. EDUARDO MONZÓN
Date : 1999

PROJECT: ESCALÓN APARTMENTS TOWER, SAN SALVADOR, EL SALVADOR 
Architectural design : SEIS ARQUITECTOS
General Coordination : CARLOS CASTELLANOS
Date : 2000

PROJECT: MASTER PLAN NEW CITY OF EL NARANJO 
Architectural design : SEIS ARQUITECTOS, in collaboration with CORREA, VALLE & VALLE

PROJECT: MASTER PLAN PASEO MIRAFLORES 
Architectural design : SEIS ARQUITECTOS
General Coordination : CARLOS CASTELLANOS

PROJECT: PEDREGAL DEL NARANJO 
Architectural design : SEIS ARQUITECTOS
Structural design : MABY DE ROSALES, SIGFRIDO ARRIVILLAGA
Hydraulic design : TOYCA
Builder : ISA
Date : 1997

PROJECT: LAS CASCADAS HYPER-MALL SHOPPING CENTER, SAN SALVADOR, EL SALVADOR 
Architectural design : SEIS ARQUITECTOS
Structural design : ENG. FERNANDO CONLLEDO
Hydraulic design : ENG. OTTO HERNÁNDEZ
Electrical design : ENG. NERY MEJÍA
Builder : CONSTRUCCIONES NABLA, S. A. DE C. V.
General Coordination : CARLOS CASTELLANOS
Date : 2002

PROJECT: ROOSEVELT PYRAMIDS 
Architectural design : SEIS ARQUITECTOS
Date : 2002

PROJECT: PALÍN – FLOR DE CAMPO 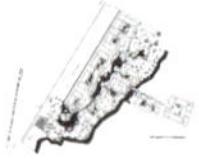
Architectural design : SEIS ARQUITECTOS
Date : 2001

PROJECT: MASTER PLAN HARCARMEL CITY 
Architectural design : SEIS ARQUITECTOS
General Coordination : CARLOS CASTELLANOS
Date : 2001

PROJECT: GALERÍAS MIRAFLORES SHOPPING CENTER 
Architectural design : SEIS ARQUITECTOS
Structural design : ENG. MARIO YON
Hydraulic design : ENG. GUSTAVO ORTÍZ
Electrical design : ENG. RUDY CIFUENTES
Builder : ICONSA
General Coordination : CARLOS CASTELLANOS
Date : 2002

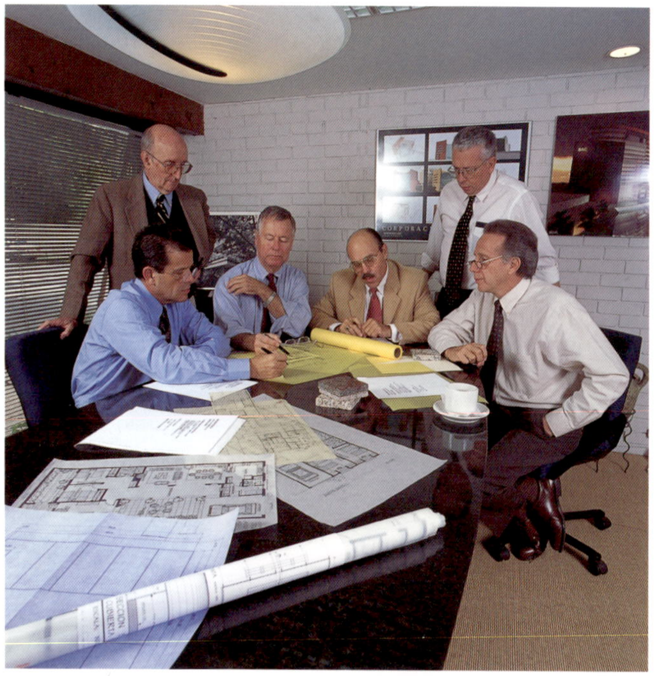

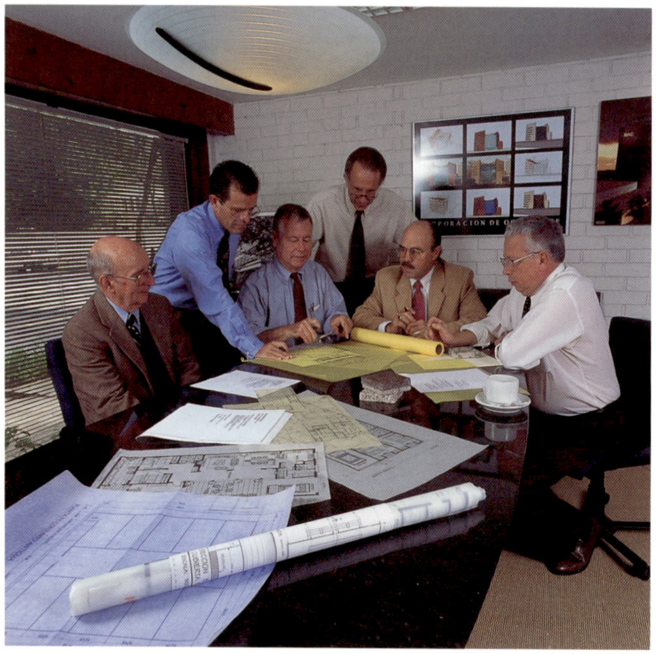

seisarquitectos

Seis Arquitectos, S. A., came into being as a strategic alliance among a number of Guatemalan architectural firms with a broad experience and an established reputation. This alliance became consolidated when the firms joined into a company which is oriented toward dealing with the process of globalization and undertaking projects which, by virtue of their dimensions and importance, benefit from the joint experience of its six members. Legally founded in 1997, the firm unites the knowledge, experience and prestige of the architects who founded it: Peter Giesemann, Carlos Lara, Raúl Minondo, Ernesto Porras, Rodolfo Solares and Rafael Tinoco.

Projects developed

- Master Plan, Nueva Ciudad del Naranjo, Guatemala
- Master Plan, Sector Comercial Sur de Miraflores, Guatemala
- Master Development Plan, Condado Concepción, Guatemala
- Master Plan, Nueva Ciudad de los Altos, Quetzaltenango, Guatemala.
- Master Plan, Ciudad Montecarmelo, Guatemala.
- Master Plan, Finca Retana (Antigua), Guatemala.
- CFI Banco Agrícola de El Salvador, San Salvador, El Salvador.
- Club House, el Recreo Golf Club, Guatemala.
- Apartment Tower, Escalón, San Salvador, El Salvador.
- Calle Real de Concepción shopping center, Guatemala.
- Pedregal del Naranjo, Guatemala.
- Alamedas de San Miguel, Guatemala.
- Alamedas de Santa Clara, Guatemala.
- Houses in Antigua Guatemala, Guatemala.
- Casa Elgin, Guatemala
- Miraflores shopping center, Guatemala
- Roosevelt-Tikal Tower, Guatemala
- Hiper Mall Las Cascadas shopping center, San Salvador, El Salvador.
- Cenma shopping center, Guatemala
- Shopping center in San Cristóbal, Guatemala.

solares&lara

Solares & Lara, Inc., is a firm located in Guatemala City, made up of Guatemalan professionals who are dedicated to all aspects of architecture.

The company is based on the idea of adapting itself with complete flexibility to the successful realization of projects of any dimension. This flexibility allows it to strengthen itself with the professional staff needed to execute any project, at any time, in the way that is most advantageous to the client.

Its permanent staff and the associated professional and technical team that may be called upon to reinforce its work in a given moment give Solares & Lara the strong cumulative experience that is required to offer the best professional services in the areas of architectural design and engineering, as well as consultancy and supervision of the same.

Projects Developed

- More than 350 private homes in Guatemala City and the rest of the country.
- 2001. Remodeling of Hotel Antigua, Antigua Guatemala.
- 2001. "Bosques de Las Luces" residential complex, carretera a El Salvador, 200 homes.
- 1999. "Las Rotondas" residential complex, Carretera a El Salvador, 48 homes.
- 1998. "Las Luces 1" residential complex, carretera a El Salvador, 249 homes.
- 1999. "Broken Sound" residential complex, Zone 10, 75 homes.
- 2001. "Las Vistas de Elgin" residential complex, Zone 13, 18 homes.
- 1994. "Cantabria" Condominium, Zone 13, 26 residences.
- 1999. "Cañadas del Castor" residential complex, Zone 15, San Lázaro.
- 1997. "Buganvilias de Cayalá". Zone 15, 40 homes.
- 1999. "Las Lomas" residential complex, carretera a El Salvador, 46 homes, Sausalito, Fraijanes
- 1980. "La Punta de la Cañada" residential complex, Zone 14, 15 homes.
- 1995. "Montelimar" residential complex.
- 1993. "Los Eucaliptos" residential complex, Zone 15, 5 homes, Monterrey.
- 1976. "Los Altos" residential complex, carretera a El Salvador, 60 homes.
- 2000. "El Escorial" residential complex, Zone 14, 6 homes.
- 2001. "Piemonte" apartment building, Zone 14.
- 1997. "L'Excellence" apartment building, Zone 14, 38 apartments.
- "Victorias Suites" apartment building, Zone 14, 15 apartments.
- 1992. "Tiffany" apartment building, Zone 10, 65 apartments.
- 1993. "Torrelianas" apartment building, Zone 15, 60 apartments.
- 1999. "San Ignacio" apartment building, Zone 10, 2 towers.
- 2002. "Atrium" apartment building, Zone 10, 140 apartments.
- 1991. "Atlantis" building, Zone 10.
- 1993. "Murano Center", Zone 10.
- 1998. Corporación de Occidente building, Zone 9.
- 1995. Banco Internacional, Zone 10.
- 1996. Banco Reformador, Zone 9.
- 2000. "Plaza G & T" building, remodeling, Zone 4.
- 1990. "SCI Centre" building, Zone 9.
- Commercial and residential condominium (project), Zone 11.
- "Autorama Sales Room" (project), Zone 9.
- "Bolerama" bowling center, Zone 13.
- Commercial building, Zone 4.
- Central Offices: Hertz, American Express, Clark Tours and Guatemalan Travel Advisors, Zone 9.
- 1990. "Megacentro", Zone 11.
- Burger Shops Gemínis 10, Zone 10
- Mac Donald's, Zone 4.
- "Plaza Blanca", Zone 9.
- 1995. Banco Internacional, Zone 15.
- "Cristal Towers", Zone 10.
- Cervecería Centroamericana, carretera a El Salvador.
- 2001. Hotel Antigua, Antigua Guatemala, 24 rooms.
- 1978. Hotel Ramada Antigua, Antigua Guatemala, 156 rooms.
- Hotel Posada del Sol, Izabal, 100 rooms.
- Hotel in Chichicastenango, Chichicastenango, 30 rooms.
- Flores, Petén, 100 rooms.
- Hotel Lacandón Paradise, Flores, Petén, 50 rooms.
- Salón Las Naciones, Zone 10, Design and construction.
- Hotel El Dorado, Zone 10, Design and development of blueprints.
- Car park building, Hotel El Dorado, Zone 10, design and development of blueprints.
- Bedroom, Camino Real, Zone 10, Design and construction.
- 1997. Hotel Princess, Tegucigalpa.
- Club Cabaña, Hotel Marriott, Zone 10, Design and construction.
- Car park building, Camino Real, Zone 10.
- Sports and cultural center of the Colonia China.
- 1997. Hotel Ramada Antigua, Antigua Guatemala, Remodeling and decoration.
- Hotel Club Villas del Pacífico, Escuintla, Chulamar.
- Hotel Ramada Guatemala, Guatemala City.
- San Isidro Golf Club, Zone 16.
- Remodeling offices of Pacific Industrial Bank, Zone 10.
- Remodeling offices of Westrust Bank, Zone 14.
- Remodeling of Mac Donald's, Zone 9.

carlos m. lara castillo

February 7, 1947

Studies
- **Degree in architecture,**
  Universidad de San Carlos de Guatemala - Colegiado 141.

Professional and executive posts
- Pro-secretary of the Board of Directors, 1974-75
- Official delegate to the Central American Congress of Architecture, held in San José, Costa Rica, August 1975.
- Member of the Society of Guatemalan Architects.
- Member of the College of Guatemalan Architects.
- Member of the Federation of Central American Architects.
- Member of the Federation of Architects.
- Member of the Administrative Council of Corpa, S.A.
- Architectural consultant to the Ministry of Public Health and Social Welfare, 1974-1975.
- Head architect of the Engineering Department of the National Committee for national school construction, 1974.
- Architect of the Corpa, S.A. firm, 1975-1992.
- Architect of the Solares & Lara, S.A. firm, since 1992.
- Architect of the Seis Arquitectos firm, since 1998.
- Advisor to Los Eucaliptos Investment Corporation.

See works and projects carried out by the firm Solares & Lara.

rodolfo**solares**ortíz

September 11, 1947

Studies
- **Degree in architecture,** Universidad de San Carlos de Guatemala - Colegiado 138

Academic activities
- Professor, introductory course, Instituto Feminino de Estudios Superiores –IFES – USAC, 1973-1974.
- Professor, graphic expression III, Faculty of Architecture, Universidad Rafael Landívar, 1974-1975.
- Professor, design I, Faculty of Architecture, Universidad Rafael Landívar, 1975.
- Member of the commission in charge of drafting the plan of studies for the Industrial Design course, Universidad Rafael Landívar.
- Professor, design VII, Faculty of Architecture, Universidad Rafael Landívar.
- Professor, architectural design II, Faculty of Architecture, Universidad Francisco Marroquín, 1978.

Professional and executive posts
- Member of the Tribunal of Honor, College of Architects, 1975-1976.
- Member of the College of Guatemalan Architects.
- Member of the Society of Guatemalan Architects.
- Member of the Pan American Federation of Architects.
- Member of the Central American Federation of Architects.
- Member of the Administrative Council of Corpa, S.A.
- President of the Tribunal of Honor of the Autonomous Sports Federation of Guatemala, 1998-2002.
- Design and supervision of "Carpintería Rivera", 1968-1970.
- Architect of the Corpa, S.A., firm, 1975-1992.
- Architect of the Solares & Lara, S.A., firm since 1992.
- Architect of the Seis Arquitectos, S.A., firm since 1998.

See works and projects carried out by the firm Solares & Lara.

minondo&giesemann

Founded in 1970, this firm of architects offers services of design and planning, integrating a broad experience and technology into the visual, economic and ecological aspects of each project.

Projects Developed

- 1999. "Excellence Prize", awarded by the Cementos Progreso company and the Guatemalan Chamber of Construction, for expression, creativity, identity and use of concrete.
- 1998. Colegio Tecnológico del Sur, Escuintla, Guatemala.
- 1997. Camino Real Tikal (project), Petén, Guatemala.
- 1995. (Roosevelt) Pediatric Hospital, Clínica del Niño Sano.
- 1993. Las Margaritas Business Center, Towers 1 and 2, Zone 10, Guatemala.
- 1993. Banco del Agro, S.A. (Central headquarters), Zone 9, Guatemala City.
- 1992. Juncayá Condominium, Atitlán, Guatemala.
- 1987. Pantaleón, S.A. Las Margaritas, Zone 10, Guatemala City.
- 1986. Pantelco building (project), Zone 9, Guatemala City.
- 1981. Galerías Reforma building, Zone 9, Guatemala City.
- 1980. Montúfar-Liberación shopping center (project), Zone 9, Guatemala City.
- 1979. Miraflores shopping center (project), Zone 11, Guatemala City.
- 1978. Viviendas Camino Real condominium, Atitlán, Guatemala
- 1978. Aeroclub de Guatemala, Zone 13, Guatemala City.
- 1977. Plaza Lorenzo shopping center, Zone 9, Guatemala City.
- 1976. Convista building, Zone 15, Guatemala City.
- 1975. Plaza El Roble, Zone 9, Guatemala City.
- 1974. Colegio Evelyn Rogers, Zone 15, Guatemala City.
- 1972. Extension, Camino Real and Biltmore, Zone 10, Guatemala City.
- 1971. Extension, Colegio Alemán, Zone 11, Guatemala City.

Projects developed in collaboration with Minondo & Giesemann

- 1998. Atlantic building, Zone 10, Guatemala City.
- 1989. Anacafé buidling, Zone 14, Guatemala City.
- 1972. Reforma Obelisco building, Zone 9, Guatemala City.

petergiesemann

June 12, 1939

Studies
- Harvard College, Cambridge, Mass., B.A., 1961.
- Harvard Graduate School of Design: Master in Architecture, 1965.
- **Architect,** Universidad de San Carlos de Guatemala, Faculty of Architecture, 1968.

Academic activities
- Professor of the Faculty of Architecture, Universidad de San Carlos de Guatemala, 1969-1973.
- Member of the Tribunal of Honor of the College of Guatemalan Architects, 1969-1970.
- Member of the Board of Directors of the College of Guatemalan Architects, 1970-1971.
- Member of the Faculty Council, Faculty of Architecture, Universidad Francisco Marroquín, 1972-1992.
- Professor of the Faculty of Architecture, Universidad Francisco Marroquín, since 1975.

Publications
- *Architectural Record*, Jan. 1969.
- *Architecture Plus*, April. 1973.
- "Indumentarias y tejidos mayas a través del tiempo", (Mayan dress and textiles throughout the ages). *Crítica* magazine, No. 99, Grupo Crítica, Guatemala 1995.
- "The Fabric of Life", Museo Ixchel, by J. Dugdale, revista *World Studio Sphere*, New York, Spring Issue, 1996.
- Television interview, "People and Arts" channel. The Casa de Cristal was chosen for its program, "Casa Latinoamericana", 2000.

Projects developed in individual practice
- 1996. Banco Agrícola Mercantil, Zone 9 (Central headquarters), Guatemala City.
- 1995. Banco Agrícola Mercantil, Zone 1 (Pasaje Enríquez), Quetzaltenango, Guatemala.
- 1994. Self-service bank, Banco Agrícola Mercantil, Zone 3, Quetzaltenango, Guatemala.
- 1993. Banco Agrícola Mercantil, Zone 1 (Remodeling), Guatemala City.
- 1991. Banco Agrícola Mercantil, Zone 15, Guatemala City.
- 1982. Sidasa offices, Zone 9, Guatemala City.
- 1980. Offices, Ingenio Concepción, Zone 11, Guatemala City.
- 1974. Cobella apartments, Zone 14, Guatemala.
- 1967. Seminario Mayor de Guatemala. Convent, dormitories, dining room and church.
- Has developed more than 500 homes with a constructed area of between 500 to 2,500 square meters.

Projects developed in collaboration
- School of Music, Amherst College, Massachusetts, U.S.A., 1967
- In collaboration with Benjamin Thompson Associates.
- Kirkland Clinton University, U.S.A.
- In collaboration with the Architects Collaborative, Cambridge, Massachusetts, U.S.A.
- Topke building, Zone 4, Guatemala City. In collaboration with the architect Adolfo Lau, 1971.
- Ixchel Museum, Campus of the Universidad Francisco Marroquín, Zone 10, Guatemala City, 1992. In collaboration with the architects Lau, De León, Pemueller and Cohen.
- Medical Offices (Project), Jacarandas de Cayala, Zone 16, Guatemala City. In collaboration with the architects Lau, De León and Cohen.

See works and projects carried out by the firm Minondo & Giesemann.

raul**minondo**herrera

October 1, 1924

Studies
- Harvard College, Cambridge, Mass.: B.S. Engineering Sciences, 1946.
- **Civil Engineer**, Universidad de San Carlos de Guatemala, Faculty of Engineering, 1947.
- Harvard Graduate School of Design: Master in Architecture, 1949.
- **Architect**, Universidad de San Carlos de Guatemala, Faculty of Architecture 1950.

Academic activities
- Professor, Faculty of Architecture, Universidad de San Carlos de Guatemala 1964-1968.
- Member of Board of Directors, College of Guatemalan Engineers, 1964.

Publications
- *Architecture Plus*, April, 1973.

Projects developed in individual practice
- 1975. Hotel del Lago (Barceló Del Lago), Atitlán, Guatemala.
- 1972. Real América shopping center.
- 1971. Real Reforma building, Zone 9, Guatemala City.
- 1970. Instituto La Asunción, Zone 10, Guatemala City.
- 1970. Fiasa building, Zone 9, Guatemala City.
- 1970. Hotel Chulamar (Santa María del Mar), Escuintla, Guatemala.
- 1970. Hotel Camino Real, Zone 10, Guatemala City.
- 1970. Helvetia factory, Zone 11, Guatemala City.
- 1965. Ducal factory, Zone 18, Guatemala City.
- 1965. Herrera Llerandi Hospital, Zone 10, Guatemala City.
- 1961. Kern's factory, Zone 17, Guatemala City.
- 1960. Bandesa Reforma, Zone 9, Guatemala City.
- 1960. Herrera building, Zone 1, Guatemala City.
- 1960. La Curacao building, Zone 9, Guatemala City.
- 1960. Canella building, Zone 4, Guatemala City.
- 1960. Fabrigas building, Zone 4, Guatemala City.
- 1960. Centro Médico hospital, Zone 10, Guatemala City.
- 1960. Capri cinema, Zone 1, Guatemala City.
- 1960. Café Incasa, Zone 17, Guatemala City.
- 1960. Channel 3 of television, Zone 11, Guatemala City.
- 1958. Tropical cinema, Zone 8, Guatemala City.
- 1958. Las Ameritas cinemas, Zone 13, Guatemala City.
- 1957. Crédito Hipotecario Nacional, Civic Center, Guatemala City.
- 1956. Trébol cinema, Zone 11, Guatemala City.
- 1955. Banco de Guatemala, Civic Center, Guatemala City.
- 1952. Bauer building, Zone 1, Guatemala City.

See works and projects carried out by the firm Minondo & Giesemann.

tinoco&porras

Projects developed
- Plaza Obelisco shopping center, Avenida Reforma, Zone 10, Guatemala City.
- El Domo sports center, Zone 10, Guatemala City.
- Ibero Plaza building, in collaboration with the architect Guirola, Los Próceres, Zone 10, Guatemala City.
- Preuss Sterkel residence, Guatemala City.
- Dalton residence, Antigua Guatemala, Guatemala.
- Group of Dalton houses, Antigua Guatemala, Guatemala.
- Bella Vista development, Antigua Guatemala, Guatemala.

ernestoporras

April 9, 1942

Studies
- **Architectural degree**, Universidad de San Carlos de Guatemala, 1971.

Academic activities
- Professor and director of School of Interior Design (Escuela de Diseño de Interiores), 1970-1976.
- Secretary, College of Architects, 1972.
- Professor, Faculty of Architecture, Universidad Rafael Landívar, 1977.
- Professor, Faculty of Architecture, Universidad Francisco Marroquín, 1977-1991.
- Exchange Professor, College of Architecture, University of Florida, 1986.
- **Dean**, Faculty of Architecture, Universidad Francisco Marroquín, since 1991.

Projects developed
- 1971-1995. In collaboration with the architect Jorge Montes: Design of private homes, apartment and office buildings.
- Plaza de los Cuatro Arcos building, Zone 14.
- Corporate building, IDS de Guatemala, Zone 10.
- Altamira Suites building, Zone 9.
- Centro Ejecutivo building, Zone 10.
- 1992. In association with Benjamin Thompson Asscoiates, Cambridge, Mass.: Los Próceres shopping center.
- 1995. In association with the architect Rafael Tinoco: Design of homes and buildings.
- Plaza Obelisco shopping center.
- Polideportivo building, Zone 13 (Dome).
- Ibero Plaza building (under construction).

rafael**tinoco**alvarado

October 17, 1942

Estudios
- **Architectural degree**, Universidad San Carlos de Guatemala, 1967 - Colegiado 59.
- Masters degree in sculpture, Rome, Italy.

Academic activities
- Professor, Universidad San Carlos, 1969-1972.

Professional and executive posts
- Member of the board of directors of the Society of Architects, 1969-1970.
- Member of the firm Tinoco, Lacape and Ogarrio.
- Founder-CEO of Architects Tinoco and Lacape, S.A.
- CEO-Owner of Architect Rafael Tinoco and Associates.
- Partner of Architects Tinoco and Porras.

Projects developed in collaboration – Tinoco & Lacape & Associates:
- El Triángulo building, 7ª Avenida Zone 4, Guatemala City.
- Plaza del Sol building, 12 Calle Zone 9, Guatemala City.
- Hotel Guatemala Fiesta, 13 Calle Zone 10, Guatemala City.
- Banco Industrial building, in collaboration with the architects Valenzuela, Benchoam and Haeussler, 7ª Avenida Zone 4, Guatemala City.
- Centro Capitol building, 6ª Avenida, Zone 1, Guatemala City.
- La Torre building, 7ª Avenida and 2ª Calle Zone 9, Guatemala City.
- Marosa apartment building, Zone 14, Guatemala City.
- Oakland apartment building, 12 Avenida Zone 10, Guatemala City.
- Colegios Profesionales building, in collaboration with the architects Arroyave and Herbruger, Vista Hermosa, Zone 15, Guatemala City.
- Building for the Presidential Guard, Zone 1, Guatemala City.
- La Montaña country club, in collaboration with the architects Montes, Rosales and Porras, San Juan Sacatepéquez, Guatemala.
- Parque Tikal, in collaboration with the engineers Cordón and Mérida, Guatemala City.
- Permanent centers for INTECAP, Zone 12 and five departments of Guatemala.
- Girasol residential complex, 20 calle Zone 10, Guatemala City.
- Las Acacias residential development, 3ª Calle Zone 10, Guatemala City.
- Johanis housing development, 10ª Avenida, Zone 10, Guatemala City.
- Development of urban design and houses, Lomas del Sur, Villa Nueva, Guatemala City.
- Redesign Clínicas Médicas building, Obelisco, Guatemala City.
- Lomas del Sur housing development, 200 houses, each of 120 square meters, Villa Nueva, Guatemala.
- JUAMA, offices and factory, Avenida Hincapié, Zone 13, Guatemala City.
- Galerías del Sur office building, Avenida Aguila Batres, Zone 11, Guatemala City.
- Covadonga apartment building, Avenidas Las Américas Zone 13, Guatemala City.
- Novella Town Houses complex, 4ª Avenida Zone 14, Guatemala City.
- Las Mercedes store premises, Zone 10, Guatemala City.
- Clínicas Médicas building, Torre Marfil, Zone 10, Guatemala City.
- Hotel Petex Batún, Lake Petex-Batún, Petén, Guatemala.
- Torre Alba apartments condominium, Zone 14, Guatemala City.
- Villa Magna hotel and offices, 1ra. Avenida, Zone 10, Guatemala City.
- Amadeus apartments condominium, Oakland Zone 10, Guatemala City.
- Torre Granito building, Avenida Los Próceres, Zone 10, Guatemala City.

See works and projects carried by the firm Tinoco & Porras.

Design
CARMEN LUCÍA SOLARES

Solares studied art and drawing in the Fortmann Studios, Florence, Italy and Italian language and the history of Florentine art in the Istitutto Michelangelo, Florence, Italy.
She did her university studies in graphic design at Endicott College, Beverly, MA., the Academy of Art College, San Francisco, CA., and Sacred Heart University, Fairfield, Ct. (BA). She currently works as a freelance designer in Guatemala City.
info@designcs.com

Texts
AXEL PAREDES
Paredes studied architecture at the Architectural Association of London (AA), the Escuela Técnica Superior de Arquitectura (Higher Technical School of Architecture) of Madrid and the University of Utah, United States. He currently works as professor of architecture in the Francisco Marroquín University of Guatemala and is the director of the magazine *ArquiT+*.
axelp@email.com

CARLOS CASTELLANOS
CEO of Seis Arquitectos

Coordination of content
LUIS PEDRO ARROYAVE
Arroyave is a graduate of the Faculty of Architecture of the Francisco Marroquín University, Guatemala City.
luisparroyave@hotmail.com
CARLOS CASTELLANOS

Architectural drawings
JEANNE SAMAYOA, LUIS PEDRO ARROYAVE and RODRIGO CABRERA.

angebourda

Photo-reports:
- International Photo-Journalism: Report on a journey from Alaska to the Antarctic GEO (1976-77).
- C. Dior Collection, Paris, France, 1989, "Printemp-"ÉTÉ".
- Fotokina International Convention, Cologne, Germany, 1990.
- Expo Paris 92,Comptoir de la Photographie, Paris, France, 1992.
- Historical Cultural Center of Seville, Spain, 2000.

Exhibitions:
- "Altuarte", Patronato contra la mendicidad, Segunda Naturaleza, Galería El D'zunun, Guatemala, 1978.
- "Negativos Positivos" ("Positive Negatives", retrospective of black and white photos of 52 Guatemalan personages). Galería Sol del Río, Guatemala, 1991.

Experimental theatre, cinema and photography:
Has participated in different works of children's theater:
- *Juguemos a jugar jugando*, Experimental theater for children, with a mixture of cinema and photography. Direction and Production, 1977-1978.
- *Sebastián sal de compras*, Theater work by Manuel José Arce (1977).

Prizes:
- First International Professional Photography Prize, Puebla, Mexico. (Professional Photographers of America, Inc.), 1984.
- Degree from Escuela Nacional de Fotografía, Universidad San Sebastián, Spain, 1984.
- 1989 Jade Prizes – Best Photographer – Asociación General de Publicistas de Guatemala (General Association of Guatemalan Publicists), 1989.
- Prize for Best Creative Photography, McCann Erickson campaign, Río, Brazil, 1992.
- First National Prize for Quality. Project: silver work in Guatemala. Ediciones Jomagar, Madrid, Spain, 1994.
- First prize for creativity, category: Best Poster, World competition of the World Tourism Organization, Seoul, Korea, 2001.

Advertising campaigns:
Among the most important, he has worked as a photography director and producer for the advertising agencies:
- BBDO
- Eco Young & Rubicam
- Leo Burnett Comunica
- McCann Erickson, Guatemala and Central America (since 1980).

Has participated in the following publishing projects:
- A & C Internacional, *Revista Internacional de Arquitectura y Diseño* 1996.
- *World Architecture*.
- *La platería en el Reino de Guatemala, siglos XVI-XX* (Silver Work in the Kingdom of Guatemala, XVI-XX centuries). Jomagar Ediciones, Madrid, 1996.
- *Piezas maestras maya* (Mayan masterpieces), Banco G & T, Guatemala, 1996.
- *Casa Guatemalteca*, Villegas Editores, Bogotá, Colombia, 1999 (Architecture and interior design).
- *Historia del Café de Guatemala* (History of Guatemalan Coffee), Villegas Editores, Bogotá, Colombia, 2001.
- *Seis Arquitectos, Arquitectura Contemporánea* (Six Architects, Contemporary Architecture), Villegas Editores, Bogotá, Colombia, 2002.
- He is currently preparing a new book, entitled *Portraits*.

Associations:
- President of the Cultural Association of the Liceo Jules Verne, 1995-2001
- Alianza Francesa de Guatemala, 1988-2002.

The creativity of Ange Bourde does not allow him to keep still for very long. If a photographer's life is, in the best sense of the word, a restless journey over the surface of human beings and objects with the aim of discovering their most intimate secrets, Bourda is, without doubt, a true photographer.

Depicting architectural works is a specialized branch of photography. Their spaces, volumes and rising structures only reach a high degree of reality when they are caught by the lenses of a master. The best building in the world may become flat and lose its perfection when it is portrayed by the average camera or the average photographer.

The architects Rodolfo Solares, Carlos Lara, Peter Giesemann, Raúl Minondo, Ernesto Porras and Rafael Tinoco have left an indelible mark on the urban landscape of Guatemala and the full reality of their achievements has been caught by Ange Bourda, who once again proves the excellence of his work in this book. The spaces and buildings created by those architects have given Guatemala City an air of modernity and beauty that are perfectly captured by the incomparable vision of Bourda, with all of his talent, experience and skill.

Heir to a tradition implanted by Durandelle, Paul Strand, Eugene Atget, Henri Cartier-Bresson, Robert Doisneau, Jacques-Henri Lartigue and others, Ange Bourda fully lives up to the postulates of Le Corbusier, who stated that restraint and a sense of equilibrium are the key elements in highlighting the beauty of architecture.

Ana María Rodas

In photography, as in architecture, everything begins with the perception and the conception of space. It is from this essential point – from this recognition of a reality of rhythm, lines and forms – that the image and the work are born. This interpreting, adjusting, taking hold of and changing of balances and centers of gravity has been an unforgettable experience, shared for the past three years with the team of Seis Arquitectos (and mainly with Rodolfo Solares and Peter Giesemann). This book is the fruit.of that experience. It results from the endeavors of the whole team and should be seen, in its entirety, as a single photograph.

Ange Bourda